Critical Praise for David Carter's *Stonewall*

"Meticulously researched."　　　　　　　　　　*—Time Out New York*

"No matter what you may believe about the event, you will gain new insights. Historically important and socially significant."
　　　　　　　　　　　　　　　　　—The Dallas Morning News

"A terrific piece of nonfiction, a satisfying and illuminating document that will be referred to time and again."　　　　　　*—The Advocate*

"Among the most important books in the gay canon."　　*—The Villager*

"Reads more like a novel than a research document."*—The Texas Triangle*

"Fascinating."　　　　　　　　　　　　　　　　　*—Out*

"The first legitimate historical account of the Stonewall riots . . . valuable."
　　　　　　　　　　　　　　　　　　　　　　—Gay Today

"Highly recommended."　　　　　　　　　　　*—Library Journal*

"This was a riot heard around the world, and Carter has done it proud."
　　　　　　　　　　*—Jonathan Ned Katz, author of *Love Stories:
　　　　　　　　　　　　　Sex Between Men Before Homosexuality

"Carter . . . writes very much like, well, not God, but Moses certainly . . . [*Stonewall*] ought to be in the library of every literate queer who likes an argument."　　　　*—James McCourt, author of *Mawrdew Czgowchwz*

"A major work of narrative history."　　　　　*—The Weekly News*

"Moving."　　　　　　　　　　　　　　　　*—Frontiers*

"Brings life even to passages about the actual bricks and mortar of the Stonewall Inn."　　　　　　　　　　　*—Chicago Free Press*

"Enlightening."　　　　　　　　　　　*—New York Newsday*

"A gripping, hour-by-hour reconstruction . . . this definitive account is long overdue but well worth the wait."　　　　　　　*rks*

"Read it and be inspired."　　　　　　　　　　　　*ess*

STONEWALL

STONEWALL

THE RIOTS THAT SPARKED THE GAY REVOLUTION

DAVID CARTER

ST. MARTIN'S GRIFFIN ❦ NEW YORK

STONEWALL. Copyright © 2004 by David Carter. All rights reserved.
Printed in the United States of America. For information, address
St. Martin's Press, 175 Fifth Avenue, New York, N.Y. 10010.

www.stmartins.com

The Library of Congress has cataloged the hardcover edition as follows:

Carter, David.
    Stonewall : the riots that sparked the gay revolution / by David Carter.
        p. cm.
    ISBN 978-0-312-20025-1
    1. Homosexuality. 2. Lesbianism. 3. Gay liberation movement—
United States. I. Title.

HQ76.C3155 2004
306.76'6'0973—dc22

                                                          2004040226

ISBN 978-0-312-67193-8 (trade paperback)

Second St. Martin's Griffin Edition: May 2010

        D   10

To the gay street youth
who fought and bled at Stonewall

I have no doubt we shall win,
but the road is long, and red with monstrous martyrdoms.

—OSCAR WILDE,
LETTER TO GEORGE IVES

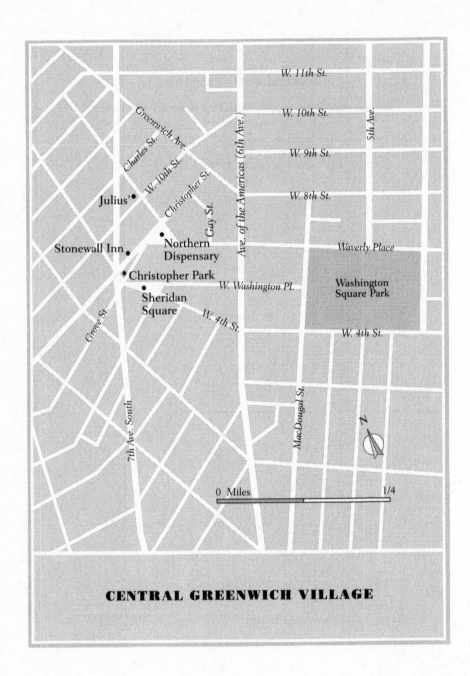

W. 11th St.

W. 10th St.

W. 9th St.

5th Ave.

W. 8th St.

Greenwich Ave.

Charles St.

W. 10th St.

Christopher St.

Gay St.

Ave. of the Americas (6th Ave.)

Julius'

Stonewall Inn

Northern
Dispensary

Christopher Park

Sheridan
Square

W. 4th St.

Grove St.

W. Washington Pl.

Waverly Place

Washington
Square Park

W. 4th St.

7th Ave. South

MacDougal St.

N

0 Miles   1/4

CENTRAL GREENWICH VILLAGE

CONTENTS

Prologue

The Stonewall Riots were a series of violent protests and street demonstrations that began in the early morning hours of June 28, 1969, and centered around a gay bar in the Greenwich Village section of New York City. These riots are widely credited with being the motivating force in the transformation of the gay political movement. Everything else about these riots—how they started and who was responsible; who were the patrons of the Stonewall Inn; who were the owners; what happened at the riots; who was there and who was not; and pretty much everything else revolving around these riots—has been a bone of contention between various individuals and interest groups within and without the gay world. This book attempts to bring together everything that is known about the Stonewall Inn, the riots themselves, and the life and times of the people involved (gay men, lesbians, transvestites, and others) to present the clearest possible picture of what happened and why.

It was only a few decades ago—a very short time in historical terms—that the situation of gay men and lesbians was radically different from what it is today. At the end of the 1960s, homosexual sex was illegal in every state but Illinois.[1] Not one law—federal, state, or local—protected gay men or women from being fired or denied housing. There were no openly gay politicians. No television show had any identifiably gay characters. When Hollywood made a film with a major homosexual character, the character was either killed or killed himself. There were no openly gay policemen, public school teachers, doctors, or lawyers. And no political party had a gay caucus.

It is common today to trace the tremendous gains made for lesbian and gay rights since the early 1970s back to the Stonewall Riots of 1969, when gay men, transvestites, and lesbians fought the police during a routine raid on a popular gay club in Greenwich Village. It is also commonly asserted that the riots, which continued on and off for six days, marked the beginning of the "gay rights movement." Gay people had founded a political movement for the rights of gay people prior to Stonewall, although of modest means, and it was the Stonewall Riots that resulted in the birth of the Gay Liberation Front (GLF) and later of the Gay Activists Alliance (GAA). These exemplars of a new kind of gay organization, imbued with the militant spirit of the riots that engendered them, soon inspired thousands of gay men and lesbians across the country—and ultimately around the world—to join the movement for gay civil and human rights.

The immense changes precipitated by the Stonewall Riots make us want to know more about this event and to understand its causes. Yet the riots have seemed to a large degree inexplicable. Why did a sustained resistance occur when the police raided this particular club? Why did gay men take a stand at that time and at that place?

Research conducted for this history revealed that the riots occurred for a number of reasons having to do with timing, social history, cultural changes, and local history and geography, as well as political events. Moreover, many of these causes were as subtle as they were real and thus have long eluded notice. The factor of time further complicates determining the event's causes: not only did these causes and contributing factors not occur simultaneously but they were spread out over wide vistas of time, with some of the underlying causes occurring decades prior to the event while others were as fresh as that week's headlines. How these various strands eventually came together to create a turning point for the gay rights movement is the subject of this history. Given the varied nature of the riots' causes, their origins at different points in time, and their multiplicity, the way in which these factors converged to create the Stonewall Riots is an intricate story. Yet almost all the causes lay where the riots took place, in America's bohemia, Greenwich Village.

SETTING

THE

STAGE

Greenwich Village, USA

In the late 1960s, Tony Lauria, known to his friends and associates as Fat Tony, the son of an important Mafioso named Ernie, decided to open a gay bar in Greenwich Village. He did so despite the unhappiness it caused his father, a man so conservative that it was said that meeting with him was almost like having an audience with the pope. Ernie had made his fortune in traditional Mafia operations such as the carting business and felt that running a "fag bar" was for people on the lower echelons of the Mafia hierarchy. The father had high ambitions for Tony and sent him to Xavier, a Catholic preparatory school. Despite the quality education Tony had received—as shown by his good diction—he preferred to hang out on the street with other neighborhood boys whose thick Italian accents made them sound like actors playing mobsters. The father's success, his lofty aspirations for his son, and his displeasure at his son's barroom venture suggest that an archetypal father-son conflict may have been behind Fat Tony's decision.[1]

Fat Tony's father owned the apartment building on the southwest corner of Waverly Place and Sixth Avenue, in which he and Fat Tony lived. An impressive structure, the proud building towers over its neighbors and displays knights carved in stone on its facade. At seventeen stories it is high enough that its upper floors command a fine view of the neighborhood.

Looking east, Washington Square Park, for many the very epitome of

the Village, is just a block away. The popular park has a history hardly suspected by the many New Yorkers who think of it only as a pleasant place to
walk, little knowing, for example, that the golden leaves they enjoy strolling
through in the fall have grown out of the bodies of other New Yorkers. In
the city's early days, when most of New York's population still inhabited
Manhattan's southern tip, a marsh covered the park. During the 1798
cholera epidemic the city desperately needed an out-of-town paupers'
graveyard and drained the marsh to meet this exigency. On the northwest
corner of Washington Square an extremely tall English elm tree stands
only about ten feet from the park's edge. A straight line drawn west from
this tree would practically hit the front of Tony's father's building. Some
say the tree on the corner is the oldest tree in the entire five boroughs. Oldest or not, the Hanging Elm earned its name when Manhattan established
a public gallows and chose it as the site for executions. Perhaps the city
chose the tree because of its proximity to the paupers' graves, which allowed the city authorities to dispatch its least valued citizens without bothering to haul the bodies away. When the graveyard had consumed ten
thousand bodies, the poor were not even shown the minimal respect ordi-
narily granted a final resting place, for the graveyard was converted into a
military parade ground. Eventually, the beggars and the criminals had their
revenge. When the army brought in their heavy artillery to show it off, the
weight proved too much for the decaying bodies to support and the
weapons collapsed into the unmarked graves of the poor. After that unexpected defeat, the city turned the site into a park.

To the west of Ernie's building lay another vista with a compelling past.
The street that runs from the Hanging Tree to the front of the mob-owned
apartment building intersects Christopher Street just where Fat Tony's new
business was situated—but not before passing the Northern Dispensary,
the city's oldest clinic, where Edgar Allan Poe had been a patient. (Poe
would no doubt have appreciated the irony that immediately adjacent to
the building where sick people had gone seeking to escape the grave there
was once a sausage factory; in recent years, as if inadvertently betraying its
ancestry, the ground floor of the same building housed a leather clothing
store.)

Fat Tony could hardly have found a street with a more colorful history
than Christopher Street for his new business. The oldest and longest street
in Greenwich Village, Christopher Street at one time extended beyond its
current length to about the middle of what is now West 8th Street between
Fifth and Sixth avenues. Where Christopher Street used to begin was the
location of the Eighth Street Bookshop, the most influential bookstore in
Manhattan for Beat literature. In 1964, when Allen Ginsberg—better
known to some for being openly homosexual than for his poetry—returned

from his long stay in India, he stayed in a room above the store while look-ing for a place of his own. It was at the Eighth Street Bookshop that Al Aronowitz, the *New York Post* reporter who had written some of the first ar-ticles on the Beats, dropped by one day with a young folk singer he wanted Ginsberg to meet, namely, Bob Dylan.[2]

Given Christopher Street's length and history, it is not surprising that a walk down even a couple of its blocks can provide a sampling of the long Village tradition of bohemian life and its influence across time. In walking from where the Eighth Street Bookshop stood to the Northern Dispensary on Christopher Street, the short physical distance traveled suggests a par-allel journey of ideas over a vast expanse of time. Allen Ginsberg found in-spiration in the work of Edgar Allan Poe, calling him "the first psychedelic poet," making this short tour all the more suggestive, for while 8th Street had the Eighth Street Bookshop as a cutting-edge literary presence in the 1950s, in the late 1960s the street became one of the main purveyors of psy-chedelic posters and clothes.

Where Christopher Street begins today, at its intersection with Green-wich Avenue, we find the former site of Luke Connor's, a popular gather-ing place for the actors and writers of the Provincetown Players, an association of some of the twentieth century's most important talents in the theater, such as Eugene O'Neill. A few doors in from Greenwich Av-enue is 11 Christopher Street, where the influential poet e. e. cummings once lived. Farther down the block, just two doors west of where the Stonewall Inn would open, was the Lion's Head, a pub popular with writ-ers. This bar offered refuge for creative spirits from playwright Lanford Wilson and composer David Amram to writers James Baldwin, Norman Mailer, and Frank McCourt. At the end of this block of Christopher Street, at the corner of Seventh Avenue South, *The Village Voice*'s office was in a building whose jutting triangular shape resembled a ship's prow, suggesting the forward-looking aspirations of the innovative writers and artists who worked for *The Voice;* among them, photographer Berenice Ab-bott, underground filmmaker Jonas Mekas, and poet Frank O'Hara. Through its encouragement of Off Off Broadway theater, *The Voice* helped to expand the very concept of theater.

In a subtle way, another element of the avant-garde history of these few blocks ties into this history. Just as the Village's population rose and fell over the decades and centuries, so did its reputation as a bohemian quarter. (It was the Village's reputation for unconventional lifestyles that first at-tracted gay people to the area around the turn of the century, as they sensed that a place known for wide tolerance might even accept sexual nonconformists.)[3] When both Seventh Avenue and the Seventh Avenue subway line were extended south into the Village, the new easy access led to a rediscovery of the area as a bohemian enclave. This in turn led to a burgeoning of the real bohemian scene and the birth of a tourist-trap imitation one. It was in part because of the propinquity of the new subway station that Sheridan Square, close by Christopher Street, became the epicenter for both kinds of venues. These were composed mainly of clubs and another Village institution, tearooms, which were very modest restaurants that often catered to a particular clientele.

With the onset of Prohibition, artists, intellectuals, and gay men and lesbians began to socialize more and more in tearooms, since bars could no longer serve alcohol. Among the rare early American books to depict lesbian love is the autobiography of "Mary Casal," *The Stone Wall,* published in 1930.[4] That same year, two former stables at 51 and 53 Christopher Street were merged into one building at the ground-floor level and became Bonnie's Stone Wall, which soon gained a reputation as one "of the more notorious tearooms" in the Village, a reputation not easily earned in a time when tearooms were routinely raided by the police. It seems reasonable therefore to assume that in naming her "notorious" business Bonnie's Stone Wall, the owner, presumably Bonnie, was alluding to the new memoir to send a coded message to lesbians that they would be welcomed there.[5] The tearoom's notoriety does not seem to have harmed business, for Bonnie's Stone Wall was one of the rare cases of a tearoom that not only survived but also evolved into a full restaurant. Decades later, Bonnie's Stone Wall had lost its rebellious edge and become a popular place to hold wedding receptions and banquets and had even become a particular favorite of policemen. By the 1940s its name had already changed to the more bucolic-sounding Bonnie's Stonewall Inn, and by the 1960s it had been changed again to the Stonewall Inn Restaurant. It was the former Stonewall Inn Restaurant that, in 1967, having sat vacant for some time after a fire gutted it, metamorphosed into the gay club the Stonewall Inn. While the staid restaurant's uproarious origins were quite forgotten by the second half of the twentieth century, it seems as if fate had marked the place from its very beginnings as a site of homosexual rebellion.[6]

Christopher Street's origins go back to the time when the area that became Greenwich Village seemed remote from Manhattan's southern end, where the Dutch founded the city. When the Dutch government wanted to reward Wouter Van Twiller, the third director of New Amsterdam, with a farm, he was given two hundred acres of land within the present-day Village, near the Indian settlement known as Sapponckanican.[7] With the passage of time, the original Dutch farmland was subdivided and resubdivided as the population of farmers slowly grew. The tempo of populating this portion of Manhattan sped up dramatically when a series of four epidemics of yellow fever and cholera struck lower Manhattan between 1791 and 1805.[8] Early New Yorkers fled to what was then seen as an outpost so distant that they could not imagine a plague following them that far.

These flights from plague eventually transformed the Village from a rural country hamlet into an area so populous that it became necessary to lay down roads. From their earliest days, Villagers have shown a certain appreciation of their own traditions and a willingness to defend them. Perhaps the earliest manifestation of this trait occurred when the first Village roads were planned by the residents who were careful to see that the roads followed the footpaths left by the original Indians as well as those added by the early settlers. A number of the Village's original streets were therefore laid out because Indians and farmers, with their close ties to the earth, had followed paths that seemed natural to them, so that the Village's streets were created for the convenience of human feet and not for wheeled vehicles.[9] When an attempt was made in 1817 to impose a grid plan on all of Manhattan's streets, the citizens of Greenwich Village successfully resisted the plan and the Village became the only part of Manhattan north of the Wall Street area where the new street plan was not implemented. This resistance shows that the Villagers' sense of their community as a unique place and their resistance to conformity have deep roots. To understand Villager psychology, this ingredient of feistiness must be factored in. Villagers have long been willing to fight for what they want as well as to applaud those who have the courage to stand up for their beliefs. When the antecedent to the subway trains, elevated trains (the "el"), were built too close to Village residences, housewives angered by the trains' loud racket are said to have stacked bricks in their kitchens to throw at the passing trains. Villagers were so proud of a leader of a riot that they named a street for him: Gay Street was named for attorney Sidney Howard Gay, the editor of the *Anti-Slavery Standard,* to honor him for his role in the 1834 abolition riots.[10]

The New York Public Library has a collection of 54,000 photographs of old New York, taken between the 1870s and the 1940s. The first appearance in this collection of the two buildings that would one day become the Stonewall Inn bar is a photograph taken in 1899 that shows two white horses drawing a trolley as they approach 51 and 53 Christopher Street. It is appropriate that a pair of horses are featured in the earliest image of these buildings, since they were both built to serve as stables in an era that relied heavily on animal muscle for transportation. The horses bespeak a period when Americans lived closer to the land, a slower time when people were not so alienated from their own natures or from their fellow beings. Even in bustling Manhattan, businesses took the time to pay attention to the amenities: of these two Christopher Street stables, one was home to the all-black horses that delivered goods for Saks Fifth Avenue, and one of the stable keeper's duties was to paint the horses' hooves black to match their coats.[11]

However, 1899 was also the year that Henry Ford started the Detroit Automobile Company and that New York City got its first fleet of taxicabs. The next image in the library's collection of these buildings is taken in 1928, and 53 Christopher Street is a French bakery. Number 51 still has "The Jefferson Livery Stable" emblazoned on its facade, but these words are obscured by a larger poster nailed on top of it proclaiming that the building is about to be altered into "most desirable STUDIO APARTMENTS." A clear view of 51 and 53 Christopher Street is blocked by a car and a delivery truck.[12]

While Greenwich Village grew by fits and starts—and had occasional declines—it maintained a certain level of isolation until well into the twentieth century because its irregular street plan impeded a direct flow of traffic into the Village. The increasing popularity of both the automobile and the recently introduced subway system added to the public pressure to extend Seventh Avenue. At the close of World War I, Seventh Avenue, which used to end at 11th Street, was extended south, with its new section named Seventh Avenue South.[13] *The Greenwich Village Historic District Designation Report*, which documents 1969 Greenwich Village in detail, states that due to the extension south of both Seventh Avenue and the West Side subway line, "the physical isolation of Greenwich Village from the main traffic routes of the City was lost forever."[14] As horses and stables became rarer and rarer, gas stations and automobile supply stores filled up the small triangular plots the cut-through had made along Seventh Avenue South.[15] The triumph of impersonal mechanical speed over a gentler and more natural mode of transportation meant that the last horses at 51 and 53 Christopher Street were evicted, and in 1930 the two buildings became one.

At the west end of the block on which the Stonewall Inn club would later open, a number of streets—Christopher, Seventh Avenue South, West 4th, Sheridan Square, and Grove—crisscross and converge. The resulting effect of a traffic hub in an entertainment district with busy pedestrian traffic has struck more than one observer as a scaled-down version of Times Square. Running underneath the surface of Christopher Street, a PATH commuter train connecting the Village to New Jersey runs at almost a right angle to the Seventh Avenue subway line, dropping off passengers both on lower Christopher Street, close to the Hudson River, and on 9th Street near Sixth Avenue, only about 150 feet from where Christopher Street begins. The Sixth Avenue subway was extended south at the end of the 1920s, and an entrance to the West 4th Street station, with its seven subway lines, is only a little farther away from the Stonewall Inn's door than the Christopher Street station. All in all, the Stonewall Inn was only a block away from eight subway lines, only about two short blocks away from a PATH train station, and between three major avenues: Sixth Avenue, Greenwich Avenue, and Seventh Avenue South. More significantly, the club was only a short city block and a half from Greenwich Avenue, the premier cruising ground for gay men in New York City in the 1960s. Moreover, the new bar was located the same distance from what these men called The Corner, the intersection of Greenwich Avenue and Christopher Street, the most popular meeting place for gay men on all of Greenwich Avenue.[16] The new bar could not possibly have been more centrally located.

In addition to the highly centralized location of the Stonewall Inn, its immediate geography also had some unusual features for New York City. First, by Manhattan standards there is an unusual amount of empty space around the Stonewall Inn. Directly in front of the club lies Christopher Park and, just a little to the east of the park, the area around the triangular Northern Dispensary is fairly open, being the intersection of three streets (Grove, Christopher, and Waverly Place). Indeed, *The Greenwich Village Historic District Designation Report* noted the way the geography of Waverly Place by the Northern Dispensary gives "the feeling of openness, so rare in our streets today."[17]

That feeling of openness sprang from the Village tradition of citizens standing up to those in power to protect their interests, for Christopher Park had formerly been the site of an awful tenement. When it burned to the ground in a fire that killed more than forty persons, Villagers protested the idea of another residential building being built there and insisted that the land be turned into a park.

Other events in the history of the immediate area surrounding the small park demonstrate the Village's long history of open-spiritedness. Near the base of the triangle formed by Christopher Park is 59 Grove Street, where Thomas Paine died. Paine's pamphlets played such a vital role in starting the American Revolution that Thomas Jefferson praised him as the only American who could write better than himself, and William Blake put him in a class with Jesus as a worker of miracles for overthrowing "all the armies of Europe with a small pamphlet." In spite of these accolades, Paine was so unconventional as a freethinker that he often ended up in trouble. After he went to France to support the French Revolution, he was imprisoned. When New York State gave him a free home in New Rochelle to honor him for his role in the American Revolution, his unconventional beliefs so outraged his conservative neighbors that they tried to kill him several times.[18] At the end of his life when he needed a refuge, the Village provided it.

On the south side of Christopher Park, directly across from the buildings that became the Stonewall Inn, was the home of Phillip Stokes. Stokes had a great interest in Eastern mysticism, and so, in 1932, he invited the Indian spiritual master Meher Baba to stay in his home. It was there that Meher Baba first met the American public. He had been observing silence since 1925, communicating by means of a small board he carried on which the letters of the alphabet were painted. At the gathering at the Stokes home, Meher Baba pointed to the letters on the board to spell out his message, saying that he was observing silence only so that he could one day break it, which he said would bring about a spiritual upheaval: "America has tremendous energy, but most of this energy is misdirected. I intend to divert it into spiritual and creative channels." Asked how his speaking would help such current social problems as those of politics, economics, and sex, he answered that when he spoke the results would be gradual and would affect all aspects of life. "New values and significance will be attached to matters which appear to baffle solution at the present moment," he asserted. He later explained that constructive and creative forces were being released that, although working silently, would "bring about the transformation of man."[19] Harbingers of radical change—artistic, political, and spiritual—surrounded the diminutive triangular park.

At the west end of the block where Stonewall was located, there is a confusion of street names: Seventh Avenue South is generally called Seventh Avenue, and Sheridan Square—shaped like a triangle in spite of its name—is commonly referred to as West 4th Street, while everyone calls the park across the street from the Stonewall Inn "Sheridan Square," even though its official designation is Christopher Park. That a statue of General Philip Sheridan looks out over Christopher Park—and not Sheridan Square—may have caused the confusion, whereas the statue of a Civil War general opposite an establishment named Stonewall caused at least one person to assume that the statue represented Stonewall Jackson.

The several one-way streets intersecting around Christopher Park confuse even Village residents. Someone sitting in Christopher Park, facing west and surveying the corner lampposts on the park's western end, will see that some of the lampposts have two signs, each saying ONE WAY. Because of the oblique angles at which streets intersect there, the one-way signs seem to point in opposite directions. The way streets come together into a hub here results directly from the extension of Seventh Avenue farther south. When the extension was created, it cut through the existing crazy-quilt pattern, created a century earlier when the Villagers fended off the imposition of the grid plan. With the "quilt" being cut again, its pattern became even crazier around the sheared-off edges, and nowhere more so than around Christopher Street, where a person standing today can see the almost surrealistic shape of some buildings sliced apart by what Villagers referred to with dread as the cut-through.

The east end of Christopher Park can be just as confusing. There Waverly Place achieves the distinction that makes it unique among all the streets of New York City: the only street in the city to wrap around itself, it does so where it crosses Christopher Street, throwing itself around the three-sided Northern Dispensary (as a New Yorker once put it, "Where Waverly intersects Waverly intersecting Waverly"). From this point, as if having succeeded in confusing itself, Waverly takes a sudden sharp bend like the irregular path of a drunk and continues east to Sixth Avenue. But not before running into Gay Street on its northern side, a surprisingly short street that in its own diminutive existence of one block cannot keep itself straight, veering back upon itself at an odd angle, only to turn back into Christopher Street.

Christopher Street became so gay in the 1970s that some gay men wrongly assumed that Gay Street had been named in their honor. Still, from a turn-of-the-century perspective, this confused knot of streets could certainly be termed, however anachronistically, a queer geography. It was in the midst of this tangle of irregular streets and triangular open spaces that the largest gay club of the 1960s opened.

To comprehend the club's significance, however, it is first necessary to understand the various social and political forces that were shaping the specific features of the homosexual world that the Stonewall Inn would inhabit. Some of these forces were national, and many of them were specific to New York City. These factors provide the context that explains why the Stonewall Inn became a special place for gay men in general and for particular subsets of the gay population in particular. A survey of the legal situation of homosexual men and women in the United States and particularly New York City in the 1950s and 1960s will provide a framework to understand the dynamics at work in both the local gay population as well as the history of gay political organizations in New York City. The successes and failures of gay political activism did much to influence the reception and fate of the Stonewall Inn—and even influenced the kind of club it would be.[20]

THE LAW

The homosexual is an inveterate seducer of the youth of both sexes, and . . . is not content with being degenerate himself; he must have degenerate companions, and is ever seeking younger victims. . . . Some male sex deviants do not stop with infecting their often-innocent partners [with homosexuality]: they descend through perversions to other forms of depravity, such as drug addiction, burglary, sadism, and even murder. Once a man assumes the role of homosexual, he throws off all moral restraints.

—*Coronet*, 1950[21]

This history is one in which almost all the action takes place in the 1960s. The phrase *the sixties* inevitably brings to mind images of freedom and rapid social and political change. The irony is that for almost the entirety of that decade homosexual men and women, far from experiencing a great burst of freedom, found themselves in the worst legal position they had been in since the republic's birth.

Because of a Puritan heritage, America's laws had traditionally oppressed those who engaged in same-sex lovemaking. With the increasing shrillness of the far right after World War II, exemplified by both a rabid anticommunism and the demand for total conformity that characterized the 1950s, laws aimed at homosexuals became so harsh that at times they were draconian.

The Defense Department hardened its policy of excluding homosexual servicemen and -women, tripling the World War II discharge rate and, in a reversal of prior practice, generally giving less-than-honorable "blue discharges." These punitive discharges stripped thousands of veterans of the benefits that had been promised them in the GI Bill of Rights. After Lt. Roy Blick of the Washington, D.C., vice squad testified before the Senate in 1950 that 5,000 homosexuals worked for the government (a figure he had invented), the Senate authorized a full investigation into the matter by a subcommittee chaired by North Carolina senator Clyde Hoey.[22] The Hoey subcommittee's report said that "those who engage in overt acts of perversion lack the emotional stability of normal persons." Having concluded that "one homosexual can pollute an entire office," the subcommittee urged that the military's recent purge of homosexuals be the model for civilian agencies.

The Civil Service Commission and the FBI complied by initiating an intense campaign to ferret out homosexuals by, for instance, correlating morals arrests across the United States with lists of government employees and checking fingerprints of job applicants against the FBI's fingerprint files.

After Eisenhower became president, he signed Executive Order 10450, in April 1953, which added "sexual perversion" as a ground for government investigation and dismissal. The government shared police and military records with private employers, resulting in the dismissal of hundreds.

While McCarthyism encouraged the toughening of laws toward homosexuals because they were believed to be security risks, America's Puritan tradition was producing hysteria over child molestation. Homosexuals were believed to be the main culprits. As the right-wing demonization of homosexuals proceeded apace, the negative qualities attributed to them overlapped until it became a common assumption that any homosexual man or woman was so beyond the pale that he or she must also partake of the most forbidden ideological fruit of all: communism. Homosexuals thus became handy scapegoats for both of these postwar obsessions. Antihomosexual laws were correspondingly made more severe.

States passed new laws that either stiffened the penalties for homosexual sex or created new categories to criminalize. For example, California governor Earl Warren thought the sex offender problem so serious that in 1949 he convened a special session of the state legislature to deal with the issue. That session passed laws that increased the penalties for sodomy and invented a new crime: loitering in a public toilet. The name of anyone convicted of spending too much time in a toilet was registered with the state. Twenty-nine states enacted new sexual psychopath laws and/or revised existing ones, and homosexuals were commonly the laws' primary targets. In almost all states, professional licenses could be revoked or denied on the basis of homosexuality, so that professionals could lose their livelihoods.

By 1961 the laws in America were harsher on homosexuals than those in Cuba, Russia, or East Germany, countries that the United States criticized for their despotic ways. An adult convicted of the crime of having sex with another consenting adult in the privacy of his or her home could get anywhere from a light fine to five, ten, or twenty years—or even life—in prison. In 1971 twenty states had "sex psychopath" laws that permitted the detaining of homosexuals for that reason alone. In Pennsylvania and California sex offenders could be locked in a mental institution for life, and in seven states they could be castrated.[23] At California's Atascadero State Hospital, known soon after its opening as "Dachau for Queers," men convicted of consensual sodomy were, as authorized by a 1941 law, given electrical and pharmacological shock therapy, castrated, and lobotomized. *Gay Law* author William N. Eskridge Jr. summed up the legal status of homosexuals at the beginning of the 1960s: "The homosexual . . . was smothered by law."[24]

Nor were transvestites spared. In New York State an old antilabor statute, passed in the nineteenth century to suppress tenant farmers who donned disguises to demonstrate against their landlords, was dusted off to use against men and women who dressed in the clothes of the opposite sex. In practice, New York police used the guideline that any person wearing fewer than three articles of clothing appropriate to their sex was, according to subsection 4 of section 240.35 of the New York Penal Code, "masked . . . by unusual or unnatural attire or facial alteration" and thus subject to arrest.[25]

It has often been pointed out that no specific statute outlawed being homosexual, that only homosexual acts were illegal. While this is technically true, the effect of the entire body of laws and policies that the state employed to police the conduct of homosexual men and women was to make being gay de facto a crime. The very harshness of the laws made judges generally unwilling to sentence homosexual men, lesbians, and transvestites to such inhumane punishment. Instead, judges tended to hand out light fines or to place those convicted on probation. But the random or selective use of far harsher penalties and the potential threat of their use, combined with other sanctions and harassments, major and minor, official and nonofficial, more than sufficed to keep the vast majority of homosexual men and women well within the lines that society had drawn for them. Thus lesbians and homosexual men lived in an uneasy state of fear and spiritual suffocation.

Once all manner of sanctions had been created to make it difficult for homosexual men and women to meet their own kind, the police aggressively patrolled the few places where homosexuals could mingle: bars and bathhouses (both private and public) and outdoor cruising places such as streets, parks, and beaches. Agents planted microphones in park benches and used peepholes and two-way mirrors to spy on homosexuals in public rest rooms.[26]

While the law classified homosexuals as criminals and the scientific establishment used psychology to medicalize homosexuality into an illness, gay men and lesbians found almost universal moral condemnation from religions, whether mainstream or obscure. Thrice condemned—as criminals, as mentally ill, and as sinners—homosexuals faced a social reality in post–World War II America that was bleak, if not grim.

Doric Wilson had come to New York in 1958 from Washington State to pursue a career as a playwright and often came to the Village to meet other gay men. One Sunday he circled a block on Greenwich Avenue. He had circled the block twice already and hadn't met anyone. In the early sixties it could be hard to meet someone, the encounter was so ritualized. The shops were closed on Sundays, but he circled the block looking at the shop windows; then he walked by without looking. Then he went around the block again, passed an attractive man, and stood and feigned a studious interest in the goods displayed in the window. Would the good-looking fellow stop and also stare? Maybe the other man would signal his interest by tapping his foot as they both window-shopped. Then Doric could ask the other man if he knew the time or had a light for a cigarette? They started the long, drawn-out procedure of approach. Did he live here? What did he think of the Village? And so forth. Suddenly Doric felt a sharp pain in his back. The blow was accompanied by a command: "Move on, faggots! Move on!" Doric didn't bother to argue with the police officer. He just moved on.

One reason Edgar Allan Poe went to the Northern Dispensary was because it was practically next to the small row house where he had found a very inexpensive apartment. The house where Poe lived happens to be across the street from the building Fat Tony's father owned. Barry Miles wrote that "American bohemianism is said to have started with Edgar Allan Poe,"[27] and the incongruous juxtaposition of the mobster's large apartment building with the bohemian's small row house in some ways parallels the paradox in which gay New Yorkers in the 1960s found themselves trapped. As word increasingly got out nationwide that there were large numbers of gay people in Greenwich Village, more and more gay men and lesbians were drawn to New York City. Eventually New York had the largest gay population in the United States, and the Village increasingly served as a center for the growing homosexual subculture. Sociologists Martin Weinberg and Colin Williams, who studied New York's homosexual population in the late 1960s, wrote that they found twenty-six bars, twelve nightclub/restaurants, four hotels, and two private clubs that catered to homosexuals, as well as all five of the city's lesbian bars, in the Greenwich Village area. They added: "Cruising areas abound."[28]

Paradoxically, New York was also the city that most aggressively and systematically targeted gay men as criminals. George Chauncey's *Gay New York* traces the rise of a visible gay population in the city from the 1890s to 1940, as well as the rise of powerful antivice societies to combat prostitution, alcohol consumption, homosexuality, and other behavior viewed as immoral.[29] In response to the great influence that these societies exerted over politicians, police vice squads—which New York City was the first to create—attempted to control homosexuals by observing locales where they congregated, using decoys to entice them, and raiding gay bars and baths.[30]

When Prohibition ended in 1933, the state passed many laws to regulate the sale and consumption of alcoholic beverages. As the word *Authority* in its name suggests, the laws that created the State Liquor Authority (SLA) made it undemocratic, giving it practically total leeway in administering and enforcing these laws. The SLA interpreted the laws so that even the presence of homosexuals—categorized as people who were "lewd and dissolute"—in a bar made that place disorderly and subject to closure.[31] The result made New York City the "most vigorous" investigator of homosexuals before World War II.[32] Responding to right-wing pressure after the war, New York City modernized its stakeout, decoy, and police raid operations, and continued to haul in thousands of homosexuals, sometimes just for socializing at a private party. More commonly, the police arrested gay men at bars and in cruising areas. By 1966 over one hundred men were arrested each week for "homosexual solicitation" as a result of police entrapment.[33]

Making it illegal for bars to serve homosexuals created a situation that could only attract organized crime. The Mafia entered into the vacuum to run gay bars, which in turn set up a scenario for police corruption and the exploitation of the bars' customers. These victims were not likely to complain, because they had nowhere else to go and because they feared the mob. Moreover, the involvement of the Mafia in gay clubs further increased the legal vulnerability of gay men and lesbians.

In the mid-1960s—the very time when a wave of freedom, openness, and demand for change was cresting—New York City increased its enforcement of antihomosexual laws to such an extent that it amounted to an attempt to impose police-state conditions onto a homosexual ghetto.

RESISTANCE

Throughout much of American history lesbians, homosexual men, and transvestites at times offered resistance—however weak, fleeting, or ineffectual—to the social and legal institutions that oppressed them. The first sustainable political resistance began in 1950 in Los Angeles when Harry Hay founded the Mattachine Society. This marked the birth of the homophile movement. The founders of the Mattachine Society used the word *homophile* because they believed that this new term, with its incorporation of the Greek word for love, could help counter the stereotype of homosexuals as obsessed with sex. The Mattachine Society took its name from medieval societies in which those playing the role of fool could speak truth to those in power.

Hay and his colleagues articulated in a statement of purpose a plan of action in which homosexuals who lived "isolated from their own kind" were, first, unified and then "educated" in order to develop an "ethical homosexual culture" similar to that of other minorities. After progress had been made toward the first two goals, the intent was "to push forward into the realm of political action." The Mattachine Society began taking political action sooner than planned when a police officer entrapped one of its founders. The new organization resolved to fight the charge, a radical idea at the time. Astonishingly, Mattachine won, making their name renowned among California homosexuals and spurring a membership surge.

Not long afterward, however, word began to circulate of the radical politics of some of the Society's founders, most notably Hay who had been a member of the Communist Party. When it became clear that the organization would falter if Hay did not withdraw from it, he did so at the Mattachine Society's 1953 national convention. The organization then incorporated as an educational and research group, espousing the belief that by providing accurate information about homosexuality to the public it could "eliminate discrimination, derision, prejudice and bigotry." The Mattachine's new leaders, including those in New York City, reasoned that since they had no validity in society's eyes, they could borrow from those who did, namely, psychologists and psychiatrists, the supposed experts on homosexuality. The vision of political activism was lost.[34]

In Chicago, sixteen-year-old Craig Rodwell, a high school junior in 1957, left his mother's apartment each weekday to walk to school. Although he had the money to pay the bus fare, he walked the entire distance. Craig walked to and from school on days when it was hot as well as on days when the stiff winter winds that howled in off Lake Michigan blasted the city, making pedestrians scurry to escape the misery outdoors. Money was hard to come by for Craig, whose mother's salary as a secretary was stretched thin to support him and his older brother. But Craig was a very determined young man, and he was especially eager to save all the money he could. The more he saved, the sooner he could realize his dream. Besides saving money by walking to school, Craig started asking for money for his birthday and for Christmas.

On many days after arriving at school, he walked to the library, went straight to the unabridged dictionary resting on its stand, and began to turn the pages. He continued looking until he came to the word. The word he had come to the library to see over and over again. *Homosexual.* He stared at the word as if to make sure that it was still in the same place and on the same page where he had so often seen it. To Craig, it proved that he existed.[35]

Needing to stare at a word in the dictionary to validate his very being showed just how radically Rodwell's experience of his sexuality had changed. Only a few years before, he had easily expressed his sexuality with other boys, for he had spent much of his childhood and early adolescence in an all-boys institution run by the Christian Science church. "We lived for our free time when we could go out in the woods. We liked the kissing and the holding hands and other things too. It was all very natural," he recalled. When a housemother occasionally saw Craig being intimate with another boy, she would tell them that they could not do what they were doing. Her injunctions always angered Craig.

As for Craig's being at the institution, there, too, money had played a role: his mother had sent him there after her husband had deserted her. With no income, she had to spend all her time working to support herself and her sons. And so Craig was sent away to the Christian Science School until he was fourteen, when he returned to Chicago to live with his mother. By this time his mother had remarried, and the family economic situation had improved enough that Craig could take ballet lessons.

Some months after returning home, Craig was walking one night to the el with Frank, a gentle Italian dishwasher, when suddenly two police cars, their lights whirling, converged on the two. Policemen got out of the cars and separated and questioned Craig and Frank. The police refused to believe that it was the fourteen-year-old Rodwell who had picked up the older man. The district attorney put heavy pressure on Craig to lie by saying that the older man had approached him and given him money. Craig refused. Frank was sentenced to five years for having sex with a minor, even though Craig explained that he had claimed to be older. No doubt it was Craig's noncooperation with the authorities that caused them to recommend he be sent to a reformatory.

This was more than Craig's mother could bear after she had already been separated from him for so much of his life. She broke down crying and screaming, got down on her knees, and begged the juvenile hearing officer to have mercy. The officer relented and said that if Craig's mother sent him to a private psychiatrist, she would place him on probation instead of sending him away. Despite the arrest and barely escaping reform school, Craig's confidence in the rightness of his behavior was not shaken. On the contrary, he now became, in his own words, "an angry queer."

About two years later Craig met a man named Harry at Chicago's gay beach. Harry told him about the Mattachine Society and showed him some of their publications. Craig was immediately fascinated with the idea that gay people were actually organizing to do something about the way they were treated. Craig decided to go to the Chicago chapter of the Mattachine Society right away. Once at the address listed in the publication, his heart sank as he scanned the building directory in vain for the words *Mattachine Society*. He wandered the halls looking for a door with the word *Mattachine* on it. Finally he realized that what he had imagined as a large, busy headquarters was just a mailing address. Craig felt the bottom fall out of his life.

Not long afterward he heard that all queers lived in Greenwich Village. He immediately decided to move there as soon as possible, which meant after graduating from high school. He started walking to school.

In the nation's capital, on some evenings in 1959 Franklin Kameny lay awake in his bed unable to fall asleep. Malnutrition had caused him to lose so much weight that his bones hurt where they touched the mattress. Less than two years before, he had had a good job, as befitted someone with a Ph.D. in astronomy from Harvard. The job had come from the U.S. government, which had hired Kameny to make more accurate maps for the military.[36]

He had once served in the military himself, having left college in 1943 to fight in Europe on World War II's front lines. Frank was intellectually precocious, so that when he started studying astronomy after the war, he made steady progress in his field. In the 1950s he went to a Tucson observatory to do the research for his Ph.D. thesis. After he had completed his research, he decided to travel around the country by bus on his way back to Cambridge. On a stop in San Francisco a stranger had approached him as he walked through the bus terminal. When the man walked up to Frank and groped him, plainclothes police officers emerged from their hiding place and arrested Frank and the stranger. Unfamiliar with legal proceedings, Frank did not fight the charge, since he was told that after being on probation for three years, his arrest record would be expunged. Because of the promise of expungement, Frank had not worried about the old arrest record when he applied for a job with the military.

At the end of 1957, while working on a military project in Hawaii, Kameny received a phone call summoning him to Washington immediately. Once there, he met with a representative of the Civil Service Commission.

"We have information that leads us to believe you are homosexual. Do you have any comment?"

"What's the information?"

"We can't tell you."

"Well, I can't give you an intelligent answer if you can't tell me, and in any case, I don't think it's any of the government's business."

Soon after that terse exchange, Kameny received a standard dismissal letter. Frank decided to fight back. In the meantime, he could not find a job, because almost all the positions for observational astronomers such as himself were with the U.S. government. Unfortunately, Frank did not know anything about working at jobs other than the kind for which he had been trained. As Frank pursued his solitary fight, his funds dwindled, and he lived on food such as Jell-O, hot dogs, and mashed potatoes. On the best days, he had a pat of butter to put on his mashed potatoes. On the worst days, he had nothing to eat.

He followed the administrative appeal process all the way through to its end without success. After twenty months, Kameny finally found a science and engineering job that did not require a security clearance. For almost anyone else, that would have been the end of the fight. It was perfectly clear to Frank, however, that while he had done nothing wrong, the government had. Frank Kameny decided that the United States would have to change its policies.

Randy Wicker was so determined to unravel the mysteries surrounding homosexuality in order to understand himself that he majored in psychology and sociology. He was disappointed in his studies, however, for in the academic literature he found only case studies and the standard theories of the day, such as the Freudian orthodoxy that male homosexuality was caused by a son having a weak father and a dominant mother. Yet all Randy's reading about homosexuality ultimately paid off in a different manner than he had expected when he read about a very large place where homosexuals went to meet one another: Greenwich Village. The following summer, he traveled to New York to explore the Village. Hanging out in his first gay bar, Lenny's Hideaway, Randy heard of a mysterious and very powerful organization called the Mattachine.

Thomas Lanigan-Schmidt grew up in the sister towns of Linden and Elizabeth, New Jersey, towns that, while having their own governments and boundaries, blend into and overlap each other on the ground. These are gritty industrial towns, whose chief industries in the 1950s and '60s were represented by companies like Singer Sewing Machine, General Motors, and Gordon's Gin. Growing up there in a time before there were any laws against air pollution, Tommy had trouble seeing how to drive his paper route through the pollution that mingled with the morning fog. The gray air that engulfed Tommy penetrated his nostrils with a sulfurous stench that reminded him of rotten eggs.

Perhaps Tommy drew with bright colors to make a contrast with his gray surroundings. He loved to make pictures of parrots and peacocks. When he depicted tropical fish, he favored Siamese fighting fish because of their rich, vibrant colors.

Tommy attended a Catholic grammar school. There the nuns noticed Tommy's talent for drawing and put him in charge of decorating the bulletin boards. Unlike the nuns, who encouraged Tommy's artistic temperament, Tommy's father feared his son's interests indicated a lack of masculinity. In an attempt to change Tommy, his father had persuaded him to work the paper route. His father had explained that this was the path to independence and promised Tommy that he could buy anything he wanted with the money he earned.

Tommy set his heart on an object in the local Woolworth's that he considered an item of rare beauty: a little opalescent pink-and-gold teacup made of very thin china, with a delicate stem on its bottom and an elaborate gold handle. He dutifully saved the small amounts of money from his paper route for its purchase.

When the great day finally came, Tommy proudly carried the cup home. Rather than being pleased at seeing Tommy use the money to buy something he wanted, his father was enraged that his son had bought a lady's teacup. The next morning Tommy found the teacup in the middle of the kitchen table, lying on its side, its small pink bottom snapped off. Tommy carried the broken teacup up to his room, carefully placed it in an Easter egg box, and hid the box.

The agitated twenty-four-year-old with a trim build, blue eyes, and brown hair was practically yelling at Dick Elman, WBAI's public affairs director. "Why do you have these people on that don't know a damn thing about homosexuality?" he demanded. The furious young man's piercing voice, the result of a deviated septum, certainly was irritating. Randy Wicker continued, "They don't live it and breathe it the way I do. . . . I spend my whole life in gay society." Wicker was infuriated because the previous night New York's progressive radio station had broadcast a program on homosexuality in which the only persons talking had been straight psychologists and psychiatrists. Predictably, they had given the psychological establishment's party line on the subject. Elman replied, "Get a group together, and I'll come up and do an interview."

These were words Wicker had been waiting to hear. For years Randy had tried everything he could think of to get out accurate information about homosexuals and homosexuality. His first brainstorm had come in 1958 when he had persuaded the Mattachine Society of New York (Mattachine–New York) to publicize its lectures. Randy had printed and distributed hundreds of flyers, which had drawn an overflow audience. He also captured the attention of the police, who then pressured the Mattachine Society's landlord into throwing the organization out on the street. The loss of the brand-new quarters was especially painful because members of the society had just spent months renovating them. Half of the organization's fifteen members thought more firebrands like Randy were just what the organization needed and pointed to all the people who had come to the lecture. The other half pointed to the lost lease as evidence that rabblerousers like Wicker would doom the organization.

Wicker's next venture took place about three years later when he learned of a public forum called a speak-out that was held on the corner of Mac-

Dougal and West 3rd streets. A speaker could stand on a soapbox and talk about issues considered radical or offbeat. Randy trembled as he mounted the box, fearful that the crowd might stone him. He decided to talk about a gay bar that operated just down the street. He explained that the bar paid off the cops and that this was not in the interest of the cops, for it corrupted them. In turn, the cops corrupted the city government. It therefore served everyone's interest for homosexuals to have the right to gather in their own places. To Randy's amazement, his peroration was greeted with a round of applause. After another positive encounter at a speak-out, Randy concluded that whatever the shortcomings of their government, the American people were accepting and wanted to be informed.

Randy became most angry when he read the misinformation printed whenever the media discussed homosexuality. They carefully fed the public images of homosexuals as communist spies, child molesters, or men who played a stereotypical "queen" role by plucking their eyebrows and speaking in a high voice.

In his determination to break the media silence on homosexuality, Wicker tried everything from having matchbooks printed with a one-line homosexual rights message to advertising unsold homophile publications for a nominal price as a "sample packet of homosexual publications," ads that were rejected by most newspapers and magazines, including *The Village Voice*.[37]

When Randy had buttons made that said "Equality for Homosexuals" and wore one to a gay party, he sold a button to everyone there. Usually, however, he had little luck in promoting the cause in the homophile community. He also found the machinery of group decision-making inordinately slow for his taste and concluded that a considerable number of the Mattachine's members were either too frightened or brainwashed to fight for their rights. The group that exemplified this overly cautious mentality for Randy was the West Side Discussion Group, a gay social group sponsored by the Mattachine Society that tended to be home to the most conservative members and affiliates of the homophile movement. The liberal attitude toward homosexuality in the late fifties and early sixties was that homosexuals were not criminals but mentally ill people who might be cured if given understanding and a lot of expensive therapy. The West Side Discussion Group was so conservative, however, that some of its members were not even able to digest the liberal theory. One of them said to Wicker, "How can we expect the police to allow us to congregate? Let's face it; we're criminals. You can't allow criminals to congregate." Randy blew up at the man, saying, "It disgusts me. Why do I have to sit here and listen to idiots like you say things like that? You've let society brainwash you."

In the spring of 1962[38] Randy finally got so fed up that he formed his own one-man operation, the Homosexual League of New York. He had business cards printed and presented himself to WBAI as the public relations director of the "organization."

On a humid spring night several weeks after Wicker had confronted Elman, the WBAI public affairs director arrived at the Upper West Side apartment of a friend of Randy's. With the windows open, the eight men Wicker had assembled sat on the floor with Elman to tape a candid discussion of their lives. Realizing that it was breaking new ground, WBAI sent out a press release about the broadcast, bringing the event to the attention of Jack O'Brian, a columnist with the *New York Journal-American*. O'Brian was deeply offended by the very idea of such a program. Labeling Wicker an "arrogant, card-carrying swish," O'Brian suggested the station change its call letters to WSICK.[39] The media-savvy Wicker realized that he had just been handed an opportunity and, with characteristic energy, carried copies of O'Brian's article to newspaper and magazine offices until it had reached the desk of every news editor in the city.

The New York Times did two stories on the broadcast. In a review headlined "Radio: Taboo Is Broken," *The Times* pronounced that the program "succeeded . . . in encouraging a wider understanding of the homosexuals' attitudes and problems." *Newsweek* gave the event a full page. *The Realist* used several of its issues to print an entire transcript of the ninety-six-minute program. And *Escapade,* a *Playboy* imitator, printed a condensed version of the transcript. The *New York Herald Tribune* and *Variety* carried favorable articles as well.[40]

The immediate payoff had been golden, but the resourceful Wicker leveraged it into platinum. He assembled copies of the transcripts and the extensive press coverage and sent them to writers whom he continued to buttonhole, offering "field trips" into homosexual New York.[41] As historian John D'Emilio noted, the coverage of homosexuality in the national media from 1962 to 1965 increased markedly as a result of Wicker's campaign. Articles on the subject in the *Reader's Guide to Periodical Literature* increased sixfold between 1962 and 1963 alone.[42] A crack had been made in the wall of media silence.

Arthur Evans took his belt off, went to the closet in his small dormitory room, and opened the door. After scrutinizing the clothes bar in the closet, he decided his idea would work. He could attach his belt to the bar, wrap the belt around his neck, and end his life.

Most people would have figured that a student in his junior year of college at an Ivy League school who was bright enough to be there on a full scholarship would have everything in life to look forward to. All the more so considering that he had come from a poor, working-class family in a dismal neighborhood of York, Pennsylvania.

Arthur was tortured by his overpowering feelings of attraction toward other boys. He had experienced these feelings since age eleven, when puberty hit early and hard. He knew that his longings were dangerous and was careful not to act on them, believing that if other boys found out how he felt he'd be beaten up or killed. When he tried to read about homosexuality in the school library, he found only Freudian theory; in the Bible, condemnation.

Arthur felt he had to escape York. He found the means to leave when he won a scholarship from the local paper company to study chemistry at Brown University. Though Brown at that time enrolled only males, Arthur at first found no sign there of other men who felt as he did.

Arthur was beginning to be interested in political activism. He started the Free Thinkers Society of Brown with his roommate, Michael. While Brown was a secular institution, it had a weekly chapel service at which attendance was compulsory. Considering themselves militant atheists, Arthur and Michael hatched a plan to protest the service. They demonstrated in front of the chapel, handing out leaflets and urging those who agreed with them not to stand but to sit through the chaplain's prayer. Arthur and Michael got five students to join them. This surprised Arthur, for this was before campus protests became common.

The protest made the front page of one of Arthur's two hometown newspapers. The Glatfelter Paper Company, which had given Evans his scholarship, was run at that time by Christian fundamentalists. After the article on the protest appeared, Glatfelter informed Arthur that it was revoking his scholarship. Arthur then got in touch with Joseph Lewis, the millionaire head of the National Free Thinkers Society, and explained the threat Glatfelter had made. Lewis wrote to Glatfelter saying that if they terminated Evans's scholarship, he would sue them and drag their name through the mud in the media. Glatfelter then backed down. This victory over the paper manufacturer became a shaping event for Arthur's future.

Evans's triumph convinced him to change his major to political science. Arthur concluded that the confrontation with Glatfelter offered several lessons for successful political activism: take a principled stand, be smart about it, get a lot of media attention, and have some friends who can pull strings for you.

Meaningful as it was, Evans's victory did not solve the problems of loneliness and sexual frustration. Instead, the feelings intensified. Even worse, other students were coming on to him. Evans couldn't believe they were like him, so they could only be coming on to him because they wanted to get him to give himself away. This was more than he could bear.

Evans decided to act. He went to the closet and had just started the preparations for ending his life when a wave of deep dread came over him. An image of standing on the edge of a precipice above a pit so deep it had no bottom welled up before him. A sudden wave of nausea swept over Evans, and he stepped back from the edge.

Soon afterward, in the spring of 1963, Arthur picked up a national magazine and read in it that a lot of homosexuals lived in Greenwich Village. That he was not alone after all was a complete and sudden revelation. Evans decided to give up his scholarship and move to New York City.

Dick Leitsch was born in Kentucky, which he called "the land of horse-shit, tobacco and the mint julep."[43] His Kentucky childhood was in many ways typical. For example, on Saturdays he went with his friends to the movies. But while his companions fantasized about being cowboys, westerns failed to engage Dick's imagination. He was, however, mesmerized by the great screen actresses of the forties and fifties. The lives they portrayed in urban settings made Kentucky seem decidedly lackluster. Dick began to dream of "going to New York, drinking cocktails, smoking cigarettes, and having stupid love affairs, just like Bette Davis."

While Leitsch may have found Kentucky lacking in cultural sophistication, there was some sophistication about homosexuality, both in the larger society and in Dick's Catholic family. Dick's mother had gay male and lesbian friends who were couples and came over to the house and visited. His parents were totally accepting of his homosexuality when the first man with whom Leitsch had sex indiscreetly sent him flowers the following morning with a love note attached.

His mother asked, "Is it true? Is this your boyfriend?"

"I had sex with him last night."

"Well, Father Valentine used to be a chaplain in a prison and said that you would probably grow up to be a homosexual. We've been watching and thought that you probably were. I guess he was right."

Dick's parents continued to be supportive, urging him to introduce them to his friends. Meanwhile, Dick's childhood fantasies about New York as the epitome of sophistication had continued to grow as he listened at night to live radio broadcasts from the Stork Club and the Copacabana.

After moving to Cincinnati in 1958, he and Derrick, a man who had lived in New York but had not liked the city, became lovers. Leitsch ultimately persuaded Derrick to give it another try. Derrick went back first, got reestablished, and wrote to Dick to come join him. Arriving at Pennsylvania Station in early 1959, Leitsch was greeted by Derrick. They got into a taxi and, as the cab passed through Times Square, Dick saw the crossroads of the world and felt intensely happy. It looked just as he had imagined it, except that in color it looked, if possible, even better.

On Sundays Tommy Lanigan-Schmidt often went with his friend "Mark" Vag to the Greek Catholic church Mark attended.[44] Tommy had easily embraced the Catholic church in which he was raised, but when the nuns sent him to the grammar school library to do his bulletin board artwork, he discovered the highly mystic traditions of the Russian and Greek Orthodox churches. The school library had Greek Orthodox volumes because there was a local population of Greek Catholics, who belonged to a branch of Catholicism that blended Roman Catholic and Greek Orthodox teachings.

Tommy had been shocked as a Cub Scout when his den mother, in spite of Mark being a member of the den, had warned them to stay away from the local Greek Catholic church because the priest there had a wife. He also felt sorry for Mark because the local toughs would mock his name, walking up to him and saying loudly, "Hey, Mark FAG!"

Good male friends were not plentiful in Tommy's young life. The tougher kids in school picked on him. Between classes they would walk up to him and hit him hard in the stomach.

Tommy had befriended Mark, and Mark in turn invited Tommy to attend his church. The rich fabric used by the priests, the highly ritualized ceremonies, and the abundant use of incense immediately appealed to Tommy's spiritual and aesthetic sensibilities. The local Greek Catholic church had held an air of mystery for young Tommy, especially when he saw its doors standing open on Easter mornings.

Now that he was in high school, he was old enough to stay up till midnight, the symbolic hour of deepest darkness, when the Greek Catholic Easter service begins. As Tommy entered the church, something seemed odd. Gradually, he realized that no candles were lit. A life-size portrait of Jesus on a piece of cloth was arrayed over a large coffin-shaped box. A priest emerged and told everyone to leave the church. As the worshipers left, they intoned slowly and repeatedly, "Christ is risen from the dead," in a droning dirge that was deep and sad.

As they left the church some worshipers stumbled in the darkness. By late night in a factory town like Linden, the air smells heavy because the factories release much of their effluvium in the evenings, and by this time of night the polluted air had settled down to street level. The foul odors intensified the plainsong's sadness.

The chant continued mantralike until all the congregants were outside. Then the singing stopped and the words were intoned. The pace of the chant quickened until it was almost frenetic. Suddenly a priest holding a large gold Bible stepped forward. He was wearing the brightest vestments Tommy had ever seen: gold embroidery spangled with silver threads shimmered in the candles' light. The priest read the story of Jesus' disciples going to the tomb and seeing the angel who said, "He is risen." The crowd repeated, "Christ is risen." The priest approached the church's double doors and knocked loudly on them with his crook: *Bang! Bang! Bang!* And the doors sprang open.

Their candles lit, there was a rush of fire as the churchgoers hastened inside, chanting, "And on those in the tombs bestowing life!" a moment in the ritual that represents being brought back from death's realm into life. Inside, Tommy found the church transformed: every chandelier was turned on, all of the church's bells began pealing, the choir started to sing, and the church, previously bare, was filled with flowers. As he stepped back outside the church into Linden's foul air, Tommy had an inexplicable feeling of hope. This moment was to return to him unexpectedly years later.

Soon after his arrival, Dick Leitsch was introduced to New York City's gay scene, including the neighborhood he initially settled in, the Upper West Side. Curiously, many of the places that were pointed out to Dick had recently been closed down, from Milano's, a rough trade bar, to the All-State Café, a dance bar, to Omega, a hustler bar, as well as many others. This shuttering of gay businesses was the result of a recent and massive campaign of police harassment under Mayor Robert Wagner. During the crackdown the licenses of gay businesses had been revoked. Many people had been arrested, and many more had been entrapped and harassed. The mayor's campaign against gay men was the main topic of conversation in the gay male world. Although Leitsch found a much bigger homosexual scene in Manhattan than he had known in Louisville, he noticed that it was more underground. "I just couldn't believe that was happening in New York, which I thought was the capital of civilization. It had never occurred to me that it was going to be more conservative than my hometown."

As Arthur Evans settled into his new life in New York City, he often went to Washington Square Park to sit and read. Politics remained very much on his mind, and as he contemplated the park's arch, built to honor George Washington, he noticed a quotation by the revolutionary inscribed on the arch's top: "Let us raise a standard to which the wise and the honest may repair." Whenever he returned to the park, he read the inscription, which seemed to speak to him.

2

Oppression, Resistance,
and Everyday Life

Dick Leitsch went to Greenwich Village from time to time, but he found gay men there a bit cliquish and self-consciously bohemian. He found a real communal social life with other gay men in the area along Central Park West, where homosexual men went to relax by socializing at evening time.

"Every night after dinner we'd go walk on Central Park West and we'd run into all of our friends, the people we worked with, and half the West Side gay people—which were thousands—on Central Park West between 59th and 86th. In those days, there was one long bench from corner to corner, solid with gay men. Hundreds and thousands of them walked back and forth singularly, in couples, and in groups."

The huge chattering crowds made a considerable din, which led to complaints from nearby residents, and the police would make from three to five sweeps along the park most nights. A sweep might consist of a single car or as many as six at a time, each with large bright lights mounted on its top. While driving by and shining the lights on the gay men, the police used megaphones to order, "Move on. Keep moving, faggots. Keep moving." Dick recalls that the gay men would all get off the benches and walk up the street very slowly, as though they were going home. Once the police cars disappeared from view, the gay men would scramble back to the benches, wait for the police to circle again, and repeat the same charade.

Late in the winter of 1962 a suave, tall, and handsome thirty-two-year-old Wall Street banker was cruising Central Park West. When he reached 88th

Street, he noticed an attractive man and approached him. The banker's name was Harvey Milk and the man he had cruised was Craig Rodwell.

Craig Rodwell and Harvey Milk had little in common. Milk was Jewish and a native New Yorker, whereas the midwestern Rodwell described himself as a Christian Scientist. The banker held the right-wing political values common in his profession, while the young ballet student was politically progressive. Whereas Rodwell was eager to take on the whole world's prejudice against homosexuality, Milk was very secretive about his sex life.

When Craig had arrived in New York in the late summer of 1959, he was only eighteen, yet he felt it had taken him forever to get to a city with an active Mattachine chapter. On arriving at the Mattachine–New York office, Rodwell was told that he could not join because he was too young: he would have to wait until he was twenty-one. Craig could not wait that long. On his own he made up flyers urging people to join the Mattachine Society and put them in the mailboxes of Village residences with two men's names on them, figuring that the recipients were probably a gay couple.

While Rodwell was studying at the American Ballet School thanks to a scholarship, he had little money left over for living expenses.[1] He got a low-paying job in a flower factory and did not make enough money to go to gay bars. One night while he was cruising in Washington Square Park a police officer gave Craig the usual order to move on. Rodwell retorted, "This is harassment of homosexuals." The officer immediately arrested him and took him to jail. Craig's resistance was unprecedented. That night in jail one policeman after another came by Rodwell's cell to see the upstart homosexual. "What'sa matter, lose your purse?" baited one. Craig shot back, "What'sa matter, never seen a faggot before?"

Rodwell continued to haunt Manhattan's cruising grounds until he met Milk, with whom he would have his first serious romance. Each morning, Milk, a born romantic, gave Craig a wake-up call invariably accompanied by a joke. On Christmas morning, Harvey, the son of Orthodox Jews, arrived early, laden with presents that showed thoughtfulness and a romantic touch. Craig was soon swept off his feet.

But the pair's divergent politics tested the romance. While in his early teens Rodwell had idolized Adlai Stevenson, Milk had championed Barry Goldwater. When Rodwell told Milk about another of his evening forays putting flyers into mailboxes, Milk yelled at him, "You shouldn't do that to people! Getting those in mailboxes will make people paranoid that everyone knows about them being gay."

"You're just thinking about how you would react if it showed up in your mailbox," Rodwell retorted.

There were other problems beyond politics. When Milk discovered that he had gonorrhea, he concluded Craig had been unfaithful, for Milk had not slept with anyone else after the two had started dating. When Milk confronted Rodwell, Craig admitted to having sex with other men, even though he was in love with Harvey.

It was not only homosexuals from out-of-state who heard about the Village and found their way there. Jerry Hoose recalls his first trip there as an eighteen-year-old: "Around the end of '63 or the beginning of '64, I heard about Greenwich Village. I was living in Brooklyn and kept dreaming about finding other gay people. One day I just said, 'I got to find it!'

"And I got on the train and got off at 8th Street. I got to Sixth Avenue and 8th Street, at that time the Mecca: it was Greenwich Avenue from Sixth Avenue to Mama's Chick'N'Rib on Charles Street. I crossed Sixth Avenue and I saw all these very gay-looking people, and I said, 'Well, I've found my world.'"

Tree is another native New Yorker who discovered the Village as a gay place in his teen years. His favorite place was not a bar but the restaurant many gay men from the era still remember affectionately, Mama's Chick'N'Rib. With perhaps a touch of hyperbole, Tree remarks, "It was considered the gay hangout of the world." Tree was at Mama's so often he ended up working there in the late 1950s.

"This place was more crowded than any bar. Of course the bars in those times were all owned by the Mafia—they charged you to get in, watered down drinks, a little roughing up if you got too drunk. But Mama's Chick-'N'Rib was a home. We had a waiter there named Jack. They called him Joan Crawford. And there was myself, Jerry, Garth, and a few others.

"Now, certain nights, when it was all friends in the place, we wouldn't let anybody in. We would lock the door because we were packed. And we'd fog up the windows by turning the heat and air-conditioning on, so there was a little dancing, a little kissing here and there. Everybody would eat and drink for free all night long and then in the morning when everybody knew Mama was coming, Jack would pass around two boxes, one for the register and one for the tips. Everybody would throw money in both of them. And at the end of the night Mama looked in the cash register and she was so happy. She made five, six hundred dollars and Jack and Garth and everybody that worked there was happy because they made like fifty, sixty dollars for their tips, which is a lot of money in the fifties. Mama never knew the difference.

"She was a little old Greek lady that you had to love her or hate her. . . . In all the years she had Mama's she only wore two dresses. One was blue and one was black. She had a favorite strand of pearls and wore them every day. She looked on all the customers in her place as her children. It was 'my boy' this, and 'my boy' that, and as she talked to you she always played with her pearls. She could hold a handful of coins for a minute and then tell you to the penny how much was in her hand. . . . She counted french fries, sliced tomatoes that you could read a newspaper through. If you dropped food on the floor, it went back on the plate. It was that kind of place, but movie stars were seen in there."

Even though Mama's was not run by the Mafia, as the place catered to gay people, Mama still had to pay off the police. "Brown bag Friday it was called. Cops would come around to bars and restaurants that catered to gay people, and they would have a little brown bag like a container of coffee with no coffee in it. It was all full of money for the neighborhood precincts—uptown, downtown, midtown. 'You want your windows broken?' 'No.' 'Well, you let all these fags hang out in there.' So, we had to give a little envelope every once in a while."[2]

On Labor Day weekend of 1962, Craig Rodwell headed for the beach like millions of his fellow Americans. The beach Craig chose, however, was the one at Riis Park, where thousands of gay men and lesbians congregated. After he had enjoyed the beach for a while, he headed for the bathhouse, where hot dogs and soda were sold. Craig had heard the talk on the beach that since this was a homosexual beach, on Memorial Day and Labor Day the police enforced a blue law written early in the century that outlawed a man wearing a bathing suit that did not cover his navel and reach at least the midway point between his knees and his groin.

Craig left the beach without a towel nonetheless. When he reached the boardwalk, the policeman stationed there started writing him a ticket. Craig protested that this was harassment of homosexuals and that they all knew what was going on, it was a quota system, and . . .

A crowd began to collect.

The policeman quickly grabbed Craig and hustled him into a small room maintained by the police inside the bathhouse. As soon as the policeman had Craig behind the closed door, he slammed him down on the hard floor. "Faggot!"

Craig Rodwell had always been told to tell the truth as part of his Christian Science upbringing. He had learned that following that precept could be dangerous for himself as well as for others. When Frank had been arrested in Chicago, he had lied, saying he was Craig's uncle. Craig had told the truth and the dishwasher had been sent to prison for years. The district attorney had told Craig to lie and he had not, which was why his mother had had to get down on her knees, crying, to keep her son from also being sent away.

After being arrested at Riis Park, Craig appeared before a judge who gave him a court date. The kindly judge who had taken him into his chambers said the fine would be routine and to be sure and bring the amount to pay it, around twelve dollars. Two weeks later Craig went to court carrying the cash. He found, however, that a charge of inciting to riot had been added to the charge of violating the dress regulation. Asked by the judge what had occurred, Craig said that the charge of inciting to riot made no sense, that he'd been immediately hauled into a small room away from the public. The judge dismissed the charge. Asked about the other violation, Craig turned to look into the face of the judge, who was sitting right next to him. Craig explained how the law worked, that it was an old law currently used only to harass homosexuals.

Craig saw the immediate change in the judge's eyes on hearing the word *homosexuals*. His face turned beet red as he banged his hammer down on the gavel, looked away from Craig, and gave him the maximum penalty, twenty-five dollars. Since Craig did not have that much money on him, he had to go to jail for three days.

Rodwell remembered that after his arrest in the park, the police had come by his cell for hours to taunt him. He knew they had been looking for an excuse to work him over, so he had held his tongue except for the one mild rejoinder when he had asked the guard if he was the first "faggot" he had seen. He also remembered that when he'd been asked his name at Riis Beach, after he had answered, the officer had taunted him by asking him to give it over and over again.

Asked his name at the prison, he refused to give it. Within a short time, a huge guard walked into the holding area where Craig was.

"All right, where's the guy who won't talk?"

Someone pointed to Craig. The guard slammed Craig's head against the wall, took his wallet from his pocket, and held it upside down so that its contents fell out.

"Pick it up!"

His head bleeding, Craig got down on his knees to gather up the pieces of paper. Through his tears, he could make out the photograph of his mother.

Several days had passed since Craig had not returned home, and Collin, Rodwell's roommate, had no idea what had happened to him. The phone rang and Collin answered. Harvey Milk again. No, Collin still didn't know where Craig was. Milk had slowed down on calling Craig after he had gotten gonorrhea from him, but with Craig gone and his roommate having no idea why, he was very concerned.

When Craig was released from prison, he got together with Harvey. Craig noticed Milk's strange expression on seeing Rodwell's shaved head. When the wake-up calls came even less frequently, Craig understood that in the eyes of the conservative Milk, he was now not only unfaithful but also a marked man who might endanger Milk's very successful career.

Shattered over the end of the relationship, Craig decided to take his life. He got rid of his cats, gave notice at his job, and dropped out of school. He bought a bottle of the depressant Tuinal. When Collin went out to a double-feature movie one night, Craig started taking the pills. He'd already written a note asking Collin to call Craig's aunt on finding the body. Above all, Craig didn't want his mother to get the news from a policeman.

When Craig Rodwell opened his eyes in Harlem Hospital, he saw a police officer. Although Craig was tied down, the very sight of a cop so infuriated him that he bolted upright with enough energy to break the restraints. His roommate, Collin, had been bored at the movies and come home early and found Craig unconscious. Chance had caused his attempted suicide to fail, but he wasn't sure he wanted to be alive.

A long difficult period followed. After a month in the Bellevue psychiatric ward he was transfered to St. Luke's psych ward. Then a wandering period in which Craig moved to Pleasantville, New York, Chicago, and on to Hollywood. As soon as he got off the bus in Los Angeles, Craig realized he'd made a mistake. He stayed for about a month, during which time John Kennedy was assassinated. By January 1964 Craig was back in New York.

Striving to give meaning to his life, Craig decided to work for the gay movement and volunteered to work full-time at the Mattachine Society. At the Mattachine office he typed the newsletter, edited it, stuffed envelopes, and did anything else that needed doing. He found using all his free time in this way "just thrilling." Craig Rodwell had found his life's calling.

The marginal quality of homosexual existence was rendered literal in the Village along the waterfront. While the shores of oceans, lakes, and rivers are still used in many cities by gay men as places to meet because of the privacy they afford, in the postwar Village the banks of the Hudson River became a meeting place because of the trucking industry. Commercial trucks that hauled produce and other cargo into the city usually unloaded their goods either at warehouses or at the waterfront loading docks. While the trucks were waiting for a load to take back out of the city, the empty trucks were parked unattended, with the backs unlocked.[3]

Marle Becker recalls the orgies that took place in the trucks: "There was no fence. The trucks would back right up to the river and it was pitch-dark in there. Every now and then you could see somebody with a cigarette in back of a truck. There would sometimes be two or three hundred people in them." While Becker enjoyed the sex in the trucks, he adds: "If we had our druthers we would have been happier checking into a hotel like any other couple, but that wasn't always an option for us." As for the criticism aimed at homosexual men by heterosexuals for having sex along the riverbank, Becker remembers how on his first visit to New York City he and his lover had been refused a hotel room because they were gay: "There wasn't any place for us to go. If you didn't have an apartment or if you had roommates or what have you [the only option] was to have sex in Central Park or the trucks or some out-of-the-way place where hopefully you didn't get caught and arrested." Even an invitation by another person to his place could be problematic: would the other person turn violent or turn out to be a plain-clothes policeman? "It was like, should I trust this person, shouldn't I trust this person? You didn't know from one minute to the next what was going to happen. So it was safer to be with two hundred people in the back of a truck."

Adding to the Village waterfront's appeal as a gay outpost, there were at various times in the postwar era a few waterfront bars that catered to homosexuals. The best-known of these, Keller's, operated in the sixties as a seaman's bar during the day and a gay bar at night.

In the postwar era, even in the Village, most social life for gay men took place in bars. Under increasing police pressure, the gay male bar and cruising scene migrated from West 8th Street to Greenwich Avenue between Sixth Avenue and Seventh Avenue South, until eventually in the early 1960s Greenwich Avenue became gayer than 8th Street.

Although police pressure had been very severe in 1960, it probably reached its apogee beginning in 1963 under the administration of Mayor Robert Wagner as the city began a concerted drive to make homosexuals invisible in time for the 1964–65 World's Fair in New York City.[4]

Philip Bockman arrived in New York City in 1963 after falling victim to a campaign of harassment at the University of Michigan. Called into the dean's office the day after he had refused to give the names of other gay students to a police officer who had roughed him up, he was told that un-less he "changed his ways" he "really should not be registered at the school." He recalls, "I did come to New York, only to find that Mayor

Wagner had this crackdown on the gay bars. Everything was closed up when I got here. The only gay bar open was the Cherry Lane. There were a few others that operated very surreptitiously. In 1964 for the World's Fair they started entrapping people as much as they could to clean up the homeless, the prostitutes, and the homosexuals. A lot of people were caught in that dragnet. I remember going to bars and some of the under-cover policemen got to be known because they would always be in the bars and some people got to know who they were. I remember a couple of in-stances where we would form a circle around them and we'd spread the word to everybody in the bar. Sometimes we'd even follow them from bar to bar."

Edmund White, who came to New York in 1962, recalls: "During the World's Fair time, the mayor didn't want there to be a gay image to the city so he closed virtually all the bars. It felt to me, like whereas gays used to cruise in a rather furtive way on Greenwich Avenue, they were now coming down Christopher Street and moving farther and farther down toward the water."

It seems likely that gay men who cruised Greenwich Avenue and did not find a sexual partner had established the practice of circling the block again, and Christopher Street was one of the most convenient places to turn back for such a maneuver. The sex scene at the trucks and one or two waterfront bars also began to draw men there, and the most direct route from Greenwich Avenue was down Christopher Street.[5]

One winter night in 1964 Dick Leitsch was walking down Greenwich Av-enue and spotted a boy who struck him as very pretty standing in the door-way of a bakery at the corner of Greenwich Avenue and Christopher Street. It had been almost two years since Leitsch's love affair with Derrick had ended when Derrick decided for the second time that he did not like New York City and had decamped for Florida.[6] The young man Leitsch had eyed started walking down Christopher Street, stopped, and leaned up against a building. The maneuver struck Leitsch as odd, for gay men cruised on Greenwich Avenue and on 8th Street, not on Christopher Street.[7] Nonetheless, Leitsch followed him. The two men struck up a con-versation, and Dick accepted Craig Rodwell's invitation to his apartment.

Craig and Dick started seeing each other, but when Rodwell told Leitsch that he was in the Mattachine Society, Leitsch laughed at him. Dick had been to a Mattachine–New York meeting in 1962 and heard Al-bert Ellis, a psychologist on the board, give a talk on homosexuality as ill-ness and was appalled when Ellis got a standing ovation from the membership.[8] Leitsch may have been bemused by Rodwell's involvement in Mattachine, but he soon learned that it was total. "Every time I called Craig and said, 'You want to go to the movies,' he said, 'I have to go to Mattachine.' Finally, just to be with him, I started hanging out at Mattachine."

Concerning the relationship between Leitsch and Rodwell, there is little that the two men agreed on except that it did not last long and ended badly. Rodwell maintained that he never wanted more than a sexual relationship and that Leitsch was obsessed with him to the point of being violent; Leitsch states the opposite, that it was Rodwell who "decided that he was going to be my lover. . . . He seizes on you and won't let go."[9] Whatever the truth of the matter, the two agree that it was because of their sexual involvement that Leitsch got involved in Mattachine–New York.

Although Rodwell had not been able to join formally because of his age, he had been active in Mattachine prior to 1964. He and Randy Wicker strongly advocated that the organization abandon the educational and research approach and take a militant stance. Frank Kameny had, with Jack Nichols, founded the Mattachine Society of Washington (Mattachine-Washington) in 1961. After Kameny and Nichols met Rodwell and Wicker, the four of them worked together to share strategies and support one another in their quest for a militant homophile movement. They were further supported by and worked with a lesbian couple, Barbara Gittings and Kay Tobin.

Lesbians had started their own organization, the Daughters of Bilitis (DOB), not long after the Mattachine Society was founded. If lesbians were less likely to draw the attentions of the police than homosexual men, that was in part because they had fewer institutions, whether social, political, or cultural. The needs of American lesbians were so basic in the 1950s that DOB turned inward to try to meet those needs by providing discussion groups and get-togethers. Barbara Gittings founded the New York chapter of DOB in 1958 and served as its president until 1961, the same year she met Kay Tobin. When Gittings met Frank Kameny in 1963, he greatly influenced her thinking and attitudes. "If you take the position that Frank has (that homosexuality is fully on par with heterosexuality) then you get a very clear view of what you have to do. He really crystallized my thinking." In 1962, Barbara had become editor of DOB's publication, *The Ladder*. Influenced by Kameny's and Wicker's militancy, she used her editorship to try to edge DOB toward an activist stance.

As a dialogue got under way between militants Rodwell, Wicker, and Kameny and members of the Mattachine–New York board, the board began to listen more seriously to what the militants had to say. One board member in particular, Julian Hodges, a rising star within Mattachine–New York, seemed more open than the others. When he became the organization's president-elect (the equivalent of vice president) he invited Kameny to give the organization's 100th public lecture.

In July, Kameny came up to New York from Washington, proclaiming like a fiery Old Testament prophet the message that a militant civil rights and social action approach was the way for gay men and lesbians to achieve their rights. Kameny argued that the homophile movement should be modeled on the black civil rights movement as formulated by nonviolent militant leaders such as Rev. Martin Luther King Jr. Kameny warned of the dangers inherent in the position that homosexuality was a mental illness. Having used his scientific background to study the psychological literature, Kameny stated that "until and unless valid, positive evidence shows otherwise, homosexuality, per se, is neither a sickness, . . . a neurosis, a psychosis, nor a malfunction of any sort."

Kameny courageously carried his logic to its conclusion, saying, "Not only is homosexuality . . . not immoral, but . . . homosexual acts engaged in by consenting adults are moral, . . . right, good, and desirable, both for the individual participants and for . . . society."

The effect of Kameny's passionate and eloquently argued speech was electric. Dick Leitsch, who read Kameny's speech over a dozen times, credited it with making him political for the first time in his life.[10]

Leitsch started putting in so many hours volunteering at the Mattachine office that Hodges asked him to become his assistant. Leitsch became editor of the organization's newsletter as well and used it to further the militants' agenda by emphasizing coverage of legal, political, and governmental events that bore on homosexuality and by writing in support of the black civil rights movement.

Hodges and his supporters decided to run a slate of militant officers in the 1965 Mattachine–New York elections. Hodges's slate included Kameny, the progressive psychologist Dr. Hendrick Ruitenbeek, and Dick Leitsch. Their ally Randy Wicker, ever the individualist, ran for the office of secretary as an independent. Leitsch was urged to run for president-elect and accepted the nomination in spite of not wanting the position. (Leitsch had urged Rodwell to run for president-elect, but Rodwell refused.) In his campaign statement, written by Rodwell, Leitsch promised to work to end police entrapment, discrimination by government and private agencies, and discrimination and prejudice in general against homosexuals.[11] The militants won the May election in a sweep, making Julian Hodges the president of Mattachine–New York.

Those were heady times for the insurgent activists. Having elected a slate of militants to run New York's Mattachine Society, they pressed forward with what were probably the two most controversial (and for the militants exciting) ideas in the homophile movement: public demonstrations in support of homosexual rights and an attack on the psychological establishment's position that homosexuality was a mental illness.

Picketing proved to be the most exciting experience for the militants. The first picketing was to protest against Castro's plans to put homosexuals in concentration camps. These protests—one in Washington, D.C., at the White House and one the next day in New York at the UN—went so well that the activists decided to mount a series of picket lines at strategic sites in Washington. The participants found the experience to be so liberating that they felt elated.

Craig Rodwell considered the picketing at the White House to be "the most wonderful day in my life." Saddened that the series of picket demonstrations was ending, he had a sudden brainstorm: the activists should picket once a year on July 4 in Philadelphia, where the United States had been born, to remind the American people that there was one minority group that still lacked basic rights. Rodwell's idea was accepted, and in 1965 activists traveled to Philadelphia to march in what came to be called the Annual Reminder.

It was during the time when Leitsch was just getting to know Julian Hodges that, out on a walk one day, they came across a politician who wanted to talk to them. The politician was campaigning to be district leader of the Village Independent Democrats (VID), then a new organization. He told Leitsch and Hodges about how Illinois had decriminalized sodomy and why New York should also do the same. The politician went on to say that adultery and divorce should be legalized as well. Although both men agreed with his position, Leitsch had walked away feeling that there was something very obnoxious about the politician, whom he had not taken very seriously. The politician lost the election, and his attempt to win elected office was derisively labeled "the SAD Campaign" because of Ed Koch's emphasis on legalizing sodomy, adultery, and divorce.

Doric Wilson, feeling miserable as well as confused, entered the Cherry Lane Bar. His play *And He Made a Her,* an Off Off Broadway hit, had just been moved to the Cherry Lane Theater as part of that theater's Monday evening playwrights series. Doric had considered this move to the well-respected Cherry Lane as proof of the professional theater world's stamp of approval. But the version of the play he had just seen did not at all resemble the one he had previously seen performed at the Caffe Cino. The new director had killed all the play's humor. Doric felt total despair, for he now saw his future endangered instead of assured. A drink in the Cherry

Lane Bar, where gay men often gathered, would give him a chance to collect himself.

A stranger came up to him and offered to buy him a drink.

"No, leave me alone. I'm in a rotten mood," was Doric's terse reply as he exited the bar.

Wilson walked to another bar. The same man who had approached him in the Cherry Lane had followed him and again walked up to Wilson. Doric said, "No, get away from me!" He left that bar and found a third one.

By the time he entered the third bar, he was beginning to calm down. The man from the Cherry Lane Bar showed up again. Feeling better, Doric yielded to the persistent fellow and accepted the drink, though it seemed only fair to warn him that he was not open to any further advances.

Doric faced his would-be suitor: "Look, I'm not interested in you. I've had one of the worst days of my life, but if you're going to follow me around, yes, you can buy me a drink, but I'm not going to be good company."

The man took out a badge and announced that Doric was under arrest.

One day in October of 1964 Leitsch picked up *The New York Times* and read the headline about Greenwich Village. He learned that Ed Koch had made a 180-degree turn: he and Carol Greitzer, Democratic leaders of the First Assembly District, were demanding that something be done about "the problem of . . . homosexuals who have been congregating on Village Square at Eighth Street and the Avenue of the Americas." Two days later *The Times* reported that Koch was "head[ing] a drive to rid the area" of homosexuals "and other undesirables." The article explained that after Koch had met with Police Commissioner Michael J. Murphy, Murphy had announced "plans to increase surveillance of Greenwich Village to curtail loitering and solicitation by homosexuals." In the article Koch boasted "that Commissioner Murphy had assured him that more 'effective' measures would be taken to curb activity of homosexuals."

The drive Koch and Greitzer launched led to the closing of a number of gay bars and the entrapment of hundreds of homosexuals, leaving many of them unable to get licenses or well-paying jobs for years into the following decade. In April of 1965, Koch asked Wagner for another "cleanup" of the Village and got it, during which more gay bars were closed and thousands of gay people were harassed on the Village's sidewalks. Three months later, Koch got yet another drive started, this one targeting Christopher Street.[12]

Entrapment was an issue much on Dick Leitsch's mind as he continued to volunteer at the Mattachine headquarters. At times in the midsixties the phone would ring in the Mattachine office all evening with calls for help from desperate men trying to save their families, their livelihoods, and their reputations. As Leitsch talked to one victim after another, he noticed certain patterns.

Leitsch realized that the police explanation for arresting gay men—that they were locking homosexuals up because they were prowling the city making unsolicited advances—was patently false. The entrapped men had been arrested by police officers in plain clothes who had gone into gay bars and cruising areas dressing and acting as though they were interested in sex. When the gay men had responded in kind, the cops arrested them. Gay men also noticed that the policemen who did this kind of work tended to be very attractive men who dressed provocatively for the occasion. The policemen who went into public bathrooms were not supposed to display themselves, but Leitsch heard over and over from those arrested that the men they met in a toilet often not only were displaying their penises but also had erections and were masturbating to look as inviting as possible.[13]

Other patterns emerged as well as Leitsch continued to answer the calls for help. For example, it was not uncommon for the police to suggest the names of certain attorneys who might be able to defend the men arrested for solicitation and/or loitering. When those charged consulted the attorneys, they were asked to pay exorbitant fees, far beyond the normal charge for such an infraction.[14] Leitsch also noticed that after the charges had been dropped, the police officers, previously so serious and gruff, suddenly became quite amiable. Entrapped gay men commonly concluded that one reason for the high fees charged by the lawyers the police steered them to was to grease the wheels of "justice."

Leitsch had run for president-elect of Mattachine–New York on a platform of ending entrapment. This issue was arguably the most pressing in the homosexual community, and it also seemed to Leitsch that it should be the easiest to address since it was so obviously unpleasant and went against everything that most Americans stood for. Once Leitsch had been elected, the question was how to go about ending entrapment.

Gay men in New York had learned that besides major events such as a world's fair, elections were also likely to trigger an increase in police entrapment. In May of 1965 John Vliet Lindsay, the six-foot-three lean, good-looking Republican congressman from New York's Silk Stocking District, announced that he would run against the incumbent mayor, Democrat Robert Wagner.

As the election campaign grew heated in the summer of 1965, Leitsch was in the Mattachine–New York office one afternoon when a reporter from the *New York Post* (then a paper with progressive politics) named

Joseph Kahn came by to discuss a proposed change in the sodomy law that was under consideration in the state legislature. As Leitsch and Kahn tried to talk, they were constantly interrupted by the phone ringing with calls from entrapped men. When Leitsch explained to Kahn both how entrapment worked and how common it had become within the male homosexual community, Kahn reacted skeptically. Leitsch made the reporter an offer: would he like to talk to some entrapment victims?

Tommy Lanigan-Schmidt graduated high school in 1965 and went to New York City to apply to the Pratt Institute to study art. At the end of the application process he was told that they would let him enroll because he drew so well but that he wasn't going to graduate because he lacked self-discipline.

When Tommy enrolled at Pratt he found the instructors uninspiring and the way they taught very limiting. Moreover, the art movement held up as a model in the classes Tommy took was Bauhaus, the antithesis of the medieval art he loved. With money a problem, he also did not see how he could complete a degree. Tommy made a conscious decision: to keep his dignity, he would stay in Pratt and learn the material taught, but he would make sure he failed.

In June of 1966 he received an official letter of dismissal. On that day, he returned home to Linden and showed the letter to his father, who was exasperated by the news.

Tommy's father determined to take matters into his own hands. Within hours, he took Tommy to downtown Linden and had him sign up on a ditch-digging crew. It was summer work that through the right connections might eventually lead to a union job for his son. Maybe it wasn't too late to make a man out of Tommy after all, his father thought.

On signing up to join the crew, Tommy saw that the other crew members were some of the tougher kids he had gone to high school with. Tommy knew it would have given them all a laugh to bury him alive. On leaving the office, he walked outside, took the dismissal letter out of his pocket, and looked at it. He already considered the letter his own personal declaration of independence. A moment of great clarity came to him, and he knew what he had to do.

Tommy went home. His father asked him, "You want to go get the newspaper?" Tommy said yes, and his dad handed him seven cents. He had sixty-five cents in his pocket. Seventy-two cents wouldn't get him to New York from Linden, but it would from Elizabeth. Tommy walked to the train station in Elizabeth, bought a ticket, and climbed aboard. Arriving at Penn Station, he headed down to the Village. He'd make it as an artist on his own somehow.

Change seemed to be everywhere in the air in the fall of 1965 as John Lindsay was elected mayor. An aura of excitement pervaded the city as the new mayor prepared to take office, his youthful good looks inspiring comparisons with John Kennedy, whose election had likewise inaugurated a season of hope. New York's homosexuals also felt cautiously hopeful about the new mayor. They had fared worse under the Wagner administration than under any other in the city's history. Maybe conditions would improve for them with Lindsay.

Although Dick Leitsch was also curious about how the new mayor would treat the gay community, a major change had already taken place in his life. As he remembered, one day Julian Hodges had come to him and said that they had to talk. Hodges confessed to Leitsch that he had been misappropriating Mattachine–New York funds.[15] Leitsch replied that Hodges must inform the organization's treasurer of this wrongdoing. Mattachine–New York's treasurer, the head of a major Wall Street accounting firm, agreed to make up the shortfall but told Hodges that he would have to leave town. Mattachine–New York accepted Hodges's resignation, which made Dick Leitsch the organization's president just in time for the Lindsay administration.

On a March night in 1966 the top brass of the new Lindsay administration were having a tough time keeping order during a raucous meeting at Judson Memorial Church in the Village. Police Commissioner Howard Leary, Chief Inspector Sanford Garelick, and Lindsay's human rights commissioner, William Booth, had all come there to pour oil on troubled waters after a cleanup campaign aimed at drug use, noise, congestion, and homosexuals in the Village had made some very public pratfalls. Two weeks prior, Garelick, New York's highest-ranking uniformed officer, had personally supervised an attempt to seal off an entire section of the Village around MacDougal Street, where young people drawn to the city went looking for a good time. The chief of police had ordered fourteen blocks around MacDougal Street closed to traffic on a Friday night, a peak time for the rowdy youths who came to enjoy the nightlife. Soon 1,500 youths were sitting in the middle of the empty streets, clapping and chanting, "Up with the Village and down with the police." A half hour later cars were allowed inside the area. The press had a field day mocking the police, and residents were up in arms.

Crowded into the church, Villagers had their boisterously independent spirit on full display as various political factions vied to control the agenda and the evening's tone.

Garelick was getting discouraged by the chaos when suddenly a nasal voice sounded from the room's rear. "I'm from a minority group in the community that is rarely heard from. Why aren't private nonracketeer businessmen allowed the legal right to run restaurants for homosexuals just as they run restaurants for heterosexuals?" asked Randy Wicker.

Sanford Garelick, speaking in his best professional tone, replied, "We have to enforce the law on licensed premises. You say repression; I say enforcement . . ."

Wicker was having none of it. "Are sexual deviates supposed not to eat? And what about those plainclothesmen, whose psychology even the homosexual doesn't understand, who come into places dressed in tight pants to lure people into illicit acts?"

"Entrapment," intoned Garelick, "is a violation of our rules and a violation of our procedure."

When Wicker pointed out that many solicitations in gay bars were made by plainclothes policemen, Garelick denied it. This prompted Aryeh Neier, the NYCLU's executive director, to walk up to the podium and say that Garelick showed "a certain naiveté" in denying that entrapment occurs, before adding, "It's alarming to think that the Chief Inspector doesn't know that a large number of police spend their duty hours dressed in tight pants, sneakers, and polo sweaters . . . to bring about solicitations." The audience erupted into a loud ovation and shouts of "Bravo!"

Pressed on how frequently police officers tried to entrap homosexuals, Garelick demurred but stated, "I'm very severe in my condemnation of entrapment." Looking obviously uncomfortable, he added that he hoped that if incidents of entrapment did occur, the public would report them to the police "as they would crimes."[16]

Dick Leitsch had to allow himself a smile. His plan of placing Mattachine members in the audience to ask the right questions had worked beautifully, as had the entire campaign he and other Mattachine–New York members had relentlessly pursued since Lindsay had taken office. The timing of the Kahn series on the vice police in the *New York Post* had been perfect. The Wagner administration had ignored the articles and all the questions they raised, but Kahn had confronted Police Commissioner Walsh on the entrapment of homosexuals in particular and Walsh had said that entrapment was not police department policy. The *Post* had then run an editorial calling for an end to entrapment. Leitsch and other Mattachine members had called the *Post* to urge them not to let the issue fade, and the newspaper had promised to keep the heat on. They did, exposing both the seamy nature of such police operations as well as how wasteful they were of city resources and police manpower.

When Garelick left Judson Memorial Church that evening, he no doubt felt relieved that the meeting was over. Unfortunately for him, his troubles about homosexual entrapment were not. When Dick Leitsch arrived home late that evening, his phone rang. He picked it up and heard the voice of John Lassoe, an Episcopal priest and Mattachine–New York supporter. The information Lassoe had was perfect: a vice plainclothesman had just entrapped a heterosexual priest at Julius', only a few blocks away from where Garelick had been speaking. Leitsch hung up the phone and started calling reporters to make sure they had the story in time for the next day's papers.

The New York Times put the story of Garelick's request that the public report instances of entrapment to the police next to a story about the entrapment occurring simultaneously in the same neighborhood. Shortly afterward the *New York Post* ran a story detailing a typical instance of bathhouse entrapment: a policeman, standing by his locker, dressed in his underwear, clutched his groin as he moaned. When a forty-year-old Brooklyn tailor asked him if he was ill or needed help, the tailor was arrested. Columnist Pete Hamill spoke with the man's devastated wife, who asked as she sobbed what would happen to her husband. In spite of her crying, she managed to speak softly so that her children would not hear the conversation.

After he had read the press reports about the entrapment at Julius' coinciding with Garelick's denunciation of entrapment, Leitsch rolled a sheet of paper into the typewriter and started a letter to Sanford Garelick. He had, after all, asked to be informed of any instances of entrapment.

Leitsch's cleverness, while understandable, had not been needed. By now the new administration had clearly gotten the message, which was confirmed when Lindsay invited Leitsch to a meeting. The meeting brought together various factions: officials of the Lindsay administration, Village politicians, and representatives of Village groups that had been harassed by the recent police drives. The meeting took place at the Village Vanguard and got off to a humorous start when Allen Ginsberg voiced concern about poets and avant-garde theater people caught in the cross fire of the Mafia, the police, and the city's cabaret laws. Ginsberg told Lindsay there had to be someone in the License Department who could handle culture.

"He's right behind you," Lindsay answered, indicating the deputy commissioner from the License Department.

"But is he culturally hip?" Ginsberg pressed.

"I can assure you," Lindsay deadpanned, "he is not."

When the subject of entrapment arose, the mayor said that "he had told the police department that the practice would stop immediately and would not be resumed" so long as he was mayor. Ed Koch grew red-faced, jumped up, and started yelling in protest. Leitsch smiled broadly as he sat next to the apoplectic Koch. He and Mattachine–New York had won the war on entrapment.[17]

SLA POLICY

Even before the success of the campaign to end entrapment, Leitsch had already started an effort to end police harassment of gay bars, which he saw as the second-most pressing problem facing the local gay population.

According to both Dick Leitsch and Randy Wicker, in the late 1950s there were a considerable number of gay bars that operated openly in New York City. Leitsch puts the number of gay bars at "more than forty" in 1959 and says that they were businesses that had been around for a long time and were controlled by "private individuals." But a great wave of bar closings began in 1960, which Leitsch felt was the fallout of a large investigation into corruption within the State Liquor Authority (SLA). When the New York City Police began a systematic campaign in 1960 to close all gay bars, they all lost their licenses, with one exception, the bar of the Cherry Lane Theater (though even that bar finally lost its license during Koch's 1966 antigay crusade).

The result of the 1960 crackdown, according to Leitsch, was that "the organized crime syndicate saw an opening and rushed in, opening bars all over town." Leitsch claims that "during one period" Mafia gay bars were able to remain open by paying off "strategic people" but that "when that became more difficult after the scandals in the State Liquor Authority, the bars began to operate only until they were raided, at which time they would pick up the entire operation, bar, employees, clientele and all, and move to another place in the same neighborhood, with the licenses in another name."[18]

Leitsch later commented in a lecture that whenever a crackdown occurred, "homosexuals knew the 'Mafia' would find some way to supply us with a place to meet and socialize. The sad philosophy of the gay world was that expressed by Brecht's Mother Courage: 'Our only hope lies in corruption.'" Leitsch saw the problem as the SLA having "surround[ed] the liquor business with so many rules and petty restrictions that honest men cannot survive," so that the business "reverts to the hands of those crooked enough to have the knowledge and lack of scruples to ferret out and work with crooked liquor agents."[19]

With so many powerful interests having so much at stake, how could

Mattachine–New York go about making gay bars legal? To try to determine how to approach the problem, Mattachine–New York paid an attorney to do a detailed study of New York's Alcoholic Beverage Control (ABC) Law. The memorandum that was prepared found: "Contrary to the contention of many bar operators, there is no provision in New York which flatly prohibits homosexuals from gathering in bars and there is no provision which flatly prohibits bars from serving homosexuals." However, the memorandum's author immediately added, Section 106(6) of the law, which prohibited a licensee's premises from becoming "disorderly," had been interpreted as not allowing licensed premises to serve homosexuals or for homosexuals to gather in drinking places as "a reflection of the attitude of the State Liquor Authority and . . . most of our courts."[20] As Leitsch and his colleagues studied the memorandum, it seemed to them that before they could get very far in trying to make gay bars legal, what was initially needed was some clarity about the New York State Liquor Law. The liquor law's vagueness with regards to serving alcohol to homosexuals rendered the issue murky.[21]

Danny Garvin ordered a beer and settled against the bar to relax with his navy buddies. He felt a tap on his shoulder and was told to turn around and face the bar. "Why?" Danny asked. The bartender explained that this was the bar's rule to prevent being closed on charges of solicitation. Danny did not understand how he was supposed to cruise if he was facing the bar. Wasn't that the point of coming to this bar, to meet other men?

Danny remembered the first time he had walked into Julius'. Some of his navy mess mates had brought him here, perhaps to show off their worldliness. They had said that though he was only seventeen he would not have any trouble getting a drink. The bar had seemed so ordinary that Danny had no inkling that it was a homosexual bar until a rather stereotypically feminine-looking older man, seeing Danny and his buddies' haircuts, had spoken to them: "I bet you three are servicemen. I can tell fortunes. Let me see your palms." Taking one of each of their palms, he had pretended to study them before announcing, "Well, I'm going to tell you, one of you is homosexual, but I'm not going to tell you which one. I'm going to give all three of you my phone number, and the one that is will know to call me!"

That was how it always seemed to work out for Danny: the only men approaching him were older men whose sole interest in him was sexual. That was just fine, he told himself. He was mainly interested in getting his rocks off, and men seemed more sexually available than women.

One reason the all-male crowd at Julius' hadn't struck Danny as unusual was that it seemed like any of the neighborhood bars where men went to socialize in Inwood, the middle-class immigrant neighborhood he had grown up in. An all-male gathering in a corner bar was common enough in Inwood, perhaps in part because of the strong Irish presence there. So much of Danny's identity seemed wrapped up with his Irish heritage. His grandfather James, freshly arrived in America, had helped to assemble the Statue of Liberty, and Danny's father, Michael, had smuggled messages for the IRA in Ireland until he was caught. It was only because Michael had been born in America that the British had released him, but only on the condition that he return to the States.

Another part of Danny's Irish heritage was the guilt that seemed to come with growing up in a devout Catholic family. When he reached puberty his older sister had told him that if he ever started to have an erection or experienced a wet dream, he should get out of bed, fall to his knees, and pray to the blessed virgin Mary. No, he wasn't really gay: he was just getting his rocks off. At least he hoped so, because judging from all he knew of it—the older men who had come on to him in public toilets or theaters—it seemed a very seamy life. It was such a confusing scene, too, with all the lingo he didn't understand, like men calling each other she and Mary Duggan. And there were strange terms like *flame queen* and *scare drag*. Sometimes he couldn't even follow it.

"The closet door was so tight back then." That's how he would try to explain it years later.

The stratagem Leitsch and his colleagues devised to seek clarity on the state's liquor laws revealed the extent to which they modeled their activism on the black civil rights movement. In a move that was both creative and ingeniously simple, they determined that several members of the Society would enter a bar, announce themselves as homosexuals, and ask to be served. If they were refused service, as they expected to be, they would make a complaint against both the bar and the SLA for violating their constitutional rights to free assembly and equal accommodation.[22] To make sure that they made their point, they invited the press along.

They sent telegrams to the press announcing that three Mattachine members would show up at noon on April 21, 1966, at the Ukrainian-American Village Restaurant on the Lower East Side to ask for drinks. That restaurant had been targeted because it displayed a sign saying: "If You Are Gay, Please Go Away."

While the conception of the challenge to the SLA may have been ingenious, it seems to have been ill-fated from the start. By this time Craig Rodwell had quit the Mattachine Society because Mattachine–New York's board would not agree to some of Rodwell's proposals to do more public outreach. However, Leitsch had planned to mount his challenge with John Timmons, and Timmons had insisted on inviting Craig along, to which Leitsch reluctantly agreed. Craig, in turn, told Randy Wicker about the event and Wicker, ever eager for publicity, showed up uninvited. Wicker's presence annoyed Leitsch, for although it was Mattachine–New York that had coordinated the gay challenge at the Judson Church and Wicker was the organization's secretary, he had identified himself that night as speaking for his own one-man operation, the Homosexual League.

The four men arrived at the Ukrainian-American Village Restaurant later than planned and found it closed. The press had informed the manager of the planned action and asked how he would respond. The manager had thwarted their plans by simply closing shop. The activists then walked over to a Howard Johnson's on Sixth Avenue and 8th Street, where Dick Leitsch read a statement identifying the group as homosexuals and asking for service. The manager, Emile Varela, doubled over in laughter and ordered a waiter to bring the men bourbons, saying that he knew of no regulation against serving homosexuals. Having failed twice, the men improvised a third target, the Waikiki, another Sixth Avenue spot popular with gay men. There the men were again served. After huddling yet again, the men walked two blocks west to Julius', where the bartender was also willing to serve them. Leitsch talked to the manager, who explained that as they were already facing a license suspension he did not want any more trouble. When Leitsch explained how valuable his refusing to serve them could be and promised that Mattachine–New York would help get them legal assistance with their current case, the manager agreed to play along. Refusing to serve the men, he told the press that since the men had said they were homosexual, he would not serve them, saying, "I think it's the law." Dick Leitsch then told the press that he would file a complaint in Mattachine–New York's name with the SLA.[23]

Mattachine–New York got extensive media coverage for what *The New York Times* dubbed a Sip-in, but the SLA refused to play their part in the game the organization had set up. The day of the Sip-in, the media asked the SLA's chief executive officer, Thomas Ring, about his agency's policies concerning homosexuality. After years of suspending and revoking licenses when homosexuals had been entrapped in bars, Ring said that the SLA "do[es] not discriminate against homosexuals" and claimed that their regulations "leave service to the discretion of the management." Four days after the Sip-in, the SLA told the press that it "would take no action against bartenders or liquor licensees who refuse to serve drinks to homosexuals." The SLA chairman, Donald Hostetter, asked about the Mattachine–New York complaint, answered, "We would take no action on such a complaint," but added, "This might be a matter for the [New York City] Commission on

Human Rights." The SLA had decided to pretend that it did not discriminate and had no oversight over such discrimination, while shuffling the problem off to another entity. Commissioner Booth was eager to cooperate and, based on the city's law that outlawed discrimination on the basis of sex, declared that "[d]enial of service to a homosexual . . . would come within those bounds."[24]

Subsequent events and explanations would eventually clarify that the SLA's new line was that homosexuals could be in bars and be served liquor as long as they were not "disorderly," by which the post-Sip-in SLA meant that homosexuals who behaved largely as heterosexuals were allowed to—kissing, touching each other intimately, or dancing in an overtly sexual manner—were a disorderly presence and hence could endanger a bar's license. In the meantime, Booth had been reluctantly forced to conclude that the New York City Commission on Human Rights was limited by law to investigating sex discrimination only in the field of employment and so was powerless to take action against a bar that refused to serve homosexuals.[25]

The publicity gained by the Sip-in did have the effect, however, of inspiring a number of bars outside New York City, especially in New Jersey, to get in touch with Mattachine–New York and request its assistance in fighting their own state liquor authorities. Over the coming years Mattachine–New York would continue to whittle away at the tools the police and the region's state liquor authorities used to harass bars and restaurants that served a lesbian and/or gay male clientele. Most significantly for New York City, the police department could no longer use entrapment against gay men as a tool to deprive a business of its liquor license.

For all that had been achieved by Mattachine–New York under Dick Leitsch's leadership, there were a lot of strains and divisions among the leading East Coast homophile activists. Leitsch had been furious when Mattachine-Washington did not pay what he saw as their portion of the cost of producing both a 1965 regional conference and the *Eastern Mattachine Magazine*, a joint publication venture of the two organizations. After a falling-out over this matter, Leitsch felt alienated from Kameny.

Randy Wicker had made so much money selling his gay buttons that he was busy preparing to launch a shop that would specialize in political buttons, and he began to withdraw his energies from Mattachine–New York.

By the spring of 1966 Craig Rodwell had become alienated from the Mattachine Society because of a disagreement over a project he had proposed. Rodwell had wanted Mattachine–New York to open a storefront operation to make the organization more visible and accessible. His idea was that from such an office the organization could make available pamphlets and magazines published by the homophile movement as well as books on the subject of homosexuality. When the board rejected the idea, he quit Mattachine–New York in protest and began to spend his summers working on Fire Island cleaning rooms at a hotel popular with gay men. He planned to save his money and open his own bookstore.

After two seasons of working at Fire Island, Rodwell had enough money to open a bookstore that would stock only gay and lesbian reading material. Rodwell named the store the Oscar Wilde Memorial Bookshop. He intended the store to function as a center for the gay and lesbian community at a time when there was no such community center in New York. After quitting Mattachine–New York, Rodwell took a leaf from Randy Wicker and started his own organization, which he named HYMN, for Homophile Youth Movement in Neighborhoods. While the organization never had more than a few members, it gave Craig a public platform. Rodwell emphasized the idea of identity and activism by setting up the organization so that "memberships are not sold . . . you 'join' by being gay—because this is a *movement*," as he explained to a reporter.[26] A few months after opening his bookstore, Craig started publishing a newsletter that he named the *Hymnal*, which he intended to use to inspire gay men and lesbians to become politically active. As Barbara Gittings had done with *The Ladder,* Rodwell highlighted news of militant actions and major successes, especially from Europe, where the gay legal and social situation was much better than in America. The *Hymnal's* first issue informed readers that Britain's House of Commons had given initial approval to a law that would legalize homosexual sex.[27]

"Why don't you just tell them you're queer?"

Danny Garvin, only 17 in early 1967, just shook his head once from left to right. He couldn't believe what he was hearing. First Chuck says that Danny has to leave because he's AWOL and under eighteen and Chuck could get arrested, and now Chuck's telling him to tell the navy he's homosexual!

It seemed that everything that could go wrong in several hours had. After getting drunk the previous night he'd overslept and not reported back to base on time. Then he discovered that he'd left his military ID in the liquor store where he'd picked up the booze for the impromptu party last night. When he had called his sister, she'd said the FBI and the CIA were looking for him. That was when he had really panicked. Now he'd run to Chuck, the one gay person his own age he'd gotten to know, and he's telling him to get lost. Danny left Chuck's, went to a drugstore, and bought some razor blades.

The Mattachine Society of New York had had a partial success in legalizing gay bars through the so-called Sip-in, beginning a legal challenge to the practice of denying licenses to the bars that served homosexuals. The incomplete victory created ambiguous results. While the SLA had retreated into a strategy of obfuscation instead of joining the battle, the success of Mattachine–New York in ending entrapment and changing the SLA policy so that businesses with liquor licenses could serve homosexuals resulted in legitimate businessmen beginning to invest in non-Mafia clubs. In March of 1967 Mattachine won a very significant ruling from New York's highest court: the SLA could not revoke a license on the basis of homosexual solicitation. The SLA's ability to prevent bars from serving gay men and lesbians was being eroded.

The Mafia apparently could read the writing on the wall just as well as the SLA. Running gay bars would become increasingly like running any other bar, and so the profits would go from exorbitant to ordinary. The Mafia was not interested in ordinary profits.

A year after these Mattachine successes, *The New York Times,* always eager to be the first to spot a new trend, reported on its front page that because of the declining profits in the gay bar business due to the encroaching legalization, the Mafia had a new strategy: operating gay bars as private clubs. Since they were private, the paper explained, these clubs enjoyed "the same legal sanctuary as an individual's home against police inspection without a court warrant." *The Times* reported that some of these new clubs charged high annual dues, extra fees for admission to special rooms, and high prices for setups or illegal liquor.

This strategy created new challenges for the police. Courts were refusing to issue search warrants "without specific complaints and evidence," and patrons of these businesses were generally unwilling to give the police the kinds of detailed information needed for warrants. When plainclothes police tried to enter the clubs to gather evidence, they had "been ejected bodily when they failed to pass a recognition test." These new kinds of operations, *The Times* reported, "have tight security and member identification."[28]

Danny Garvin looked at the piece of paper the U.S. Navy wanted him to sign. It seemed a reasonable exchange: he wanted an honorable discharge; the navy didn't want to pay any benefits. By this time he'd had enough of both the navy and psychiatric wards. After he had cut himself with two razor blades and only succeeded in scratching his wrist up, he knew that he couldn't bring himself to commit suicide. He had then gone to Bellevue on the advice of a psychiatrist and asked to be admitted. The navy had come and picked him up from Bellevue and transferred him to St. Alban's Naval Hospital.

There had been plenty of strange moments during the three months he had spent at St. Alban's. Volunteering as a movie projectionist, he had shown the film *Gigi* seven or eight times a week to soldiers just back from Vietnam who were missing legs or whose faces had been burned away. Only a few weeks ago when he'd obliged a nurse by helping to take a body to the morgue, workers there had grabbed his hand and slapped it on the ice-cold chest of a corpse that had been stored there for God knows how long. But by far the most absurd aspect of Danny's hospitalization was his inability to discuss what troubled him the most, his homosexuality, because he wanted the honorable discharge.

Danny picked up a pen and signed the general release. Hours later he walked out of St. Alban's Naval Hospital, where he had turned eighteen. He was the same age his father had been when the British had given him his freedom, also in exchange for getting something they had wanted.

It seemed appropriate therefore that it was also St. Patrick's Day. Danny had touched death, but he was alive.

He would go to Julius' that night to celebrate.

3

On the Street

While gay men and women in the 1960s were pressured into keeping their sexual lives very closeted, they succeeded in creating a diverse subculture. Then as now, the lesbian and gay male community had its own divisions and subcultures based on everything from sex, to sexual proclivities, to class and race. While it is not within the scope of this history to survey all or even most of these groups then existing in New York City, one group that demands our attention was a band of very young gay men whose social life existed mainly on the street. Although these youths stood in contrast with the activists because of their lack of respectability, the two groups shared two common traits beyond their sexual orientation: the social life of both was centered on the Village, and the members of these two groups were among the very few homosexuals of the era who chose to be visible.

When Tommy Lanigan-Schmidt arrived in New York City, he had no plan about how he was going to survive, let alone realize his dreams of becoming an artist. He did not know anyone who could help him get a job, and he initially looked to other homeless gay youths to help him survive.[1] With no money and no job, Tommy turned to panhandling.

One cold night a man walked up to him and asked, "Are you all right, Mary?"

Tommy, confused, protested, "I'm not Mary!"

"Mary, Grace, Allison—what difference does it make? After all, we're all sisters. Aren't we?"

"But I'm a man!?"

"Listen, Jesus would not want someone freezing in the street. If you need a place to stay, I have one."

The street queen who had so kindly offered Tommy lodging was alternately known as Opera Jean, because of his love of opera, and Sister Tooey, as he was infamous for going through people's medicine cabinets searching for the downer Tuinal.

Tommy soon found a very inexpensive apartment, thirty-five dollars a month, on the Lower East Side. It was in a terrible building, with around six of its apartments burned out. He had almost no money at all after paying for his rent and food, and so he lived very close to the street and found his friends there among the drag queens, street queens, and runaways.

There was Stanley, a queen who was always in drag and prone to bizarre pronouncements. When Stanley told Tommy that he had gone to a famous school, Tommy innocently asked him which one. Stanley answered exasperatedly, "You're crazy! 'A Famous School' was carved above the door! We operated on lions and alligators in biology class, not frogs!" Congo Woman, a "very nasty" black queen, used to throw bricks through store windows to get whatever she wanted, usually some drag item such as a dress or a wig. She also carried a stone in her purse just to have handy to throw at people. Irish Sylvia used drugs fairly regularly, and so when he fell to his death from the roof of the St. George Hotel many assumed that he had fallen because he was high, but there were rumors that he had been pushed. Tommy recalls that "that was the first queen funeral that I went to." Bambi, who got his name because of his large eyes, was never seen without a bottle and a bag. He had a habit of standing in the middle of the street to stop traffic and then banging on drivers' car windows as he demanded change. Tommy emphasizes Bambi's unpredictability by saying that he was "a creature of the moment." Nelly, a Latino youth also known as Betsy Mae Kulo (as in Spanish for "kiss my ass"), was so young-looking that when he went hustling in drag no one would have thought him a man. Orphan Annie was so called because his white skin, red Afro, and unique eyes immediately called to mind the hollow-eyed comic strip character. He claimed to have an extremely wealthy grandmother who sent him money. Another youth who wore a Beatles haircut and had good teeth almost never said anything but always wore a suit or a coat and usually a tie. Sometimes the shirt would get very dirty, but Tommy never saw this young man without a coat and figured this was his way of trying to hold on to some dignity.

Whereas the youth with the Beatles haircut looked quite conventionally male, a few of the youths were extremely feminine. Tommy recalls, for example, one boy who, although he always wore men's clothes, had such feminine mannerisms that the overall effect—his body language in combination with his fine features, long hair, and plucked eyebrows—was decidedly feminine.

Almost all the boys, some as young as fourteen, were runaways. A few actually lived with their families and went home at night but made the streets their second home. Most of them had come from abusive families. They were predominantly white, with a few black and Latino youths.

WE WERE STREET RATS. PUERTO RICAN, BLACK, NORTHERN AND SOUTHERN WHITES. "DEBBY THE DYKE" AND A CHINESE QUEEN NAMED "JADE EAST." THE SONS AND DAUGHTERS OF POSTAL WORKERS, WELFARE MOTHERS, CAB DRIVERS, MECHANICS AND NURSES AIDES (JUST TO NAME A FEW). UNTIL PROPERLY INTRODUCED IT WAS DE RIGUEUR ARGOT TO CALL EVERYBODY "MISS THING," (AFTER THIS, IT WAS DISCRETIONARY USAGE).*

Bob Kohler is a native New Yorker who has lived in the Village almost all his adult life. After being seriously wounded while serving in the navy in World War II, Kohler worked as a talent agent. At forty, Bob had decided to take some time off from work to consider where his life was going. Kohler lived in the Village on Charles Street and had a schnauzer named Magoo that had to be walked several times daily. It so happened that Magoo's route went by Christopher Park. During his furlough, Bob went by the park so often he noticed the gay street youth who often hung out there and began to talk to them.[2]

"They loved my dog. That was the big thing. They would ask to walk the dog, and they became even younger with the dog. That became like a link, being able to walk the dog. I was old enough in those days to be their father. I think in the beginning they were very surprised that I wasn't looking for anything at all, which is one of the reasons they trusted me. I think that was basically the bond from them to me, the dog and the old person."

Bit by bit Kohler became extremely interested in the youths and their stories. Sometimes he would circle the park with Magoo and one or two of the youths. As they walked, one of the youths would betray his tender age by swinging around a parking meter that had been hit by a vehicle so that, loose in the sidewalk, it leaned at an angle. The more Bob listened to the young men talk, the more he sensed the pain they felt over having lost their connections with their fathers: "I always felt that what the kids saw in me was a father. At least for most of them that was their biggest problem."

Bob often gave them small amounts of money to buy food at Smilers

---

*The extract in full capitalization is from *Mother Stonewall and the Golden Rats,* a work of art in the form of a handbill by Thomas Lanigan-Schmidt.

Deli, a neighborhood convenience store. "You'd give them a quarter for potato salad and another quarter for macaroni salad, and you had to give them another quarter for Ex-Lax because they were so constipated from all the starches. But that's what they lived on, back and forth to Smilers. You could almost see the dent in the road."

The stories of the street youth's behavior are often shocking. As Bob Kohler explained, "They were rotten kids. Of course they had been made rotten." One young man Tommy met on the street had an enormous burn scar covering his face and most of the rest of his body. His mother had decided that she didn't want men to be "tempted" anymore by her son's good looks and had held his face in the flames herself. He was not the only one among the street youth who had been burned. Bob Kohler recalled one boy among the street youth who bore the impression of a clothes iron on one of his buttocks, also made by one of his parents. In other cases parents or other relatives had thrown boiling water on them.

WE SAT ON THE CURB-GUTTER AROUND THE CORNER FROM A DANCE-
BAR CALLED THE STONEWALL. HE HAD WOUNDS SUTURED UP AND
DOWN HIS ARMS. THE ARMY HAD REJECTED HIM FOR BEING "A
QUEER." HIS FATHER HAD THROWN HIM OUT OF THE HOUSE THROUGH
A GLASS DOOR.

Once a youth urgently said to Bob, "If I could only have my breakdown, if I could only have my breakdown, then I know they would help me." Bob asked him what he was talking about. The boy explained, "They would always help my mother when my mother had her breakdowns. They would take her away and then she would come back and she'd be fine."

Kohler recalls, "Death was a very, very common thing. You didn't miss a beat when somebody said . . . 'She died,' or 'She got shot.' . . . There were always bodies being fished out from the river. . . . I know of two that I knew. I remember one queen waking up on a very high rooftop in the blazing sun, stoned out of her mind from the night before and had slept through the whole day, burned to a crisp, and just wandered around the roof, just fell off. One called the wrong person a nigger and was murdered."

Exposure to the elements worsened their chances of survival. "They slept in doorways in the rain. They slept on the benches when it was nice. So it was a very harsh life that they lived, and in the winter especially." Tommy says simply that "most of the people I knew from back then were already dead within four years after I met them."

According to Kohler, the kids operated on a constant cycle from searching for drugs, to getting high, to crashing, back to seeking more. Many of them would take anything they could lay their hands on. Still, they had their preferences even as they bartered, stole, and begged for drugs. "The down of the day was Darvon. Then Black Beauties, Christmas Trees. The downs were to take away the pain that was always there. The ups were to keep them going, so that they could go out on tears all night. They never slept. It was just collapse, hoping they made it to a bench before they couldn't go another step."

They would shoplift from the local A & P grocery, or sometimes they would steal from Smilers. Several would enter together and two would pretend to fight to distract the staff so that a third could steal food. Another way of stealing a meal was known as "eat and tip," as in "tip out the door." This ploy was mainly used at the local Howard Johnson's when the youth wanted what for them was a really good meal. Located on Sixth Avenue at 8th Street, the Howard Johnson's was cavernous and had a very long counter with a zigzag shape. The youths would situate themselves far from the exit the waitresses used to get from behind the counter and after eating, at a signal, would all get up at the same time and run out.

As much as Bob cared for the youths, he did not idealize them. Even when they walked Magoo, he did not completely let down his guard: "I used to watch, because I thought they're going to either eat him or sell him if somebody offered them five bucks.

"I became many things. I became a father confessor. A stasher of stolen goods. I became a patsy at times, too, because these kids lived to get over, and I was no exception. Just because I was as much of a friend as they could have, I still was somebody that they wanted to get over on. So I never turned my back. But they would tell me all their troubles."

Billy, a blond youth also known as Miss Billy, was one of the boys Bob was closest to: "He was a cute, cute kid. A real tall kid and very young. He was gay, gay, gay, but he was not a drag queen. I sort of became a protector of Billy. I tried to help him more than the others. Billy leaned on me more. I bailed him out of jail a couple of times." Billy was one of the youths who lived at home but spent as much time as he could on the streets.

Just because some of the youths had homes did not necessarily mean that they had easy lives. Robert Rivera, more usually known as Birdie, for example, came from a Puerto Rican family in the Bronx. Although his Jewish father had a male lover, Birdie recalls that "my parents didn't want me anywhere near the house." He became the lover at age eleven of Joe, a police officer who became his legal guardian, but Joe, who insisted that Rivera wear dresses, also beat him.

According to Birdie, by 1965, while he was still in high school, he and other gay youth had formed their own gang, the Commando Queens. Members had to be over eleven and under eighteen. Their code of ethics was: "You had to be kind to someone every day; you had to make sure your makeup was okay; couldn't be dirty; had to protect somebody who was getting beat up, someone who was queer; couldn't wear bras or girdles, no leather."

Birdie became a very tough street youth whose philosophy was to hit before being hit. He and other street youth friends of his staked a claim to Riker's, a restaurant at the intersection of Christopher Street and Seventh Avenue South, and were intimidating enough that they "took it over from the winos." They ran wild in the subways and didn't necessarily spare other gay people, such as the old men and cabdrivers they hustled: "We used to terrorize those queens—would tease them about who they had sex with and for what. We called them 'dog food.'" Birdie's closest friends were Martin Boyce and Tommy Lanigan-Schmidt, both of whom recall Birdie's fearlessness.

When the street youth were able to get a little money they would sometimes find transient lodging in cheap hotels like the Albert, the very popular Broadway Central (until it collapsed), the Earl, the Marlton on 8th Street, the Haliburt on University Place, and the Keller.

When they were able to get into a hotel, they almost always ended up getting thrown out. Bob Kohler went to the Essex to visit Orphan Annie. After he and some of Annie's friends had been sitting and having a normal conversation for some minutes, Annie suddenly leaped up, picked up the radio, threw it out the window, and sat back down. No one acted as if anything unusual had happened, so Bob also kept quiet. Minutes later, Annie, for no apparent reason, picked up a lamp and threw it out the window.

Cross-eyed Sylvia instructed Tommy in how to make what the street queens called a drape dress, a resourceful technique for a queen who had no female attire and needed to find some in a hurry: "Check in a place like the Hotel Albert and be sure to have a shopping bag with you. Since the curtains have hems on their tops and bottoms and a lining on the back, you simply cut the seam off the top and the bottom, slip in between the cloth and the lining, put on a belt, and attach a broach. After you've put your male attire in the shopping bag, you're ready to leave the hotel in your new dress." The Broadway Central's large windows made it particularly popular with New York's street queens.

Tommy explains, however, that usually the street youth were thrown out of hotels not because of vandalism but either from generosity or their own survival needs: they either tended to let their homeless comrades stay the night or brought johns to their rooms.

The cabaret laws, laws against homosexuality, and the SLA laws complicated life at the few businesses that might have had some special appeal to these youths as gay young adults. For example, the Tenth of Always was an ice-cream parlor run by the Mafia and targeted at gay teenagers. The prohibition on selling alcohol to persons under eighteen years of age was compensated for by selling hamburgers and sodas at hugely inflated prices. The Tenth allowed dancing, an activity that attracted teenagers, notwithstanding the small size of its dance floor. But Tommy recalls how the staff would yell at customers if they even sat close to each other. Since the Tenth did not have the required license to allow dancing, when the police made one of their frequent stops by the place the Mafia staff would turn on a chandelier as a signal for everyone to stop dancing.[3]

Why had these youths been so totally abandoned? Apparently the reason is that most of them were much more feminine in behavior than the average homosexual man of the time. They were a band of youths from New York City and around the country who were generally not wanted by their families or schools or hometowns because they were so obviously queer. Hearing that the Village was the best place for them, they found their way there. At least in the Village they could find others like themselves—or so they thought—but other gay men shunned them. With the exception of Marsha Johnson, drag queens also shunned them. People in the apartment buildings around Christopher Park threw things at them from their windows. They were a world unto themselves, cut off by their age and by being so out of control. The interest Bob Kohler took in these youths and the kindness he showed them were unique.

Unfortunately, the youths directed the rage they felt at being so completely abandoned against one another. Kohler recalls, "They were constantly at odds. In a given week every one of them would stop speaking to every other one of them, and then they'd be back as sisters again. Most of them carried either a pair of scissors or a nail file, the preferred weapons because if they got arrested they would claim either that they were going to beauty school or that they were cutting people's hair and doing nail filing, assertions that the police could not disprove.

"It was nothing to be sitting there and it would be fine, and all of a sudden you'd hear a bottle break and that was always the weapon, the broken bottle, and they'd go for the face. If it was a drag queen, they'd go for the tits to deflate them. They would fight over pills. They would fight over whose bench that was. They would stake out benches.

"The fight would be about nothing. It would be over in a finger snap. Getting hurt was not important. Getting dead was not important. They'd rip their toes open wearing stupid open-toe sandals, and their feet sometimes would be so swollen up. There was no value placed on these kids by the gay community, by the medical community, by anybody, but mostly by themselves."

The boys' sense of humor helped dissipate some of the anger. Tommy recalls "When gay people talk to each other there can be this really competitive performance. Street queens have that in machine-gun motion. It's so rapid-fire in their competition because they like to get each other to laugh and they like to get each other laughing at how clever and smart and interesting they are. So usually they would rather get each other laughing than hitting or knifing each other. There was a respect for someone that could really turn a phrase in a crazy way."

Sometimes, too, camp humor could be used to express group solidarity while trying to shock heterosexuals. In a spirit of youthful fun, at times when the street youth would be cruising on Greenwich Avenue, they would spontaneously throw their arms around each other and sing to the tune of "It's Howdy Doody Time" their own gay-affirming lyrics:

> *We are the Village Girls!*
> *We wear our hair in curls.*
> *We wear no underwear:*
> *We show our pubic hairs!*

Humor was also the one weapon the street youth could use against the police.

THE COPS (SINGULAR AND PLURAL) WERE GENERICALLY KNOWN AS "LILY LAW," "BETTY BADGE," "PATTY PIG" OR "THE DEVIL WITH THE BLUE DRESS ON."

Tommy recalls, "The bubble-gum machine meant the cop car, because back then they only had one light in the middle. So someone might say, 'Lilly and the bubble-gum machine' or just 'Here comes Lil.' Because it was the sixties, sometimes she was called Patty Pig, which was more easy for the cops to interpret, so it wasn't said that much. Lilly Law they mostly didn't know. Especially when we said 'Lil': 'Lil, there she is.' Some queens called her Alice Bluegown. And she rode in the bubble-gum machine, so if someone said there were a lot of bubble-gum machines out, we knew there were a lot of cops there."

Prostitution (or hustling, as it is called in the gay world) was not only a way to get cash by trading sex but also gave the youths an opportunity to steal from johns. The youths would ask Bob, "Can you hold this?" and his apartment came to be filled with stolen items. When they would go down to the piers, they would also ask him to hold their money—if they had any—because they themselves were often robbed while hustling.

According to Kohler, "Very, very few, if any, were drag queens. They lived by panhandling, stealing, and hustling down at the piers at night. This is the only time that they ever went in drag, and it was pathetic drag. I mean, they had no money. They sometimes were able to steal wigs from 14th Street." Being very young, with their features not fully formed, many of them succeeded in impersonating women by using their own natural looks with just a little makeup and a few additions to their own clothing. With long hair being the style for young men in the mid-1960s, many of them could even dispense with wigs or falls. In the summer they usually wore shorts and at other times flowing bell-bottom pants, which was the fashion for young men at the time Bob met the street youths: "The street kids had bag-woman drag. They wore sandals and tied their blouses or shirts in a big knot midriff, and that was basically it. The drag queens that were down at the piers couldn't have fooled a blind man. It was just ragged, hausfrau drag, whatever they could get together." Some simple jewelry like earrings might be added and the bell-bottoms would sometimes be in a lightweight, sheer material, so they looked like a long gown.

An example of a young man who hustled at the waterfront, though not in drag, was Jackie Hormona. He enhanced his natural good looks by dying his hair blond, putting on a little facial powder to make his skin appear smoother, and applying a touch of eyeliner. Although his overall appearance was masculine, like most of the street boys he was a bit more feminine in comportment than most gay men of the time. While Kohler explains that Jackie was known as Hormona because he wanted to take hormones, Jerry Hoose thinks otherwise, attributing the name to camp humor: "Even his name, Hormona, was sort of like a put-on, really. Because he really wasn't that outrageous, like a drag type. The 'Hormona' was an exaggeration, sort of a goof. A lot of us back then took on exaggerated kinds of names and things just to be outrageous. But I don't think he had any plans on changing his sex or anything." While Hoose recalls the subtle use of makeup, he never saw Jackie wear a dress or use lipstick.[4]

One of the more enigmatic of the street youth, Jackie seems to have maintained a certain emotional distance between himself and others. Tommy knew him so little at the time that he didn't even know his street name: "She was always walking by and waving and then kept walking." Jerry Hoose agrees, saying that although he always got along with Jackie, "Not really many people were very intimate with Hormona. She was sort of a loner, more than the rest of them." Hoose remembers havng the impression that Jackie was from the South, for there seemed to be a slight southern twang in his speech. Hoose also recalls that Jackie "always gave the impression like he was from money. Whether that was true or not, who knows? But that's the impression he gave a lot of us, that he's living on the streets and doing all this shit because he wanted to, but not because he had to."

Hoose knew Jackie from cruising areas: "Jackie was a regular on Greenwich Avenue—and on Christopher Street, sitting on the stoops, getting drunk. I saw Jackie drunk many, many, many times. You know, bottles in a brown paper bag, stuff like that."

Hoose links the constant drinking to another of Jackie's characteristics: "He would just do anything to make a splash. He really had no fear. He was extremely wild, one of those I-have-nothing-to-lose kind of characters."

Just how wild Jackie could be Hoose remembers from the place he saw Hormona most often, the trucks: "The trucks used to be raided like two or three times a night. Out of nowhere police cars would come from all directions, with the police smashing their nightsticks against the trucks. Everybody would fly out. They'd beat us—try to grab people, smash people in the head with the nightsticks. People would run in all directions, but there'd be a small crowd of people here and there like me that screamed back, but I remember he would like go a little further than me—throw things at the police. He was pretty fearless. Jackie wouldn't just sit around and take it."

Beyond Jackie's nothing-to-lose attitude, an additional explanation for his resistance to police oppression may lie in an attribute that Tommy recalls in Jackie, that of simple fairness: "Jackie had good moral leverage, being someone who wouldn't get into fights or wouldn't encourage stupid fights. He was the kind of person that if two people are fighting would say something like 'You know, it's not worth fighting about' or 'It's your friends, so why are you acting like this?' He was one of those people that had the nerve to tell people they should treat each other better. Most people were more expedient than fair. There was a very typical kind of opportunism among street queens, who were robbing each other a lot. So if someone could step in and get people to be a little more levelheaded, I always respected that. And it was unusual, because that person had to have a certain presence and confidence to not get murdered doing that. I would just be quiet and fade into the background because I didn't know who was going to go off, but Jackie would say, 'Don't do that to people.'"

Another of the street youth who hustled and did so in drag at times was a black male known as Nova or, more fully, Zazu Nova, Queen of Sex. A good-looking man, Nova had a strikingly soft complexion of rich color, with a long nose and a distinctly African silhouette. A bit aloof, he carried himself almost as if he were royalty.[5] Jerry Hoose thought he looked good as a man but made a rather masculine woman, for Nova was a very tall, muscular man with large hands. Tommy heard that Nova came from upstate New York. A staunch Unitarian, he took great pride in his religious upbringing.[6] By all accounts, Nova had a fierce temper, even to the point of having a violent nature. The word on the street was that Nova not only had been in prison several times; there were also rumors that he had served time for murder.[7]

One of Tommy's best friends from the era is Martin Boyce, who lived at home but socialized on the streets. Martin knew Nova was a force to reckon with, for he had seen her in action. Boyce was exiting Grand Central Station at three o'clock one morning when he ran into Nova on 42nd Street. As Martin greeted Nova, he grabbed her breast because it looked real and he wanted to see what it was made of. He didn't realize that five men had surrounded them. When one of them said, "Look at that. He's touching that tit and doesn't get nothing out of it," Martin realized that he and Nova were about to be jumped. Fortunately, Nova was prepared: "She had in her purse a chain that could tie up a truck. She swung that fucking thing—it really looked like an anchor was attached to it. She whipped that fucking thing out and they fled."[8]

While Marsha P. Johnson was not one of the street youth per se, she was very much of the street. Born in Elizabeth, New Jersey, the city Tommy Lanigan-Schmidt grew up in, Malcolm Michaels Jr. moved to New York the same year Tommy left home for good, 1966. The two youths also shared a deep religious sensibility, but Marsha Johnson was deeply disturbed, so that while her religious pronouncements could have the oracular tone of direct experience, they also had the unsettlingly weird quality of statements made by persons suffering from psychosis: "Sometimes I have visions. In one of them, there were ten suns shining in the sky, gorgeous and freaked out, like the end of the world. I love my saints, darling, but sometimes the visions can be scary." Her off-center nature is also shown by the way she used materials she found on the street for her wardrobe: costume jewelry earrings became ornaments not for her ears but her hair, sometimes she wore red plastic high heels, and she might deck herself out in flowers, either real ones discarded by flower merchants or plastic flowers or artificial fruit from a five-and-dime. But this describes Marsha years after she arrived in the Village. In the early days she tended to go out mainly in semidrag and called herself Black Marsha. (When she later dropped the *Black* and started calling herself Marsha P. Johnson, she explained that the *P.* stood for "Pay it no mind.")

That energy and craziness were essential characteristics of Marsha's life is seen in her acknowledgment that by 1979 she had had several attempts made on her life by johns, eight nervous breakdowns, and innumerable arrests—after one hundred she had stopped counting. But the characteristic most often cited by those who knew Marsha best was her essential goodness. Tommy remembers seeing Marsha stealing a loaf of bread early one morning from a delivery left behind a shopkeeper's gate and then passing it to a homeless person. Randy Wicker flatly stated that Marsha "was the most generous person I ever knew." And a volunteer at a thrift shop where Marsha bought her outfits, recalling "the fella that used to buy all the gowns," described Marsha as a "wonderful, sweet person."

But Robert Heide recalls another side to the childlike Marsha, who could be both helpless and charming. He sometimes saw a demon emerge, especially when Marsha was in his male persona as Malcolm. "I think we all have that to some degree, but apparently in Malcolm/Marsha's case there was this real duality and it would take hold. There was a schizo-phrenic personality at work, for Malcolm Michaels could be a very nasty, vicious man, looking for fights. You could say hello to him and if he was Malcolm that day, he might not recognize you or you might be in trouble or a fight might even ensue." Heide's experience of this side of Malcolm is borne out by Randy Wicker, who took Marsha in as a roommate decades later. While Marsha was generally an ideal living companion, on one occa-sion she wrecked Randy's residence. A 1979 *Voice* article also reported that Marsha's "plumed saintliness" was "volatile" and quoted a Christopher Street shop manager who described her as a "bully under that soft sweet manner" and listed a roster of gay bars from which she had been banned.

Despite her toughness, the incessant police harassment stung. Marsha was as much an habitué of 42nd Street as she was of the Village water-front, and she spent much time in the cheap "hot-spring" hotels that pros-titutes favored for their liaisons. Sitting with her fellow prostitutes in the small hotel rooms, she had a recurring fantasy, that one day they would be able to walk around and not get busted by the police: "That was a dream we all had, sitting in those hotel rooms or in the queens' tanks of the jails."[9]

4

The Stonewall Inn

There were some lesbians, hustlers, married people, single people,
some transvestites, but not too many. It was the heart and soul of the
Village because it had every kind of person there.
—Philip Eagles

Opening the Stonewall Inn was a venture that took little money and even less imagination. When the Stonewall Inn Restaurant closed after a fire in the midsixties, the building sat empty for some time, until Fat Tony converted the space into a gay club with a minimum of effort. Harry Beard, a waiter at the Stonewall, recalls "one of the managers remarking, 'Yeah, paint the joint black and give it a little class.' So, consequently, the walls and the ceiling and anything else that happened to get in the way were painted black." Apparently the color was chosen not only because so many gay bars at the time were painted black but also because one coat of black would cover the burned wood and save the expense of replacing it. An extensive contemporary description of the club noted: "There's a certain hastiness about the look of the place. It seems to have only recently been converted from a garage into a cabaret in about eight hours and at a cost of under fifty dollars."[1]

This early reviewer was correct in his estimation that only a small amount of money had been used to open the bar. Chuck Shaheen, who helped Fat Tony open the Stonewall Inn, estimates the total spent at less than a thousand dollars. However much money may have been expended on remodeling, Shaheen is precise about how much cash was used to start the club: "Tony invested $2,000 and three guys invested $500 each, and that's what started the Stonewall. I remember distinctly the $3,500 being the exact amount . . . because Tony always said, 'We did this on $3,500.'" For his partners Tony chose Zookie Zarfas, who was in the firecracker business, "Tony the Sniff," and "Joey," apparently because all three were childhood friends. But there was another more significant partner who did not have to put up any money: Matty Ianello, known as Matty the Horse, had been given control of that section of the West Village by the Genovese family and so, according to Mafia protocol, automatically got a cut from mob businesses in that territory. Without investing a dime, he was considered "the real boss, the real big boss." The modest investment would soon make the four partners who did put up money a tidy fortune.[2]

The mobsters did have the white Greek Revival columns that had graced the entrance to the restaurant demolished, perhaps so they could more easily install the heavy doors they wanted to provide security for their new bar. Around this same time, a fresh coat of stucco was applied to the building's exterior, hiding the brick that had become exposed as the building had deteriorated during the Stonewall Inn Restaurant's decline.[3]

Not even much imagination was used in naming the new "club": all that Fat Tony did was lop *Restaurant* off the name of the former enterprise, which allowed him to keep the enormous rusting sign hanging just above the club's entryway. Fat Tony did not even bother to have the word *Restaurant* painted over.

In spite of recent modifications forced upon the SLA, because Fat Tony intended to serve a clientele that he could not legally sell liquor to he needed a ruse. The ploy that Fat Tony used was a common Mafia ploy for running a gay bar, the fiction that the operation was a bottle club, a private club serving its members. To that end a charter that had been issued to the Red Swan Social Club in 1929 was obtained for the new club. In a true bottle club, members could bring their bottles and leave them at the club with their names on them. Waiters at such a club could pour a drink from the member's private stock and the club members would tip the waiter for doing so. But the staff of the Stonewall Inn just made up names, wrote them on strips of paper, and attached the strips to bottles to fool the police. In practice, the club served anyone the doormen admitted.[4]

If little imagination was used to create the Stonewall Inn, the club did break new ground by being a large gay club in a rather open area and on a main thoroughfare, instead of on a side street, as was more typical in New York City, which is what Tommy Lanigan-Schmidt remembers noticing about the Stonewall Inn the first time he saw it.

A customer entering the Stonewall Inn would see that the entrance was in the middle of a brick edifice, directly under the hulking metal sign and between two large horizontal windows that, as was true of the windows of almost all street-level gay bars in New York City at the time, were blacked out so that the police and the public could not see inside, providing the clientele privacy and security. For extra protection, the windows were reinforced from the inside with plywood, which was further reinforced with two-by-fours to prevent the police from being able to simply break through the windows and rush inside.[5]

The thick oak doors were rendered more secure by steel doors inside them and several inside locks intended to slow down the police in a raid. Each of the front doors had two small vertical openings cut into it at eye level. One of the four openings served as a peephole to screen potential customers, giving the establishment somewhat the feel of a speakeasy. Dawn Hampton, a black heterosexual woman and former torch singer who had worked in many gay clubs, remembers that "at that time there was a lot of entrapment going on, police coming to the door and pretending they were of that life." Chris Babick, a frequent customer, recalls that "the door of the Stonewall had wrought iron bars across this little peephole, a little wooden thing that slid open. And the man inside would look at you and, if you looked like you belonged there, would let you in."[6]

Another technique used to screen out undercover police or heterosexuals who might not blend in well was to ask would-be customers to describe the inside of the Stonewall Inn as proof they had been there before. The most common test of entry, however, was simple recognition by the doorman. Blond Frankie, who had worked at a number of gay clubs before working at the Stonewall, had a nearly photographic memory for faces, which earned him a spot at the door. Harry Beard remembers that "a favorite ploy of the vice cops was to pass themselves off as a typical patron, and the Stonewall . . . would always say, 'This is a private club, for members only.' I assume that the standard response in those days was, 'Well, I've been here before.' And Frankie would just look at their face and go, 'Well, no, you haven't.'"[7] The entrance's final defense was a switch that the doorman could throw to turn on the bright white lights inside as a signal that the bar was being raided.

When a customer had passed inspection, the door was opened and the bouncers would be found sitting at a table to collect $1.00 for admission on weekdays and $3.00 on weekends. On the weekends after a patron plunked his money down, one of the doormen would tear two tickets off a roll and hand them to him. Each ticket could be traded for a drink. (Rolls of tickets of different colors were rotated to prevent customers from cheating on readmission and/or holding unused tickets for a later weekend.) A special lamp was also used for door control: customers wanting to step outside and return later could tell the doorman they were coming back, and he would stamp their hands with an invisible ink that would show up under the lamp's blue light.[8]

Customers were asked to sign a book as part of the Stonewall Inn's fiction of being a private club. The book-signing ritual served in part to prevent straight people from entering. One regular club goer remembers that in the summertime the front doors to the Stonewall Inn would sometimes be open. "They would stop straight people who were coming in: 'No, this is a private club.' That's the reason for the book to sign in."[9] Theoretically, the book could also have been introduced in court as evidence of the Stonewall Inn being a bottle club. Perhaps it functioned too as a kind of prop to mock or try to confuse the police. Certainly some customers were in on the joke, for they scrawled campy names such as Elizabeth Taylor and Donald Duck in the book. But there was also a measure of self-protection in using the false names: if the police did seize the book, it could not implicate anyone as a "deviate."[10]

Upon entering, those who wanted to check their coats turned to the left, where the checkroom was located on the left side of a dead-end corridor, directly behind one of the large windows. Hampton remembers that homosexual men dressed more formally then than in the years after the gay liberation movement launched a more casual and identifiably gay style of dress: "Most of the men were wearing outer jackets. They weren't wearing so much leather back then or so much denim at that time. There was a whole different mind-set: there were some men who wore hats in those days."

Being a heterosexual woman did not stop Hampton from enjoying a warm relationship with the club's clientele: "I wasn't hitting on anybody. I wasn't trying to straighten anybody out or anything like that, so I was very accepted. A lot of the kids called me Mommie. It used to be a fine joke for me when someone would say something to me about having children and I said, 'I have a ton of them.'"

To get into the main bar—located on the east side of the Stonewall Inn—those with nothing to check simply turned to the right at the end of the lobby, passed through an inner door that was usually open, and stepped down one step.[11]

A customer who had gotten this far was now into the Stonewall Inn's largest room, whose most prominent feature was a long bar, with many round stools.[12] While the clientele was generally in their upper teens and lower twenties, those at the front bar tended to be white men in their upper twenties and lower thirties, with men over the age of thirty-five being unusual, though by no means unheard of.[13] On the wall in back of the customers seated at the long bar was a narrow ledge on which customers could rest their drinks.[14]

At the end of the bar was an area reserved for dancing, with the music provided by a jukebox stocked with singles, which could be played for ten cents a song or three for a quarter.[15] The music made it possible for customers to dance, which was the Stonewall Inn's main attraction from the day it opened its doors.

On St. Patrick's Day of 1967 Danny Garvin headed downtown, figuring that he would enjoy an evening at Julius' before heading to Chicago to stay with his sister. He would go to Illinois to pull his life back together, but being Irish, he would never have considered not celebrating the holiday. An older man walked up to the fresh-faced youth and demanded, "What are you doing in here?"

"Well, I'm having drinks."

"You should be around the corner with all the chicken."

More language confusion. Danny gave the older man a quizzical look.

"That new bar that opened up around the corner tonight, Stonewall. They're all over there."

Danny walked one block over to the Stonewall Inn and entered. The place was "fairly well packed" with young people, but what really struck Danny was that people were "dancing all over the place." Shocked anew, he thought, *Men don't dance with other men! This will never last!*

Chris Babick was also impressed the first time he went to the Stonewall Inn by the sight of men dancing, but for him the reaction was positive: "And there were men dancing with men. And when I [saw] the two men—there were several couples dancing together—I had such a thrill in my stomach. It was . . . like an electric shock. And it was so fucking exciting."

Dawn Hampton recalls, "I was there when they originally opened it as a dance palace. People came there because they loved to dance." *The Homosexual Handbook,* published in 1968, said: "The younger, more agile and more sensationally demi-dressed, jerk and bump on the rather large dance area at the end of the [front] room. . . . Spotlights are pointed directly down and they light the dancing youths dramatically." All contemporary accounts of the Stonewall Inn are unanimous in their agreement on the centrality of dancing to the club.[16] Dawn Hampton told an interviewer, "It's not like the places that had back rooms in the last twenty years. It was just a place where they loved to dance. They loved to be together and wanted to be with their own kind."

An habitué of the club concurs: "There was a sense of community feeling in the Stonewall. You would meet your friends there. It was a fun time, a good time. There was a warmer feeling in the bars, a nicer feeling, I'd say, than there is now [1989]. Maybe because bars are advertised now. . . . You didn't know then, so someone had to point the Stonewall out to you, or let you know, or somehow you just happened to see a bunch of men walking in there. Because you wouldn't see two guys on the street holding hands then, so it was more of an in place. Gay people were different back then. Guys would ask you to dance."[17]

Of course dancing was not the only activity that went on in the front room. Vito Russo remembered the front room as a place for cruising and camping.[18] For people who wanted to sit, there were some tables set up in the club, usually for two, with little candles on them.[19]

Drinks were priced at a dollar each, a high price for the era. There was pressure from the Stonewall staff to order a drink very soon after entering: "You got a ticket, but they wanted you to buy your drink *zip* when you went in and that was the main bar," recalls Chuck Shaheen. On weekend nights, after customers had gotten two drinks by trading in their tickets, the staff would then pressure them to buy more. Even though drinks were priced high, the mob was only passing out watered-down drinks. Even so, the staff was pouring liquor that had been stolen or obtained from bootleggers. Shaheen remembers that it all "came from Matty the Horse's company," explaining that "none of the liquor was brand-name liquor. We would go in the back at the beginning of our shift and take Dewar's bottles and pour whatever swill we could get into it. The same with vodka. It wouldn't be Smirnoff. Nothing would be what it said it was." The club kept one bottle each of a couple of call brands for favored customers. According to Shaheen, everything that was sold in the Stonewall Inn came only from Mafia suppliers, the liquor, the cigarettes, and even the music on the jukeboxes.

The lighting was very dim throughout. The first room had a low ceiling that combined with the darkness to create a cavern-like feel.[20] Smoky air filled the bar,[21] for the club's only ventilation came from several small, inadequate air conditioners.[22] However, the men liked to wear perfumes, such as Tabu and Ambush, both marketed to women, whose aromas gave the place a rich, saturated atmosphere.[23]

In the wall dividing the front from the back room was a doorway with swinging black doors through which one passed, stepping up one step, to the back room. There was one other route between the two main rooms—through the bathrooms at the club's rear. The rest rooms had doors on both ends, which allowed them to be used as passageways.[24] The women's room was distinguished by having a red lightbulb, which irritated some of the scare queens (men who affected a feminine presentation without trying to pass as women) and transvestite club goers, for the dim light made it difficult for them to adjust their makeup.[25]

The men's room was distinguished by having its own attendant. Beard remembers him as "an old black guy named John. He used to dispense colognes and underarm deodorants, and razors and soap and towels and toilet paper and such." Michael Fader remembers John as heterosexual. He sat in the corner, at the ready to give a club goer a shot of cologne on his neck for a tip.[26] A rest room attendant in a place as down-at-the-heels as the Stonewall Inn sounds improbable; however, he may have been there to discourage men from having sex in the rest room and making the Stonewall even more legally vulnerable.[27]

Whether reached via the main doorway or by cutting through one of the club's rest rooms, a customer who reached the Stonewall Inn's second room found himself in a setting different from the front room. While the first room was dominated by its long bar, the second room was much smaller and had only a small bar and even dimmer lighting.[28]

Harry Beard recalls that the back room had "a service bar with a few stools around it." The back room had some cheap wood paneling, a ledge to set drinks on, and a few tables, with a bench against the wall providing additional seating. While usually only one floor waiter circulated in the front room, a number of floor waiters worked the back room, and they pushed drinks very aggressively.[29]

Tommy preferred the music on the jukebox in the back room. There the records were releases by artists who put a lot of feeling into their songs, such as Otis Redding and Stax recording artist Carla Thomas (called the "Queen of Soul" by Redding). In the front room, the jukebox offered more mainstream performers such as the Beach Boys. The back room, with its more soulful music, made up in spirit whatever it lacked in size. Its lively feeling derived from its being the favored place of the homeless youth, as well as of young blacks and Puerto Ricans. Tommy Lanigan-Schmidt recollects how some people called the front room "the white room," because of its racial makeup and its music. For similar reasons, patrons dubbed the back room the "black" or "Puerto Rican room."[30] Always crowded, the younger and the "in" crowd claimed the back room as their domain.[31] The back room's flagstone floor gave it an advantage for energetic dancers.[32]

Just a few feet inside the doorway[33] one found the Stonewall Inn's most unexpected feature, a full-sized wishing well constructed of stone and cement.[34] Surrounded by benches, the five- or six-foot-tall well had a roof over it.[35] In the days when the club operated as a restaurant, the wishing well had often graced wedding receptions,[36] and many pictures of brides and grooms had been carefully posed with the well as a prop. Now the well stood incongruously in the dim light amid the jukebox's constant blare, its potential for romance and charm not even noticed by the Stonewall staff, who used its interior as a makeshift storage space. Tommy recalls how he never knew what he might see inside it: bags of ice, empty boxes, or boxes full of beer temporarily parked there on the way to being consumed.[37]

The back room had its own social geography, with the street end being where the most marginal of the Stonewall's customers congregated, includ-

ing Tommy: "It was where the most down-and-out queens hung out, because that was the furthest out place."[38]

The question of different parts of the Stonewall being favored by different clientele raises the long-debated issue of what kind of club it was after
all. Who went there and who did not? Did some group or groups predomi-
nate so that it can be categorized as a particular kind of gay bar?

While the clientele was mainly male and young, Hampton says that the
bar had "some of everything . . . a lot of them were businessmen and didn't
want their families to know, naturally." She states that the mixture included
various ethnic groups: "They were mixed Spanish, whites, and blacks, but
there were more whites than the others." Tommy Lanigan-Schmidt agreed
that "somehow, it covered the range . . . the whole mixture of everyone gay
at the time." Robert Bryan said the mixed clientele reminded him of how a
gay bar in a small city would draw all kinds of gay people "and you get the
women, and the leather, and the collegiate, and the drag queens," and he
felt the similarity was explained by a corresponding cause, that the
Stonewall Inn "was *the* gay bar in the city."

Fader says that "eighty percent [of the crowd] you wouldn't know anybody there from [somewhere] else," before making the critical point for understanding the Stonewall Inn: that "anyone who was in the margins of gay
society would be free to go there, because they were totally accepted."
Bryan says: "The street queens were the predominant force in there, although there were all types of people," with the result that "it did have an
overall kind of a trashy reputation, and certainly, that was the predominant
ambience: trashy, low, and tawdry." Vito Russo similarly recalled: "It was a
bar for the people who were too young, too poor or just too much to get in
anywhere else. The Stonewall was a street queen hangout in the heart of
the ghetto."[39] Perhaps Allen Young characterized it best when he said the
club was the "favorite hang-out of the freest of the gay people—those most
likely to be labeled 'fag' and 'drag queen.'" The nature of the Stonewall's
crowd made Young so uncomfortable that he "preferred the more up-tight
and sedate (read, 'masculine') crowd at Danny's, a few blocks closer to the
waterfront."[40]

One of the more disputed points about the Stonewall clientele is to
what extent women went there and how many of those were lesbians.
Hampton says that "all gay men went there. Very few, if any, gay women at
all. Usually I would practically be the only woman around." Shaheen said,
"It was 98 percent men."

Certainly some of the women were heterosexual. One Stonewall regular
recalls, "Some women who would go to the Stonewall were hippie straight
women, or some woman who would look like a drag queen."[41] One gay man
who went to the Stonewall Inn with a female—although a very young

one—was Chris Babick. When Chris started going there in 1968 he was a seventeen-year-old high school senior but looked so much younger that he relied on his fifteen-year-old friend Peggy to buy him drinks. Shaheen adds that "the floormen [waiters who circulated selling drinks] always loved girls to come in because [the floormen] were straight."

Early Stonewall researcher Tina Crosby concluded in 1974: "The screening process at the door effectively excluded women; each person I talked with remembered the Stonewall as an exclusively male bar, with the only exception being an occasional tough lesbian or female friend of one of the male patrons."[42] Jennifer "Hardy" (not her real last name) remembers seeing a lesbian of this very type on her first visit to the Stonewall Inn as a seventeen-year-old runaway: "There was this woman in there, and she was big. . . . That's not what I was looking for. I didn't want somebody that would control me and beat me up and that's kind of the impression I got from her, that she was strong and that she was mean. I don't know if she was a bouncer or what she was, but I steered clear of her."[43] The presence of this kind of lesbian at the Stonewall reflects the predominance in the lesbian social scene at that time of the butch-femme model.

The one dissenting voice about the kind of lesbians who frequented the Stonewall is Shaheen, who remembers beautiful hairdressers, which suggests that "femme" lesbians patronized the Inn and raising the intriguing possibility that they might have been mistaken for heterosexual women or even for "fag hags," since they brought along their male homosexual counterparts: "There were lesbians and they were not of the very butch type of lesbians in those days. Remember that its biggest clientele were hairdressers. . . . They were big tippers, and some of them were women and some of them were gay."

The last hotly contested issue about the clientele is the extent to which transvestites came to the Stonewall. The general consensus confirms the usual presence of a few. Certainly all credible witnesses agree that the Stonewall Inn never became a "drag queen bar." But what determined if a drag queen was admitted? Shaheen said simply that "it all had to do with the doorman knowing you." Some of the drag queens Shaheen recalls going to the Stonewall Inn are Tiffany, Desiree, Spanola Jerry (a hairdresser), and Tammy Novak, but he quickly added, speaking of the first three, "They were spenders. That's why they got in," making it plain that not any transvestite could walk up to the door at any time and be admitted. As for Tammy Novak, she clearly belonged to a special category, having lived with Fat Tony and Chuck Shaheen.

The presence of drag queens at the Stonewall Inn has been much exaggerated over the years for a number of reasons.[44] One of the first is a terminology problem. The word *queen* was more widely used in the late sixties to indicate any gay man who was not conventionally masculine, whereas today the word usually occurs in the phrase *drag queen* or indicates a very feminine gay male. Thus when a contemporary person reads about "a whole bunch of queens," the picture that may come to mind is one of transvestites, whereas the 1960s usage probably simply indicated a group of gay men, with the understanding that none of them were totally straight-acting.

Complicating the picture is the existence in the late 1960s of gay men known as *scare queens* or *flame queens*. One of the club's regular customers explains the meaning of these terms that describe a kind of gay male who became practically nonexistent not long after 1969: "What you had back then was the flame queens, which were very similar to the character Emory in *The Boys in the Band*: they were supereffeminate, hair would be teased, they would wear eye makeup, Tom Jones–type shirts, maybe hiphuggers, bright colors. A good example of this was Brandy Alexander, who used to perform at the 82 Club and who was an extra in the movie *Midnight Cowboy*. I remember Brandy saying to me she would have to go up there and do the streets, and even then, even though Brandy was a performer in drag—in the movie [when] they would show you the drag queens on 42nd Street, they're flame queens. You couldn't do the whole drag thing [in the film], because that's not how people dressed: you would be arrested. So as far as the Stonewall being all these drag queens, no, there were flame queens. Even Barbara Eden [a male, Barbara Eden being a camp name] who worked there in the coat check didn't do drag except once in a blue moon."[45]

This distinction helps resolve some of the seemingly contradictory accounts about how many transvestite and transsexual customers patronized the Stonewall. For example, Chris Babick spoke to Michael Scherker as if the transvestite population at the Stonewall was quite sizable. However, when Babick describes what he wore, it fits the description given earlier of "scare" or "flame" queens: "I had bleached hair and I started wearing makeup [because] I had this acne problem. My favorite outfit was these black pair of hiphuggers, bell-bottoms, and my straight girlfriend embroidered daisies on the bottom of them, this trim. . . . And I had this favorite cotton satin-type shirt. . . . And I'd wear that with this big belt with a big buckle and my boots." It also seems clear that while there was high drag at the Stonewall, there was also low drag, which practically fits into the previously mentioned category of "flame queen," as is the case with the following person Edmund White saw there: "There was one [drag queen] that was always there, this very tall black one who I called the whirling dervish because he would get out by himself on the dance floor and turn around with his leg just shooting through the air. He was under thirty and would wear pedal pushers and a midriff shirt and maybe a wig, but the kind of thing that he could take the wig off and put it in his pocket and look kind of like a boy, because I think a lot of times these boys had to go back to Harlem at night. They could make the transition pretty quick—maybe they carried shopping bags and checked those. I'm not quite sure, but I have a feeling they did a quick change on the subway as they were going up to Harlem late at night." From White's description, one can imagine that someone who saw the whirling dervish with his wig on might describe him as a drag queen (with the understanding that he was not trying to pass as a woman), but someone who saw him without the wig would undoubtedly consider him a "flame queen." Perhaps the most accurate way to characterize the Stonewall Inn in terms of what we currently call transgender identity is that while there was a lot of gender transgression going on there, this was largely a reflection of the male homosexual world of the time, that most men who went there were conventionally masculine, but that there was a considerable minority of men there who ran the gamut from men effeminate in their mannerisms, to scare or flame queens, to a few transvestites and some transsexuals.

Finally, the most important point about the clientele at the Stonewall Inn is that all segments of the gay and lesbian community, including a strong representation of the more marginal elements, defined the Stonewall Inn as a special place in the homosexual world of greater New York, giving it a unique status at that time. Tommy Lanigan-Schmidt was so struck by this feature on his first visit that he described the Stonewall as a kind of temple of homosexuality: "If the Tenth of Always was like a little parish church, the Stonewall would be like St. Peter's in Rome. . . . It was big in its scope. . . . Somehow, it covered the whole mixture of everyone gay at the time."

With two dance floors, the Stonewall Inn became wildly popular. Harry Beard recalls, "We had a real healthy segment of people with cash, a lot of people from the bar business, since at that time we were the largest gay club anywhere in the country, probably the largest club period."[46]

And so it was that when the Stonewall Inn opened its doors for business on the night of March 18, 1967, immense profits began to pour in.[47] Chuck Shaheen recalls that "we used to take out of there between $5,000 and $6,000 on a Friday night and [again] on Saturday." With the initial investment being $3,500 and the monthly rent only $300 a month, the Stonewall Inn made back all of its investment and then some the first night, so that after a few hours of operation it was essentially pure profit every day for nearly two and a half years. Shaheen explains that to prevent the loss of such large sums of money, part of the bouncers' job was to "go around and pick up our banks," an errand on which they carried baseball bats. The money was kept in cigar boxes, which had several advantages over cash registers. The first time the police raided the club they seized the cash registers as evidence of the illegal sale of alcohol. After that, the club used cigar boxes, not only because the expensive machines would be lost in future raids, but they could also be used as evidence against the owners, who, as operators of a purported bottle club, were not supposed to be selling anything. After removing the money from the cigar boxes, the bouncers wrapped rubber bands around the rolls of cash and casually tossed them into the Stonewall Inn's office.[48] Chuck Shaheen eventually moved up from being a bartender and lived with Fat Tony as a kind of man Friday, and one of his duties was to run the money over to "the family bank," the Bank of Commerce on Delancey Street, where "most of the money was put through."

Of course it was impossible to make so much money in such a public setting without being noticed. The huge profits certainly caught the eye of Craig Rodwell. Since practically the only social outlet gay people had in New York City was bars, it infuriated Rodwell that these places were controlled by the Mafia and not by the gay community. "Bars have always been our only place, our haven in a sense. I was always furious that the mob controls so much of our social life." Having worked in gay bars, Rodwell had learned how much the management loathed their gay customers: "They like our money and hated our guts. And that was one of the major issues around the Stonewall. There was that collusion between the cops and the mob, and we were like caught in the middle all the time."[49]

Characteristically, Rodwell took an activist approach to the bar situation. Having his own publication and the opportunity to distribute it in his bookstore, he used the *Hymnal* to critique the implications of the Mafia's control of the gay bar scene. About the Stonewall's finances Rodwell wrote that the bar was "one of the . . . more financially lucrative of the Mafia's gay bars in Manhattan."[50]

Such heady profits also interested the police, who felt they had a right to a piece of the pie. It was common knowledge when the Stonewall Inn opened that it was run by the Mafia and that the police were paid off by the club, the standard practice for lesbian and homosexual clubs in New York City. One reason that the payoffs were common knowledge is that, as Kevin Brew noted, "It's the kind of thing you don't see in actuality. You don't see the bartender paying the police, but you knew something was going on because they left the bar alone (after the payoff)."[51] Craig Rodwell noted the same thing in *Hymnal* in his list of characteristics that explained how to tell if a club was Mafia run: "Policemen will make periodic and mysterious appearances to talk with the goons at the door."[52] Shaheen confirms this method of payment: "The police were very much on the payroll of the Stonewall. . . . The Sixth Precinct. I can only account for the Sixth Precinct." Asked how often the police came by to collect, Shaheen replied, "Once a week. There were two [envelopes]. Because in those days there was an officer and that was his beat, and then someone in the precinct, usually the captain or the desk sergeant, would get an envelope." As for the amount paid, Shaheen said he did not know the exact amount but was positive it was hundreds of dollars a week.

The Stonewall was in Manhattan's Sixth Precinct, and from all available evidence, there is no reason to doubt that the Sixth Precinct was paid off by gay bars and clubs. For example, Tim Callahan, who worked at the bar Danny's for around six months during the time the Stonewall was open, said that he saw the precinct captain come by several times. Each time the same thing happened: the captain would have a drink with the bar's owner during which time they seemed to have a congenial conversation, after which they would both walk out to the captain's car. While Tim never actually saw money change hands, he had no doubt that this was taking place. During his time at Danny's, these friendly visits from the captain were the only times Tim ever saw a policeman enter the bar.

Other rare contemporary evidence of the police receiving bribes comes from a letter Dick Leitsch wrote:

> Those two cops who came to visit us . . . have informed me that they discovered one of the cops whose name I gave them was taking payoffs from that club [the Stonewall Inn], and he's been dismissed from the force. The other one is still under investigation and surveillance, though they think he's clean. They're not going to take any action against the Stonewall.[53]

The amount the Stonewall Inn paid to the Sixth Precinct was $1,200 per month, according to a *Pageant* magazine article on police corruption. The article was published less than five months after the Stonewall Inn opened. While the article did not name the bar, it sounds like the Stonewall Inn: "a rather shady bar serving homosexuals." The article added that in terms of payoffs, the bar was the largest contributor to the police department. Proof that the bar mentioned was the Stonewall Inn comes from the $1,200 figure being given three times afterward as the amount of the Stonewall's monthly payoff (twice in 1978 and once in 1988) by Ed Murphy, who was associated with the bar.[54]

That the Stonewall Inn was a Mafia club had many ramifications. While homosexual men were provided with a place to socialize, the downside could be considerable, for the Mafia had little or no concern for their clientele's welfare. But as one person on New York's gay scene in the fifties and sixties explained, since clubs were closed down so often by the police, gay people were desperate for places to meet and usually had to settle for dirty and dangerous environments.[55]

The Stonewall had both. Chuck Shaheen explains the Stonewall Inn's main affront to hygiene: "We had no running water behind the main bar. We were unable to clean the glasses. We had two sinks. We filled them up at the beginning of the shift with water. Today you need to have all kinds of hot water and detergents. We didn't use that. Because of the volume, we would just take anybody's glass and run it through the water and refill it and serve it to anybody else." This practice apparently caused an outbreak of hepatitis among the Stonewall's customers.

The lead article in the *Hymnal*'s first issue attacked Mafia control of gay bars, with the Stonewall Inn serving as the epitome of all that was wrong with such clubs. The article included a report on a hepatitis outbreak: "New York HYMNAL received a report . . . that the Stone Wall was going to be closed by the Health Department because it was alleged that a number of cases of Hepatitis (which has reached epidemic proportions among the homosexual community) had been traced to the Stone Wall's bar." As the lesbian publication *The Ladder* pointed out, such risk to customers came as a natural consequence of the SLA's ban on licensing businesses to sell alcohol to homosexuals: "Since the SLA refuses to issue licenses to gay bars, these bars are generally run . . . under unsanitary conditions."[56]

The Mafia's refusal to invest in basic amenities literally spilled over into other inconveniences for customers. The front bar had a regular built-in sink and for a second sink made use of a rubber tub. At the beginning of the shift, each was filled with clean water. With hundreds of people passing through the bar on a weekend night, the water eventually got dingy enough that even the Mafia felt compelled to freshen it. "Mike" the porter remembers that one of his jobs was to empty the rubber tub. Since the club lacked the proper facilities for doing so, he would take the tub to the men's room and empty the contents in a toilet.[57] Eventually, with the Stonewall's many customers flushing the toilets before and after the water from the rubber tub had been poured in, the total volume would exceed the capacity of the club's pipes and the toilets would overflow. The result was that the bathroom floors, as Lanigan-Schmidt recalls, seemed constantly wet "with an unpleasant-looking water."[58] Rodwell's *Hymnal* lamented the "filthy john" and called the Stonewall Inn "the tackiest joint in town."[59] Robert Heide and his friends referred to it as "The Cesspool."

However, the Stonewall Inn posed an even greater physical threat to its customers: the building had no fire exits. Given the crowds that gathered there on the weekends,[60] that the club had no rear exit, that it had only one doorway between its front and back rooms, and that customers fleeing a fire would have had to pass through a narrow lobby before exiting the building, a fire in the Stonewall could have had terrible consequences.[61]

Not satisfied with the huge profits made from diluted booze, the greedy Mafia owners also dealt in drugs. Rodwell explained that "of course in any of those [Mafia bars] there's going to be a huge drug crowd. The drugs are pushed in there like crazy. That's one reason the syndicate keeps their control of gay bars. Just selling liquor is one of the minor things they do in those places."[62] Vito Russo agreed, writing: "It was possible to buy any known substance available in capsule form."[63] Shaheen recalls that "all the hairdressers were very into Desbutols, which was actually Desoxyn, but it was mixed with Nembutol," a combination intended to "smooth you out as it helps you up." One club goer who helped supply some of the drugs denied that hard drugs were readily available: "It would be the place you would go to cop. If you knew the right person in there, that's where you would get your acid . . . marijuana or whatever. Nothing like heroin or anything like that."[64]

The chief purveyor of drugs at the Stonewall was the legendary Maggie Jiggs.[65] (Though everyone called him Maggie, he did not work or live in drag. Tish, a female impersonator from the era, explained, however, that "you knew she was gay when you saw her.") Tish had gotten friendly with Jiggs in Providence, when Tish was living in Connecticut and commuting to Providence for school. One night as Tish took the commuter bus home, he was surprised to see Jiggs. "I said to her, 'Where are you going?!' and she said, 'I'm going to New York.' I say, 'Really?' She says, 'Oh, yeah. I just robbed a john and I got $100, and I'm going to go to New York.'"

Despite being chubby, having a receding hairline and a clubfoot, and standing only about five and a half feet tall, Jiggs had an outgoing personality that made him hugely popular. When Tish moved to New York, he was surprised to find Jiggs a ubiquitous presence in Manhattan's gay bars.

"I start going to the clubs, and I see she's behind the bars. I would go to some new bar and I would [say], 'Well, Jesus Christ, Jiggs, what are you doing here!?' 'Oh, well, they sent me over here.' And every time I'd go to another club, Jiggs was there! Then we'd leave that club, and we'd go to an after-hours club: Jiggs would be behind the bar! She had a following. If a new bar opened up, the boys—as I like to call them—would say, 'Send that Jiggs there; he's got a good crowd.' You know, we all liked Jiggs."

Jiggs had a prop that he always used in his work, a tall gold-colored chalice set with stones, which normally sat on the bar. Tish used to tease Jiggs about it. "I'd say, 'A little offering! Drop it in.' And I'd say, 'Don't forget: Jiggs is going to go to Europe, a little offering for Jiggs.'" After circulating with the chalice, Tish would then turn to Jiggs and say, "Well, so far, Jiggs, you've got just enough to get to the airport. You've got to work a little harder."

"She'd slip you the drinks and you'd give her the money and after a time she wouldn't ring it up; she'd put it in her cup, you see. So we all said, 'Oh, she's such a conniver!' But we all liked her and the bosses always knew, if you're working in a gay bar, you're going to take a little off the top."

Jiggs was even better known for the cigar box he always carried, which served among other purposes as a container for the drugs he peddled. (Jiggs was so well known for the cigar box he used that when he died, his ashes were buried in one.)[66]

Stealing from the Mafia was dangerous, even for a popular bartender. Tree recalls that "the person who collected the entrance fee, or the door-man, or the guy in the shiny suit . . . walked around watching to see if the bartenders were ringing up the drinks or if the waiters were reselling the entrance tickets. . . . Arms and legs were broken on a few bartenders and waiters when they got caught."[67] In spite of her well-known light fingers, Jiggs survived unharmed because, Tish explains, "Jiggs knew just about how much to take."

Even with police payoffs, illegal bars were raided on an average of once a month but more frequently during an election campaign when politicians, eager to impress the electorate with how "clean" they were keeping the city, pressured the police to be more vigilant. Why did the police raid after being paid off? Because they were ordered to, because it was their job, and because of complaints from the Stonewall Inn's neighbors, never very happy with the gay men the Inn drew to the neighborhood.

The Sixth Precinct did at least warn the Stonewall that a raid was imminent. Chuck Shaheen explains: "We would be alerted that we were going to be raided before we opened, so all kinds of things could be done. There was always less money on the premises. There was always less liquor . . . because what they would do when a bar was raided in those days, if you had cash registers, they would impound the cash register . . . [and] the liquor, and . . . let all of the customers leave. They would try and identify the people who worked there. It was never, and I repeat never, any of the real management or owners. The bosses would disappear very quickly. That's why they always had a gay person on the door, because that's the person who had to take the heat and actually get arrested.

"The white lights on the dance floor would go on and . . . we would have time to jump from behind the bar and mingle. And people would get rid of their drugs and all that stuff. But they were never really interested in looking for drugs and things like that, unless you still had it on your person or something, if you were one of the unlucky people to be chosen—supposedly at random from the crowd by the police—as an employee. We [employees] would immediately jump from behind the bar and try and take the money out of the box [and] put it in our pocket. We'd jump over the bar because we knew they had to break through the front door, which was a very strong door. [The Mafia owners] didn't want them to get the money. They would hold it as long as they could."

There was such close cooperation between the police and the gay bars that the police would time the raids to minimize the disruption to the bars' business. Shaheen explained, "A normal raid would be before midnight, which would enable us [to prepare for it] . . . we really never got busy until after midnight on the weekend. Or they would raid it on a Tuesday night. Whoopee. If they raided it on the weekend, it was always that we would know it was going to be before midnight, before we even officially set up."

Although the Stonewall Inn employees (as opposed to the owners) were occasionally taken away by the police, arrest was not viewed with any alarm. "We were never frightened of being arrested. The police would just randomly pick people off and say, 'You, you, you, and you.' If we were arrested and taken into the Sixth Precinct, which we were many times, we automatically knew we would be out in a matter of hours. Many times it would happen that people who did not work there were arrested. But the lawyers had them out so quickly, they never even left the precinct house." The lawyer the Stonewall Inn used was a "family lawyer," Enid Gerling.[68]

While there was dancing in both of the Stonewall's rooms, dancing had more of a communal character and was more expressive in the back room. Tommy Lanigan-Schmidt feels that the real power of the Stonewall for its admirers had its genesis in the music played there. From his perspective as one of the gay street youth, he saw three main ingredients at play: being gay; being unconstrained, because these youths were living from day to day; and being adolescent, they had tremendous sexual energy. Tommy explains, "The music is carrying the articulation of this emotional need that can't be articulated on the outside publicly. You picture a bunch of kids and the towns they came from: they hear the songs on the radio, Diana Ross or the Shangri-Las, and the way they relate to it is they identify it as someone of their own sex, but they're not telling anyone. But the song is articulating that feeling both through the music and the words. At the Stonewall, all these kids who had to hold this inside in high school can now articulate this completely. At the Tenth of Always I was very conscious of their stopping people from dancing: you were never allowed the full flow of that. The Mafia people there were very gruff about telling you not to dance; they'd really treat you like queers, like you were disgusting. At the Tenth of Always it was always a little tiny dance floor and you'd hear the Shangri-Las' song—something like 'walk across the room and give him a great big kiss'—and you could look across the room and see sexy Vinnie over there and you could get into all the longing, but you couldn't go over and ask him to dance.

"At the Stonewall Inn the articulation becomes much more complex because not only could you ask him to dance, but a lot of other people could ask him to, so then you could get into *all* of the feelings, like feeling sorry for yourself in a really beautiful way like a teenager is supposed to. A teenager loves to have that frustration articulated: 'Oh, I wanted to ask him to dance, and he doesn't even know I exist! And there he is dancing with that awful queen!' 'Cause I would get into this thing: 'That queen doesn't know what's good for that man, and I know what's good for him.' And then I'd go and articulate other things that I heard in a movie like, 'Oh, you have hands like Michelangelo's *David*,' and the guy would look at me and say, 'So what?' But the usual articulation coming in there was not from Michelangelo; it was from the Supremes and Martha and the Vandellas. So there's this really tremendous articulation seeping into people's subconscious and deepest needs, plus the place becoming a refuge and a strength."

Three months after Danny Garvin left New York City to stay with his family in Illinois, he returned.

"I was at the point that I would have sex with men, but I wouldn't kiss; I was still in the early stages of coming out. Then I ran into this guy one night who picked me up in a Bickford's [a chain restaurant], and he was with a few friends of his. His name was Charlie, and I stayed overnight. The following night we went to the Stonewall and Charlie asked me to dance. And I said, 'No, no, no. I don't dance with men; I don't do that.' So he said, 'Why?' I said, 'I don't want anyone to see me.' He said, 'But you know, everybody in here is gay.' And it was just the fear, you know?

"So as the night went on we had a few more drinks; he asked me if I found any of the men who were with him attractive; I said 'Yeah, Frank.' And I started crying, 'cause nobody had ever asked me.

"The following night we went back to the Stonewall, and then Frank came over to ask me to dance. And I realized if I didn't dance with this guy, we probably wouldn't get it on together. It was the first man I was attracted to; it was the first time I danced. I felt embarrassed and nervous, and I realized that I liked this guy. You know, it was my first love. So we dance. It was nice. We slow danced to 'Let It Be Me,' which became our song. That was the first time I allowed myself to dance, to be part of gay life. To go ahead and kiss a man in public."

Lanigan-Schmidt feels that the appeal of the Stonewall Inn came not only from dancing to music but also from the songs' lyrics. He cites the lyrics of several songs performed by Martha Reeves and the Vandellas as examples of lyrics that could have a particular resonance for those who went to the Stonewall Inn. One example is "Third Finger, Left Hand." In this song the singer exults that although "friends said it couldn't be done," she has succeeded in marrying the man of her dreams.

Tommy found magic in the lyrics, applying the idea of the attainment of something said to be impossible to his own situation as a gay man. "It translates the same way it would to a heterosexual, but it also has other translations, because the whole thing is, it says: 'Friends said it couldn't be done.' I really would think things like, *Here we are dancing!* because I was very aware of looking and saying, 'There's men dancing with each other and dancing slow dances with each other.' That entered very consciously in a way that impressed me. So a song like this would be like a big, celebratory thing, every word."

Tommy analyzes "Forget Me Not" as a poignant example of how pop music could speak to gay people. The song is written from the point of view of a woman telling her boyfriend good-bye as he prepares to sail for Vietnam. The singer tells her lover that he should remember her when he is away so that when he feels lonely or in despair they will still be united.

Tommy points out that not only did people generally never think of gay men as having soldiers for lovers and being separated from them by the war but that "someone could go out and have a one-night thing with a soldier and hear that song and that song could be the way they hold on to that forever. Or they could actually have a regular steady boyfriend in the army. To have that affair or quickie sex and then come to a place and be able to dance that into a song was a major innovation of the Stonewall, because it wasn't happening anyplace else.

"Another thing in gay life that happens since you're a little kid is the ability for self-ridicule that we developed to survive, which is about laughing at ourselves with a certain poignancy. You've got all these queens in the street, and they can be pretty mean to each other, but we all get laughing. And these songs can play into that, too. All teenagers make up their own crazy words for what is not in the song. The street queens would do it, too. That song 'Trains and boats and planes are passing by to Paris and Rome for someone else but not for me,' by Dionne Warwick or someone. And these street queens would go, 'Faggots and dykes and queers are passing by; it means a trip to Paris and Rome for someone else but not for me.' Now, you could analyze it as hopes and dreams to go to Paris or Rome, or someone else is getting it, but I'm not, but it's not so serious-sounding that you couldn't laugh at it.

"At the Stonewall people would invent a line like that and then it would spread like wildfire, where a bunch of people could scream out that line while they're dancing and get into it. And it might fade away in a couple of days or it might be something they'd say forever. I think the best metaphors for Stonewall are words like *home,* because when you're not living any-where regularly, home becomes where you make it. A bunch of queens singing that gives each other a mutual strength, and that familial sense of the street queens, it's a kind of tribal loyalty."

Dick Leitsch also noted the special place the Stonewall Inn held for the gay community's most rejected members:

The "drags" and the "queens," two groups which would find a chilly reception or a barred door at most of the other gay bars and clubs, formed the "regulars" at the Stonewall. To a large extent, the club was for them. . . . Apart from the Goldbug and the One-Two-Three, "drags" and "queens" had no place but the Stonewall. . . .

Another group was even more dependent on the Stonewall: the very young homosexuals and those with no other homes. You've got to be 18 to buy a drink in a bar, and gay life revolved around bars. Where do you go if you are 17 or 16 and gay? The "legitimate" bars won't let you in the place, and gay restaurants and the streets aren't very sociable.

Then too, there are hundreds of young homosexuals in New York who literally have no home. . . .

Jobless and without skills—without decent clothes to wear to a job interview—they live in the streets, panhandling or shoplifting for the price of admission to the Stonewall. That was the one advantage to the place—for $3.00 admission, one could stay inside, out of the win-ter's cold or the summer heat, all night long. It also saved the kids . . . from getting arrested as vagrants.[69]

The tribal energy that Lanigan-Schmidt noticed might express itself in any of a number of ways while dancing. For example, Tommy remembers how the pin spotlights in the front room were playfully used: "Queens used to use this expression, 'Give me vogue.' They would do these poses that they figured were like models. They'd suck in their cheeks, but they'd try to get just where the pin lights near the jukebox came in. The queens from the back room would go into the front room to show off because in the front room they'd be noticed more."

Danny Garvin also remembers how music at the Stonewall Inn fostered communalism, especially in the back room: "In the back room—because the room was large enough—is where you'd find most of the people would do their line dances. I can remember learning a dance there called 'The Spider.' And it would be a camp, because they'd get ten or fifteen of us all lined up and we'd all go across and somebody would scream, 'Hit it, girl!' and everybody would go down and touch the floor and get back up, and move on."

And the back room had all the right ingredients to make it the more sexually charged of the two rooms: it had dimmer lighting, was the favored hangout of the street youths, and had better music and dancing. Harry Beard recalls, "The back bar was for the socializers and talkers and people that wanted to play touchy-feely under the tables."

Charles Burch found the dancing in the back room so sexual as to be inspiring. An avid reader of Walt Whitman, he believed in the poet's vision of love in its physical aspects as so free that it was universal. To him the Stonewall seemed "terribly wonderful" because it was a place to sexually connect with strangers, the realization of his Whitmanesque fantasies. "To me it's nice when they play a slow tune that you could use for the kind of dancing where you get up close. 'Cause then I could do my sex dancing with some utter stranger. And that was what I loved."

Another testimony to the power of dancing at the Stonewall comes from Danny Garvin. Asked when it was that he first became aware of being different and how he felt about it, he responded, "It would have been in the Stonewall that night when I first danced with that guy. I knew I wasn't drinking. I knew I wanted to go to bed with him. I was so scared to [dance with him] . . . And there was that fear of 'suppose somebody from my neighborhood sees me.' You know, the closet door was so tight. . . . There were no positive role models. Who'd know what the Mattachine Society was at seventeen? . . . So, yeah, the Stonewall's the first place where I started to accept myself being gay."

While other clubs and settings may have offered places for socializing and making romantic and sexual liaisons and while there were a number of clubs where people could dance, the Stonewall was the only sizable place where gay men could express their sexuality freely and openly for sustained periods of time. Bathhouses offered places where gay men could actually have sex—that was the bathhouses' sole purpose—but socializing there was largely incidental to sexual activity. In other words, the Stonewall Inn was the only place where gay men could express all sides of their personalities. Not only could gay men dance freely, but there also could be a certain expansiveness about their dancing, given the physical size of the club and the tight security provided by the Mafia.

Tommy Lanigan-Schmidt succinctly sums up the meaning of the Stonewall Inn in this regard when he says, "It was as real as the street, and also—what was the biggest step in there—at the Tenth of Always, when you'd dance with someone, you always knew that any minute the chandelier would flick on and you'd have to go sit down. At the Stonewall, everyone just kept dancing. It was open a few years before those riots. It sunk its roots deep because it had longevity and because you were never told not to dance."

With its owners interested only in exploiting gay people, the Stonewall was not an ideal place for gay men. Yet it offered its patrons three crucial things: space, security, and freedom. Added to these were longevity and the continuity that longevity made possible. Through the power of music and dance, the club fused these elements to create among most of its regular customers a sense of gay community and identity and thus a loyalty to the Stonewall Inn.

5

The Skull

While Chuck Shaheen clearly stated in his interview with historian Martin Duberman how Tony Lauria and his three partners became the prime movers behind opening the Stonewall Inn, when he discussed another of the Stonewall's underworld managers, he never explained how Ed Murphy, a shadowy figure known as The Skull, came to be a manager at the Stonewall Inn. This is fitting for Murphy, who seems to have been so ubiquitous in the gay bar scene in Manhattan that his presence was often taken for granted. Danny Garvin remembers seeing him "just hanging out" at the Stonewall Inn and at Danny's. Tommy Lanigan-Schmidt describes him in a similar vein at the Tenth of Always: "He was always there like a Buddha. You know, he had that presence. I never saw him do anything but sit where he was. Wherever he sat, he sat and that was Murphy." It was as if Murphy, an obese man with a gray beard and gray suit, had a knack for insinuating himself into the gay bar scene.

While the Stonewall Inn had its negative aspects, for most of its customers these were not usually major issues, especially when weighed against what the club had to offer on the positive side or, for that matter, when compared to most of the other New York City gay bars then in operation. But as it turns out, some of the Stonewall's patrons had more to fear from the club's operators than high-priced weak drinks and occasional police raids.

One warm evening as Tommy Lanigan-Schmidt headed up Greenwich Avenue with several of his friends, he was delighted to see one of his heartthrobs, Tano, a masculine, good-looking Puerto Rican youth. In spite of his attraction to Tano, the reason for Tommy's glee in spotting him was not because he hoped it would lead to anything romantic or even sexual. Gay men on the street passed the word to each other that Ed Murphy fancied the youth as a favorite boyfriend. Tommy had heard many different rumors on the street about Murphy, suggestions that he was powerful and connected and owned lots of gay bars. To Tommy it all boiled down to "vague rumors of bad things," and so he had kept a certain distance from Tano in spite of his strong attraction. Tano's only response, however, to Tommy's circumscribed friendliness was complete aloofness. Frustrated, Tommy decided to play sour grapes by calling Tano Miss Polka Dot, for Tano often wore polka-dot shirts, like the one he had on this evening. Tommy took a perverse pleasure in baiting him, for it upset Tano enough that Tommy could see the very masculine Latino fighting down an urge to attack him. When Tommy noticed Tano that night, his first thought was, *Oh, good! I'm going to get to call him Miss Polka Dot again and see his angry, sexy face.* But on approaching the youth, Tommy heard the screech of an automobile's brakes and noticed a dark car from which several men emerged. They pulled Tano into the vehicle before speeding off. It was the last time Tommy saw Tano.

In the coming weeks two versions of a story emerged on the street to explain the youth's disappearance, both of which connected his kidnapping to Ed Murphy. In one version, Tano had stolen something from Murphy. The second rumor was that he had enraged Murphy by becoming involved with someone else. The kidnapping of a man right in front of his eyes had startled Tommy, but when he remembered that he had heard Murphy could have people rubbed out the event no longer seemed so surprising.[1] The suspicion that Murphy was involved in the murders of youths goes back at least to the early sixties. Stephen van Cline recalls, for example, that Murphy had been involved with the early 1960s waterfront gay bar called Dirty Dick's, where, he says, a number of young men were seen for the last time.[2]

Edward Francis P. Murphy had become a hellion at a tender age. Repeatedly thrown out of Catholic schools, he came to the attention of the police at age nine when he attacked the owner of a neighborhood banana store and trashed his fruit stand. After several other brawls, Murphy was sent to a special problem school on nearby Hudson Street. The time he spent there with other juvenile delinquents did not improve his temperament, for he later hit a police officer over the head with a milk bottle in a dispute over

Murphy's shoeshine box. For this infraction he was packed off to a reform school in Dobbs Ferry.

When Murphy was released from reform school in 1943, he entered the army after a short stint in the gay bar business at the Pink Elephant, an establishment run by the Jewish Mafia. After combat in France, he left the army in 1946 and worked as a bouncer at the Moss Bar on Eighth Avenue.

Apparently it was his work as a bruiser for hire that led the ambitious and physical Murphy into a wrestling career. Murphy realized that he had a "tough top" and decided to make his head do double duty. He shaved it, anointed himself Skull, and put his cranium to work as a battering ram. The tactic worked well enough to get him into professional wrestling, where spectators came to know him for his special death hold. Murphy's aggressive style seemed to make him a natural for wrestling. A television viewer from the era recalled seeing him rip the microphone out of the announcer's hands, stomp on his opponent's head when he was unconscious, and throw chairs at old women who booed him.

By the late 1940s Murphy had teamed up with a gay friend to rob dentist offices, targeting them for their shipments of gold from dental laboratories. After robbing seventy-three dental offices, Murphy was finally caught in 1947 and served ten years in prison, the maximum time, spending much of it in isolation for assaults.

When he left prison, he worked as a bouncer in gay bars such as the Cork Club, the Bali, Mais Oui, Sans Souci, the 415, the Terrace, and Artie's.[3] Murphy seems to have had a penchant for moonlighting, for he also began to work as a hotel house detective.

While the preceding record of Murphy's early career is taken from his own accounts, it was in his work in the hotel business that he first came into the public record in a way that has a direct bearing on gay history. In August of 1965 the police arrested Murphy while he was working for the New York Hilton as a house detective. He was charged with being the head of a ring that had preyed on hotel guests, extorting $100,000 from "rich playboys and executives."[4] While the newspaper report made it clear that sex had been used in the extortion scheme, only those who read between the lines would understand that the blackmailers had targeted homosexual men.

Six months later Murphy's name hit the New York media in a much bigger story that was explicitly connected to homosexual victimization. This time Murphy was accused of being involved in a ring of blackmailers that preyed primarily on homosexual men. The ring had been centered in New York and Chicago, although its reach was nationwide. While the scale of the extortion ring was known to be large from the beginning, by the time the investigations were completed its scope and size were staggering: having operated for almost ten years, the ring had victimized close to a thousand men and taken in $2 million. Equally impressive was how many of these men were highly successful. Among those listed at the time or in more recent newspaper reports were the head of the American Medical Association, two army generals, Admiral William Church, a Republican member of Congress from New Jersey, a Princeton professor, "a leading motion-picture actor," "a musician who has made numerous appearances on television," heads of business firms, "a much-admired television personality," and "a British producer."[5] None of the individuals named here were identified in the contemporary press coverage of the blackmail ring, a credit to both the men prosecuting the cases, Andrew Maloney and Robert Morgenthau, as well as the newspapers that covered the story.

The investigation began with a fairly routine arrest, when a man impersonating a detective in Grand Central Station was apprehended by a real detective, James McDonnell.

Although the ring used several scams, by far the most common one was to send attractive young men into hotels where wealthy homosexual men came to meet such youths.[6] The decoy would lure the man to a hotel room, attack him, and run out of the room with his wallet or other valuables and identification. Then, weeks later, after having found out which men had the most to lose, whether in terms of their families, professions, or reputations, other members of the ring, usually a pair, would call on those deemed vulnerable. The pair would produce police badges from New York or another jurisdiction and an arrest warrant. The "policemen" would then threaten to arrest the victim, exposing him as a homosexual. They would soon offer to "forget about it" if the victim would give them anywhere from a few hundred to several thousand dollars.

The nerve the blackmailers displayed was breathtaking. Tracking their victims down in their hometowns and calling on them in their homes was routine for the ring. They called on the New Jersey congressman on Capitol Hill and marched him out of his own office door so he could fly home to pick up $50,000. A surgeon was pulled out of an operating room. Members of the ring went to the West Coast and got inside a nuclear plant. The extortionists were discussing the price of their silence with a nuclear scientist when the scientist's superior walked into the office. The fast-thinking victim introduced the blackmailers as two detective friends of his who were visiting from New York. The scientist, thinking he was dealing with real detectives, suggested that they might want to see the plant. His superior approved and the extortionists were taken throughout a plant that was normally under the heaviest security strictures. When the scientist was invited to New York to testify against those who had victimized him, he at first refused to believe that they were not detectives, saying he was disgusted with the New York police. After all, as the Mattachine Society pointed out at the time, this operation did resemble the New York Police Department's use of police decoys to entrap gay men.

Not surprisingly, these stories sometimes ended tragically. When Admiral William Church, the head of the New York Naval Yards, was approached by Detective McDonnell in Washington, D.C., he refused to accompany McDonnell back to New York to testify before a grand jury. Church told McDonnell that he would drive up the following day. Instead, he drove his car to a Maryland motel and put a bullet in his head.

A particularly noteworthy feature about the contemporary news accounts of this story is that the initial newspaper stories listed Edward Murphy as one of the arrested extortionists, but afterward his name disappeared from the newspaper coverage. For example, in nine *New York Times* articles on the case published between February 18, 1966, and July 12, 1967, Murphy was never mentioned again after the initial February 18, 1966 story.[7] Yet the initial news story made it clear that Murphy was one of three ringleaders, if not the head of the entire operation. In March of 1968 the *New York Mattachine Newsletter* asked why Murphy had not been sentenced for his role in the blackmail ring. The newsletter stated that not only had Murphy served several prior prison terms, but he also had recently pled guilty under a federal indictment to extortion charges and was under "a number of indictments" at the state level. After pleading guilty to the federal extortion charge, Murphy had merely been put on probation for five years. The newsletter reported that Mattachine–New York "had been informed that Murphy's sentence has been so often postponed because he had made a 'deal' to turn state's evidence, and the delays are to work out another 'deal' to lighten his sentence."

Murphy apparently did give evidence against the two other main figures in the ring: John J. Pyne, a Chicago police officer, and Sherman Chadwick Kaminsky, a Bronx native who also went by the name of Paul Vargo.

However, that Murphy, after having been to prison several times before, could get off with serving only part of a five-year sentence merely for giving evidence against his co-conspirators, despite shaking down approximately one thousand men over almost ten years—including a number of men of very eminent social rank as detailed earlier—is astonishing. Moreover, while several names emerged in the newspaper accounts as key players in the scheme, word on the street said that the gang had one ringleader. The *New York Mattachine Newsletter* of March 1968 named Ed Murphy as that person. The theory of a single person at the head of the enterprise is bolstered by a letter from Richard Inman, a homophile activist battling police extortion of homosexuals in South Florida, written to Mattachine-Washington cofounder Jack Nichols in 1965. In the letter Inman stated that he knew via a friend inside the FBI that there was one "boss man of the syndicate's homo shakedown detail for the whole U.S." That Inman wrote the letter before the police uncovered the national ring adds to its credibility.[8]

The law of averages dictates that the more prominent and wealthy (and therefore correspondingly more vulnerable) the men Murphy targeted, the more likely he was, on average at least, to get the blackmailer's ultimate prize: men who had the most to lose by any publicity while also having the most money to spend on silence. But Murphy did even better in the waters he trawled: he landed the biggest fish of all, one whose value exceeded even that of money, because this one had the ability to keep law enforcement off his back. Murphy's operation landed none other than the nation's top law enforcement officer, J. Edgar Hoover. The same net that hauled in Hoover brought along a bonus prize: J. Edgar Hoover's "longtime companion," Clyde Tolson, who was, moreover, an associate director of the FBI.

Allen Ginsberg, a man who loved both to gather and pass on gossip, had known since the late forties that J. Edgar Hoover was homosexual. A friend of Ginsberg's happened to be in Washington, D.C., when he ran into the FBI chief. Hoover grabbed the man through his pants, inspiring Allen to write about being "groped by the FBI in the halls of Congress."

As he recalled homosexual life in the era before Stonewall, Ginsberg explained, "There was one very tall young guy, rather portly, who later became an insurance executive, who went down to Washington and was wandering through the upper corridors of some very good hotel right near the White House and was accosted, for erotic purposes, by J. Edgar Hoover no less, and told me about that in 1947. So I always had Hoover's number, although it was very difficult to prove. Like Cardinal Spellman, another gent who was supposed to be a closet queen and supposedly had young men accompany him on his trips. That was, of course, never breathed in the newspaper, although both of those guys were fervent anti-Communists and heavy moralists and all in favor of all sorts of censorship. Nonetheless, among the underground or elegant gay world, there were many rumors about them, and even, as I say, one or two encounters, particularly with J. Edgar Hoover."[9]

That Hoover was homosexual and Clyde Tolson his lover is currently generally accepted. The history of *The Homosexual Handbook*, published in 1968, shows, however, that by the late 1960s, not only was Hoover's homosexuality whispered rather widely in the homosexual world but also that Hoover was, understandably, extremely sensitive about any public suggestion of this information. The book's last chapter, titled "Uncle Fudge's List of Practical Homosexuals Past and Present with Very Short Biographical Notes—A Hearsay Reference Work," includes Hoover's name:

> J. Edgar Hoover: *Celibataire,* the director of the Federal Bureau of Intelligence [sic], he has for several decades remained the *eminence froide* of our national great society.

After the book appeared, pressure from the FBI caused it to be withdrawn. The publisher soon reissued the book, but with Uncle Fudge's list one name shorter.[10]

Knowing that J. Edgar Hoover was homosexual, Ginsberg made an intuitive leap to explain Hoover's odd and consistent denial of the existence of organized crime. Why would the head of law enforcement for the entire United States claim to know less than what the average citizen knew from reading the newspaper, that organized crime certainly did exist, and abundantly? In 1987, well before a witness came forward to talk about Hoover appearing at parties dressed as a woman, Ginsberg explained his surmise to Obie Benz: "[Hoover] insisted there was no organized crime. In fact, in those years [the late 1940s] I had the fantasy that the Mafia might have secret movies of J. Edgar Hoover in the basement with some big, hairy Mafia Lothario and were blackmailing him so he'd lay off organized crime, because he insisted there was no organized crime."[11]

From information published in the 1993 book *Official and Confidential: The Secret Life of J. Edgar Hoover,* by Anthony Summers, Ginsberg's intuition has been proved correct. Not only did Summers discover that the Mafia had photographic evidence implicating Hoover in homosexual activity, but it also came to light that Hoover at times dressed in female attire. Research conducted for this book strongly suggests that Ed Murphy had one or more of these photographs, which allowed him to avoid serving time in prison for leading an extensive national blackmail ring.

John Paul Ranieri, a former prostitute interviewed for this history, provided critical testimony for corroborating and better understanding the larger implications of Murphy's criminal enterprises for gay history. Ranieri said that as a youth from Westchester County he had been forced by blackmail and Mafia-supplied drugs into a prostitution ring in which he remained active for three years before he escaped the mob's control. He claimed that a number of youths in the ring had disappeared after they got careless with talk, for while most of the customers were more or less average homosexual men with money, the regular clientele, according to Ranieri, also included famous men such as Malcolm Forbes, Cardinal Spellman, Liberace, U.S. senators, a vice president of the United States, one of the most famous rock musicians, and J. Edgar Hoover. The mob's order, according to Ranieri, was strictly "Keep your zipper open and your mouth shut."

Ranieri said that he met J. Edgar Hoover at private parties at the Plaza Hotel and that Hoover's name was never mentioned. Hoover was always in drag, and Ranieri said he could tell that the FBI director was sure that no one recognized him. Ranieri said that he had ensured his own survival by having in his possession a photograph of himself with Hoover, given to him by the photographer.[12]

How does the preceding information link Ed Murphy with J. Edgar Hoover? The connection is made evident in a news story written shortly after Hoover's homosexuality and transvestism became public. When Summer's book was published, a newspaper story about the 1960s national homosexual blackmail ring suddenly appeared after a quarter of a century of silence on the subject. Without mentioning Murphy's name, it quoted law enforcement sources who had worked on the case as saying that their investigation into the nationwide blackmail ring had turned up a photograph of Hoover "posing amiably" with the racket's ringleader and had uncovered information that Clyde Tolson, Hoover's lover, had himself "fallen victim to the extortion ring." After federal agents joined the investigation, both the photograph of Hoover and the documents about Tolson disappeared.[13]

Information uncovered in researching this history suggests that having the goods on Hoover, Ed Murphy continued to blackmail homosexual men, using the Stonewall Inn as a prime locale for this new extortion operation. There he targeted professional gay men, especially those working on Wall Street.

According to the same 1968 *New York Mattachine Newsletter* that asked why Ed Murphy had not been sentenced for his role in the national blackmail ring, Murphy had an interest in several gay bars in New York, including the Stonewall Inn—the only club identified in the article—and these clubs' membership lists had been used for blackmail:

> MSNY has also been informed that Murphy has an interest in the Stone Wall, a club on Christopher Street, and several other gay clubs in New York. Our source claims that the membership lists of some of these clubs are used to further extortion and shake-down schemes.[14]

Stronger evidence of Murphy using the Stonewall Inn for blackmail comes from a 1969 publication that quoted the Mattachine Society of New York. In the 1960s it was not easy to find gay bars and so, as a service, the

Mattachine Society of New York began compiling lists of these bars. Eventually a local guide was published by a small business venture as the *Gay Scene Guide,* and the publishers, on friendly terms with Mattachine–New York, quoted material from that organization's newsletter. Still, the bar lists remained just that, lists of gay bars, with but one exception: In the 1969 *Gay Scene Guide,* after the entry for the Stonewall Inn, there was a long quote from the *New York Mattachine Newsletter* inserted in the midst of the brief descriptions of gay bars:

The following news item was reported in the March 1968 *Mattachine (N.Y.) Newsletter,* and is presented here in condensed form . . . the Mattachine Society Inc., of New York, was instrumental in aiding D.A. Frank Hogan's office with information that led to the arrests of a number of blackmailers:—"Edward F. P. Murphy, an ex-convict who is alleged to have been the head of the national ring which recently was active in extorting money from homosexuals . . . has served prison terms for larceny and for carrying deadly weapons, and was arrested for impersonating an officer, and for extortion . . . under Federal indictment on extortion charges . . . permitted to plead guilty and received a five-year probation. On a number of indictments in the state courts, Murphy pleaded guilty on May 16, 1966 . . . sentencing has been postponed six times . . . he could get up to 15 years in prison as a second offender, on the robbery charge alone. MSNY has also been informed that Murphy has an interest in the Stone Wall, a club on Christopher Street, and several other gay clubs in New York." We *caution our readers NEVER* to use your real name when cruising, NEVER to give your address to a questionable bar or club, and remember, that trick or hustler you've just picked up may be "working" for the management! We urge you, if you've been intimidated or blackmailed in the past, to report it to the D.A.'s office, or to M.S.N.Y.[15]

That a local guidebook took the unusual step of inserting a warning against giving out information to employees of the Stonewall Inn in the middle of a bar listing is more than suggestive. Indeed, several years later Dick Leitsch was quite forceful about Murphy's role at the Stonewall Inn, writing that he "seemed to be the manager of the place."[16]

The Homosexual Handbook reported that the "burly" at the door of the Stonewall Inn "keeps boxes that hold, or are rumored to hold, thousands of cards upon which are printed the particulars of the many thousands of customers,"[17] which echoes some of the ideas found in the *New York Mattachine Newsletter* article and may explain part of how the blackmail routine operated: did some customers naively believe that they were really being screened for membership in a private club and that this screening would protect them by both excluding police officers and helping to establish the identity of the place they patronized as a legitimate private club?

Beyond Murphy's involvement in the Stonewall Inn and in blackmailing gay men, he was deeply involved in male prostitution. Chuck Shaheen, who had a very high regard for Murphy, told Martin Duberman, "I knew Eddie Murphy for a long time. . . . He was into young boys. Most definitely. And was very, very involved with procurement of young boys."[18] Danny Garvin recalls how he would "always see these hustlers hanging out with [Murphy]. He had connections, and these hustler kids would hang out with him."[19] Tommy explains why the Mafia would operate the Tenth of Always as an ice-cream parlor in terms of Murphy's predilections: "The Tenth of Always had a kind of particular feeling, that you knew you were there because Murphy liked chicken. In there I felt like I was in some surreal Catholic Youth Organization dance, because everybody was like my age or younger, and the drag queens just looked like regular high-school girls, and the hustlers looked like regular high-school boys. And then it really looked crazy because everyone was sitting, sipping these sodas, and it was like—there's no word to describe—it wasn't a brothel, a bawdyhouse, or whatever. It was like the pickings of johns: that's what it was set up for."[20] Bob Kohler, who hated Murphy passionately, cited as evidence of Murphy's loathsomeness that he paid the youths he pimped with counterfeit money.[21]

Research on this book uncovered a couple of elusive references to a prostitution ring that was run on the second floor above the Stonewall Inn.[22] When one looks at all the available evidence today, there is little doubt that such a ring operated out of the floor above the Stonewall Inn, although few knew it existed. But by Murphy's own account, "upstairs the Mafia retained a room."[23]

Craig Rodwell's *Hymnal* provides rare contemporary evidence that the Mafia recruited youths specifically at the Stonewall Inn for their criminal activities. Continuing its campaign to warn gay men against Mafia exploitation, the *Hymnal* reported that "some of the 'queenie-boppers' on Greenwich Ave. and at the Stone Wall have been approached to be [heroin] delivery boys."[24]

One day, as John Paul Ranieri strolled around the Village during an interview for this history, he pointed out various places that he remembered from his life there in the late 1960s.[25] As we wandered the area around Christopher Street, walking east on West 10th Street, we passed a parking garage on the northern side of the block where the Stonewall Inn used to be. Ranieri then pointed to a door in the reddish-brown wall a few steps above the sidewalk and said that door was the one he always passed through, entering via West 10th Street, to go to the second floor above and to the rear of the Stonewall Inn to pick up his orders. The office above the Stonewall Inn was, he said, one of two locations to which he reported for instructions on his assignations.[26]

According to several articles written by the gay bartender Tree, who worked as a page boy on the floor of the New York Stock Exchange in the early sixties, it was "the world's biggest closet." "Between the dirty ol' men brokers, married and single, and the employees of the NEW YORK STOCK EXCHANGE there were more gay men than in any gay bar at a single time." And if the stock exchange itself was the world's biggest closet, it also boasted, according to Tree, in the men's room on its third floor, "one of the best T-ROOMS [public rest rooms used for sex] around . . . spoken about with affection all over the world." As if in evidence of the T-room's international pull, two 1990s articles that Tree wrote specifically about homosexuality in the Wall Street area in the 1960s include photographs of Konrad, a beautiful blond youth. The articles explain that Konrad had come on vacation from Durban, South Africa, when Tree met him in the crowded T-room. "We fooled around a little but the traffic in the men's room was too much." Apparently the stock exchange T-room was so popular that it could become practically impossible even to get into at times. As Tree explained, "Word passes on from one to another."[27]

Barry Perrin, a Stonewall Inn habitué, remembered the warning he had been given about blackmail after he came out: "Of course, there was a lot of blackmail. You heard about that sort of thing going on if somebody found out you were gay. I didn't know it then [in the late 1960s]. I found out since [in the early 1970s] that even the bartenders at Stonewall did that. That I didn't know, but they didn't bother with me, I suppose, because I was nineteen and they didn't expect me to have much of a career at that point, or money to give them.

"The Stonewall staff apparently—and this is not from my memory but from what I've heard since—used to talk to guys that probably looked like they were a little more successful, probably a little bit older. If they found out that you worked for a law firm or a stock brokerage firm or anything like that, you were blackmailed . . . especially in the stock market areas—it's not that large—you could be blackballed from a whole industry, and that was absolutely so.

"The good-looking bartenders in Stonewall, who were probably connected to the Mafia—they themselves were probably not actually Mafia, but those were their bosses and they were told to do this, and they did it— the good-looking waiters would get friendly with guys and then find out where they were. It's really so insidious, when you're talking to somebody that you find nice—he's being nice, pleasant finally. Eventually you tell him where you work, and then all of a sudden this happens. It's just so awful."[28]

According to Perrin, blackmail at the Stonewall worked in a manner parallel to the national ring: those who later became blackmail victims were initially victims of a robbery that included taking documents. The ring then researched which men might be wealthy enough to be vulnerable to extortion. At the Stonewall the waiters did the research.[29]

But beyond the Stonewall being linked to blackmailing Wall Street employees and blackmailer Ed Murphy being connected to the Stonewall Inn, is there any piece of evidence that directly connects Murphy himself to blackmailing men on Wall Street? There is: In the late 1970s, a friend of Murphy's told Morty Manford that Ed Murphy said that he had been informing on the mob to the FBI. Murphy's friend went on to explain that because the mob had discovered that The Skull was an informer, Murphy had decided to come out, stop working with the mob, and quit informing because he "wants to become a good guy." Manford reacted skeptically to Murphy's claim of being an FBI informer by saying, "I've heard . . . that he was involved . . . in a ring that was blackmailing homosexual men down at Wall Street."[30]

Deputy Inspector Seymour Pine had not been moved to Manhattan's First Division of the Public Morals police for long before being summoned to a meeting with his commanding officer. Detective Charles Smythe, who shared joint responsibility for Morals First Division, accompanied him. Pine was glad to have Smythe as his partner, as they knew each other quite well, having fought side by side in World War II. The men enjoyed the comfortable trust old army buddies who have been through combat together naturally feel toward each other.[31]

The war had considerably disrupted Pine's life, but being Jewish, he had not minded: he was eager to make his contribution to the fight against Hitler. In fact, it was Pine's religion that had determined his career as a police officer, for while he had wanted to join the FBI, his father had discouraged him, knowing that it was difficult for Jews to become FBI agents. Encouraged by his father to become a police officer instead, Pine had taken courses in government and public administration at Brooklyn College before graduating from there in 1941. He entered the police department right away and also enrolled in St. John's Law School but was drafted before finishing his probationary period in the police department.

The young draftee proved to be quite a catch for the army. Pine had been captain of his college's wrestling team, played football, been president of the school's athletic association, and studied judo in the police department. With such a diverse athletic background and his training in fighting, it is understandable that during his basic training at Fort McClellan in Alabama he readily spotted deficiencies in the army's hand-to-hand fighting techniques. After he convinced his superiors that there were better ways to train soldiers in hand-to-hand fighting, he was sent as an instructor to infantry school. There he wrote a manual on hand-to-hand combat for the infantry soldier that became the army's official manual on the subject. Pine's accomplishment in writing this manual was considered proof at the time that someone who had not gone to West Point could make important contributions to the military.

From infantry school Pine was sent to officer candidate school, graduating from the Provost Marshal General School as a second lieutenant and then being immediately assigned to teach hand-to-hand combat there. But Pine longed to be in Europe fighting, and so when he was ordered overseas he turned down an offer by the school to remain there as an instructor. Shipped to Europe at the end of June 1943, Pine was assigned to the Allied Military Government of Occupied Territories (AMGOT) both because he had been a police officer and because he had a knowledge of Italian. He served in AMGOT for a year in Sicily and Italy before being reassigned to the American School Center in England, where he instructed servicemen who were going to be running a military government in the event of victory. He was next transferred to General Patton's staff in military government but requested service in an infantry unit. His request was granted, and he was assigned to a Massachusetts outfit, the 26th Infantry Unit.

Serving in AMGOT, he had seen his share of hard combat. "We would try to capture records so that we could preserve the towns. We would have to be up near the fighting when they were ready to go in, and if the shelling would start very often we would get into a foxhole with somebody else, and they were very happy that we would get in with them, when the ground was shaking and the shells were dropping—you felt as if you were going to explode. You would feel the walls of the foxhole actually shake against you, reverberate, 'cause these shells were falling all around you." Pine was tough enough that not only could he keep his cool under such intense fire, but he also was able to calm other soldiers down. "In between [the shelling] you'd go around and talk to your guys and break that tension, this tremendous fright, where everybody is crapping in his pants."

In Europe, working as a liaison with the underground forces, he was injured in a mine explosion, after which he was hospitalized for approximately thirteen months. Released from the hospital, he retired from the army as a captain and resumed his civilian job as a police officer on limited duty, as he needed hospital treatment three times a week for the following two years.

As his years in the police force passed, Pine rose through the ranks, eventually attaining the rank of deputy inspector. Before Pine's last promotion he was a captain in Brooklyn's Tenth Division. He impressed Chief Inspector Sanford Garelick by how he handled himself in a tricky situation in a Coney Island race riot. Garelick offered Pine a promotion, but Pine refused it, explaining to Garelick that he had organized a program in which he and all his officers volunteered to work with brain-injured children in patterning: manipulating the arms and legs of the children in an attempt to help them learn how to crawl. As the program was strictly voluntary and Pine had organized it, he felt that if he left the area the program would come to an end. In 1967 Garelick promoted Pine against his wishes but kept him in Brooklyn's Tenth Division. This meant moving him into Public Morals, the only opening to which Garelick could promote Pine and keep him in the Tenth Division.

Pine had great success in fighting the mob in Brooklyn and was known not to tolerate any corruption by his officers, and so in the spring of 1969 Garelick transferred him to a troubled unit, Manhattan's First Division Morals.[32] The First Division included all of Manhattan from 35th Street down to Battery Park at the island's southern tip.[33] The types of crime he had to deal with in Manhattan were generally similar to those he had investigated in Brooklyn, except that now he became involved in cases of pornography, censorship, and gay bars. He was also told that it was his responsibility to meet with representatives of the Mattachine Society, which he did from time to time.

At this particular meeting with their First Division commanding officer, Pine and Smythe learned that financial irregularities discovered in Europe reached back to the deputy inspector's bailiwick. Interpol had noticed that an unusual number of negotiable bonds were surfacing in foreign countries and had requested that the New York Police Department look into the matter: were these legal or counterfeit? The NYPD investigation had found evidence of a collusion between the Mafia and the employees of depositories to steal large numbers of bonds. Moreover, it appeared the Mafia was able to put the squeeze on certain people with access to the bonds because the Mafia had learned that some of them were homosexual. From studying the police reports on various gay clubs the commanding officer had concluded that the center of this activity lay in the general area of the city in which the Stonewall Inn was located. The commanding officer singled out the Stonewall for particular attention: police reports stated that a lot of big cars stopped in front of the club to drop off wealthy straight people who went into the Stonewall. A source of outside money?

The commanding officer made his wishes clear: He wanted those clubs put out of business. Particularly the Stonewall Inn.

6

Dawn Is Just Breaking

As Craig Rodwell sat down to write an article for the *Hymnal*'s fourth issue, due out in May of 1968, he felt the homophile movement was stalled locally. It was natural then that he turned to events on the West Coast, which he found inspiring. As he warmed up to what he felt could be accomplished in New York, he extolled the accomplishments of the Society for Individual Rights (SIR) in San Francisco: "In three years, it has opened a community center with varied social activities, a theater, a storefront, and has become a force to be reckoned with in San Francisco. Candidates for public office seek their support." After mentioning that SIR had 3,500 active members—Mattachine–New York then had about 550—Rodwell wrote: "The same thing can and must be done in New York City."[1]

By the mid-1960s San Francisco already had a rich history of homosexual activism. In 1961, in response to San Francisco gay bars being shaken down by the police and alcohol authorities, an openly gay drag queen, José Sarria, ran for the position of city supervisor by circulating a petition among the city's gay population, helping to set off "developments that fed a steadily growing stream of gay political activity in San Francisco," as historian John D'Emilio has written. One of the new endeavors sparked by Sarria's campaign was the formation of a group known as the League for Civil Education (LCE), which began printing the *LCE News*, "the first sustained attempt to bring the movement into the world of the gay bar . . . its circulation in San Francisco alone [after one year] exceeding nationwide figures of *One, The Ladder*, and the *Mattachine Review*." In spite of the *LCE News*'s militant tone, by 1963 three mayoral candidates had purchased ads in it.[2]

In 1962 bar owners and employees had formed the Tavern Guild, which retained a lawyer and bail bondsman for anyone arrested in or near a gay bar and coordinated the fight against California's Alcohol and Beverage Control Department (ABC). Soon SIR formed with a more open and democratic approach than that used by the LCE and California's Mattachine organization "to create a community feeling that will bring a 'Homophile Movement' into being." Recognizing the social needs of gay men, SIR held not only dances and parties but also meditation groups and art classes. It ran a major education campaign on venereal disease with the support of the city's public health department and held voter registration drives. The Guild also published an attractive magazine, *Vector,* which was sold on newsstands throughout the city. In 1965 the Guild began holding candidates nights each fall where political office seekers faced a gay audience that endorsed pro-gay candidates, including those who have since become leading figures in San Francisco and California politics: Willie Brown, John Burton, and Dianne Feinstein. So successful was SIR that in 1966 it opened the country's first gay community center. By 1967 it was the country's largest homophile organization.

Critical to the success of organizations such as the LCE, SIR, and the Tavern Guild, however, was the Council on Religion and the Homosexual, or CRH, a coalition of homophile leaders and clergy, which, through providing the "cloak of the cloth," as San Francisco historian Paul Gabriel has phrased it, lent an aura of credibility to these organizations.

CRH had incorporated in 1964 and is especially known for the events that unfolded at one of its first undertakings, a New Year's Eve ball at California Hall to raise money for the homosexual community. When the ball was held, the San Francisco Police Department showed up in force and staked out California Hall with paddy wagons, huge klieg lights, movie cameras, and photographers. As guests entered the dance, the police filmed and photographed every one of the hundreds of attendees. Finally, the police, who had promised the clergy not to interfere, found a pretext to shut the dance down and arrested several persons who had helped organize the event. This only galvanized the ministers who had put on the affair, having learned firsthand that what they had been told about homosexuals being harassed and oppressed was not an exaggeration.

While the story of California Hall is sometimes celebrated as "San Francisco's Stonewall," the story of Vanguard and Compton's Cafeteria is a similarly compelling one and also has its roots in both CRH and the Glide Memorial Foundation. The Foundation had been started by the wealthy Lizzie Glide to fund a church in the Tenderloin, her vision being of a church that would serve sailors and itinerant workmen.

By the 1960s, San Francisco's Tenderloin had turned into a district very much on the down-and-out. Its cheap hotels and restaurants made it the section of town where runaway youths gravitated. There homeless gay youths sold themselves, as did transvestites and female prostitutes. Drugs were widely available, and it was a center for police corruption, as its very name suggested: The term *tenderloin* was imported from New York, where it denoted a district so rich in graft that a police officer who worked there could afford to buy his family a choice cut of meat. As more and more families left the area around Glide for the suburbs, Glide Memorial Church, with its very large endowment, was left with a small and aging congregation. In the 1960s young people were attending church less often, and so churches began to reexamine what forms their ministries should take. In this progressive era, many churches responded to the drop in attendance by emphasizing social services. A number of denominations started inner city ministries to reach out to youths, helping poor youths deal with such problems as drugs, job training, and housing, almost always among black populations. Many of the ministers who did such work became interested in rethinking theology and in getting involved in protest movements.

Louis Durham was sent from Nashville, the national education and training headquarters for the Methodist Church, to lead the effort to revive the dying Glide Memorial Church. After performing an evaluation, he hired three young ministers, the first being Ted McIlvenna, considered a rising star. He had had a personal vision, giving him the belief that in the twentieth century, and especially since the Second World War, a huge biblical revelation, like that found in the Old Testament books of prophets was happening. The vision that had been revealed to McElvena was of a coming into consciousness of the divinity of human sexuality. Ted saw his life's work as opening the world to this revelation. Constantly on the go, he met with everyone on the forefront of sexuality issues, from Kinsey to the leaders of the Mattachine Society.

In 1963, Ted began to work with young homosexuals in the Tenderloin, where he met a youth who had been castrated by an adult. McIlvenna was appalled, but seeing the disfigured adolescent made his commitment to gay youth total. As McIlvenna began to investigate the youths' situation, he realized that there were no services available for them: no overnight shelters or counseling or vocational services.

Ted McIlvenna then brought ministers Don Kuhn and Cecil Williams, the latter a black minister fresh from battling segregation in Kansas, to Glide in 1964. The work these men were doing in the Tenderloin was soon supplemented each year by a church intern who also did youth outreach work. Especially key was Ed Hanson, the youth intern from 1965 to 1966.

After years of work, the Glide Foundation ministers were able to bring together members of the homophile movement and Tenderloin neighborhood activists to form the Central City Citizens Council (CCCC). The CCCC published the *Tenderloin Report*, which documented the lack of education among those living in the Tenderloin, as well as the high poverty and the lack of social services and housing. The CCCC also fought for and won a portion of federal poverty program funds that had been designated for San Francisco.

The funds were used to create the Central City Poverty Program. And so the interns and the minister set about helping the street youth, the runaways, and the hustlers to organize themselves. Although the ministers hired by Glide had worked primarily with black and other ethnic minority populations, they believed that the approach used in those communities should work with a population of inner city youths who were mainly homosexual. The ministers had found that it was much more effective to hire someone from a disadvantaged group to organize that community to help itself rather than bringing in an outsider to do the same work.

Neil Secor, the first intern to work with the Tenderloin youths, began by inviting them to meet weekly in his living room. The first sessions were almost like consciousness-raising sessions, meetings that served for heterosexuals and homosexuals to get to know, trust, and understand each other. Once they were able to work together, Secor got the youths to organize, and then they began to use Glide's offices. When Secor left and Hanson arrived, the youths were ready to formalize their organization as Vanguard.

The group of mostly gay youths chose the name of Vanguard by July of 1966 and elected one of their own, Jean-Paul Marat (a pseudonym), as Vanguard's president.[3] An issue of *The Berkeley Barb*, an underground newspaper, gives a thumbnail portrait of Marat as thin and pale, with wavy black hair, reddish cheeks, and thick, babyish lips.[4] Vanguard soon started a magazine, called *V*, which, like many underground newspapers of the time, featured original and compelling artwork, all done by Marat. The only requirement for membership in the group was that a person be "a kid off the street." Vanguard embraced the belief of self-empowerment advocated by the Glide Foundation's young, idealistic ministers. The first known news article about the group quotes a member as saying, "We believe we can take care of a large portion of our problems without the interference of the federal government, head shrinkers or older people, most of whom do not at all understand the problems of the kids."

A flyer put out by the group describes their understanding of the problems facing them and how to solve them: "We protest police harassment of youth in the area when the big time speculators seem to work openly and receive *no attention*. . . . We protest being called 'queer,' 'pillhead,' and being placed in the position of being outlaws and parasites when we are offered no alternatives to this existence. . . . We demand justice and immediate corrections of the fact that most of the money made in the area is made by the exploitation of youth by so-called normal adults who make a fast buck off situations everyone calls degenerate, perverted and sick."[5]

It is remarkable that Vanguard had from its inception the militantly unapologetic tone that would characterize the gay liberation movement, which would not be born for another three years. *V* is also remarkable for its common use of the more affirming *gay* as opposed to *homosexual* or *homophile*. Similar to the later Gay Liberation Front's (GLF's) emphasis on self-criticism, the youths showed a willingness to address not only society's shortcomings but their own as well.

An editorial on prejudice by Marat talked about the gay youths' difficulties in accepting one another: "Day after day I hear complaints about the prejudice that the straight society has against the gay society. Let's look at our own prejudices. We ostracize people because they do this or that or the other in bed. We make snide comments about the drag queen who isn't quite convincing enough. The 'leather boys' are the butt of many jokes and much ridicule. . . . If we want society to accept us as we are, we are going to have to start accepting ourselves and others like us."[6]

Besides self-help articles, listings of organizations to go to for assistance, and articles on politics, *V* also featured many articles written by the youths about their own experiences. One of the most poignant pieces is a poem titled "The Hustler" that was sent in anonymously and published under a photograph of an attractive young man with a resigned and sad expression:

I sell my love for dollars,
If you can spare the time,
A hug is but a nickel,
A kiss is but a dime.

I'll go to bed for twenty,
All night for just ten more.
Now don't get the idea
That I am just a whore.

For if I didn't sell my love,
Where else would it go?
I have no one to give it to;
No one who'd care to know.

So open up your wallet
And show me what you've got.

> *And whether I should love you*
> *A little or a lot.*

One of the few hangouts available to the street youths in the Tenderloin was a branch of a local chain restaurant called Compton's, especially popular with gay youths, hustlers, and transvestites. According to Tamara Ching, "It was just a place that we would come and hang out. If you didn't manage up a trick that night, it's where you would hang out with your friends. We'd stay there and then eat breakfast and go home and sleep until it was time to get up and go out on the prowl again." Crema Ritz even compared Compton's to "a community center."[7]

Historian Susan Stryker has found that the gay youth were tolerated at Compton's for years because the evening manager was an older effeminate homosexual. When he died suddenly in the spring of 1966 and new management came in, a decision was made to discourage the patronage of these poor customers who sat for long periods of time and ordered little food. The diner hired Pinkerton security guards to harass them, and invited the police inside for the same reason. The security guards insulted the gay and transvestite customers and manhandled those who did not drink their coffee fast enough. On July 18, the newly formed Vanguard organized a picket line at Compton's to protest the harassment and discrimination. Around twenty-five persons picketed in the evening, from ten o'clock until midnight.

On a hot night the following month, when a policeman grabbed the arm of a transvestite, she threw a cup of coffee in his face. As if on signal, other gay customers began throwing cups, saucers, and trays at the police and security guards. Compton's immediately closed, "and with that, the gays began breaking out every window in the place." As other gay men ran outside to escape the breaking glass, the police tried to catch them and put them in patrol wagons, according to the only known written account of the disturbance. Those leaving Compton's fought hard, with gay men hitting the police in their groins and "drag-queens smashing them in the face with their extremely heavy purses." One police car had all of its windows broken and a newspaper stand close to the restaurant was burned down as "general havoc [was] raised that night in the Tenderloin." The following night, when the restaurant turned away transvestites, another picket line of "drag-queens, hair fairies [West Coast equivalent of 'scare drag'], conservative Gays, and hustlers" picketed the cafeteria. The conflict ended when the restaurant's newly installed windows were smashed a second time. [8]

Given that the riot at Compton's occurred when the gay street youth of the Tenderloin were receiving significant support from Glide Memorial Church ministers, it is reasonable to conclude that the support these youths, who were regularly abused, received from Glide emboldened them to resist oppression by the police and security guards. No record exists of any resistance by gay or transgendered men on a similar scale prior to the event at Compton's. Susan Stryker, who has studied the history of services available to transgendered persons in San Francisco, offers an additional reason for the Compton's incident. Shortly before the disturbance, a doctor in the area became the first in the U.S. to offer sex-change reassignment surgery. Since his office was only five blocks from Compton's and since transgendered persons took a leading role in the disturbance, Stryker concludes that this new service may have played a role in triggering the riots: transgendered men, a highly despised minority within a minority, were being given hope for the first time ever and thus felt assertive enough to resist oppression.*

Craig Rodwell circled around in the 100-degree heat for at least the twentieth time. There was nothing he could do about it being summer or the lack of shade. He had, after all, chosen this time and this place to protest. Having come all the way to Philadelphia for the Annual Reminder, he wasn't going to miss picketing. He wished, though, that he didn't have to wear a coat and tie. But Craig lost this argument every year. He and some others thought that the idea of a strict dress code for a picket demonstration was absurd. Still, others, particularly Frank Kameny, argued that since they were picketing to establish their right to employment, they must look employable. Maybe next year Rodwell could persuade his colleagues to loosen the rules controlling every aspect of their behavior as they picketed. Meanwhile, he just kept circling.

When Arthur Evans had moved to Greenwich Village he began to read a lot of poetry, which changed his understanding of life: "William Blake had a big impact on me, and I got very excited about Blake. His vision of the recovery of sex is related to the struggle against imperialism and industrialism and the machine: the reaching for the organic, getting down to sinewy nerves and muscles that go way back into history before the mind. And they're more than a machine. . . . It's the living pulse of the planet coming out."

Walt Whitman inspired Evans with his celebration of the body electric and his vision of democracy: "Whitman speaks of democracy as spiritual practice, something that you have to live and practice the way you would prac-

*This account of the history of Vanguard, the Council on Religion and the Homosexual, and the Compton's revolt is based upon unpublished research by Paul Gabriel and Susan Stryker.

tice a musical instrument, with the same degree of passion and commitment. That sensibility, I think, is in Walt Whitman and it involves sex as well."

When Evans chanced upon Allen Ginsberg's work, he recognized a kindred spirit to his beloved Whitman: "Ginsberg has influenced my basic perceptions of things more so than any other living thinker, but it's hard to put it into conceptual words because it's more than that. It affects feelings as well. I was electrified by his poetry. First of all because I thought it was very powerful poetry, and secondly because I thought he was drawing on things that were very important to me. The Vietnam War was not just a conflict. It was saying something significant about American history and it was saying something important about human spirituality. Where did the Vietnam War come from? It came from America's spiritual history and from its sexual history. These things—sex, politics, history, personal life— all these things are interconnected, and Allen Ginsberg, as I saw it, was articulating this vision, expressing these connections between things."

For Evans, as for so many others of his generation, the national conflict over the Vietnam War did much to define him. In 1967 he had enrolled in Columbia University's doctoral program in philosophy. Evans loved philosophy and no doubt in quieter times would have completed his Ph.D. in several years, but Columbia University was, like many others, roiled by the decade's political upheavals. Columbia had claimed it was not supporting the war in Vietnam, but the Students for a Democratic Society (SDS) did research that proved that Columbia was lying, which was one of the reasons for the uprisings there.

During the student occupation of the campus in May of 1968, Grayson Kirk, the university's president, chose the middle of the night to call in the police, who beat hundreds of students and faculty members. Although Evans did not happen to be present when the police violence occurred, the next day he saw lots of professors and students going around campus with bandages on their heads, a sight that changed Evans: "That was a radicalizing experience. At that point I realized the administration of this university is the enemy. They're part of the military-industrial complex. These people are not supporters of learning. They are not my friends."

In August Arthur went to Chicago to protest the war in Vietnam at the Democratic Convention. Many thousands of protesters were heading to the Windy City, for it seemed certain that Lyndon Johnson's vice president, Hubert Humphrey, would get the Democratic Party's nomination to be president although antiwar candidate Senator Eugene McCarthy had won more votes in the primaries than Humphrey had. Mayor Richard Daley, the quintessential machine party politician, was determined to prevent the protesters from demonstrating.

In the weeks before the convention Allen Ginsberg had had an increasingly bad feeling about how things would turn out in Chicago. He had been one of those who had suggested holding the Festival of Life in Chicago as a counterexample to Democratic Party machine politics, and still felt that he should attend in hopes of minimizing the violence that seemed likely. He and longtime colleague Ed Sanders held exercises in Chicago to train protesters in breathing and chanting techniques that if—and only if, Ginsberg well knew—practiced by a large portion of a crowd could help maintain calm when violence and confusion threatened to erupt. Ginsberg also paid attention to more mundane matters, such as meeting with city officials to try to get a permit for a sound system so that those trying to maintain calm could communicate with those protesting.

As Evans took part in a protest in one of Chicago's parks and was attacked by the police, he noted the event's surreal quality. Simultaneous with the ground attack, he saw tear gas canisters flying through the air with gas beginning to emerge from them even as he heard Ginsberg chanting the Hindu mantra "Om."

Evans found that Ginsberg's chanting "gave it a sense of significance, that this wasn't just a bunch of people running around. Very important values were at stake here, about meaning and life and our proper role in history and how to deal with violence. All these issues were hanging in the air, and he sort of put that into context by that very simple gesture. These demonstrations were a meditative act, and we were crossing the boundary between politics and spirituality."[9]

In 1968 at the Stonewall Inn one night, Danny Garvin met a man named Craig who invited him to visit him in the gay commune where he lived at the corner of Bleecker Street and Sixth Avenue. This commune, having no grand overarching vision or structure, was rather nonchalant, mainly a place where young gay men and their friends lived and hung out while enjoying hippie culture.

Yet the commune was not simply a gay male crash pad. Its members discussed and debated the great issues of the day such as the war in Vietnam, women's rights, consciousness-raising, and the legalization of marijuana. Their standard reading material was the local alternative publications, *The Village Voice* and the *East Village Other*. Members and their friends listened to albums by the favorite musicians of the day, such as the Beatles, Buffy Sainte-Marie, and the Jefferson Airplane. At other times, a friend might drop by with a guitar and everyone would sit around singing popular songs as they shared bottles of wine.

Danny remembers the end of the sixties as a time of rapid changes: "All of a sudden men were growing longer sideburns. It was happening throughout society, but it was happening in the gay community a little bit quicker. Gay men all of a sudden would wear bell-bottoms. Clothes became unisex. Men wore hip-huggers. Jewelry became somewhat unisexual, too, because you had men and women wearing love beads and chains and bells." When Danny went wearing a bell to meet Frank, the man he had first danced with, Frank began to lose interest. "You're not becoming one of those, are you?" he asked.

Remarkably, although the members of the commune had debated the war in Vietnam and the oppression of women they had never discussed the meaning of being gay, even though they lived in a gay commune. Danny recalls that even at that time he figured that he would eventually "settle down with a woman." Garvin attributes the lack of such political awareness among his gay hippie friends to just how oppressive the situation was for homosexuals. Garvin recalls a practice, common at the time, called dropping dimes, in which one gay man betrays another by calling his parents and telling them that their son is gay. "I knew gay men, usually in their later twenties or early thirties, who eventually got married and would just all of a sudden step out of gay life." The generation gap also affected gay men: the older gay men in suits and ties presented an image rejected by young gay hippies in the Village.

Gay men suffered from self-hatred as well. While pop and rock music celebrated (hetero)sexuality with joy and abandon, gay men still gathered in bars to listen to "The Ballad of the Sad Young Men," a song that portrayed gay life as morbidly as its title suggests. They also threw acidic lines from Edward Albee's *Who's Afraid of Virginia Woolf?* at one another and often quoted the depressing line "Show me a happy homosexual and I'll show you a gay corpse" from an Off Broadway play of the period, *The Boys in the Band.* Danny recalls that "gay life didn't seem a very positive thing to grow old into."[10]

The Stonewall Inn had modified its decor in response to the changing times, though only in the front room. Black lights were added to the dance floor in the first room and a light show was installed behind the bar: lights underneath lit up dark and light squares in a checkerboard pattern. But the main innovation was go-go boys who danced on weekends in gilded cages at each end of the bar. As they danced in paisley or silver or gold lamé swimsuits or bikini underwear, light projections swam over their nude bodies. Their cages were perched on top of rickety platforms behind the bar where customers could see but not reach them.[11]

According to a number of witnesses, though not all, the clientele at the Stonewall Inn had changed with the passage of time as well. Edmund

White felt that the patrons included more blacks and Latinos and that drugs had become much more popular at the club. Two persons interviewed by Tina Crosby in the early seventies told her that "by 1969 it was getting a 'burnt-out feeling' and was past the height of its popularity." However, most persons from the era recall few, if any, changes in clientele over the years. The *1969 New York City Gay Scene Guide,* published by the Mattachine Society, wrote: "It continues operating amid persistent rumors of closing. Observers note that 'go-go boys' . . . have failed to attract the dwindling crowds." But maybe this was wishful thinking on the Mattachine's part. After all, Rodwell had written practically the same thing a year before in the June–July 1968 issue of the *Hymnal:* "The Stone Wall . . . is still in operation, unfortunately. Hoping to save their declining business, the Mafia management instituted 'go-go boys' on platforms."[12]

As the decade approached its end—and especially in 1969—the subject of homosexuality was more and more in the air, whether in the context of the arts or political events or merely as a topic of conversation. To give but several examples, in mid-July of 1968 *The Wall Street Journal* published a lead front-page article that noted the growing militancy among homosexuals who were fighting for "a piece of the action" in America. The response to the article was so strong that a later issue devoted an entire "Letters to the Editor" column to correspondence about the article.[13] Craig Rodwell highlighted the article in the *Hymnal,* noting: "It is said that *The Wall Street Journal* is six months ahead of society in indicating trends." In mid-1968, Criswell, the television psychic, appearing as a guest on the *Tonight* show, predicted that within several years exclusively homosexual communities would spring up throughout the country. Whereas in 1962 Randy Wicker had made a splash in the media by going on the radio as an openly gay man, before 1968 ended, a group of gay men in New York City that included Bill Weaver and Charles Pitts began broadcasting on WBAI a weekly program on homosexuality called *The New Symposium,* "with the aim of inspiring a sense of social identification within our subculture." Every member of the program staff appeared under his own name.[14]

In January 1969, *Time* magazine published the first cover story by a national magazine on homosexuality, and *Hair,* whose lyrics contained several positive homosexual references, became the bestselling record album of the year.

Gay folk even took the number of the year as a hopeful symbol, sixtynine long having been a code word for homosexuality, based on reading the numbers as a depiction of a gay couple engaging in mutual oral sex.

Even *Hair's* most popular song, which proclaimed "the dawning of the age of Aquarius" as an age of "harmony and understanding," has as its source, no matter how few were aware of it, a myth that celebrated homosexual love. The age of Aquarius is named for the Greek server at the banquet of the gods who bears liquid refreshment to the deities, whence his popular astrological designation as the Water Bearer. But the story of Aquarius is that of Ganymede, who, in Greek mythology, was the most beautiful youth on earth. His beauty was so enchanting that even Zeus himself could not resist his charms, and the supreme god of the Greeks, taking the form of an eagle, flew down to earth, seized him, and transported him back to Olympus. After this "rape," Ganymede served the Greek deities when they dined, while Hera, Zeus's consort, grew jealous as Zeus paid more attention to the beautiful youth than to her. But being a mortal, Ganymede did eventually die. Zeus's love for the youth was so great, however, that rather than let him go the way of all flesh, he bestowed immortality upon Ganymede by transforming him into the constellation known as Aquarius.

Earl Galvin recalled how when the calendar turned to 1969, gay men began to say to one another, "Maybe this will be our year." The *New York Mattachine Newletter*'s gossip columnist, D.D., noted that according to Chinese astrology, in which each year is associated with an animal, 1969 was the year of the rooster, which pleased D.D., who saltily commented that a "year of the cock" sounded appealing. If the world was on the threshold of entering an age named to celebrate same-sex love, the coinciding of a rooster year could be portentous, for according to the Chinese astrological system, a rooster year is one in which "politically and domestically, the downtrodden make their voices heard, the aggrieved or tyrannized will stand up for themselves, and bullies will now get their due comeuppance."[15]

In New York City, apart from steady progress on court rulings that continually ate away at the SLA's ability to revoke or withhold liquor licenses from gay bars, there were few indications of progress. For example, although the New York Police Department had ceased entrapping homosexual men, the Transit Police, who were not controlled by the mayor's office, continued the practice. Then an off-duty Transit cop, Colin Kelly, killed a gay man, John Allison, and another gay man who was with him at the trucks near the waterfront. The circumstances of the killings and subsequent police conduct caused the Mattachine Society to suspect that the men had been murdered. The February *New York Mattachine Newsletter* reported that two Transit cops, after having arrested three men in a washroom, emptied out their wallets. When one of the men protested, the cop asked him how he would like to be carried out of the washroom with a "shiv" in his body. (A shiv is the crude but deadly handmade knife prisoners fashion.) The same newsletter recounted how another Mattachine member had stopped at 1:15 in the morning to talk with some friends near the Stonewall Inn. When two police officers came along and told everyone to leave, he refused to comply, pointing out that the group was neither loud nor obstructing traffic, whereupon he was handcuffed and taken to jail.[16]

Just as the Transit cop who had shot and killed two gay men at the trucks seemed about to go free, there was violence and extortion at the waterfront. Trucking firms and pier owners had hired private policemen to protect their property and vehicles from being damaged by the gay men who used them for sex, but some of the private detectives shook down the gay men. Mattachine–New York tried to alert others to the dangers of pickpockets, muggers, and blackmailers: "The area has become a mecca for uptight hoodlums looking for a 'queer' to beat up. One of their favorite games is to shove a homosexual into the cesspool known as the Hudson River. [. . .] At least four people have drowned in the filth after hitting their heads on pier footings." Another man who had performed sex on "an evidently willing partner" was beaten so badly afterward that he lost an eye. Urging gay men to stay away from the trucks to avoid physical danger as well as the chance of arrest, the Mattachine Society suggested the baths as an alternative for those compelled to seek out anonymous sex.[17]

Ironically, after Mattachine–New York had urged gay men who felt a need for anonymity to seek it in the baths rather than on the waterfront, the next issue of the organization's newsletter carried the lead headline "Bathhouse Raided." The Continental Baths, where Bette Midler would be discovered a few years later, was already becoming a fixture of New York City's gay scene. On February 20 it was raided by the police and twenty-two men were arrested. Before the police left, they wrecked the bathhouse. The bathhouse owners said that the raid had happened because they had refused to pay off the police. The newsletter also reported that Colin Kelly had been absolved of any guilt in the killing of the gay men on the waterfront.[18]

On the West Coast, militancy was increasing far beyond that displayed in previous years by SIR and the Tavern Guild. Leo Laurence, a thirty-six-year-old reporter for San Francisco's KGO radio, had covered the protests at the 1968 Democratic convention. Witnessing young antiwar protesters putting their bodies on the line had made him a radical. Laurence began writing for both *The Berkeley Barb,* an underground newspaper, and SIR's *Vector.* Early in 1969 Laurence was elected by SIR's membership to edit *Vector,* and he wrote at the time that "this is the beginning of a new revolution in San Francisco, the Homosexual Revolution of 1969. When the black man became proud, he became more militant. That same power is starting to hit the homosexual movement in the Bay Area." Laurence called for gay people to form coalitions with other militant and radical groups such as the Black Panthers and the antiwar movement.

Because Laurence believed it was important to be honest about one's sexuality, he had a picture of himself and his lover, Gale Whittington, with the latter shirtless and Laurence embracing him, published in the *Barb*. Gale, who worked as an accounting clerk at the States Steamship Line, was immediately fired from his job. Laurence soon lost his position as editor of *Vector* as well after he characterized West Coast homosexual organization leaders as "timid . . . middle-aged up-tight conservatives." The article was titled "Gay Revolution" and Laurence complained that such leaders were "hurting almost every major homosexual organization on the West Coast and probably throughout the nation." While they loved to say, "Gay is good," at gay meetings, Laurence complained, they were afraid to say it in public, which to him only made them so many hypocrites. "About the only people with that kind of courage are the new breed of young gay kids. And that's just why organizations like SIR keep them out. The old-timers are scared that these kids will come in and really create a gay revolution."[19]

Fired from his editorship position and thrown out of SIR, Laurence started a new organization called the Committee for Homosexual Freedom (CHF). Far from being intimidated by what he had experienced, Laurence kept up the attack. "We are organizing a campaign that will show the State Lines, or any other employer, that they don't indiscriminately fire homosexuals who are good employees and get away with it. . . . The social revolution that is sweeping the country has given new pride to the Blacks and is now giving fire to the homosexuals," Laurence predicted in the *Barb*'s pages. After demanding that State Lines rehire Gale, he said: "If they don't, militant homosexuals will show that company what Gay Power really means." He finished with a prediction: "The public has a big surprise coming this year if they think they can push homosexuals around and get away with it." Laurence appealed for help: CHF needed people to make signs and posters as well as to demonstrate.

Soon dozens of homosexuals under twenty-five were showing up to help, as well as heterosexuals.[20] It was decided to mount a picket line in front of the State Lines' offices in San Francisco's financial district. The picket demonstration would be held every weekday starting at noon for one hour. On the first day of the picket line over fifty people demonstrated.[21]

State Lines refused even to meet with CHF to discuss their demands. The picket line grew and soon a young minister from Los Angeles by the name of Troy Perry was trying to organize support from that city. Only six months prior Perry had held the first service for a church he was forming in

Los Angeles for homosexuals. Spirits remained high on the picket line, as freedom songs rang out, more office workers came to join in, and blacks driving by raised their fists in solidarity. One man organized a phone-in, urging supporters to call States Lines every day and ask for a different department. Michael Cooke, a twenty-nine-year-old who had been thrown out of the University of Texas in 1961 for making a speech about homosexuality, said, "Fear and intimidation have ruled the gay world for two thousand years. The only legacy this has brought me is the feeling I have precious little to lose. The time is ripe for some militancy." Just how much the social and political upheavals of the previous few years had prompted the protest at State Lines was shown not only by Laurence's own experiences in Chicago but also by the presence on the picket lines of gay people who had participated in antidraft groups, the Stanford Sit-In, and a strike at San Francisco State College, as well as other veterans of the bloody events of 1968 Chicago.

As the State Lines picket demonstration gained momentum, a gay man died after he was shot in the head by a plainclothes police officer who had tried to entrap him in a Berkeley park. When the district attorney indicated that no inquest was necessary, Larry Littlejohn, SIR's president, said, "It looks like an official coverup." A mock funeral motorcade was organized from Glide Methodist Church to the Berkeley Hall of Justice to protest the killing, as the CHF picket line grew grim . . . and spread to Los Angeles, where Troy Perry led fifteen marchers (mostly young gay men and a number of heterosexual theology students) who attracted a crowd of two hundred onlookers. Reverend Perry observed that with so many onlookers, "amazed at the courage of our people," the picket demonstration "was the biggest thing in downtown L.A."[22]

When a Tower Records store in San Francisco fired a clerk, Frank Denaro, on the mere suspicion that he was homosexual, CHF launched a weekend picket at the store specifically geared to stop customers from going inside. The tactic proved effective, as a large number of customers stopped at the picket line, then climbed back inside their cars and drove away.[23]

In May, a young leftist in San Francisco named Carl Wittman took note of all the militant actions occurring in the city and sat down to write about the events' implications. Before a year had passed, the essay, eventually titled "A Gay Manifesto," would become one of the defining documents of the gay liberation movement. In it Wittman wrote:

> San Francisco is a refugee camp of homosexuals. We have fled here from every part of the nation, and like refugees elsewhere, we came not because it is so great here, but because it was so bad there. . . .

And we have formed a ghetto, out of self-protection. It is a ghetto rather than a free territory because it is still theirs. Straight cops patrol us, straight legislators govern us, straight employers keep us in line, straight money exploits us. We have pretended that everything is OK, because we haven't been able to see how to change it—we've been afraid.

In the past year there has been an awakening of gay liberation ideas and energy. How it began we don't know; maybe we were inspired by black people and their freedom movement; we learned how to stop pretending from the hip revolution. . . .

Where once there was frustration, alienation, and cynicism, there are new characteristics among us. We are full of love for each other and are showing it; we are full of anger at what has been done to us. And as we recall all the self-censorship and repression for so many years, a reservoir of tears pours out of our eyes. And we are euphoric, high, with the initial flourish of a movement.[24]

In New York City, the month of May found Mayor Lindsay facing a tough reelection battle. Running against Lindsay for the Republican Party nomination was state legislator John J. Marchi, whom Mattachine–New York described as "one of the bitterest opponents of homosexual law reform." The Democratic candidates were not generally progressive, and some of the better-known candidates included Robert Wagner, whose dismal record regarding homosexuals was only too well known, and Mario Procaccino, who was such a "law and order" candidate that even his fellow Democrats considered him repressive.[25]

On June 17, Lindsay lost his own party's primary to Marchi. The race was thrown into a confused frenzy as Lindsay realigned himself and sought to save his political life by running a fusion campaign, with his name appearing on both the Liberal and Independent parties' lines. Mattachine–New York reported that Marchi's victory speech was "a panegyric to 'old values' of cleanliness and godliness," with much of it sounding like "a veiled warning to the sexually unorthodox, the minority groups, the people who don't abide by the 'old morality,' and others, to run for the hills." Procaccino then tried "to out-reactionary Marchi" and succeeded to such an extent that "he alarmed even former Mayor Wagner." In this context, as a growing number of bar raids took place, New York's gay population wondered if it was not seeing a return to the bad old days they had always lived through at election time.

———

What came to be called the counterculture had many manifestations, from communes, to alternative foods, to underground newspapers. One of its characteristic innovations was the alternative schools that sprang up all across America. These organizations were usually free or low-priced and very modest in scope. One of the best-known in New York City was Alternate U., a free school and organizing center founded around 1966 by Tom Wodetski. Located on the Village's northern edge at the corner of 14th Street and Sixth Avenue, its several classrooms and one office inhabited a former dance studio on the corner building's second floor. The school emphasized action, not academics, and encouraged its students to take the skills and ideas they had learned—whether in a class in Marxist theory taught by Stanley Aronowitz or in community organizing by Flo Kennedy—out into the world in order to change it. Although freewheeling, Alternate U. did have a board.[26]

In early 1969, John O'Brien volunteered at Alternate U. and was soon asked to join the board. He accepted the invitation in spite of being preoccupied with sorting out his feelings about being gay. His sexuality predominated his thoughts, for he had recently been thrown out of the Young Socialists Alliance (YSA), the youth group of the Marxist Socialist Workers Party (SWP), because he was gay.

He remembered how on his birthday in January 1969 he had been brought in for questioning by the organizers of the New York chapters of the YSA and the SWP. He could tell that they were reluctant to believe that he was homosexual: not only was he a hard-working party member, but his very masculine demeanor—including a very muscular physique—did not fit the gay stereotype. He also knew he could deny the accusation and they would believe him and the matter would be forgotten. But for O'Brien this was the moment of truth. He decided not to compromise his integrity and was summarily thrown out.

This expulsion upset him, for he had devoted his life since his early teen years to progressive and revolutionary causes. No one in the New Left could doubt his dedication: he had been demonstrating and fighting the police in the streets since his youth, when he had sneaked away from home to demonstrate for black civil rights in Alabama and returned with his hand scarred by a police dog. During the student occupation of Columbia University the SDS had put him in charge of security for one of the occupied buildings. O'Brien often pulled these sorts of dangerous assignments not only because of his muscles, but also because growing up in Spanish Harlem had made him tough.

O'Brien had not served on Alternate U.'s board long when he met a young man by the name of Bill Katzenberg. Bill also belonged to the SDS and had been referred to John by Alternate U. after showing up there saying he wanted to start a gay radical group. But starting a gay anything was about the last thing O'Brien wanted to consider given his previous experiences with gay groups: He had tried to join the picket line at one of the Annual Reminders and had not been allowed to because his clothing did not fit the dress code. A gay student group at Columbia University, the nation's first, had picketed outside one of the buildings there during the student occupation. O'Brien had joyously joined them, but the students had ignored him. Perhaps they had suspected him of being a spy or a provocateur because he didn't look gay. Sex was the only gay thing that seemed to work for O'Brien.

Katzenberg struck O'Brien as being both highly motivated and sincere. He told O'Brien that he wanted to organize radical gay people into a group and that he wanted the group to do more than just complain: it should be a group geared toward action. O'Brien was tempted but decided not to join. He would lend his name to help sponsor the group at Alternate U., and he would help them find a place to meet. Other than that, Katzenberg would have to sink or swim on his own.

But Katzenberg continued to come to Alternate U. to talk to O'Brien and finally managed to convince him to join the new group. A turning point came when Katzenberg introduced O'Brien to Jerry Hoose, who was very much a part of the sex scene at the trucks and the cruising scene on Christopher Street. Hoose, O'Brien recalls, seemed to know everyone who hung out on Christopher Street. According to O'Brien, in the spring or summer of 1969 Hoose supported the idea of a new group and introduced him and Katzenberg to other people on the street with whom they talked about gay oppression.

One of the men Katzenberg conversed with was a lithe and handsome young carpenter from Brooklyn by the name of Marty Robinson, who had no shyness about being gay. When his prominent parents had offered him a trip to Europe if he would renounce his homosexuality, he had not thought twice before turning them down. His "natural aggressiveness" had caused Katzenberg to approach him about creating a "new butch image for male homosexuals." But Marty had already experimented with the extremes of acting "ultrabutch" as well as "a little screaming and camping" before going back to just being himself. He turned down Katzenberg's proposal to start a group called the Pink Panthers, because "[t]he whole idea was a big turn-off to me. There's nothing worse than to try to be a 1950's butch!"[27]

O'Brien recalls, "We had a number of discussions, most of them actually standing on street corners on Christopher Street, mostly on the northwest corner of Bleeker. We'd stand there, sometimes on the stoops a little further down, sometimes in the Silver Dollar Restaurant, which was a big hangout for us. We met there. We started, the three of us, then were able to recruit a couple more people, becoming like five people, and we agreed on putting an ad in the paper and finally having a meeting." When *The Village Voice* refused the ad, O'Brien and Katzenberg went to the SDS-affiliated newspaper *Rat,* which accepted the small classified ad, which announced: "A group of young radical homosexuals will meet . . . to develop a critique of heterosexual supremacy, both in society and within the Movement."[28]

Mattachine–New York's June newsletter brought plenty of bad news for its readers. The body of a man, killed by strangulation, had been pulled out of the Hudson, appearing to be yet another "dock scene" victim. In the previous month and a half, three men, apparently gay, had been robbed and murdered on Manhattan's East Side. In May a new gay private club had opened in the East Fifties without any licenses. When the police raided it and arrested the management, the police were well within the law, but they then illegally arrested every customer and charged them with "disorderly conduct." The police also issued a warning: in the future they intended to arrest any person they found in an unlicensed club. Even D.D.'s gossip column had bad news: the police were unusually active in the public parks and the Hilton Hotel was "hot with private dicks."

In light of so much bad news, the newsletter's lead story—that the New York City's Civil Service Commission (CSC) had grudgingly, after fighting for two years in court, agreed that homosexuality was not an "absolute disqualification" for holding city jobs—offered little reason for celebrating. All the more since although this ruling only affected hiring by New York City itself, there were still a number of exceptions to the new policy. The Welfare Department was exempt from this ruling, and the CSC itself quickly pointed out that "it would probably refuse to hire a homosexual as a policeman or fireman." The CSC spokesman then added, "An admitted homosexual, when the acts are frequent and recent, would probably not be qualified to be a guard in city penitentiaries, a children's counselor, or a playground attendant."

As the newsletter reported that Canada was in the process of legalizing homosexual sex and that West Germany's new laws making gay sex legal would probably take effect by Labor Day, it informed New Yorkers that both *The Village Voice* and *The New York Times* had refused to accept ads for *The Homosexual Handbook,* which had just sold out its second printing of 50,000 copies.[29] While New York's homosexuals read of how U.S. allies, including Canada, were legalizing homosexual sex, they themselves were being fired, blackmailed, beaten, knifed, shot, strangled, thrown into the

Hudson, and killed. Meanwhile, the most liberal city government in a decade couldn't bring itself, even after a two-year court battle, to think homosexuals fit to fight fires or work in penitentiaries, and two of the city's most liberal publications would not even run an ad for a book about homosexuality.

Toward the end of June word spread through New York's gay community of vigilantism in Queens. A number of homosexual men had found a convenient trysting spot in Kew Gardens, a public park. When men in the neighborhood took umbrage and decided they needed "to protect their wives and children" (even though none were ever in the park in the middle of the night), they formed a vigilante committee to harass the men who went there. Using walkie-talkies to coordinate their efforts, a group of as many as forty men would patrol the park, where they surrounded and confronted gay men, shining bright lights in their faces and ordering them to leave. But gay men were not so easily cowed by the decade's end and some refused, asserting their legal right to be on public land. Neighborhood youths also took to going to the park and beating and robbing the homosexuals they found there. When gay men still showed up, the vigilantes got saws and axes and, a night or two after Lindsay lost the primary, chopped down the park's trees. When a concerned citizen saw the mayhem going on, he admonished one of the vigilantes who swung an ax at him. When the man reported the attempted violence to the police, they did nothing to stop the cutting. Other citizens reported the trees' destruction, only to see police cars drive up, and an officer get out and chat with the vigilantes, then leave without taking any action.[30]

In Greenwich Village, there was no lack of police action at the end of June, as five gay bars were raided over three weeks. Three of the five bars raided were among the most popular gay spots in town, and several bars—the Checkerboard, the Tel-Star, and the Sewer—were closed for good.[31]

In April *The Advocate* had announced the appearance of a new gay publication called *Queen's Quarterly*. Started by friends of Craig Rodwell's, the magazine had a philosophy of gay pride and empowerment that practically jumped off the magazine's pages at the reader, starting with its attractive art direction and continuing on through its editorials to articles about gay sexuality that were both frank and positive. The magazine's tenor even prompted heterosexual *Village Voice* reporter Howard Smith to refer to its readers as "healthy homosexuals."

The magazine's third issue, which came out in the summer, featured a black-and-white photograph of a beautiful youth made by the famed early-twentieth-century homosexual photographer, the Baron von Gloeden. The

photograph of the Sicilian youth was surrounded by yellow and purple pan-
sies as if to accentuate the youth's beauty while subversively standing on
its head the use of the flower's name to denigrate gay men. The summer issue featured a fashion spread on sunglasses, a discussion of wine, an article on sadomasochism, an interview with transvestite actress Mario
Montez, vacation tips, and an article on how to make a gay marriage last, as
well as an article on how to defend oneself if attacked. The article on self-
defense included photographs of a nude man with the most vulnerable
parts of the anatomy labeled, from the testicles, to the Adam's apple, to the
bridge of the nose, and advised that if the reader had "the time, inclination,
and dough, by all means—learn Karate and Judo."

The lead editorial, titled "Dawn Is Just Breaking . . . ," announced:

> QQ wants to . . . present a total picture of gay life—but we're happy
> being ourselves. . . . [W]e cannot be something we are not. . . . We
> must be ourselves. . . . Our message is simple: Stop apologizing for
> yourself . . . face the facts and accept yourself as you are . . . there is
> a real place for us in this world . . . be proud and excited about being
> gay—we have earned our place in society and it must now learn its
> lesson that we are here to stay and that our voice is loud and strong.
> Dawn is just breaking for gay guys . . . this is the age of the gay re-
> naissance.[32]

By the end of June 1969, Pine's and Smythe's campaign to close down
Mafia gay bars in the Village had been in full swing for some time. On
Tuesday, June 24, Seymour Pine led a raid on the Stonewall Inn, arresting
bar personnel and confiscating the bar's liquor. There was a lot of resent-
ment about this raid on the part of gay men in the Village who complained
about it over the following nights. Ronnie Di Brienza, a twenty-six-year-old
musician, who apparently was inside the Stonewall Inn during the Tuesday
night raid, described his feelings and thoughts about the event:

> I have had a lot of shit thrown my way, but . . . I was basically a paci-
> fist. However . . . how many times can one turn the other cheek? . . .
>   Basically, I am not gay, but I am not straight either. . . .
>   The establishment and their elite Gestapo, the pigs, have been
> running things too long. First you had the Negro riots a few years
> back, which woke up white cats like myself to the fact that, though I
> am white, I am just as much considered a nigger as the black man is.
> From those early battles came the more intense militant organiza-
> tions who, like myself, are sick and tired of being niggers, and want to
> become real and human. We have reached the bottom of the

oppressed minority barrel . . . gay people . . . too, have turned the other cheek once too often.

Di Brienza summed up the mood in the Village after the Tuesday raid by saying: "Predominantly the theme was 'this shit has got to stop!'"[33]

As Pine prepared to leave the Stonewall Inn at the evening's end one of the bar's owners sneered, "If you want to make a bust, that's your business. We'll be open again tomorrow."

The words stung Pine, in part because he knew they were true. But they also sounded to him like a challenge. He would be back.[34]

THE

STONEWALL

RIOTS

7

A Friday Night Out

"Steve" Ritter felt on top of the world as he began the day on Friday, June 27. Not only was it his birthday, but he turned eighteen that day, so he knew when he woke up that legally he had reached adulthood: he still couldn't vote, but he could be drafted, and he could drink. Other major social and personal milestones marked this legal coming-of-age: he would graduate from high school in three days; he had found a lover, a muscle builder who wanted Steve to move in with him so they could live as "man and wife"; and later that same night Steve was starting a job as a waiter at the Tenth of Always. It didn't bother Steve much that he'd be working in an after-hours place, for he was about to begin his first full-time job, and one at which he could dress in the women's clothes he felt at home in. Besides, the muscle builder had even promised to pay for the expensive process of going through sex reassignment surgery, which meant that Steve would no longer have to hide who he was.[1]

But tonight he was going to have the big blowout he'd been planning for the entire past week with Kiki, his cross-dressing hairstylist friend: they would both go out "dressed" that night to the Stonewall Inn to celebrate Steve's coming of age. Steve had been to the Stonewall and had always gotten in using phony ID, but he had registered for the draft weeks before as required by law so that on the day he turned eighteen he could begin to carry his draft card as required. Tonight he would impress the doormen at the Stonewall by showing them some real ID.

Steve spent the better part of the day getting everything he would need to dress at Kiki's ready. He went to his mother's closet and surveyed her outfits. Luckily for Steve, his mother was a full-figured woman, making it possible for him to fit into her clothes. He selected a really nice empire-waisted black-and-white cocktail dress. Almost sleeveless, the high-waisted dress had a V-shaped back that came down to the middle of his spine and featured a more modest V-shape in the front, while the garment's hem stopped several inches above the knee. All in all, the outfit combined a sophisticated look with sexiness, making it the perfect choice for the evening.

Steve took the dress to his bedroom, where he already had a pair of shoes borrowed from a friend: strapless black shoes with four-inch heels. In addition to the shoes and dress, Steve had assembled a pair of black stockings, some Cover Girl makeup that he had bought for himself, and other makeup he had stolen from his mother. Steve had longish hair, which would help it blend in with the fall he had purchased. He also had a large pocketbook, so that he could roll up a pair of "boy's clothes" and hide them there in case he needed to change in a park on the way home.

Steve arrived at Kiki's house in Brooklyn Heights in the late afternoon. They had decided to meet and dress here, since Kiki's neighborhood was a bit more tolerant than Steve's.

After exchanging greetings, the two friends began the pleasurable task of slowly transforming themselves into the women they felt themselves to be. For Steve the evening at Kiki's was one of simple fun and innocent self-indulgence: "I just spent time making up. It would take us hours, and at that time we painted for the gods: it would take us three or four hours to make up." However, the preparations were not lengthy simply because of the infinite care the boys took in applying their makeup: "We spent a whole lot of time kiki'ing around—fooling around. You'd get your hair set. We'd sit around slinging a few cocktails. I was drinking gin and tonic, then vodka and orange juice. We were slamming them back as we were getting dressed."

Hours later, having completed the transformation that left her male identity as Steve behind, "Maria" picked up her pocketbook and walked out the door with Kiki when the car service they had ordered arrived. Maria remembers, "I was nervous. People would say I was a drag queen, but I always felt like a woman, so this was more natural dress than I'd usually be in." But nervousness was not the dominant emotion Maria was feeling that night as the car sped toward Manhattan. "I felt like I had finally come of age and that I was growing up. I was going to be able to finally live the life I wanted to live. There was an exhilaration because I was growing up and finally getting some freedom."

As Friday evening came to a close, Deputy Inspector Seymour Pine was also feeling pretty good. He had seen to it that the evening's raid on the Stonewall Inn packed some extra punch. He was tired of busting these Mafia clubs only to see them reopen the following day. And now the Mafia managers had thrown a challenge in his face, one that still stung. Well, he would bust them good this time. It may not be a stake through the heart, but he'd bet it would take the Stonewall more than twenty-four hours to reopen with its bars sliced into pieces and hauled out the door. He already had the search warrant that Kenneth Convoy, the district attorney assigned to Public Morals, had gotten Judge Schawn to issue the day before, authorizing Pine to search the premises, seize alcohol, and have the bars cut up and removed along with the Stonewall's vending equipment.[2]

Pine had taken the unusual step of getting a warrant to prevent one of the Mafia's lawyers from attempting to use the lack of one as a technicality to have charges against the Stonewall Inn dismissed. He had also asked the city to send an inspector from the Department of Consumer Affairs, which they had promised to do. Having a city inspector along should strengthen the case, for while Pine was capable of citing the Stonewall for infractions of any city laws, it looked better in court if it was done by the city's own experts in overcrowding and the cabaret laws, the regulations that governed nightclubs. As usual, he had requested a federal agent from the Bureau of Alcohol, Tobacco and Firearms. While the Bureau did not always have an agent to spare, they did this night, for Pine's office had received a message stating that one of their agents would be there, which was welcome news. He had no doubt the Stonewall Inn was watering down its liquor, which was a violation of federal law. Federal charges were more serious than state violations, and if the local courts did not take these charges seriously, federal judges might. And while the state courts were subject to local political pressure, the federal courts were more likely to be beyond local suasion. Besides, the more charges, the better it looked in court. Maybe if he hit the Stonewall Inn often enough and hard enough, he just might succeed in shutting it down for good.

While Pine needed the policewomen he had requested for this raid, he particularly hated using women undercover, for it always seemed to him that they faced even greater risk than his men. The women went inside in advance, in part so that they could say in court exactly who did what: who mixed and poured the drinks, who served them, which of the men inside the club was giving orders, and so forth. While Pine's undercover men could do that, it was easier to get the women inside the clubs. But he especially needed the women to assist in the arrest of any transvestites. Any men the agents snared in women's clothes would be examined to determine if they were simply wearing women's clothes or were transsexuals who had undergone a sex change: if they had had the operation they would not be arrested. As part of their job, the women were expected to mingle with the crowd and get friendly. And if a Mafia owner leaned on one of them to be more than friendly, duty called for her to play along. Pine cringed at such awful work, and he wondered how those who were married stood it.

To make sure that all went smoothly and to minimize the risk to the policewomen, he had arranged a meeting for later that Friday evening around midnight in the First Division headquarters on East 21st Street. While such a review before a raid was routine, Pine sometimes skipped it. Tonight the review would be held: Pine wanted to be sure that nothing went awry.

When Jennifer Hardy's gay roommate headed out that evening, she decided to tag along. First they stopped to get a bite to eat and ran into some of her roommate's friends. Eventually they ended up at the Stonewall Inn as they usually did. Jennifer, only seventeen, had arrived in New York from California as a runaway a couple of weeks earlier. This was her third visit to the Stonewall. She stayed and ordered a number of drinks even though she did not really care for the Inn, which seemed oppressive to her with its extreme darkness and poor ventilation. Besides, the whole place seemed like the kind of bar one had to slink into. Jennifer also felt very uncomfortable in such an all-male environment. She wanted to find some women. On her first visit to the bar she had noticed one lesbian there, but the woman was so much older than Jennifer that she had not been interested. She wanted to find someone around her own age, someone full of life.

Around ten o'clock the car carrying Maria and Kiki pulled up by the United Cigars Store on Seventh Avenue South where the two young "women" paid the driver and headed for the Stonewall Inn. As they approached the bar they ran into a couple of Kiki's friends, gay men older than Maria. One of the men appeared to be in stage makeup, with plucked eyebrows, and a small amount of eyeliner. His appearance made Maria wonder if he was a professional actor or someone who did drag.

As Maria approached the Stonewall Inn's doors, she had her draft card out, ready for her moment of triumph. "The last couple of times that I had been there, it was like sneaking in with the grown-ups."

As she entered the Stonewall, Maria proudly displayed her draft card to the doorman.

"Look, I got proof."

"You've been here before, haven't you?"

"Yes."

"Well, you little bastard! We could have really got in trouble for that. Don't you know that we could get arrested?" The doorman would not stop his embarrassing harangue. "We could be closed down for letting you in without proof."

The verbal slap in the face was in sharp contrast to the congratulations Maria had anticipated. Crestfallen, she followed Kiki inside.

Leaving the Bleecker Street commune, Danny Garvin headed to Danny's, his current bar of choice. He walked over to Christopher Street, waited in line to get inside what was now the most popular gay men's bar in the Village, and purchased his two drink tickets. On entering, he traded in one of the tickets for a soda and then stationed himself at the short service bar in the club's rear.

After hanging out for about a half hour, he was surprised to see none other than Keith Murdoch approaching. Danny had gotten involved with Keith after he had split up with Frank, who had disliked Danny's hippie attire. While Danny had not seen Keith since he had left for college the previous summer, he had continued to long for him, in part because he found he had so much in common with Keith. Moreover, they had hit it off sexually. Keith's stunning good looks, dirty blond hair, blue eyes, and cleft chin had not hurt, either.

"Wow! What are you doing here?"

"Wow, how's it going?"

"You back in the city now?"

"Yeah. You look good."

"*You* look good."

The two friends started catching up on what had been going on in each other's lives. Danny told Keith that he had moved into an all-gay commune. They went on to talk about all the incredible social and political changes rocking the country, especially the war in Vietnam. Keith learned that Danny had attended a Be-in in Grand Central Station that had turned violent when the police had in effect rioted, charging into the crowd. Eventually they got around to comparing notes on their experiences smoking marijuana.

Keith asked, "Do you know where I can get some?"

"Well, I have some back at the commune," Danny answered. "Why don't we go back there?"

Keith agreed, and after they finished using up their drink tickets, the two set off for the commune. Their conversation turned to the subject of music, which like everything else seemed to be in a radical state of flux. Each eagerly asked the other if he had heard the latest albums by their favorite artists, including the Beatles and Judy Collins.

When they reached the commune, they smoked some marijuana and then headed for Danny's bed.

Dick Leitsch threw his suitcase on his bed and started filling it. He and his lover, Bob Amsel, were to leave for Europe on Sunday. It'd been forever since Leitsch had had any rest, so this was a trip he was really looking forward to. He certainly could not have afforded a European vacation on the meager salary he got from Mattachine–New York, but luckily Bob had a well-paying job. As Dick began packing, he turned on the radio.

At the midnight meeting, Seymour Pine reviewed the plans and his instructions for the bust of the Stonewall Inn with all those who would conduct the raid: the two women he had borrowed for the evening from Chinatown's Fifth Precinct, the five Public Morals officers besides himself, and Inspector Adam Tatem from New York City's Department of Consumer Affairs. It did not matter that the federal agent was not at this meeting, for it was up to him to get into the club on his own. After they had busted the Stonewall, the federal agent would simply identify himself to the police and then wait around while they gathered up the liquor so that he could take a sample for one of the Bureau's laboratories to analyze.

The review of the plans finished, the four undercover police officers— the two male members of the Public Morals squad and the two female police officers—and Tatem left Pine's office first as they needed time to get inside the Stonewall Inn and observe its operations.

As Kiki and Maria settled in at the front room bar for an evening of fun and celebration, Kiki ordered a round of drinks to toast Maria's eighteenth birthday. Later, with the music of the Supremes playing in the background, Maria bought a drink or two for herself while waiting for friends who had promised to come help her celebrate.

But the friends never arrived.

John O'Brien never had to think about what he was going to do on a Friday night. He was so passionate about politics that every Friday night he looked forward to going to his favorite place to discuss political issues: the east side of Sixth Avenue below 8th Street. There he'd find activists hawking pamphlets as they worked the crowds who came to buy incense and beads from hippies who sold these goods on the sidewalk. It was not only a great place to hang out and talk, but there also were a good number of gay men among the political debaters and shoppers, so it was an excellent place to cruise as well.

About half an hour after the first undercover officers had departed from the First Division office, Seymour Pine, Charles Smythe, and the two other plainclothes police officers left the 21st Street office. None of the four used police department vehicles, and Pine and Smythe traveled together in Pine's automobile. They drove to Greenwich Village, parked separately within a few blocks of 51 Christopher Street, and walked to their designated rendezvous, the interior of Christopher Park.

There the four men stood and watched the Stonewall Inn's entrance, waiting for the two undercover men to exit, which they did after a while. Everything was going according to plan, so Pine confidently waited for the female undercover agents to leave the bar, which would be his cue to raid the place.

Tommy Lanigan-Schmidt decided to visit his favorite bar late in the evening. When he got to the Stonewall, he saw that Johnny Shades was at the door. Tommy had no idea if Johnny Shades slept with men, but he found him very sexy. Johnny, however, far from even noticing Tommy, was dismissive of him. On this night, Johnny refused even to let Tommy inside. Disappointed, Tommy took off down Christopher Street.

Seymour Pine continued to stare at the entrance to the Stonewall, but the policewomen still had not come out. Had something gone wrong? Pine was aware that some members of the Mafia knew police procedure even better than some police officers, and the two female officers were carrying guns in their purses. Perhaps the women had been discovered. Were they in danger? Should he go in now or wait? As Pine nervously weighed his options, he noticed that the place seemed unusually busy and mentioned this to Smythe, who seconded the observation.

Jennifer Hardy was getting rather drunk. *Shit,* she thought. *I want to get out of here.* She walked outside, crossed the street, and entered Christopher Park to smoke a cigarette. "I was kind of milling around in the park and trying to clear my head a little bit, because I was getting a real funny feeling in my head. I felt alone that night. I felt really lonely, really alone."

Craig Rodwell and his lover, Fred Sargeant, left their friends' apartment near New York University where they had just finished a game of bridge. As they headed back to their Bleecker Street apartment, Craig noticed that it was unusually hot, even for late June.

Pine continued to wait. Still there were no policewomen. He discussed the situation with Smythe and his two men. *What could have happened?* he wondered. He decided to wait awhile longer before going inside.

Disappointed at her friends' standing her up, Maria tried to make the best of the evening by talking to some of the club goers, still eager to share her excitement about her coming-of-age and the freedom she anticipated. "I knew in my heart that I wasn't gay, but I felt that these people were more accepting than any other people I had met. I felt happy to be with them, yet sorry for myself and for them that we had to hide—hide who we were, hide who we loved, hide who we wanted to be."

A club patron walked up to one of the Stonewall Inn's jukeboxes, dropped in a coin, surveyed the offerings, and selected a song by the Rolling Stones. The androgynous Mick Jagger's voice cut urgently through the dark, perfume-scented air inside the Stonewall Inn, singing, "I can't get no satisfaction."[3]

8

"We're Taking the Place!"

Seymour Pine finally decided that he could wait no longer, for it now seemed a real possibility that the undercover policewomen inside the Stonewall Inn could be in danger. Turning to his men, he said, "Let's go, fellas."

And so it happened that around one-twenty[1] on the morning of Saturday, June 28, four plainclothes police officers from the First Division morals squad wearing dark[2] three-piece[3] suits and ties, two patrolmen, one carrying a radiotelephone, and Detective Charles Smythe, all led by Seymour Pine, walked through Christopher Park's north gate and crossed Christopher Street to raid the Stonewall Inn. Pine stopped at the Stonewall Inn's thick wooden double doors and announced, "Police! We're taking the place!" As always, they were delayed at the door for several seconds. By the time Pine, Smythe, and one of the other two officers who had been waiting in Christopher Park—the officer carrying the radiotelephone initially stayed just outside the Stonewall Inn because the bulkiness of the unit would make him too vulnerable in case something went wrong[4]—were stepping across the Stonewall Inn's threshold, they were joined by the two undercover men who had been inside earlier. Once the raiding party (except for the officer in charge of the radiotelephone) was inside, they used a pay phone to notify the Sixth Precinct of their action and ask for backup.[5]

On entering the front room, Pine caught a glimpse of Inspector Tatem sitting at the bar talking animatedly with a transvestite. Obviously Tatem was trying to put the make on her, but the officers, not wanting to give him away, merely walked by him without saying anything.

Morty Manford was dancing when the music suddenly stopped and the lights were turned up.[6] Abruptly stopping in midbeat, he noticed "some very vicious men" moving through the bewildered crowd.[7]

Michael Fader, a twenty-six-year-old insurance salesman, was confused by the white lights that he associated with closing time. He had been in his favorite club such a short while that he didn't even feel settled in yet. The Rochester native knew from experience that the Rochester police did not harass homosexuals. If someone threw a rock through a gay bar window in his hometown, the police arrested the rock thrower, not the homosexuals, so naturally Michael did not equate the arrival of the police with harassment. "It crossed my mind that it was a fire drill or something. I didn't know what to think. I learned very quickly that the police were raiding the place. It immediately flashed through my mind, *What for?*"

Philip Eagles was standing close to the dance floor by the bar in the front room, having a drink and watching the go-go boys dance in their gold-lamé bikinis, when "there was a commotion, and I saw policemen filing into the bar, and I thought, *Here we go again!*"

Joel S. remembers the night as a regular one until the lights came on. "People were just kind of standing there talking to each other, 'What's going on?'—waiting to see some kind of direction. 'Are the lights going to go off, are we going to be able to start dancing again, or . . . ?'"

As soon as Maria Ritter noticed the police, however, she did not need any elucidation. "The cops had gone into the back room and started pushing people out. I realized it was something when I saw a cop. I headed for the bathroom, hoping there was a window. If there had been I would've gone out it. I have this strange recollection of wanting to get the hell out of there." Maria went through the back room and entered the women's rest room. No sooner had she closed the door than a police officer ordered her out. When she emerged, he grabbed her by the arm, and said, "Over there!" directing her to the east side of the club's front room.

As whispers went around the club that the place was being raided, customers rushed to locate friends. "Are we going to be arrested?" one shocked young man asked. Another terror-stricken man moaned, "I'll lose my job. What will happen to me? My family! Oh no, no, no!" Then the police sealed the doors of the bar.[8]

Maria remembers that "people were trying to get out, but to no avail. It was havoc; it was chaotic—it seemed things happened Bam! Bam! Bam!" Michael Fader's recollection is similar: "Things happened so fast you kind of got caught not knowing. All of a sudden there were police there and we were told to all get in lines and to have our identification ready to be led out of the bar. And I noticed while waiting in line to leave, the policemen were running around the facilities and the room."

Another witness described how the customers felt: "I was anxious. Everybody was, not knowing whether we were going to be arrested or what was happening next. I wouldn't say that I was afraid. It was a nervous mood that set over the place."[9]

The sudden arrival of the cops and the blare of the lights had transformed the scene from one of festivity to sadness. The jukeboxes fell silent, and the shimmering go-go boys left their cages to put on their street clothes.[10]

Pine called the female police officers to the side and got information from them on whom to arrest. He first wanted to know why they had not come outside. The women explained that soon after their arrival the bartenders changed shift and, wanting to identify the workers in both shifts, they had been waiting for the change of staff to finish.[11]

As the police officers moved around the club, the four undercover agents who had been inside pointed out the managers and workers, noting which ones had poured drinks and who had served them. Other policemen gathered up the alcohol. Pine noted that many of the bottles on the bars bore labels, although none in the storage room did. As the Public Morals police moved through the club, uniformed officers from the Sixth Precinct who had been on foot patrol began to show up outside. Having checked in with headquarters on their call boxes they had been told, "Get your ass over to the Stonewall; they're going to make a bust there."[12]

Maria noticed a number of other "women" in the area where she had been directed to wait, as the police moved quickly to separate the Stonewall customers into groups according to their official interests. Adam Tatem was shocked to see the "woman" he had been putting the make on pulled to the side as a transvestite.[13]

Two decades later Pine recalled the raid's beginning: "We immediately— I don't remember who it was—'Everybody get his identity cards out,' and that kind of thing. And we began moving everybody out. In the meantime, the people who were actually working there, in the club, were isolated and put in the back [west] room, and we began taking information from them, names and so forth."

But even this early in the evening nervousness was not the only emotion customers in the bar were feeling. Michael Fader remembers that, standing in line waiting to exit, "I thought, *I don't want to leave!* That crossed my mind very strongly. I just got here and I'm supposed to leave? And stand in line to get checked for my ID? And I felt myself boiling up inside, getting more and more angry. And then I noticed the police were doing some damage to the room. The side [west] room had benches along the wall that you could sit on. They had a hollow cavity underneath—and the police were ripping apart these benches, tearing them apart. I thought, *What are they doing that for?*" Suddenly he remembered the Democratic National Convention the previous August, when he had watched on television as the Chicago police had rioted, savagely beating the crowd of nonviolent protesters gathered in front of the Hilton Hotel.

Almost immediately after entering the Stonewall Inn, the police encountered resistance. Philip Eagles witnessed customers "giving the cops lip" by saying things such as "We're not taking this" and "I'm not showing you my ID." Philip asserts that he and some other customers in the front room also initially resisted showing the police their ID or only did so with "a lot of attitude." One man refused to leave the club, and Pine demanded to see his identification. When the man complied, Pine made a note of the name to follow up on later.[14] As the customers were made to line up, word passed down the line that the police were not letting people without identification out. Those in line began to conspire together to share their identification, figuring that if a person had an extra form of ID on him and it did not have a photograph, that ID could be lent to a person who had none. Michael Olenick remembers that someone in his group of four friends had an extra Bloomingdale's credit card that he lent to a friend of theirs without ID.

Whatever grumbling there may have been from the gay men, the police soon ran into more significant resistance from other patrons in each of the two rooms.

According to Pine, "We had a couple of the transvestites who gave us a lot of flak. We'd have policemen standing at the door and most of the transvestites that frequented these places were known to us, so you sort of weeded them out and said, 'Okay, you stand over here, everybody else out.' The transvestites were picked up near where the bathrooms were, because we used to at least walk them over there, because that's where they were going to be checked. And the policewoman would take them by the elbow and say, 'Okay, let's go in and check you out,' and usually, that was it. They would say, 'All right, honey, I'm a man.' I don't think anybody really checked them. I think it was almost like we were satisfied in embarrassing them, that 'we know who you are and get out!' So you took one collar just to add to the evidence that this place was illegal. Whoever was the unlucky one was the one who gave you lip. We did have the right to check for transvestites, and as transvestites, most of them were prostitutes as well, and we were concerned about that." Still, Pine insists, "if the place didn't turn into a rhubarb, we probably would have thrown everybody out, including those we verified as transvestites, except the management. I mean, there was no plan to take these people."

However, this night, according to Pine, the transvestites resisted by refusing to go into the Stonewall's bathrooms to be "examined." "We separated the few transvestites that we had, and they were very noisy that night.

Usually they would just sit there and not say a word, but now they're acting up: 'Get your hands off me!' 'Don't touch me!' They wouldn't go in, so it was a question of pushing them in, fighting them."

To Seymour Pine, it was the transvestite resistance that made the raid take on a broader scope than its intended original targets, the Stonewall Inn's owners and employees: "So, we then decided that we would take everybody in. We collected all the liquor, and those transvestites that had given us some trouble, we decided they would stay, and everybody else out." Pine put the transvestites and some of the bar personnel into the back room to hold them, but that allowed the transvestites' insurgent attitude to spread to the Stonewall personnel under arrest.

While the police had their hands full with the transvestites in the second room, they had been getting more than lip in the front room as well. According to Philip Eagles, there were some lesbians standing against the back wall who, when approached by the police, said, "We have a right to be here," and, "What are you doing?" Philips states that the cops were "feeling some of them up inappropriately or frisking them," so it seems likely that the lesbians' challenging the cops and the police frisking of them are related, although it is impossible to say which occurred first. Either way, Philip says that the lesbians "were being pushed around and bullied" and this plus the frisking of them made "everybody generally very uncomfortable."[15]

According to all other accounts, however, most patrons in the front room only seemed aware of a long and nervous wait, which might be because they were not close enough to the lesbians to witness their plight. Manford recalled that "confusion and uncertainty reigned . . . until they were ready to move us out." Manford estimated that it was "ten or fifteen minutes" after being lined up that the club goers started to leave the place.[16]

But for many others inside the bar, whatever the actual passage of time may have been, it felt much longer than fifteen minutes. Raymond Castro, a twenty-seven-year-old Puerto Rican baker known to his friends as Ray, had been in the back room standing next to the jukebox watching a couple of drag queens dancing by themselves to a Stevie Wonder tune just prior to the raid. He remembers that the police "kept us there for so long, it was almost like a hostage situation. The police wouldn't even let you get near them. They wouldn't answer any questions. You couldn't ask them anything. They wouldn't tell you anything. The only ones you could actually still speak to were a couple of the [Mafia] bosses, and all they would tell you is, 'Calm down. Everything's going to be all right, nothing to worry about.'"

Around this time patrol cars from the Sixth Precinct began to roll up and park directly in front of the Stonewall Inn, to reinforce the two foot patrolmen already present.[17]

While most customers were waiting in line in the front room, Inspector Smythe continued to move around the club, supervising the seizing of all the alcohol from the two bars and the club's storage room,[18] he or the other officers making notes as they went along, for each bottle would need to have a tag indicating exactly where the bottle had been found, so that when the seized liquor reached the Sixth Precinct each bottle could be cataloged into the evidence book.[19] Pine was periodically checking on Smythe, one time asking him, "You're almost finished?" and a bit later, "We need another patrol wagon right now?" By the time Smythe had finished rounding up all the alcohol, he found he had twenty-eight cases of beer and nineteen bottles of liquor on his hands.[20]

The question of the seized alcohol in fact weighed directly on the need for more patrol wagons: Pine knew that alcohol transported in patrol cars often did not reach the precinct house, so he preferred that it be transported in patrol wagons. Moreover, because the Stonewall Inn had a lot of waiters and Pine had not counted on arresting several transvestites, he would definitely need more than one patrol wagon.

Pine next had to figure out how to remove the bars and the jukeboxes. After inspecting the equipment, he notified Emergency Service that he wanted both the bars inside the Stonewall Inn cut up and removed along with the jukeboxes.

Maria Ritter felt worse than nervous as she waited to see what her fate would be. By now not only had her combined coming-of-age birthday and high school graduation celebration been spoiled, but also arrest with all its dire consequences for a pre-op transsexual seemed inescapable. "My biggest fear was that I would get arrested. My second biggest fear is that my picture would be in a newspaper or on a television report in my mother's dress!" During the wait, thoughts of her father weighed heavily on her mind. Although he was a research scientist who worked for a pharmaceutical company, her father struck Maria as sounding like Archie Bunker's twin. How could she possibly explain to a man who always called her Butch how she came to be arrested in his wife's dress in a Greenwich Village gay bar on her eighteenth birthday? As awful as the prospect of facing her father seemed, there were still worse fears: "I had already heard what happens to queers in jail, so . . . take it from there."

Finally the line of detained club goers did begin to move, for Pine, having separated those he wanted to arrest from those he did not, wanted the latter out of the way so that he and his officers could finish inventorying the evidence and taking the names and addresses of those they were arresting without any interference. The process of getting the club goers who were not arrested to exit the Stonewall did not go quickly. As Joel S. noted, every one of the approximately two hundred customers held by the police had to stop and produce identification at the front desk, where the police checked "every single one" of the IDs produced.[21] "It was a tedious chore just getting out of there." Those who lacked identification[22] were herded into the coatroom to await questioning by the police.[23]

As the patrons began to exit the bar in a single file during the early morning hours of Saturday, June 28, the police officers expected them to disappear silently and gratefully into the night as had always happened after raids on homosexual bars. But this night was to be different: after the patrons left the raided club, they stood in the street, watching and waiting, their attention focused on the entrance to the Stonewall Inn.

Why did the Stonewall Inn's patrons stand in the street and watch that night? Part of the answer is probably simple: the police had chosen to raid the bar at a peak time—1:00 A.M. on a summer Saturday morning—so that with a large number of customers in the club when it was raided, there were enough people present to form a crowd. Also, the larger the crowd, the more patrons there were who might be there with friends, hence a larger number who might be inclined to wait and see if their friends were arrested—or beaten. However, a rarely noted contemporary account attributes the eruption of anger that night to the previous raid on the Stonewall Inn, noting that customers had already complained about the earlier raid:

> On Tuesday night . . . the Stonewall Inn on Christopher Street was raided . . . . The Stonewall . . . has survived . . . for the past three years . . . . However, the pigs decided to start playing political games . . . because when did you ever see a fag fight back? . . . Now, times are a-changin'. Tuesday night was the last night for bullshit.
>
> On Wednesday and Thursday nights grumbling could be heard among the limp wristed set. Predominantly, the theme [w]as, "this shit has got to stop!"[24]

Not only was the previous raid on the Stonewall Inn discussed, but so were the trees that had been cut down in Kew Gardens.[25] The gay men who stood outside the Stonewall talked about the destruction of their lovers' lane as well as about how many of their other clubs had been raided in recent weeks[26]: the Snake Pit,[27] the Checkerboard, and the Sewer.[28] Now not only had the Stonewall Inn been hit twice in one week, but also tonight's raid had come on a Friday night and at the evening's peak. Standing in the crowd, Morty Manford sighed. *Damn,* he wondered. *Why do we have to put up with this shit?*[29]

Joel S. was among the first few dozen or so patrons to be released. He remembers that "as we filed out the crowd started to gather in front of the place. I guess more and more people just started to mill around the front. People were kind of staying with friends, looking and hanging out. I mean the street wasn't packed, but there were a lot of people there, and they were spread all around in front of the bar, towards Waverly Place. I remember seeing some of the more ostentatious drags walking in twos or threes down Christopher towards the bar and hearing loud, shrieking little sentences. I don't really know what they were saying, just kind of drawing attention to themselves. They were marching along, trying to show a little anger or annoyance, trying to make some noise." Joel noticed the temperature: "It was a hot, seething night. A real New York summer night.

"I guess everybody was wondering, *What's going on?*—a little annoyed. *Is something going to happen? Why is this taking so long?* In fact, some of the drag queens were kind of chanting and skipping along. It was entertaining."

From his second-floor perch in a storage room *The Village Voice* rented on the west side of Seventh Avenue South, Howard Smith looked up from his typewriter and noticed a number of police cars on Christopher Street below. Smith kept a pair of binoculars on his desk to inspect people who asked for him at the *Village Voice* office across the street. Intrigued, he reached for the binoculars and peered at the scene. While he could not tell just what was happening, it seemed out of the ordinary. As he moved around New York City Smith had made a habit of following police cars and fire trucks as well as investigating any other interesting scene he happened upon. *Wow!* he thought. *Right here! I wonder what it is?* He also noticed the size of the crowd. "It was growing very quickly. Every time I'd blink, there were more people." His curiosity piqued, he picked up his blue plastic press pass, hung it around his neck, stuffed some notepads into his pockets, ran downstairs, and "walked up to the cops and tried to figure out what was happening. I saw that it was the Stonewall."

The commotion in the streets had also drawn Lucian Truscott from the Lion's Head to see what was causing all the racket. Truscott, an army lieutenant on leave, was also an aspiring writer and was using his time off from the military to do some occasional writing for *The Village Voice*. Observing the scene and deciding to watch for a while, he soon ran into his *Voice* colleague. Truscott and Smith talked briefly about what was going on, and when Truscott realized that he did not have a press pass Smith let him into the *Voice* office to pick one up so that he, too, could go behind police lines. The two men parted company, not to see each other again that night.

The crowd on Christopher Street continued to grow as the club's ejected

patrons reached the pavement where they also were joined by a considerable number of tourists who, having come to the Village on a Friday night
looking for excitement, had found it for free on the street.

One of those now in the crowd was Tommy Lanigan-Schmidt, having
decided that enough time had passed since that mean Johnny Shades had
refused to let him inside that he could again try his luck at getting past the
doorman. Although Tommy had been to the club more times than he could
recall, it just so happened that he had never been there during a raid, so
that coming across a raid of the club he practically considered home took
him aback: "It surprised me because it was such a secure place that I
thought, *Well, how could this happen?* I immediately felt a kind of indigna-
tion because this was like sacred."[30]

Around this time Danny Garvin and Keith Murdoch were approaching
the downtown side of Christopher Park as they headed north on Seventh
Avenue South. After they had finished making love, they had decided to
end the evening by dancing at the Stonewall. On the walk over they had
talked about what it was going to be like when the revolution they and so
many others anticipated happened: even the Beatles were singing about
revolution. "We all figured that the Black Panthers were going to start the
revolution. All of a sudden, you see people coming out of the Stonewall, so
you knew it was raided." High on pot, Garvin's first reaction was: "The revolution had started!" Garvin estimates the size of the crowd when he arrived at around 100 or 150 people.

Most patrons exited quietly, but the small crowd cheered some of the
club's favorites, many of whom camped it up. As one young man swished
by the detective posted at the door, he tossed the classic come-on line at
him: "Hello there, fella!"[31] Others of the departing men took bows and
were hailed by their friends.[32] As customers reacted to the crowd's applause, they became bolder and more confident in their outrageousness.
Voice reporter Smith described the crowd as "prancing high and jubilant,"
while Truscott observed: "Wrists were limp, hair was primped, and reactions to the applause were classic." Said one excited patron, "I gave them
the gay power bit, and they loved it, girls." Another ad-libbed, "Have you
seen Maxine? Where *is* my wife—I told her not to go far!"

The scene was not all hilarity, however. Smith, who managed to form a
bond with Seymour Pine on the spot, kept near him[33] and observed the police at close hand. He noticed that the police handled the exiting patrons
roughly, now hurrying one out quicker than he could comfortably move,
now giving another a parting kick.

As Garvin watched, he saw that "it started getting ugly. You had attitude:
'Don't touch me!,' which then would ignite the crowd: 'Go get 'em!' So then

it became a show. Who's coming out, who's exiting? No one knew that it was going to turn into a riot. In everybody's mind all it was was a bar raid. People were being kicked out of the bar, so there was going to be a little campiness, there's going to be stars coming out onto the street." Garvin recalls that some of the exiting men threw their arms up and out in a V shape as if they were performers making a grand entrance on a stage.

Around this time Tom, a young man who worked for the East Village underground newspaper *Rat*, out with a friend for a beer, stumbled across the scene in front of the Stonewall and asked some of the men in the crowd what had happened.

"They raided the joint, the fucking bastards."

"Why?"

"Operating without a liquor license."

A black man yelled, "Shit, man, they're out like always to chase us down and give us a good fuck. They ain't got nothin' else to do during the summer."

Another member of the crowd approached Tom and asked him if he wanted to buy some speed.

Noticing the crowd's "skittish hilarity," Howard Smith paused in his note taking to peer up at the moon. It was full.[34]

A paddy wagon appeared, seemingly from nowhere. It pulled up part of the way on the sidewalk in front of the Stonewall Inn, just a little east of the entrance, and parked against the flow of traffic, facing east.[35] Joel S. recalls that at this time "the area was kind of loosely crowded, and the noisy drags, walking along, attracted other viewers. The crowd started getting bigger and bigger."[36]

Craig Rodwell and Fred Sargeant were crossing Sheridan Square on their way home after a game of bridge when they saw the crowd gathered in front of the Stonewall Inn.[37] Craig and Fred approached to get a closer look and saw the patrol wagon[38] parked in front of the bar, telling them that they had stumbled upon a raid. While there was nothing new about that, Craig noticed "a feeling in the air that something was going to happen." Craig immediately decided that he was not about to miss out on this, and he and Fred climbed the seven steps to the top of the tallest stoop on Christopher Street, the one just west of the Stonewall Inn, to get a bird's-eye view of whatever was about to unfold.[39] *This*, Craig thought, *is different.*

The arrival of the paddy wagon marked the first time that evening that the seriousness of the raid came home to the men and women gathered on Christopher Street. From his vantage point above the street Craig noticed how very quiet the crowd had become.[40]

Seymour Pine exited the Stonewall Inn, prepared to begin loading his haul of prisoners and evidence to the Sixth Precinct station house on

Charles Street, but found that he had only one patrol wagon. As Pine recalls, "This presumably should have been the end of the situation, because the raid was already over. Now, all we had to do was put them in
the patrol wagon." But Pine saw that he had a problem: "The crowd had
grown to ten times the size: it was really frightening." This surprised and
confused Pine: "So many showed up immediately, it was as if a signal
were given. And that was the unusual thing because usually, when we
went to work, everybody disappeared. They were glad to get away. But
this night was different. Instead of the homosexuals slinking off, they remained there, and their friends came, and it was a real meeting of homosexuals." Still, Pine was not too concerned about the problem, for
certainly neither he nor his men had ever encountered hostility from a
crowd of homosexuals. Pine learned that only one patrol wagon had arrived, so he tried to order a second one, but when the officer with the radiotelephone made the call, a mysterious message came over the line:
"Disregard that call." This struck Pine as very odd, for the calls went via
CB to a central unit. True, anyone in the Sixth Precinct would automatically hear the announcement as well, but why would anyone want to countermand it? Pine would try again later.[41] Having cleared all of the people he
did not want to arrest outside the Stonewall Inn, Pine could now load his
prisoners.[42]

The first prisoners to be loaded inside the wagon were members of the
Mafia, who were brought out of the club one by one. As the mob members
exited the Stonewall and were shoved inside the patrol wagon, the crowd
reacted variously, sending up Bronx cheers for the hated Mafiosi, jeering
the police, and clapping.[43] Meanwhile, Craig Rodwell, watching the familiar ritual of another gay club being busted, felt the anger build up inside of
him until he could stand it no longer and suddenly let loose a yell that
pierced the night: "Gay Power!" Fred immediately nudged Craig, saying,
"Shut up!" But everyone heard the cry that reverberated through the still
night air[44] and a few took it up and repeated it. But this idea seemed too
unreal, too radical, to be taken seriously, and the newly heard slogan soon
dissolved into giggles.[45]

The non-Mafia employees of the club were the next ones loaded into the
paddy wagon: bartenders, hatcheck boys, and even John, the black men's
room attendant. As Michael Fader watched those arrested being loaded
into the paddy wagon, the only one he recognized was John, who had "always been a gentleman and helpful." As he saw this meek middle-aged heterosexual black man climb into the paddy wagon, the whole thing struck
Michael as being so absurd and unnecessary. "It was just kind of a strange
cross section of people." His sense of social justice offended, Fader began

to feel even angrier. The behavior of the police also galled the young sales-man: "They had no sensitivity whatsoever. They weren't brutal in terms of clubbing people, but there was condescension and a contempt."[46]

A few cheers went up as the bar employees continued to be loaded into police vehicles, and then someone began to sing one of the most familiar protest songs from that era of protest, "We Shall Overcome." A few in the crowd started singing along, but after a few verses this, too, seemed too dignified to be taken seriously by a bunch of homosexuals and the crowd began to camp on the solemn lyrics.[47] By almost all accounts, until some-where around this time most of the crowd on the street were largely main-taining a sense of good humor about everything that was happening.[48]

The next to enter the paddy wagon were three men in full drag, de-scribed by Truscott as being among the "more blatant queens." Bob Kohler had arrived on the scene after the patrol wagon and spotted the street kids he knew from Christopher Park standing close to the park's exit onto Christopher Street. He walked up to them with his dog, Magoo, and watched as the well-dressed drag queens were put into the paddy wagon. Kohler recalled how "the queens . . . were waving, and the kids were say-ing, 'Have a good rest,' and, 'Oh, I'm glad they're taking her. She needs a rest,' and, 'Oh, Lily Law's got you, girl!'"

The buoyant humor displayed during the riots is noteworthy, especially on the first night, as the crowd deployed its keen sense of camp. Fader re-members, "A couple of times the police would come out with someone and take him to the paddy wagon, [the crowd] would make quips to the police. There were some people with really good senses of humor, and the crowd would all crack up and laugh. That was intermingled with growing and in-tensive hostility."

The first hostile act outside the club occurred when a police officer shoved one of the transvestites, who turned and smacked the officer over the head with her purse. The cop clubbed her,[49] and a wave of anger passed through the crowd, which immediately showered the police with boos and catcalls, followed by a cry to turn the paddy wagon over.[50] Edmund White, having chanced upon the scene, noted that "the cops, used to the cringing and disorganization of gay crowds, snort off. But the crowd doesn't dis-perse."[51] Tom witnessed the same police–crowd interplay: "People began beating the wagon, booing, trying to see who was being hauled out and off. Several pigs were on guard and periodically threatened the crowd unless they moved back. Impossible to do. 'Nobody's going to fuck around with me. I ain't going to take this shit,' a guy in a dark red tee-shirt shouted, dancing in and out of the crowd." White described the temper of the crowd: "Everyone's restless, angry and high-spirited. No one has a slogan, no one even has an attitude, but something's brewing."

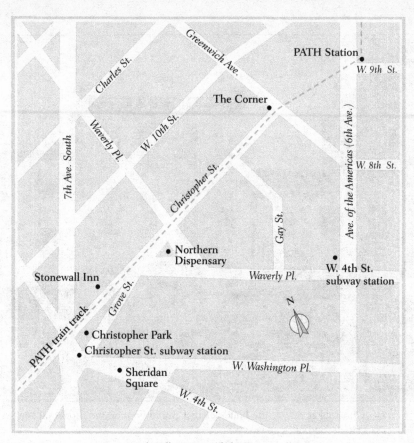

Greenwich Village around the Stonewall Inn.

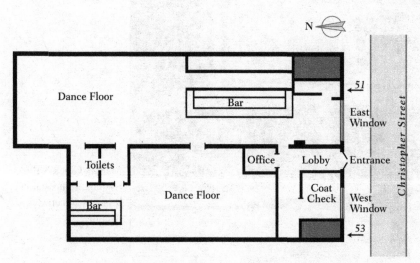

Floor plan of the Stonewall Inn, nos. 51 and 53 Christopher Street.

Nos. 51 and 53 Christopher Street, the buildings that would become the Stonewall Inn, in 1928. No. 51 is a stable, and no. 53 a bakery.

Mama's Chick'N'Rib restaurant on Charles Street at Greenwich Avenue.

Members of the Mattachine Society of New York at the bar Julius' in 1966, demanding to be served as open homosexuals. When they were denied service, Mattachine sued the State Liquor Authority. *Left to right:* John Timmons, Dick Leitsch, Craig Rodwell, and Randy Wicker.

Barbara Gittings and Randy Wicker marching in the 1966 Annual Reminder at Independence Hall, Philadelphia.

The Stonewall Inn during or shortly after the Stonewall Riots. Note the broken pane on the second-floor window just above the club's entrance.

Left: Three of the gay street youth who were in the Stonewall Riots: Tommy Lanigan-Schmidt (*top left*), Martin Boyce (*top right*), and Birdie Rivera.

Right: Gay street youth photographed in front of the Stonewall Inn during a lull in the fighting late on Saturday, the second night of the riots. *First row, left to right:* unidentified, Chris, Michelle (Michael), unidentified, unidentified, Miss New Orleans, Roger Davis, Tommy Lanigan-Schmidt. *Second row, left to right:* Sissy (with glasses), Sylvia, Black Twiggy. Perched inside window (*left to right*): unidentified, Betsy Mae Kulo.

A Gay Liberation Front march in Times Square in the fall of 1969. Jackie Hormona, among the first to fight the police at the Stonewall Riots, is on the right.

NIGHT OWL

DAILY ● NEWS

NEW YORK'S PICTURE NEWSPAPER ®

8¢
10¢ OUTSIDE I.I. AND SUBURBS

Vol. 51. No. 220   Copr. 1970 News Syndicate Co. Inc.   New York, N.Y. 10017, Monday, March 9, 1970*   WEATHER: Mostly sunny, breezy, cold.

HUNT EX-CON IN DOUBLE MURDER

— Story on Page 3

Kidnapers Free U.S. Diplomat

— Story on Page 2

Spiked on Iron Fence. Rescuers work to free man, tentatively identified as Diego Vinales, from prongs of iron fence after he leaped from second-floor window while allegedly trying to escape from Charles St. stationhouse, Greenwich Village. League and part of fence were rushed to hospital for surgery.   —*Story p. 4; other pics centerfold*

Above: Seven of the founders of the Gay Activists Alliance (GAA). *Left to right*: Arthur Evans, Fred Caballero, Arthur Bell, Peter Marlaud, Kay Tobin Lahusen, Marty Robinson, and Tom Doerr.

Left: After he was arrested in a raid on the Snake Pit, a gay club, Alfredo Vinales tried to escape from an upper floor of the Sixth Precinct police head-quarters and was impaled on a spiked fence outside. The accident enraged the gay community and ener-gized the gay liberation movement.

A GAA march in support of the Rockefeller Five. *Left to right*: Tom Doerr, Kay Tobin Lahusen, Arthur Evans, Phil Raia, Jim Owles, and Arnie Kantrowitz.

Groups from around the Northeast showed up for the 1970 Christopher Street Liberation Day march. Frank Kameny (*center, with sign*) marched with the Mattachine Society of Washington, an organization he cofounded.

Head of the Christopher Street Liberation Day march.

The end of the Christopher Street Liberation Day march at the Sheep Meadow, Central Park.

Stonewall Riots participants Jerry Hoose (*left*) and Tommy Lanigan-Schmidt were reunited after more than twenty years during a celebration at Christopher Park of the 2003 *Lawrence v. Texas* Supreme Court ruling. Since 1969 gay New Yorkers have used the site of the Stonewall Riots as a rallying place.

Gay men began to go to the many pay phones around the Sheridan Square area and call up friends, telling them to rush down to the Stonewall. Others ran throughout the neighborhood shouting that the Stonewall was being busted, and word of the raid passed through the night like a fever.[52]

Fader saw a policeman come out of the Stonewall who, though obviously "trying to disperse the crowd," had no idea about how to proceed: "He didn't know who was from the bar and who wasn't, because by then a few people had come from other areas. I was on the end of the crowd, probably closer to the Lion's Head, but close to the door. I called him a pig." Brandishing his nightstick, the policeman grabbed Fader and said, "Just say that again!" Fader's experience in many other demonstrations served him well: "I was very cool at that moment. I had some knowledge, and I thought, *I'm not going to walk into that trap. He's standing there with a revolver and a club. I'm a loser on this one.* I said, 'That would be rather silly, since you have a gun and a billy club, and I don't. I don't see any point in that!' So I remember him taking the billy club and shoving me back."

Tom noted that with every passing minute, the crowd grew angrier. "Pennies ricocheted off the van, a beer can hit the door." One reason that the crowd was becoming so angry was that they were aware that the police had other people inside the Stonewall Inn and they believed that these people were being beaten by the police. Fred Sargeant voiced this opinion soon after Friday night in a radio interview he gave to WBAI's *New Symposium II*: "The kids felt that some of the other kids were being kept inside and being beaten up by the police. I don't know whether it really happened that way or not, but the rumor spread."[53] This belief no doubt explains Tom's reporting that "the crowd . . . began shouting for different people that they knew were being held. 'We want Tommy, the blond drag queen.' Shouts went up . . . Suddenly Tommy appeared in blond wig, etc., and walked coolly out the door. Shouts and screaming. 'We want Tommy!' Tommy, not held by the pigs, smiled and suddenly took off into the crowd to the left."[54]

Rodwell, conscious as always of the Mafia exploitation of gay men, yelled, "Get the Mafia out of the bars!"

One of the drag queens about to enter the patrol wagon was Maria Ritter. "The cop who put me in was kind of teasing and flirting with me when he helped me get in. He said, 'Jesus, I can't even believe you're a boy!' I said, 'I'm not a boy! You don't understand, I'm a girl, but it's real hard for me to explain to you.' I guess he was just going by the voice and kind of like spooking me. He said, 'Come on, let's go.' I was put in a paddy wagon with a whole group of older drag queens, and I'm thinking to myself, *I'm dead.*[55] They opened the door to get a few more who were dressed in drag into the police bus, and I very gingerly stepped down and kind of shimmied out, saying, 'Excuse me.' As I was walking away the cop who put me in saw me. He said, 'Hey, you! Come over here!' He was a young guy who looked as if he was maybe interested, and I begged him, 'Please! It's my birthday; I'm eighteen. And my mother's going to kill me!' And I was crying, and my makeup was going. He almost looked the other way, kind of gave me the hand motion, and I kept walking. If he comes after me and grabs me by the scruff of the neck, he's going to do it, but if he's not, he doesn't. And he didn't."

The next bar patron to be taken from the Stonewall was a lesbian, and she was decidedly not in a good mood. The existence of this lesbian and her supposed role in the Stonewall Riots have always been among the most controversial aspects of the riots, with some prominent commentators displaying skepticism about her. It is therefore important to look closely at all the available evidence concerning her.[56] Tall and stout, with a short, mannish haircut, she was wearing pants and what one witness described as "fancy, go-to-bar drag for a butch dyke."[57] She clearly fit the role known at the time as a butch lesbian. Jennifer Hardy, who had been watching the raid from Christopher Park, remembers her as a husky "bull dyke," of "bigger size" and with a "nasty temper."[58] Steve Yates, who, like Maria Ritter, had had his birthday celebration inside the Stonewall abruptly ended by the raid, went to Christopher Park and stood outside the fence, where his friends joined him. He remembers the lesbian as a "rather beefy, good-sized woman" and a "typical New York butch."[59] Another woman who witnessed the scene and wrote about it to a friend a few days later described her similarly: "a dyke—stone butch."[60]

According to Harry Beard, a former Stonewall employee, the lesbian's fight with the police had begun inside the bar. She had been visiting a bar employee who was a friend, Beard relates, when the raid occurred. Arrested for not wearing the three pieces of clothing correct for her gender according to New York law, she was handcuffed and, while in the hallway and just a few short steps away from the entrance, was "yanked" by a policeman. She told the officer, "Don't be so rough." According to Beard, the policeman's response was to hit her in the head with a billy club.[61] (In two other versions, one given by Beard in 1980 and another one given in 1989 by Beard and two friends, Gene Huss and Don Knapp, it was a request to the police officer to loosen her cuffs that resulted in a blow to her head.[62] Yates's account might corroborate Beard's in part, for he remembers that "they were manhandling her *out the door* [emphasis added] to try to push her into a squad car." Yates also described her as "one rather beefy, good-sized woman who had probably given them a ration of shit back," which also seems to fit in with Beard's assertion that she had complained to the police while still inside the Stonewall Inn. Like Beard, Yates remembered handcuffs: "They had her pushed down with her hands cuffed behind her."[63]

There is no doubt that, furious for whatever reason, she put up a fight. Yates says, "She was giving them their money's worth," and remembers that there were three or four policemen on her. She fought them all the way from the Stonewall Inn's entrance to the back door of a waiting police car. Once inside the car, she slid back out and battled the police all the way to the Stonewall Inn's entrance. An unknown woman who recorded the scene in a letter emphasized the lesbian's fury: "Everything went along fairly peacefully until . . . a dyke . . . lost her mind in the streets of the West Village—kicking, cursing, screaming, and fighting." But after she reached the Stonewall the police pulled her back to the police car and again placed her inside it. She got out again and tried to walk away. This time an officer picked her up and heaved her inside.[64] Yates estimates that the struggle between the police and the lesbian lasted between five and ten minutes. According to yet another account, at around this time a woman—possibly this same lesbian—urged the gay men watching her struggle to help her: "Why don't you guys do something!"[65]

Bob Kohler remembers that at about this time "a couple of the kids threw some change over. I got mad and said, 'Stop throwing your money! I probably gave you that money. Stop throwing it!' The cops closed the paddy wagon, got rid of the paddy wagon, because they obviously felt something was going to happen."

As the heroic fight by the lesbian who had twice escaped the car neared its end, the crowd erupted. The anonymous author of the letter wrote that the woman's fighting "set the whole crowd wild—berserk!" Both the *Voice* reporters are agreed that it was the lesbian's struggle with the police that ignited the riot. Truscott wrote: "It was at that moment that the scene became explosive." Smith's account pinpoints the policeman bodily throwing her inside the car on the third and final attempt to put her in the vehicle as the moment "the turning point came."

The *Berkeley Barb* account seems to agree with Smith's version. Smith wrote that after the lesbian was thrown into the car, "The crowd shrieked, 'Police brutality!' 'Pigs!' A few coins sailed through the air. I covered my face. Pine ordered the three cars and paddy wagon to leave with the prisoners before the crowd became more of a mob. 'Hurry back,' he added, realizing he and his force . . . would be easily overwhelmed if the temper broke. 'Just drop them at the Sixth Precinct and hurry back.'"

Leo E. Laurence wrote, "Pigs were loading her into the wagon when she shouted to a big crowd of bystanders: 'Why don't you guys do something!' That did it. The crowd rushed the police wagon as someone yelled: 'Let's turn it over.' The pig driver drove off escaping the angry crowd."[66]

Indeed, it seems possible that it was this extremely masculine lesbian struggling with the police that *Rat* reporter Tom took for a man when he wrote that "the pigs started hauling off in a squad car a guy they had dragged outside. The crowd protested wildly, booing, shrieking, 'Up against the wall, faggots!' 'Beat it off, pigs!' A few tried jumping out to disrupt the no-man's-land between the door and the squad car, but most as yet were reticent about provoking any pig violence. Someone tried to sell me some speed, and another asked me for a knife. 'I'm gonna slice up those motherfuckers' tires.'" That the masculine-appearing lesbian was the person Tom observed seems all the more probable since he mentions that an onlooker immediately asked for a knife to "slice . . . those motherfuckers' tires," for according to Harry Beard, all four tires of the police car with the lesbian were slashed.[67]

Steve Yates and Jennifer Hardy likewise remember the lesbian's resistance as triggering the crowd's violence. Yates recalled the reaction of his friend Gino, an occasional sexual partner whom he knew only by his first name and describes as an intelligent working-class Puerto Rican "rabble-rouser": "My friend Gino had had considerably too much to drink at this point, and he started yelling at the police. They'd started dragging a woman out in handcuffs, and he started yelling at them to 'let her go! Leave her alone!' and people started yelling for them to 'let her alone,' 'Leave her alone,' 'Let her go!' I never knew her name or knew anything about her. I just remember that was the thing that Gino saw that he just could not [bear to] see. He saw it as a great injustice. There was a loose cobblestone in the pit [surrounding] a tree." Gino, who sometimes labored as a construction worker, became so enraged by the woman's mistreatment that he wrenched the heavy cobblestone out of the ground and threw it all the way across Christopher Street. It landed on the trunk of a police car with a terrible screech, "scaring the shit" out of a policeman who was standing next to the car, says Yates. "That's when the police backed in and barricaded themselves in the Stonewall."[68]

Hardy's recollection agrees with Yates's in that they both depict a gradual buildup of the crowd's anger that suddenly let loose in a violent outburst: "It just seemed like the catalyst for the whole thing to break loose was her getting out of the car and screaming and getting shoved back or thrown back into the car and then getting out again, because she was getting real pissed off. And the crowd started getting real ugly and bigger. The fun mood disappeared real fast and people started shouting. And then all of a sudden somebody said, 'Let's get 'em!' And cops just vanished."[69]

Indeed, while there seems no doubt that the lesbian who twice escaped the police car played a leading role in increasing the crowd's anger that Saturday morning in June, it seems very probable that more than one lesbian was seen resisting the police that night outside the Stonewall Inn—or was being mistreated by the police—and also contributed to the crowd's anger. Kevin Dunn, who had seen a fair percentage of the gay men leaving the Stonewall Inn camping and posing, noticed that "the lesbians who came out were not in a good humor to do a little pose. They were resistant about being busted. And they had a more serious tone, being arrested. . . . The lesbians had been thrown in . . . and sealed [inside the patrol wagon][70] and not let go of, [and] the crowd seemed to get pretty ornery about that. It was like 'Don't do this to these ladies!' It was sort of chauvinistic in a way, but it was very interesting that they got angrier, it seemed, when the lesbians were thrown in."[71] And just as Philip Eagles had seen a small clutch of lesbians inside the club, he also remembers there being more than one outside. He and his friends had gone across the street from the Stonewall Inn and stood on the sidewalk next to Christopher Park to watch what would happen. "The paddy wagon was eventually driven up in front of the bar and parked on the park side of Christopher rather than on the bar side and drag queens were pushed into the paddy wagon and the cops were roughing up some of the lesbians. I believe one of them was hurt or was bloodied to some extent. Of course, the butch lesbians were among the first to start fighting back as I remember . . . and so they were getting beaten and hit."[72]

There is no doubt, however, that at this stage of the evening many things were happening simultaneously in the angry crowd. One of the events that further stoked the crowd's fury revolved around Ray Castro. After he had been allowed to leave the club, Ray had walked around a bit and then returned to the front of the Stonewall Inn. When one of the doors opened he spotted a friend much younger than himself inside who gestured to him in a manner that said to Ray, *Do something!* Ray surmised that his friend was fearful because he did not have ID on him. Castro decided that he would try to find someone in the crowd with some phony ID so that he could go back inside and give it to his worried friend. But before Ray could do anything at all he suddenly found himself being pushed by plainclothes police.

"At that point I started pushing back and wound up with two plainclothes police pushing me. The next thing I know, there's two plainclothes cops and two uniformed police in the melee. I was knocked to the ground by one of their billy clubs, [which,] put between my legs, tripped me. At that point the handcuffs got put on me, and they had a paddy wagon right in front of the entrance to the Stonewall. When I got shoved up to the door of the paddy wagon, I had two policemen on each side of me. I didn't quite go willingly into the paddy wagon. I didn't want to be arrested. Even though I was handcuffed, I jumped up and [put] one foot on the right of the door, and one foot on the left of the door. I sprung up like a jumping jack and pushed backwards, knocking the police down to the ground, almost against the wall of the Stonewall. Well, they finally dragged me into the paddy wagon."

Ray's fierce struggle with the police was recorded by Tom: "A couple more were thrown into the van. We joined in with some who wanted to storm the van, free those inside, then turn over the van. But nobody was yet prepared for that kind of action. Then a scuffle at the door. One guy refused to be put into the van. Five or six cops guarding the van tried to subdue him with little success. Several guys tried to help free him. Unguarded, three or four of those in the van appeared then quickly disappeared into the crowd. This was all anyone needed."[73]

Fader recalls seeing some of those he had seen placed in the patrol wagon earlier escape. "The police were undermanned; they had big crowds forming. They thought everybody would just quietly go away and they'd be all matter-of-fact, but no one was in the mood to sit and be good or do whatever the cops told them to do." Fader saw the police "leave the van unattended—the doors were open, so they left." His account concurs with Tom's that the prisoners' escape excited the crowd. "That raised the emotional level, the excitement of them getting away."

Manford also witnessed prisoners being left unattended but felt that the officers had done so on purpose. "After everybody who was going to be released was, the prisoners were herded into a paddy wagon parked right on the sidewalk in front of the bar. They were left unguarded by the local police, and they simply walked out and left the paddy wagon to the cheer of the throng. There's no doubt in my mind that those people were deliberately left unguarded."[74]

It seems certain that one of the escaped prisoners was blackmailer and Stonewall manager Ed Murphy. As Murphy told the story, he was handcuffed to "Frankie" (very likely Blond Frankie) and the two escaped into the crowd and then took a taxi down to Keller's, where an S and M queen was able to free them from the handcuffs. Manford's belief that the police allowed prisoners to escape seems plausible when one considers that the Sixth Precinct was paid off handsomely by the Stonewall Inn and some of the police present must have known Murphy's role in paying them off. Furthermore, letting the prisoners escape may have been retaliation for Pine's not informing them of a raid in their precinct in advance.[75]

While at this point in the night a full-scale riot was probably inevitable, Tom credited Castro's struggle with assuring that violence did erupt.

"Several others tried [assisting][76] the guy held by the cops," Tom wrote, "but the latter escaped into the Stonewall. Soon the van pulled out leaving the street unguarded. A few pigs outside had to flee for their lives inside and barricade themselves in. It was too good to be true. The crowd took the offensive."

Danny Garvin recalls that it was the police pushing back at the crowd, some of whom were throwing money and other projectiles at the officers, that caused the gay throng to make a useful discovery: a large stack of new bricks at a construction site on Seventh Avenue South. "All of a sudden a cop would get hit, so there'd be an attitude. Then anger would start on each side. The cops then started to get a little bit physical. They would come at us with nightsticks, and we would have to disperse onto Seventh Avenue, where the people were able to see the bricks."

As the paddy wagon left, it was accompanied by three police cars with their sirens screaming. The crowd, however, was beyond being intimidated by mere sirens and the caravan had to push slowly through the furious protesters, who, enraged, pounded on the police vehicles.[77] Danny Garvin recalls the noise as "people would run over, grab the paddy wagon, and start shaking—ba-boom! ba-boom!!" Truscott heard the "cry [that] went up to push the paddywagon over, but it drove away before anything could happen. With its exit, the action waned momentarily."[78]

At least one—and perhaps more—of these vehicles had some of its tires slashed, slowing them down further.[79] Pine, noticing that the crowd was getting out of control, urgently told one of the departing drivers, "Hurry back! Just drop them at the Sixth Precinct and hurry back!"[80] After the police vehicles left for the station house, Pine had eight plainclothes detectives with him, including the two undercover policewomen who had been sent in ahead of the raid[81] and Gil Weissman, a police officer from the Sixth Precinct.[82] Weissman stayed behind with Pine and the initial raiding party, making him the only uniformed police officer left on the scene.[83]

Dave Van Ronk, a prominent folksinger, was yet a third person out celebrating his birthday on that discordant evening.[84] Two female friends had taken him out for dinner and drinks at the Lion's Head, Van Ronk's favorite watering hole, just two doors down from the Stonewall Inn. Sitting in the dining room of the basement establishment, he heard the wail of the departing police cars but, being a New Yorker, thought nothing of it. But then he began to hear "a lot of yelling and screaming" and saw people running in the street, though from his limited view out of the basement window he could see only feet and legs from the knees down. His curiosity piqued, he decided to step outside. His companions tried to discourage him, but he assured them, "I'll be right back."

Once outside he asked a man in the crowd what was happening and learned that the Stonewall had been raided. "Somebody was yelling out that they didn't pay off the cops." But then "somebody [else] said, 'Let's pay them off!' and started to throw change at them." The rain of coins began with pennies, which made pinging sounds as they hit the pavement and the Stonewall Inn's windows,[85] accompanied by jeers[86] and the shout of "Dirty Copper!"[87] While the heterosexual Van Ronk had never thought much about gay rights, he did not side with the police. "I had been involved in antiwar demonstrations where the police descended on us like armed locusts. What I saw was yet another example of police arrogance and corruption. As far as I was concerned, anybody who'd stand against the cops was all right with me, and that's why I stayed. The cops had made themselves fairly unpopular over the years with tear gas, with dogs. Every time you turned around the cops were pulling some outrage or another. I reached in my pocket and tossed a quarter or just some pennies and around that time the heavy artillery cut in. I assume that some of the street people in the park had decided to join the fray because beer cans started flying over our heads."

Shouts of "Pigs!" and "Faggot cops!" filled the night air.

As pennies and dimes pelted him, Howard Smith backed up against the Stonewall Inn's door. He noticed that by now the detectives held "at most a 10-foot clearing."

Nickels were the next thing to be thrown.

Followed by quarters.

A glass bottle was lobbed.

Then another one came flying through the dark air. And another.[88]

A flying object clipped Gil Weissman under the right eye.[89] "He hollers, and his hand comes away scarlet. . . . They (the police) are all suddenly furious," Smith wrote. Three of the officers ran into the crowd to try to scare the rioters away from the door.[90] A beer can glanced off Deputy Inspector Smythe's head.

Van Ronk decided that "around that time, I guess I'd seen all I needed to, and I thought I'd go back and have a drink and tell my friends what was going on." But at that very moment Seymour Pine suddenly leaped into the middle of the crowd and grabbed him around the waist.[91] The musician fell backward, pulling Pine down to the ground with him.[92] Van Ronk decided to put up a fight, rather than be arrested. With the help of two police officers, Pine succeeded in separating Van Ronk from the crowd and hauled him inside the Stonewall Inn.[93]

Van Ronk pointed out that at six-feet-five, "I'm pretty conspicuous—I was one of the first ones they grabbed." While Van Ronk did not precisely remember the others who were seized by the police, he felt certain that the officers did arrest several other protesters around the same time they arrested him.

Pine's version of why he arrested Van Ronk is quite different: "They were coming up and flipping coins into the faces of the policemen. I saw this one fellow come up and do that, and he hit the patrolman in the eye. He reached for his eye, and when he took it away there was blood. And when this fellow saw it, he got pretty nervous, and he immediately ran back into the crowd. And I went right after him."

The cops hauled Van Ronk, his head banging against the ground,[94] into the Stonewall Inn's front room, where they placed a handcuff on his left hand and attached the other end of the handcuff to the flange of a radiator, close to the floor. Van Ronk said he was then kicked several times.[95] He ruefully noted the irony that, handcuffed and lying on the floor, "from there on all I could get was a worm's-eye view. The episode ended as it began for me, looking at legs."

Having secured Van Ronk inside the Stonewall Inn, Pine exited the club to survey the situation. As all kinds of objects continued to crash around the police, Pine decided that his only recourse was to take refuge inside the Stonewall Inn: it was either that or risk being assaulted by a wild mob. The crowd had begun to sense the policemen's fear. Tom wrote: "A few plainclothesmen were surveying the crowd, obviously panicked," while Ronnie Di Brienza wrote in the *East Village Other* that "during the height of the action, you could see the fear and disbelief on the faces of the pigs."

Pine recalls that immediately after he hauled Van Ronk out of the crowd, "he [Van Ronk] was rushed inside the place. In the meantime we [the police] were right near the windows, near the doors . . . And then it got so bad I ordered them back into the Stonewall." Pine told his officers, "Let's get inside. Lock ourselves inside; it's safer." Before retreating inside the Stonewall, Pine turned to Howard Smith and, with a paternal tone, asked him, "You want to come in? You're probably safer."[96]

Smith felt confused by Pine's offer but knew that he had little time to choose between two clear alternatives. Smith debated in his mind, "If they go in and I stay out, will the mob know that the blue plastic thing hanging from my shirt is a press card, or by now will they assume I'm a cop too? On the other hand, it might be interesting to be locked in with a few cops, just rapping and reviewing how they work. In goes me."[97] When Smith made his choice, he thought reinforcements would arrive in a few minutes, so the risk seemed negligible. Besides, Smith had always liked seeing things closer than other people. That's why he had gotten police plates on his car, so that he could pursue anything that looked interesting.

"Oh, I'll go inside," Smith told Pine.

"Fine," Pine answered. "Come on. Right now."[98]

Smith hastened to join Pine, Smythe, Weissman, the two undercover policewomen, the four other plainclothes morals officers, and Consumer Affairs inspector Adam Tatem as they quickly retreated inside the Stonewall Inn and shut its doors.

9

Lancing the Festering
Wound of Anger

Howard Smith had never been inside the Stonewall Inn and was immediately struck by how dark and dank it was and how strongly it smelled of beer. As soon as Pine and his officers had closed the club's doors, they used the tables inside to barricade the doors. Tables and other objects were also piled up behind the wooden structures inside the Stonewall Inn's windows to reinforce them:[1] the police were now using the very plywood forms reinforced with two-by-fours to try to keep gay people on the outside that the Mafia had built to keep the police out.

But the objects used as barricades proved poor insulation against the crowd's rage, for at this time, in Pine's own words, "all hell broke loose." He called again for assistance over his portable radio and again got no response.

While Smith had taken refuge with the police inside the Stonewall Inn, Truscott had climbed on top of a residential garbage can next to the stoop Craig Rodwell and Fred Sargeant had mounted earlier to get a better view of the action. There Truscott witnessed the immediate reaction to the police retreat: "The exit left no cops on the street, and almost by signal the crowd erupted into cobblestone and bottle heaving."[2] Indeed, Truscott almost fell to the sidewalk when two men whisked the garbage can he was standing on from under his feet and threw it through the Stonewall Inn's west window, where it sat, supported by the window ledge.[3]

"Some of those guys on the streets [had been] pushing the sides of the paddy wagon and rocking it back and forth and stuff. [When] they pulled the paddy wagon away, they threw the garbage cans through the window.

When they threw the garbage cans through the window, that was it. Until then there was just a bunch of people in the street yelling and raising hell."[4]

A general assault now began on the Stonewall Inn using anything and everything the crowd outside could get its hands on: garbage, garbage cans, pieces of glass, fire, bricks, cobblestones, and an improvised battering ram were all used to attack the police holed up inside the Stonewall Inn. This was the high point of the violence on the part of the crowd of what would become known as the Stonewall Riots, a fury aimed at the police inside the Stonewall Inn, as if all those in the crowd assembled that night on Christopher Street had decided to personally revolt against the police to express a collective *cri de coeur*.

Michael Fader remembers it this way: "We all had a collective feeling like we'd had enough of this kind of shit. It wasn't anything tangible anybody said to anyone else, it was just kind of like everything over the years had come to a head on that one particular night in the one particular place, and it was not an organized demonstration. It was spontaneous. That was the part that was wonderful.

"Everyone in the crowd felt that we were never going to go back. It was like the last straw. It was time to reclaim something that had always been taken from us. It was something that just happened. All kinds of people, all different reasons, but mostly it was total outrage, anger, sorrow, everything combined, and everything just kind of ran its course. It was the police who were doing most of the destruction. We were really trying to get back in and break it free. And we felt that we had freedom at last, or freedom to at least show that we demanded freedom. We didn't really have the freedom totally, but we weren't going to be walking meekly in the night and letting them shove us around—it's like standing your ground for the first time and in a really strong way, and that's what caught the police by surprise. There was something in the air, freedom a long time overdue, and we're going to fight for it. It took different forms, but the bottom line was, we weren't going to go away. And we didn't."[5]

The police, who had blithely assumed that since they were just dealing with a bunch of fairies they would be unchallenged, found that it was as if the fey beings had suddenly and inexplicably metamorphosed into raging tigers. Pine, author of the U.S. Army's manual for hand-to-hand combat in World War II and victim of a mine explosion in the bloody Battle of the Bulge, said simply, "There was never any time that I felt more scared than I felt that night."[6] Pine's partner, Charles Smythe, who had fought alongside him in Africa and Sicily in World War II, would recall "I was still shaking an hour later. Believe me, I've never seen anything like it."[7]

While Truscott saw—indeed, felt—the garbage can being thrown, according to *Rat* reporter Tom, it was the man in the dark red tee-shirt Tom had earlier seen dancing in and out of the crowd who had the honor of throwing the opening volley after the police retreated inside the Stonewall Inn: "The cat in the tee-shirt began by hurling a container of something at the door. Then a can or stone cracked a window. Soon pandemonium broke loose." Morty Manford recalled watching one of the second-floor windows above the Stonewall Inn break: "With the shattering of glass the crowd [went] 'Ooooh!'"[8] For Manford, the breaking of the glass was "a dramatic gesture of defiance. . . . We had just been kicked and punched around symbolically by the police. They weren't doing this at heterosexual bars. And it's not my fault that the local bar is run by organized crime and is taking payoffs and doesn't have a liquor license." When Manford saw the window break, "there was a slight lancing of the festering wound of anger at this kind of unfair harassment and prejudice."[9]

Whether the anonymous man in the dark red tee-shirt was the first to throw something as the riot reached its climactic stage on Friday night or not, people closer to the street played a key role in unleashing the crowd's fury. Kevin Dunn, a nineteen-year-old gay man, dressed in hippie attire and a true believer in the peace movement, recalls how he stood thinking to himself, "'I'm sick of being told I'm sick' and went to grab something—I don't know if it was a halfway-filled milk carton—it was some kind of a carton—and I was just about ready to throw it, but I stopped and said, 'But you're not supposed to be violent, you're against violence.'" But as Kevin hesitated, "a big, hunky, nice-looking Puerto Rican guy—but big mouth—yelling out (at the police) next to me . . . took that thing out of my hand and threw it! And it was one of the first things that got thrown at the Stonewall. And I just thought after he did that, 'Ah, what the hell! Yeah!' And then I started scrambling to pick up whatever I could find." Indeed, the street element seems to have been critical from the riot's inception. According to Bruce Voeller, shortly after the police let the Stonewall patrons not under arrest leave the club, "a crowd gathered and some of the watchers jeered the police. After a few interchanges, a young Puerto Rican taunted the gays, asking why they put up with being shoved around by cops." Voeller goes on to write that according to some accounts, it was this same Puerto Rican who unleashed the barrage of objects thrown at the police by hurling a beer can, adding that it is possible that the young man was not gay.[10]

Bob Kohler agrees that the street element was important but credits the gay street kids he knew from Christopher Park: "Billy was standing next to me, and I remember the first thing, Billy started to run and I grabbed him, because Billy had a court case pending. I said, 'Stay out of this, Billy! Don't get involved!' because it just looked like it was going to be a little skirmish kind of thing. You had suddenly the taunts. It wasn't, 'Oh, there's the girls in blue.' It was nasty, and suddenly all kinds of things were being thrown. Garbage was being thrown, cans. People were fighting. People were yelling. I just remember suddenly the mood getting very ugly. I remember being taken off guard and being scared, because people were sort of running towards the cops, and it was obvious that there was going to be trouble. That I saw. A lot of the street kids started to run towards the Stonewall." Before they took off, many of them handed him their stolen wallets, credit cards, and "so-called diamond rings."

That at least three of these street kids were literally on the front line of this action is documented by a photograph taken that night by freelance photographer Joseph Ambrosini. The caption underneath the photograph—published in the Sunday edition of the New York *Daily News* just a little more than twenty-four hours after the riot began—describes the photo as showing the crowd attempting to "impede police arrests outside the Stonewall Inn." On the left of the photograph is Jackie Hormona, face-to-face with a police officer, his left hand reaching toward the officer. To his right one sees the feminine young man Tommy knew from the street with the plucked or shaved eyebrows. To the right of that youth stands the young man Tommy always saw wearing a coat or suit and usually a tie. The face of this young man, who sports a Beatles haircut, is partly obscured by another youth with his back to the camera. In addition to this photographic evidence regarding the role played by the street kids on Friday night, there is the memory of Jerry Hoose, who was summoned there by a phone call from his close friend John Goodman. Goodman told Hoose on his arrival at the scene "that Hormona had kicked a cop, maybe, or punched a cop and then threw something through the window, and then everybody got going. But he was there and he attributed it to Jackie, and I believe that because she was a lunatic. And all the other queens like Zazu Nova Queen of Sex and Marsha P. Johnson had got involved. It wasn't just the drag queens; it was the street people outside of the Stonewall."[11]

Many other credible witnesses offer similar testimony concerning the gay street youth. Lanigan-Schmidt says, "What I know definitely from my own experience is that the people who did the most fighting were the drag queens and the hustlers. [They] fought with the same ferocity they would fight with when any situation of survival put their sense of dignity on the line, very much like Bob Dylan's 'When you ain't got nothing, you got nothing to lose.'"

It is as if on the morning of June 28, 1969, America symbolically got back the anger she had created by her neglect of her most despised children: the fairies, queens, and nelly boys she had so utterly abandoned, saying she did not want them.

The question of transvestite participation in the riots is complicated by differences in the gay male community that have developed since the Stonewall Riots. Scare and flame queens hardly exist anymore, and Garvin insists that it was flame queens who contributed most to the fighting: "When people say, you know, it was the drag queens that started it, it wasn't the drag queens, it was the flame queens. The ones who were getting angriest and giving attitude were the flame queens." While Fader is a credible witness who says that "no one group did any more bravery than any other group that I saw," the preponderance of witnesses who are both credible and who witnessed significant amounts of the action agree that the most marginal groups of the gay community fought the hardest—and therefore risked the most—on this and the following nights. (It is worth noting in this context that the lesbian who set the crowd afire with her physical courage was, from all available evidence, non-gender-conforming and, very possibly, transgendered, to use today's parlance.)

Still, it is important to note that it was not only homeless or street youths who were fighting the police. Men like Robert Bryan, a middle-class college graduate, joined the fray. According to him, just before the police barricaded themselves inside the Stonewall, "every so often, they would sort of reach out and grab somebody from the crowd and pull them in, and they were beating them in the doorway with clubs. They had a circle around; they'd grab somebody at random and beat them in the doorway. I was so appalled at what was going on that I came running up behind one of these policemen who was bent over with a club and, with all my force, kicked him in the seat and knocked him over. Well, at this point, one of the policemen charged out of the crowd after me, and I took off, running. He chased me four or five blocks, almost all the way home to Thompson Street, and I finally escaped from him."

John O'Brien says that three groups were "going after the police": "You had an underclass of kids who were either hustlers or homeless and a few people like me who were political agitators and troublemakers. Fortunately that inspired some others who were students, which made up the other element of people."

While it seems beyond dispute that most of the acts of violence during the riots were committed by the more marginalized members of the gay and lesbian community, it is evident that when the police retreated into the Stonewall Inn everybody outside was angry. As Craig Rodwell recalled: "[After the police drove off in the paddy wagon] there was just like a flash of group—of mass anger. . . . And this may be five or six hundred people."

Truscott wrote that "the crowd erupted into cobblestone and bottle heaving."[12]

Manford recalled: "And it escalated. A few more rocks went and then somebody from inside the bar opened the door and stuck a gun out. Their arm was reaching out with a gun telling people to stay back. And then withdrew the gun, closed the door and went back inside."[13]

Inside the Stonewall Inn, Howard Smith heard "the shattering of windows, followed by what we imagine to be bricks pounding on the door, voices yelling. The floor shudders at each blow." As the crowd of hundreds shouted "Gay power!" and "We want freedom!" garbage cans, bottles, beer cans, and any and everything else that could be found was hurled at the Stonewall Inn.[14] Pine recalls how "now they really in earnest started to come after us. We covered everything [but] whatever we could find to put up against the windows and the doors didn't last very long. They began to batter this down and made some holes."

Smith and the police "found little holes in the wood [behind the Stonewall's windows], little peepholes, so we could look out into the street to see how big the crowd was without getting hurt because they wouldn't know we'd be looking through these little pinholes. And I took my turn and looked out. And the crowd was enormous by then." To Smith, it seemed like thousands of people.

Smith asked Pine, "Where are the reinforcements?"

"I don't know. There must be some mix-up," Pine answered.

Smith had the impression that Pine did not even want to talk about it.

As the caravan of police vehicles departed the Stonewall Inn with their prisoners, John O'Brien, out for his usual Friday night recreation of debating politics while cruising, heard the sirens but, like Dave Van Ronk, thought nothing of it. However, when O'Brien saw some young men running down Waverly Place, his interest was piqued enough to ask them what was going on. When they explained to him that the police were raiding the bars and that they were escaping, he decided to walk up Christopher Street and take a look for himself. When he arrived he walked over to the sidewalk on the north side of Christopher Park and saw an enraged crowd yelling and throwing a barrage of objects at the Stonewall Inn. When it was explained to him that the police had raided the club and were now trapped inside, O'Brien needed no further encouragement to join in.[15]

One of the first things O'Brien saw after he arrived at the scene was men stuffing pieces of paper into cracks at the bottom of the plywood inside the Stonewall's window and holding cigarette lighters to them. Seasoned street fighter that he was, O'Brien could hardly believe his eyes as he watched the youths deploy their lighters. "Some people went up to it, they'd light it, they'd run away." But at this point in the evening O'Brien says that very few people stood directly in front of the Stonewall for long, because they feared the police might fire on the crowd. "There was a little bit of unsureness about what's next, and everybody just played on the spontaneity of what happened right before that." O'Brien thinks at this point people in the crowd were "just egg[ing] each other on. We wanted to outdo the last person. . . . Nobody knew how far this was going to go." Just as Garvin recalls bricks being used for work on a building, O'Brien remembers that work on the street was being done on Seventh Avenue South close to the Christopher Street subway station and this made it easier to uproot cobblestones, which "played an important part . . . [when] people went looking for [something to escalate with]."

O'Brien noticed a group of people on the sidewalk who were trying to uproot the parking meter that the street kids used to swing on, first trying to dig it out of the ground and then rocking it back and forth to free it from the sidewalk.[16] The men wrestling with the meter looked like street people to John. "One was a dirty blondish-brownish biker type, and a couple of other guys like that. One muscular guy who was with a couple of other guys working together got it out of the ground."[17]

Several gay men now used the parking meter as a battering ram on the Stonewall Inn's doors. Danny Garvin remembers that the use of the converted parking meter got an enthusiastic response from the crowd: "It was like, 'Okay! Boom! Boom!'" It took more than one attack, however, on the Stonewall Inn's doors to force them open. As the men continued to pound the heavy doors with the parking meter, others in the crowd grabbed whatever they could find to throw. The attack on the police created a cacophony as the sounds of glass shattering up and down the street mixed with the pounding of the parking meter on the doors, while cries of "Liberate the bar!" filled the air.[18] All this was punctuated by breaking bottles thrown at the demonstrators from apartment dwellers along Grove Street who wanted to get some sleep.[19] White witnessed the continuing assault on the Stonewall's doors: "The ramming continues; the boys back up to the park fence, take a flying start, collide with the door as the crowd cheers wildly. Cries of 'We're the pink panthers!' A mad Negro queen whirls like a dervish with a twisted piece of metal in her hand and breaks the remaining windows. The doors begin to give."[20]

Several observers insist that the crowd only wanted to get back inside the Stonewall Inn to continue partying, implying that the riots had no political or historical meaning. Such a reading ignores the deeper side of this instinctual reaction of the crowd, who sensed that something valuable to them was being taken away and reacted accordingly. (Seymour Pine's intention was to shut the Stonewall down for good.) Fader explains this with considerable insight: "The crowd was really wanting to bust in and go back in; it was that strong a feeling. We felt like we'd been booted out of our home for no reason. . . . And the police were in there, and they weren't coming out. We wanted to get back at them somehow. And of course there was no way to really do that with guys who have guns and sticks, and the best we could do, and there was not too much to deal with—pavement stones and people throwing [things]—they didn't have the equipment, so that's why they used a parking meter as a battering ram. We wanted really as [much as] one could without equipment to go after the police and free the Stonewall or whatever you want to call it. And of course you couldn't. People were throwing rocks and different kinds of things. They were symbolic gestures, and they were enough. It was a spontaneous thing. It was a totally emotional—everyone having to live this life where we had to sneak in and all of that stuff, and then the place that everybody likes, to have it taken away in such a brutal way, we wanted to try and rectify this somehow to make it right and get back."

Inside the Stonewall Inn, the police and Howard Smith grew more anxious when they heard the windows being shattered, and then a loud banging made by what Smith assumed to be "bricks pounding on the door," all mixed in with yelling voices. Smith felt the floor shudder at each blow the doors received.

"Aren't you guys scared?" he asked.

The police answered that no, they weren't, but Smith noticed that they looked "at least uneasy."[21]

The night reverberated again with the boom of the parking meter on the Stonewall's doors.

While most of the crowd were expressing their anger at the police, Tommy Lanigan-Schmidt stood in wonder as he watched the scene unfolding in front of him. To Tommy, who thought naturally in terms of biblical allegories and art criticism, the big double doors of the Stonewall Inn seemed like church doors, so that when he saw them drawn shut by the policemen who had retreated inside the club, he had begun to wait. He wasn't clear exactly what it was he was waiting for but at the same time felt he was waiting "for something that you know is going to happen." Dim echoes of memories from a night years past had suddenly begun to resound inside him.

In the middle of the night: death, and a crowd that has been made to leave a building goes outside and, reluctant to leave, mills around, waiting. Words are chanted over and over, faster and faster. The yellow flames of lit candles. At the chanting's climax the priest bangs loudly on the double doors, which suddenly spring open. It is the Resurrection.

With a final loud blast, the doors of the Stonewall Inn swung wide open.[22]

Suddenly Tommy felt that it was Easter again: a new beginning in the middle of the night.

Meanwhile, Bob Kohler, still standing next to the park fence, noticed several people in the park quietly and methodically pouring a liquid into several empty Coke bottles, a couple of which were distributed by a man he knew by sight, who kept the rest of the bottles for himself.[23]

As the mayhem continued, the police inside stayed busy as they tried to keep the Stonewall's doors shut, for the mob attacked the doors again each time the police closed them. Each time the doors opened, the crowd threw all kinds of objects inside at the police. Smith wrote that "bottles and beer cans fly inside. Pine and his men immediately rush to shut it."[24] On at least one occasion, "[a] customer in the crowd picked up a shard of glass from the smashed windows and lobbed it inside. It bounced off the inner wall."[25]

Outside the Stonewall Inn, pandemonium reigned as the protesters gave full vent to their fury. Martin Boyce, who spent much of this evening with his friends Tommy Lanigan-Schmidt and Birdie Rivera, recalls how "all of a sudden the whole street now had had it, and windows started cracking, and people attacked cars and moved cars back and forth, but let the straight people out, who were in terror, really, but nobody hurt them, ever. It's amazing how controlled the rage was, even though it was so hard. This black bus driver, I remember, was caught in the middle. He was laughing, but nervously. I don't think they'd ever seen anything like that, and we hadn't either.

"Birdie was a natural-born fighter. If she could grab something, no matter what, Birdie was going to get in on it. And Birdie grabbed some oranges and spread them across this car's windshield. I was saying, 'All right, girl, go! That's my sister! Now, that's the sister I love!' But the guy inside opened the door [saying], 'You motherfuckin' bitch!'" Birdie and Boyce had assumed that because the driver was conventionally masculine-looking he was straight. They both suddenly realized that Birdie had picked on a fellow gay man in error. At that point, they both fled the enraged driver.

The riot had its surreal moments. The gay street youth kept running up to Bob Kohler now and then, loading him down with wallets and various other stolen goods. Trying to hold on to his armfuls of contraband, keep his dog, Magoo, from escaping, while restraining Billy from joining in the mayhem, Kohler at times resembled a circus clown who was pulling off an especially tricky balancing act.[26]

Somewhere around this time, Craig Rodwell and Fred Sargeant called the *New York Post,* the *Daily News,* and *The New York Times* "because we wanted to make sure this got in the papers." Craig explained, "I immediately knew that this was the spark we had been waiting for for years."[27]

The police's problem became even more complicated when the rioters started battering the Stonewall's west window's wooden subwall with the parking meter. "One of the big plywood windows gives, and it seems inevitable that the mob will pour in. A kind of tribal adrenaline rush bolsters all of us; they all take out and check pistols. I see both policewomen busy doing the same, and the danger becomes even more real," Smith wrote. Inside the Stonewall Inn, the wooden wall having almost given in so terrified Smith that, having visions of being trampled by the mob, he went searching for a weapon behind the Stonewall's long bar. There he managed to find a fire ax next to a fire hose on the wall. He quickly stuck it under his belt "like a scimitar because I wanted to keep writing notes, and Pine found that very funny."[28]

Pine's mood changed quickly when he realized how vulnerable he and his men were. "We shut the doors and tried to barricade them with tables that were in the place, and we tried to pile things up against the plywood that was backing up the windows. They broke all the windows and crashed open doors regardless. And it was at that point that I realized that my men were very nervous. And I was very apprehensive."

Outside, Kohler saw a bottle go sailing through the air and land in the Stonewall Inn, followed by a small trail of smoke emerging from the club.

The "Molotov cocktails" that the crowd began to throw into the Stonewall made Pine and his officers even more anxious: "There were bottles that came in that exploded with some kind of flame, and we were able to put those out with the fire hose that we had. We were very worried because we didn't know how long we could put these Molotov cocktails out, because they were gasoline and all we had was water. They didn't have the kind of fire extinguishers that would put out a fuel fire."

Dick Leitsch, who had cut short his packing and rushed downtown as soon as he heard about the rioting on the radio, attests to the kind of fuel being used on the Stonewall Inn: "I saw [a rioter] take a can of lighter fluid, a Ronson or something, out of his pocket and squirt it all over this plywood, over the front window of Stonewall, and put a match to it. So there were flames. They were blue and had little yellow tips, and lighter fluid is very combustible. It burns, and it's gone."[29]

Pine had no way of knowing what substance was contained in the bottles landing inside the Stonewall Inn. Given all the tension that Pine and his officers were already under, it is easy to see how they might have feared that they were in danger of dying in a conflagration.

This fear for their lives combined with the inability to communicate with the outside world put the police and Howard Smith in a frantic frame of mind: "Every time we tried to use the [portable] radio to call for assistance, a message came back, 'Disregard that call.' Somebody else apparently had our frequency in the crowd, and so we couldn't get a message through. The phone lines apparently were cut, because we couldn't use the phone."

Pine's men found the fire hose on the wall and a fire extinguisher nearby.

They unrolled the hose and used it and the extinguisher to put out the fires caused by the bottles that were lobbed inside at them.[30] However, the fire extinguisher was soon empty, leaving the police inside the Stonewall with only water to fight what Pine and his officers believed to be gasoline bombs. Spontaneously all the law enforcement agents—including the women—took their pistols out. Pine surveyed the officers under his command: "Everybody was lined up and they had their guns out, and that's when I became frightened that they would shoot, and I ordered them not to shoot, that I would be the first. You're so tense and it's the easiest thing in the world for a shot to go off at that time, and one shot going off will start everybody else off. That's what I feared, because the people were so close to us that there would have been people killed over nothing. The crime that we were arresting anybody for that night didn't warrant anybody losing his life for, and I was afraid that that's what was going to happen. I don't think there was anybody there who wasn't really perspiring—I mean *really* sweating—because it was touch and go."

The fear of a fiery death, the great din of voices from outside, and the incessant reverberations from metal and rock pounding against the walls and doors of the club were about to overwhelm the police officers when an old war memory suddenly reawakened inside Pine: "It came back to me as if it was yesterday . . . this tremendous fright, where everybody is crapping in his pants. And this was a situation that was equivalent to that."

Pine now knew what he had to do. "I went down the line with the policemen, and I started to call each man by name: 'How do you feel, Joe?'" As he addressed each officer, Pine placed his hand on him. "And they all answered. It's the only way you break the tension, once there was physical contact between them and they have to answer you, 'cause you're holding your breath.

"Then I got to the reporter, who was standing there with a fire ax in his hand, and I asked him how he was, and he said, 'I'm okay, but I'd feel a lot better if you had the ax and I had the gun.'"

Even with Pine's cool head and leadership, it was still hard for the police to withhold their fire, for in such a tense situation time seems to pass much more slowly than in ordinary life. At one point, one of the officers stationed at the Stonewall's entrance momentarily lost his composure and threw his revolver at the crowd. It hit the door frame and landed on the ground.[31] Pine remembers why the situation was so difficult: "I knew that at any moment it could break into a real killing. It was very hard to keep holding while they were attacking and you were doing nothing."

But Pine also knew the dangers of not "doing nothing": "I'd been in war situations where somebody panics and, instead of holding fire, shoots; and once that first shot is off, everybody lets go." Even so, Pine felt that if they had fired, they still would have been killed: "If they would have broken through, no matter what we would've fired they would've continued going. It's the old riot situation: the people from the back don't know what's going on in front and they keep going and we would've been killed." Smith exactly shared Pine's estimate of the situation: "It looked like they [the police] were gonna be killed. Because what if the crowd did break through and he yelled: 'Fire!' I don't think that would have mattered. There were so many people in the mob, only the people in the front would be hit and then we'd be overrun. I don't think firing would have saved anyone's life. It looked that enraged, the mob." Smith expressed this in his 1969 account by writing: "By now the mind's eye has forgotten the character of the mob; the sound filtering in doesn't suggest dancing faggots any more. It sounds like a powerful rage bent on vendetta."[32]

Howard Smith agrees that Pine's presence of mind was critical in preventing a bloodbath:

I was sure we were gonna be killed, but he was very, very good. He went from guy to guy. He made sure their guns were ready and all that. But he said, "Anybody who fires their gun without me saying 'Fire!' is gonna be in big, big trouble. You'll be walking the loneliest beat on Staten Island for the rest of your career." He was very threatening and very in control of the guys, even though it was very apparent he was scared also. But he didn't want anybody to start firing because I think he knew one cop fires, they all start, and people could really be killed. And he seemed to have a very good sense that you don't do that.

Pine was very sharp. He was definitely in command of his men. Some he specifically said: "You stand over there and don't leave that spot. You watch the door. You watch the corridor. You, I want in the back part of the bar in case there is some way in that we don't know about. You stand back there." He definitely positioned everybody. He always had at least two [police in the corridor] facing the door with guns drawn. It was the first time in my life—and ever since then when I read this in articles about any police riot anywhere—where they talk about good supervision and how important it is, how there always has to be a sergeant or lieutenant in any important cop event—I had never understood that until I saw him working in that bar. And I was very impressed. It wasn't like, "Oh, well, we're in here. They come in, we shoot them." Absolutely not. He was being very careful, but he had very little to work with.

Indeed, Pine had less to work with than Smith realized. In 1969 automatic firing handguns were rare. The officers would have only been able to fire as rapidly as they could pull the trigger, but also most of the guns the police had on them that evening would have had to be reloaded after firing five or six shots. As angry as the crowd was, Pine did not feel that he and his men could have stopped it with only several shots each. Moreover, Pine's own gun, a .38mm Smith & Wesson with a wooden handle, had a very short barrel, only about one inch long, reducing its range of accuracy to only about eight to ten feet.

While a couple of officers remained posted at the Stonewall's door, Smythe and some other officers and even Smith searched for an escape.[33] Among the prisoners held inside was a bartender who had the keys to the place, and Pine intermittently barked questions at him, demanding to know what various things were and peppering him with queries about the club's layout.[34]

Outside, Garvin recalls, "it was like being in a war. People were crying. People were cut up. I mean, people would throw bricks, but you didn't always hit a cop. Sometimes you'd hit another queen. So you didn't know when you saw someone cut were they cut because the cop hit the guy or were they cut because of running and falling or what? It was great, but you didn't want to get hit by nightsticks. Yet I had to see what was happening. I had to see! This was unbelievable. My God! It was like—these are the guys at the Stonewall who were—my God, look at . . . They busted open the doors. I can't believe it."

Finally the police succeeded in finding a vent in the back up near the roof, and they struggled to get the smaller of the two policewomen outside through this opening. Pine instructed the woman to go across the roof and to climb down—but not on Christopher Street—report the fire at the Stonewall to the firehouse on the adjacent block, and use a telephone to send an emergency signal for assistance.

The crowd outside again focused its fury on the Stonewall's western window. Tom watched as "a sort of wooden wall blocking out the front plate glass windows was forced down."[35] Smith wrote: "One of the big plywood windows gives, and it seems inevitable that the mob will pour in."[36] But just then the police inside turned the Stonewall Inn's fire hose on the crowd, hoping to stop the rioters. From the inside, Howard Smith reported: "The detectives locate a fire hose, [but] can't see where to aim it, wedging the hose in a crack in the door. It sends out a weak stream. We all start to slip on water and Pine says to stop."[37] Outside, Truscott saw the youths "cavort in the spray" in "momentary glee."[38] Tom wrote scornfully: "The pigs carried futility to the extreme and turned the fire hose on the mob through the door. Jeers, derision. One of the kids shouted 'Grab it! Grab his cock!'" While the police did momentarily stop the siege, they did so only because they had provided some entertainment—at their own expense—for their tormentors, adding yet another humiliation to the already considerable roster of such embarrassments the raiders had already suffered that evening.

The ineffectual fire hose could divert the crowd for only so long, and, as Truscott observed, the rioters soon "were able to regroup forces and come up with another assault,"[39] apparently a simultaneous one on both the door and the west window. Edmund White wrote: "The door is broken down, and the kids, as though working to a prior plan, systematically dump refuse from waste cans into the Wall, squirt it with lighter fluid, and ignite it. Huge flashes of flame and billows of smoke."[40]

Finally, it seemed to Pine that he and his officers might have to open fire on the crowd to have any chance of saving their lives: "We're inside and the fires are coming in and we're putting them out—all the time we're dodging the bricks that they were throwing in—and then they crashed through with this parking meter. And then I was sure we were gonna have to fire, but I was very reluctant to give the order, and I still kept saying, 'Nobody fire! Nobody fire! Let's back up if we have to. Help's going to be coming.'"

The crowd outside repeatedly attempted to set a fire through the now-gaping hole where the west window had been. "Some then lit a trash can full of paper afire and stuffed it through the window. Flames leaped up."[41] Morty Manford witnessed the same event: "People took a garbage can, one of those wire mesh cans, and set it on fire and threw the burning garbage into the premises. The area that was set afire is where the coatroom was."[42] That night the closet was set on fire both symbolically and literally.[43]

While watching the riot, Truscott had heard more than one person say, "Let's get some gas," yet he still found it a "shock" when "the blaze of flame . . . appeared in the window of the Stonewall." Di Brienza watched as "some small, scrawny, hoody-looking cat threw a can of lighter fluid through the broken window, and lit it up."[44] On the other side of the Stonewall Inn's brick front, Smith saw an "arm at the window. It squirts a liquid into the room, and a flaring match follows. Pine is not more than 10 feet away. He aims his gun at the figures."[45]

"Then," Pine recalled, "as luck would have it, we heard the sirens."

The sirens that Pine, his officers, and Howard Smith heard inside the club did not belong to the police but to two fire trucks that circled the area, no doubt because they could not get through the packed streets.[46] White wrote: "Two fire engines pull up," accompanied by the patrol wagon Pine had urged to "hurry back."[47] Manford saw the "fire engine [start] coming down the block,"[48] evidence that the policewoman who had managed to escape the Stonewall had informed the fire department that the Stonewall was burning.

Howard Smith recalls, "When I heard the sirens, I was pretty damn happy." Pine remembers all the tension disappearing "because we knew the Tactical Patrol Force would come in very large numbers." The Tactical Patrol Force, then known as the TPF or, more commonly, the riot police, was an elite group of police held in reserve in various parts of the city where trouble might be expected to break out. They had special riot equipment such as tear gas and shields and instead of hats wore helmets with plastic visors.[49]

Those trapped inside the Stonewall Inn felt relieved on hearing the sirens, but they had been so unnerved by the fury of the crowd that they were reluctant to venture outside. Smith recalls: "We made sure there were really a lot of cops there, and then we went out." The first reaction of the police and Smith was to check each other to see that each of them was all right. After the head count, they giggled for several minutes to release all the pent-up tension. As the laughter died down, Smith began catching up on his note taking and jotted down: "The people around me change back to cops. They began examining the place."[50]

The Sixth Precinct police began to move the crowds away from the Stonewall's doors, and Pine, his officers, and Smith walked outside the club into the welcoming night air.[51] Smith, still shaken, stuck close to Pine. "I didn't want trouble from the newly arrived cops, and I didn't want trouble from the crowd. I was very afraid. I felt I had to find a safe way to re-go through the crowd and back to my office so people wouldn't think 'There goes a cop!'"

Several local radio patrol cars pulled up with their red lights dancing,[52] and one of them soon sent out a mobilization signal, either a 10-13, which means "policeman in trouble—respond," or a 10-41, which would bring the TPF. Whether in response to the signal just sent by the patrol car or to the earlier telephone call by the policewoman who crawled through the vent, police cars from the Fourth, Fifth, and Tenth precincts soon arrived bearing seventeen officers—one sergeant and four or five patrolmen from each of the precincts[53]—all of them predesignated to respond to emergency calls.[54] The seventeen joined the handful of officers who had already shown up from the Sixth Precinct. Pine next used the radio cars to call for an ambulance to take Gil Weissman[55] to nearby St. Vincent's Hospital to have the wound to his eye taken care of.[56]

Although the TPF had not yet arrived, Pine now had the patrol wagon he had so sorely been lacking and decided to go ahead and load the alcohol and the remaining prisoners in it. He had the prisoners marched out of the Stonewall Inn to the patrol wagon, parked on Christopher Street near the corner of Seventh Avenue South,[57] presumably because enough of the crowd had not yet been dispersed for the patrol wagon to park right in front of the Stonewall Inn.

Amazingly, Pine still had not learned from the fiery experience he had just been through: "Even though we had just had all this trouble from these docile homosexuals—who weren't docile anymore—we still didn't think that anybody wouldn't go peacefully." He let the prisoners leave the Stonewall with only Van Ronk handcuffed.

Van Ronk vividly remembered leaving the Stonewall Inn: "I heard sirens. The door opened. Some cops came in and they rousted us, 'Up, out!': that was it. The cops made us [into] sort of a flying wedge to get through [the crowd] to the paddy wagon. There were more people out there when I came out than when I went in. Things were still flying through the air, cacophony—I mean just screaming and yelling, sirens, strobe lights, the whole spaghetti. From what I saw, that mob was not cowed. It would have taken something to get them to disperse. They were loaded for bear."

Pine recalls, "Fights erupted with the transvestites, who wouldn't go into the patrol wagon. Some [transvestites] who hadn't even been in the Stonewall came over and started a fight with our guys." Marle Becker witnessed the transvestites fighting from across the street: "All I could see about who was fighting was that it was transvestites and they were fighting furiously."[58] Becker's report of the fury with which the transvestites fought is believable, as Pine says that "some of our policemen [were] roughed up by the transvestites. The only fighting we did with anybody was putting them into the patrol wagons, and that was only the transvestites. The other guys went peacefully." The new transvestites were added to the haul Pine had already made.[59]

There is another possible interpretation of the preceding account: Pine says that no transvestites went on the first patrol wagon trip, but reliable accounts recorded in 1969 have transvestites being loaded on the patrol wagon before Pine and his officers were barricaded inside the Stonewall Inn. Also, Van Ronk said he does not recall any transvestites being in the patrol wagon on his trip over to the police station. It is possible therefore that Pine's memory is inaccurate and that the incident he remembers is actually the combined accounts of the two times the patrol wagon was loaded that evening. In this case, Becker's witnessing of the transvestites fighting the police would be not of the second but of the first loading of the paddy wagon. The problem with this solution of the puzzle, however, is that Becker's positioning of the patrol wagon matches Van Ronk's recollection of where the patrol wagon was when he entered it: up close to Seventh Avenue South rather than directly in front of the Stonewall Inn, where it seems the first patrol wagon was loaded. Either way—whether the transvestites resisted being loaded into the patrol wagon on the first or second trip (or, more improbably, on both trips)—it is probably more significant to note that the transvestites fought as they were put inside the patrol wagon and that the crowd was still not cowed when other police officers rescued Pine and his officers from inside the Stonewall Inn.

Before the patrol wagon left Christopher Street,[60] the TPF arrived in two buses. They came down Christopher Street from the west—against the flow of traffic—and parked between Seventh Avenue South and the Stonewall, close to the corner. Bob Kohler watched as the TPF got off the buses. "I had been in enough riots to know that the fun was over. These guys had helmets and lived to break heads." Moreover, they had special reason to be angry that evening: "The cops were totally humiliated. This never, ever happened. They were angrier than I guess they had ever been, because everybody else had rioted. Everybody in America who had a beef had already rioted, but the fairies were not supposed to riot. And nobody else had ever won. The cops realized that just by having to call in reinforcements, just by barricading—no other group had ever forced cops to retreat before, so the anger was just enormous. I mean, they wanted to kill."

Concerning the TPF, Pine himself recalls, "They were not gentle," but offers another rationale for their anger: "They saw the damage that was done to the place, and we had had this policewoman tell them that they were throwing fire bombs in there, and so they were prepared for real action. They scattered the crowds, and then they [the crowd] regathered. They were swinging their nightsticks at the crowd, breaking up these groups of people, and that's when we took off. But that was where my job ended." As he left the scene Pine still does not seem to have grasped the meaning of what had happened as the result of the raid he had just led: "There was no inkling, when the TPF came, that this was going to be a protracted operation that was going to last not only through the night but the following day and night." Pine and Smythe left for the Sixth Precinct station house to log in the evidence they had gathered and process the prisoners they had arrested.

Howard Smith also left, returning to his desk overlooking Christopher Park. "I could see it all from my window when I went back upstairs as it continued for a while, and I tried to write it right away."

Craig Rodwell was part of the crowd that the TPF was deployed on Christopher Street to clear. "They appeared in a **V** wedge, coming up Christopher Street towards Seventh Avenue because cars couldn't get through or nothing. And we slowly backed up—the same speed as they came forward. And they got to the Square.[61] But meanwhile all of us had just gone around the block and were behind them the other way. And they didn't know that at first. They had just assumed, *Well, we'll just show all of our billy clubs and all of our men's equipment and then the faggots will go home and that would be it.* But it wasn't it. And it's like a tug-of-war that went on for a few hours that night. They would chase us down the street and we'd just go around the block and come back and chant things and throw bottles."

O'Brien remembers that "when they tried to clear the streets is when people resented it, 'cause it came down to 'Whose streets are these? They are our streets. And you cops are not from this area; this is our area. It's gay people's streets.' And I think that was the attitude expressed in different formats."

O'Brien feels certain that some of the crowd, both gay and nongay, including those on the streets and those in cars, were purposefully not moving, pretending to merely be curious or helplessly stuck in the crowd. "People just came by to see what's happening and they couldn't [move] because there were rows of people behind them and the rows behind deliberately [would not move]. A lot of them knew that they were interfering with the cops, and [that] was that passive kind of resistance by a lot of gays. They just stood, but it was their way of showing resistance, and some of the people the cops went after just for standing there, because they want the streets cleared, because then they can bring more police cars in." O'Brien adds that it "was brave to do even that, and it allowed people like me [who wanted to engage the police more directly] to take advantage of the police having to respond to the crowds to go after the police. Because every time their attention was turned towards trying to clear the streets and their backs to us we'd be throwing things at the cops or in front of the cops, going after us."

The police objective was to clear the streets, and given the crowds and the narrowness of the one-way street in front of the Stonewall Inn, the police did not have an easy task, whereas all the crowd had to do was block the section of the street in front of the Inn and traffic was brought to a standstill. To this end a car was overturned, approximately in front of the stoop next to the Stonewall. As O'Brien explained, "You can wail your siren all day, you're still not getting through if those vehicles aren't moving, and they're not moving if one's overturned and there's a crowd there."

As the TPF and the crowd faced off, some of the youths called upon their street repertoire, probably inspired by the sight of the TPF advancing on them in a line formation. Suddenly the gay street youths linked their arms around one another and kicked Rockette style as they sang their old reprise, but this time changing the word *Village* to *Stonewall*:

> *We are the Stonewall Girls,*
> *We wear our hair in curls.*
> *We wear no underwear:*
> *We show our pubic hairs.*

Perhaps the street youths' humor was more effective than they hoped, for now the fire trucks were used not for firefighting but to help disperse the crowd. Their hoses were turned on the crowd, scattering them.[62]

Being hosed down was only a temporary setback for the protesters. Over and over that night they re-formed, playing a game of cat and mouse with the TPF, for as Garvin accurately states, "because of the location, there was no way to contain us." The confused geography of the Sheridan Square area of the Village worked very effectively against the TPF. As Bob Kohler watched, the street kids "were constantly getting over on the TPF. The TPF would chase somebody this way, then the kids would start something behind them so that attention would be taken, and then the TPF would come [the other] way, and then more kids would start something behind them. So the TPF were constantly off guard. It was keeping them on the run constantly."

The kick-line routine was used two or more times that night. Kohler, as well as others who watched, were amazed at the courage of the street kids who dared to mock the TPF to their faces: "The TPF were down at one end of the street, and the kids lined up in their little Rockette line, and they would kick their legs up, and the TPF would run after them. Suddenly these kids were coming from the other end, and there were maybe four [of them]. They had their arms linked and they were doing Rockette kicks and going towards the TPF. They were taunting them, calling them 'the girls in blue' again and 'Lily Law,' and they would get about as close to them as they felt they should. Then they'd start to run. Some of them, of course, didn't run fast enough."

Two who did not run fast enough were Martin Boyce and Birdie. Boyce recalls, "We started taunting the cops, 'We are the Village girls, we wear our hair in curls, we wear our dungarees above our nelly knees, and with the constables, we simply hypnotize,' and we're going on, and the police rushed us, and that's when I realized this is not a good thing to do, because they got me in the back with a [night] stick. And I said, 'No, that's not for me.' Miss Birdie was more emboldened by all that, but I wasn't. I split from Birdie at that point."

But others in the crowd did not get off so easily. According to Kohler, "People were beaten who had no part in it. I remember a very good-looking kid who said, 'What's going on? What's going on?' I said, 'Just stay out of the way.' He said, 'What's it all about?' 'It's a little too complicated.' About twenty minutes later, I saw him being dragged into a police car with blood all over him. He had just come down to find out what's going on, but it was indiscriminate. They lashed out at anybody, at anything."

Danny Garvin also witnessed police brutality. So fascinated was he by the evening's events that at one point he went into an apartment building at 98 Grove Street that overlooked the most open area near the Stonewall Inn, the area where the triangular tip of Christopher Park narrows down to a daggerlike point and where Waverly Place juts west around the Northern Dispensary. A friend of his lived in the building, and Garvin thought that from there he could get a better view of all that was happening.

"I saw a bunch of guys on one side and the cops over there, and the cops with their feet spread apart and holding their billy clubs straight out. And these queens all of a sudden rolled up their pants legs into knickers, and they stood right in front of the cops. There must have been about ten cops one way and about twenty queens on the other side. They all put their arms around one another and started forming a kick line, and the cops just charged with the [nightsticks] and started smacking them in the heads, hitting people, pulling them into the cars. I just can't ever get that one sight out of my mind. The cops with the [nightsticks] and the kick line on the other side. It was the most amazing thing. What was more amazing was when the cops charged. That's when I think anger started. And the cops were used to us calling [them] Lily Law, so the cops were used to some kind of camp coming from us. And all of a sudden that kick line, which I guess was a spoof on their machismo, making fun of their authority. Yeah, I think that's when I felt rage. Because . . . people were getting smashed with bats. And for what? A kick line."

John O'Brien was one of those the police were running after. He was in a group of about fifteen or twenty people who banded together and continually taunted the police into chasing them. O'Brien remembers that initially there were two different bands taunting the police, with O'Brien's group repeatedly running up and down Christopher Street from in front of the Stonewall Inn down to Waverly Place and then turning left on Waverly. O'Brien saw that among those who made up the band he had joined up with were some of the youths he and Bill Katzenberg had talked with about the need for gay people to organize. He quickly shared his knowledge of street-fighting tactics by shouting as he ran, "No, not that way! Don't go up that street, because the cops can follow us. Go down this street and go around. Go opposite of the cars and go through the cars!" O'Brien explains that "as someone who had fought the police for a long time I knew that you do not help the police by running in the same direction as the traffic: you go the opposite so they can't get to you in the cars, so the police had to go on foot."

The protests continued into the night. Angry gay men set fires in trash cans and broke store windows[63] and then desperately scoured for more objects to throw. Bob Kohler saw Craig Rodwell go by screaming, "Gay power! Gay power!" Occasionally Kohler and some of the street youths would take refuge in Christopher Park, because, for whatever reason, the police did not pursue people into the park that night.

Tommy Lanigan-Schmidt's experience must have been typical of many who did not fight but ran along with the crowds through the streets: "I myself was more part of like a mob that was waving in and out like the ocean. I was part of a mob that had a kind of deep identity and was acting as one force." Tommy tended to stay with his friends Martin Boyce and Birdie. Tommy noticed that evening that time took on a special quality. "[A riot] creates its own time, like weddings, funerals, wakes. A wedding or funeral has something that isn't the time of a clock ticking. It's a time of its own system. It also probably has a time like something of a dream, too." Interestingly, Michael Fader noticed the very same phenomenon: "There was no sense of time; it was all ongoing."

Although Danny Garvin had lost track of Keith Murdoch "as soon as the bricks started flying," Garvin had continued to participate in the evening's action: "People kept wanting to come back around to see what was happening. They would chase us up on the end [to] Seventh Avenue; we'd come back around on Tenth Street. They would push us down Christopher Street; people would just sneak around Gay Street and shoot back up onto Christopher."

While some of the people in the crowd of protesters were having fun and others were frightened, some, such as Ed White's friend Charles Burch, found a certain joie de vivre and exaltation in fighting the TPF: "They represented an invincible force, which was really fun, because I am enough of a masochist and a romantic that I love the idea of going up against people that you could never look bad losing to, because they were invincible. So you could just try to hurt them and not get hurt yourself if possible. And I developed, in that first encounter, a sense of street-fighting tactics, of how to harass and get away with it; of how to taunt and provoke a response and somehow try to not get hurt. And just years and years of all the resentments and humiliations and things that can come down on the head of a gay person were really—I was really experiencing liberation and radicalization and everything, *bang!*, right then and there."

When Jerry Hoose arrived on Christopher Street that night, in response to the phone call from John Goodman, his first response was: "Thank God!" Hoose explains that "I was a very angry person. I'd been waiting for this to happen. I knew it was going to happen. I said, 'Great!' I was the happiest person on the face of the earth; I'm sure I had tears of joy. And I was willing to do anything. I wanted to get into it. Everybody was angry. We were angry people, and we had a lot of reason to be angry. Lot of reason.

"It was just, to me, more of a feeling of joy, and I think it was to a lot of people. It was like, 'It's about time.' We had finally done something. I was a little sad because I didn't think that we were going in the right direction. I wanted to get the crowd to move down to City Hall and all that, but at least we had done something. And the thing I was most worried about was [that] this would be it. I said, 'This can't be it! This can't be it!' because we were mad. Everybody I knew was mad."

O'Brien agrees, "What was exciting was other people wanted to fight, too. What excited me was that I finally was not alone, that I had found my gay brothers. Until then I had been isolated and alone."

Eventually, the riot began to peter out, mainly because the rioters were tired or bored. But even as it ended, there was a palpable excitement in the air. William Wynkoop, who lived at 146 Waverly Place at the foot of Gay Street, had been awakened around two o'clock in the morning by the sound of people running. Hearing intermittent shouting as well, he had decided to go outside and investigate. After he had looked around awhile and stood in front of the Stonewall Inn talking with a witness about the evening's events, he noticed that the crowd was beginning to disperse: "All through Sheridan Square there were people who had been in the crowd and watching what was going on in the bar, [and they] had moved away, I gather, and were standing in groups talking on Christopher Street, all around Sheridan Square, on Seventh Avenue, and over on Grove Street on the other side of Christopher Park, just standing around in groups talking. And here it was, the middle of the night! . . . They were . . . moving away because the excitement was over, but they were still so fascinated by it that they were stopping in groups and talking about it. I finally went to bed, probably about four. And when I left, there were still people standing in groups, talking."

When Kevin Dunn had heard all the sirens, he moved away from the immediate scene, but remained in the area: "I went back after when things had calmed. And the one thing I remember is that there were little groups of people, maybe like a handful or two on different corners, talking about what had happened and there was this very quiet kind of excitement and buzz in the air. You know, about [whispering], 'Boy, did you catch what happened?'"

Indeed, the feeling was so real that it could be felt by someone happening across the scene, even if that person was not gay. John Fisk, a heterosexual man who lived in the neighborhood and who had a job in the arts that ended late at night, had a ritual of walking to Smilers for a sandwich after work. As he walked to Smilers that evening, although Fisk did not see any fighting nor any police around, he did notice more than the usual number of people sitting on the stoops and noted an electricity in the air that he felt to be positive in some sense. When he went into Smilers, the counterman made him the largest sandwich he'd ever seen and handed it to him without a word but with a huge smile.[64]

Dick Leitsch remembers that "after a while, everybody thought, *Well, this is boring. All we're doing is running around the block, here. We've done it ten times now and it's dull. Let's do something else.* So we sort of vanished. I remember Christopher Street being so empty, except for the cops, and seeing very few civilians anywhere around. Then I remember the sky being very dark, and there being a terrific moon, and the Village being eerily quiet."

Near dawn a number of the individuals who had witnessed the riot lingered on. Bob Kohler recalls, "We were sitting across the street at the park, and you would see smoldering [garbage] baskets and the street was broken glass. The Stonewall window was smashed, and there were cops all standing around like storm troopers. You'd look a block away and you could see trash cans still smoldering.

"It was very surreal; it really was. This didn't look like the Village. It didn't look like Christopher Street. We were sitting there, and a couple of kids were bleeding. Nobody really knew what happened. It was like, 'Oh, wow. What was that all about?' It was that kind of thing. The kids had some makeshift bandages. None of the kids were hurt that badly. Other people did get hurt very badly. But that was the end."

Martin Boyce's recollections of the end of the night portray a dawning sense of pride: "Morning came on Christopher, and those broken windows and pieces of cloth inside and diamondlike glass all over. It was a riot, no doubt about it, and there were just exhausted survivors looking dazed. We knew what happened. We all did it. It was like, 'Oh.' Because, you know, the low skyline. There was a certain beauty to the aftermath of the riot. It was a very extraordinary kind of beauty, something to make art out of later. Not directly, but Tommy Schmidt, I'm sure, could see the beauty of shattered glass and certain kind of fag decorations being blown in the wind, by the window. It was obvious, at least to me, that a lot of people really were gay and, you know, this was our street."

"Christopher Street Belongs
to the Queens!"

SATURDAY NIGHT

Chris Babick had gone out Friday night with Bob, the twenty-seven-year-old antique dealer he was dating, for Chinese food and had decided he didn't want to deal with the hassles he often ran into in bars as a seventeen-year-old who appeared even younger. Instead they had decided to just go home. Bob woke up first on Saturday and turned on the radio. Soon he was yelling at his still-asleep boyfriend, "Chris! Chris, you're not going to believe what happened!"

Chris tried hard to focus. "What? What?"

"They rioted. The police raided the Stonewall and they were rioting!"

Chris could not believe his ears. "And I—it was incredible. Incredible. The fucking queens had rioted." Chris later admitted that he did not know what he would have done had he been at the Stonewall the first night, "But I know what I did the rest of the weekend: Saturday and Sunday nights I was there. Of course Bob and I called our friends."[1]

Throughout the day, as the streets were swept and the smashed windows of the Stonewall Inn were boarded up and painted black, the unbelievable news was spreading rapidly through New York's gay grapevine. Many who heard about the insurrection were so excited that they headed down to the Stonewall Inn to see for themselves what had happened. Others sensed that there would have to be some kind of follow-up that night and wanted to be part of it.

As gay men and women trickled down to the Village, numerous slogans began to appear on the Stonewall Inn's boarded-up windows and the bar's brick facade (some of which were obviously written by the Stonewall Inn personnel), including: "We are Open," "There is all college boys and girls in here," "Support Gay Power—C'mon in, girls," "Insp. Smyth looted our: money, jukebox, cigarette mach, telephones, safe, cash register, and the boys tips,"[2] "THEY WANT US TO FIGHT FOR OUR COUNTRY [BUT] THEY INVADED OUR RIGHTS,"[3] "GAY PROHIBITION CORUPT$ COP$ FEED$ MAFIA,"[4] "How Can Inspector Smythe Drive a $15,000 Car on HIS Salary?",[5] "Support Gay Power,"[6] and "Legalize Gay bars and lick the problem."[7] Also attached to the front of the club were two copies of the *Daily News* story about Friday night's events, which struck *Voice* reporter Lucian Truscott as odd, given the highly negative reporting.[8]

By around nine o'clock in the evening, enough gay men and lesbians had shown up around the Stonewall Inn to form small groups on the sidewalks.[9] As their numbers steadily grew, police officers in the area would not let them stand still but kept them moving, hoping to prevent a repeat of the previous night's events.[10] But within two to three hours,[11] those numbers had grown into at least a couple of thousand.[12] One lesbian reported that so many people came on Saturday that "all over the Village . . . hippies joined the queers & straight places turned gay for. the week-end—it was complete madness in NYC."[13]

The Stonewall Inn was the initial focal point for the gathering of mostly gay men along with a few lesbians and a sprinkling of straight supporters.[14] The crowd reached its greatest size late in the evening, probably between ten o'clock and midnight.[15] After the protesters had gathered, they began to sing—including the "We are the Stonewall Girls" tune used the night before[16]—and chant, facing off with police officers in front of the Stonewall Inn. The initial chants were slogans such as "Gay power," "We want freedom now," and "Equality for homosexuals,"[17] but before long the rallying cries became more militant as the demonstrators shouted: "Christopher Street belongs to the queens!" and "Liberate Christopher Street!"[18] Some protesters denounced the police for harassing homosexuals.[19] As members of Mattachine–New York and Craig Rodwell handed out literature[20] and people talked excitedly about the meaning of the previous night's events, the area around Christopher Park took on the air somewhat of a political fair—or even a political free-for-all. Edmund White wrote the best and fullest contemporary account of the scene:

> A mad left-wing group of straight kids called the Crazies is trying to organize the kids, pointing out that Lindsay is to blame (the Crazies want us to vote for Prococino [*sic*], or "Prosciutto" as we call him). A Crazy girl launches into a tirade against Governor Rockefeller "Whose Empire must be Destroyed." Straight Negro boys put their

arms around me and say we're comrades (it's okay with me—in fact great, the first camaraderie I've felt with blacks in years).[21]

Truscott described the crowd as being made up of "onlookers, East-siders, and rough street people who saw a chance for a little action."[22] Leitsch saw them as "gay people from all over town, tourists, Villagers, and the idly curious,"[23] adding that while the crowd had been entirely gay in the beginning, as tourists came along they would inquire about what was going on and, when told that the protest was against the shutting down of a gay club, would become very supportive and either stay to watch or join. Leitsch saw one middle-aged woman, there with her husband, who, after telling a policeman that he should be ashamed of himself, shouted at him, "Don't you know that these people have no place to go, and need places like that bar?"[24]

Truscott recorded the raucous scene of speeches and chanting spiced by a lot of camp humor and openly gay behavior:

> Hand-holding, kissing, and posing accented each of the cheers with a homosexual liberation that had appeared only fleetingly on the street before. One-liners were as practiced as if they had been used for years. "I just want you all to know," quipped a platinum blonde with obvious glee, "that sometimes being homosexual is a big pain in the ass." Another allowed as to how he had become a "left-deviationist." And on and on.

Little wonder then that a sizable number of the somewhat older gay men who watched, including some who had returned from Fire Island just to see what was going on, "had strained looks on their faces and talked in concerned whispers as they watched the up-and-coming generation take being gay and flaunt it before the masses."[25] Not all those who took a dim view of Saturday night's events were conservative or older: the young radical Ronnie Di Brienza wrote that "Saturday night was very poor. Too many people showed up looking for a carnival rather than a sincere protest. Queens were posing for pictures, slogans were being spouted out, but nothing really sincere happened in the way of protest."[26]

Craig Rodwell disagreed: "Generally [on Saturday] it was an angry mood, a lot of chanting, a lot of hand-holding, a lot of assertion of being gay . . . it was a way of saying, 'We're tired of hiding, tired of leading two lives, tired of denying our basic identity.' A general assertion [by] gay peo-ple [of] newfound collective pride."

Chris Babick had a similar reaction: "It was an absolutely exhilarating experience to know that . . . they had defied authority. And it was . . . like the beginning of a lesbian and gay value system. From going to places where you had to knock on a door and speak to someone through a peephole in order to get in. We were just out. We were in the streets. I mean, can you imagine? And when you went to the Stonewall—people did hang out in [Christopher Park] . . . but you didn't make a lot of noise because the cops would harass you, beat you, whatever. So it was just a matter of two or three people at a time would walk up the street, ring the bell or knock on the door . . . and . . . disappear into this cavern, this place called the Stonewall in which there was lively, lively activity. But all of a sudden we were out on the streets. We were there. And I was there. . . . Here's the homosexual standing on the streets. And it was incredible. And . . . gay men and lesbians came from all over."[27]

While the protests continued outside the Stonewall Inn, the Mafia owners were doing their best to attract customers back inside. The owners seem to have realized that the entire context of running their particular business had changed, for not only had there been a riot the previous night, but also the allegations of their illegal activities were in the media and there was a police presence right outside their door. No wonder that when they reopened on Saturday they served only soft drinks, which they gave away.[28]

Outside the Stonewall Inn the chants were repeated louder and louder and more and more frequently. In the midst of this rising emotion, the club owners stepped outside and addressed the gay crowd: "C'mon in and see what da pigs done to us. We're honest businessmen here. We're American-born boys. We run a legitimate joint here. There ain't nuttin bein' done wrong in dis place." In spite of the new sign on the door stating: "This is a private club. Members only,"[29] the owners invited "Everybody" to "come and see."[30] But the crowd was growing restless.[31]

It had also grown to a multitude. Craig Rodwell recalled that "thousands of our people came down . . . all around 10th Street and all the way up Christopher and around the Square [and] Seventh Avenue."[32] Dick Leitsch saw an old woman trying to make her way through the throngs who, while refusing the help of many who tried to assist her, was apparently bewildered and frightened by the unimaginable sight of masses of homosexuals openly gathering in the streets, for she trembled with obvious fear as she walked, all the while muttering to herself, "It must be the full moon, it must be the full moon."[33] The crowds came in spite of the terrific heat. While the previous day had been hot and humid, Saturday was worse: it would be the hottest June 28 in New York City history.[34]

When the sidewalks could no longer contain the crowds, people started spilling over into the streets.[35] It was at this point, Rodwell recalls, that "we decided to block off Christopher Street."[36]

Rodwell and hundreds of others chose the beginning of Christopher Street at Greenwich Avenue as the place to stop traffic simply because that was where most vehicles entered Christopher Street. Both Rodwell and his lover, Fred Sargeant, say the decision was made to turn Christopher Street into a gay street by saying that no straight people were allowed on the street: taxis and buses would not be admitted unless they were carrying gay people,[37] a turning of the tables intended to make heterosexual people think twice about the nature of discrimination based on sexual orientation and a militant statement that gay people were entitled to something of their own: if America was going to force lesbians and gay men into ghettos, then the ghettos' inhabitants would insist on running them.[38]

Apparently the blockade began not so much as an attempt to stop traffic as to harass the occupants of vehicles who were not gay or who would not indicate support for the demonstrations.[39] Rodwell recalled that "cars that came through and buses, we just rocked them back and forth." Leitsch witnessed a showdown between the crowd and a city bus:

A bus driver blew his horn at the meeting, and someone shouted, "Stop the Bus!" The crowd surged out into the street and blocked the progress of the bus. As the driver inched ahead, someone ripped off an advertising card and blocked the windshield with it. The crowd beat on the sides of the bus and shouted "Christopher Street belongs to the queens!" and "Liberate the street."

Leitsch reports that while the police intervened and were able to persuade the crowd to let the bus pass, the demonstrators immediately came up with a new tactic to slow down the traffic: a human chain was formed across the street and cars were only let through one at a time.[40]

While the demonstrators were serious about their intent, an incident with a taxi driver was a warning that they needed to exercise some caution. Unaware of what was happening, a taxicab turned onto Christopher Street from Greenwich Avenue and immediately was caught up in the crowd, the demonstrators apparently not realizing that the challenge to them was unintentional. As the crowd started rocking the taxi back and forth, Rodwell looked in the taxi and saw that both the passengers in the backseat and the cabdriver were terrified, "scared out of their skulls." It seemed to Rodwell and others that the driver was having a heart attack, so a number of demonstrators joined arms to protect the taxi, and it backed up and out onto Greenwich Avenue.[41] Bob Kohler and Craig Rodwell would later hear that the taxi driver died, apparently the only fatality from the riots.[42]

In an apparently separate incident with a taxicab witnessed by Jamake Highwater, when the cabdriver turned into the crowd, demonstrators banged in the sides of the taxi, jumped on the cab's hood, and paraded on its top. When the driver got out and attacked some members of the crowd, "about fifteen jumped him. Meanwhile, about 15 others were trying to let the passengers get to freedom."[43]

Around this same time, a little farther west, Rodwell saw a barrage of bottles being thrown, apparently by crowds gathered on the Grove Street side of Christopher Park at the police on the other side.[44] One Christopher Street merchant stood in her shop's doorway and berated the police, telling them to behave themselves. Whenever the police headed toward her, she ran into her shop and locked the door. As some of the policemen began acting nasty toward members of the crowd, one youth found garbage can lids and threw them discus style so that they bounced "neatly off" the cops' helmets.[45]

Rodwell saw this period of time on Saturday night as similar to the time the previous evening between the lesbian resisting arrest and the crowd trying to break back into the Stonewall Inn: so much was being done simultaneously by so many different people that there is no way any one person could have taken it all in. Although the chronology of events is more straightforward on Saturday night than it was on Friday night, there were many more participants spread over a larger area on the second night. If on the previous night gay people had been angry in reaction to the police raid, tonight they were on the offensive. In claiming Christopher Street for their own, they were determined to remove the police and any other hostile parties from it . . . or at least make it very uncomfortable for them to hold on to it, like territory that an army wins but can only occupy with difficulty against a hostile populace. Rodwell understood it this way: "[Saturday night] was the first time in history that there was a general assertion of anger by gay people. A public assertion of real anger that was just electric. And even the old queens just came down to walk around the block to see what was going on. They were heroes in a sense, too. Just the fact that they came down. Being there, just standing there watching, they added to the sheer magnitude of the numbers of people there, which was very, very impressive."

One middle-aged gay man who came to see the demonstrators was Dr. Howard Brown, the former chief health officer of New York City, who had resigned from the Lindsay administration in 1968. Typical of many successful gay men of his generation, he was very concerned about passing for straight. He recalled his reaction to stereotypical gay men when, in his capacity as night mayor, a new office created by Lindsay to make the city more responsive to citizens, he had been given a tour of New York City's prison, the Tombs. There he had been shown the section reserved for homosexual prisoners: "Almost all the men in the crowded cells were demonstrably effeminate. I could not identify with them, and I froze, too terrified to ask any questions about their treatment." Over the weekend the uproar from the riots was loud enough that, even though his apartment was a four-minute walk away, with his windows open he could hear the shouting. Intrigued, he left his apartment and headed for the Stonewall Inn. He found that the demonstrators:

> were like the homosexuals I had seen in the Tombs—most of them obviously poor, most of them the sort of limp-wristed, shabby, or gaudy gays that send a shiver of dread down the spines of homosexuals who hope to pass as straight. I could not have felt more remote from them. And yet, at the same time, the scene brought to mind every civil rights struggle I had ever witnessed or participated in.[46]

By now, fires were again being set in trash cans as they had been the night before. Witnesses report seeing blazes set up and down the street as if in ancient times when bonfires, prepared in advance on mountaintops, would be lit to relay important news over great distances.

Fire from another source was also being used to send signals that night. As Doric Wilson stood on the street Saturday night, he looked up toward The Corner and saw red sparks falling from on high, through the night air, as in a gentle rainfall. The sparks were coming from New York City's women's prison, the House of Detention—usually referred to as the House of D—located at the intersection of Greenwich Avenue and Christopher Street. It was a prison with a lot of black and Latina prisoners, many of whom were lesbians. The prisoners were setting toilet paper on fire and dropping it from their cell windows to show their support for the rioters. Chris Babick recalls "that whole week the women were screaming, cheering us on. . . . The whole jail, it seemed like, was alive with people, with activity, because the streets were alive with activity. Everything vibrated."[47]

Indeed, the crowd was so whipped up with anger that the police became targets. Craig Rodwell was only six feet from an empty squad car with three policemen standing nearby when he saw Marsha Johnson climb to the top of a lamppost and drop a bag containing a heavy object on the car's windshield, shattering it. After the windshield broke, the police immediately jumped into the car but then reached out and grabbed the nearest person they could—a man who had nothing to do with the assault on the car—pulled him into the squad car, and drove off, beating their hapless victim. As Rodwell lamented, "It was just the nearest faggot. You know, 'We'll teach you,' kind of thing." Leitsch witnessed a similar incident in which a police car came up Waverly Place and stopped at the intersection of Christopher Street. The car's occupants sat and stared angrily at the crowd until a concrete block landed loudly on the car's hood. The crowd pulled away and "then, as one person . . . surged forward and surrounded the car, beating on it with fists and dancing atop it." Soon after the police inside radioed for help, the crowd permitted the vehicle to leave.[48]

At one point in the evening, Leitsch saw someone attack an officer in a police car:

> Another car, bearing a fat, gouty-looking cop with many pounds of gilt braid, chauffeured by a cute young cop came through. The fat cop looked for all the world like a slave-owner surveying the plantation, and someone tossed a sack of wet garbage through the car window and right on his face. The bag broke and soggy coffee grounds dripped down the lined face, which never lost its "screw you" look.[49]

In a showdown with a bus, possibly the same one described earlier, the police persuaded the crowd to pull back but only to have themselves become the next victims of the enraged citizenry: "They descended onto the prowl car. They first knocked off the flashing red light. Then they started shaking the squad car sideways as if to tip it over."[50]

According to *The New York Times*, the Sixth Precinct had been unable to control the situation and so the TPF were called in for the second night in a row,[51] but according to Dick Leitsch, the Fourth, Fifth, Sixth, and Ninth precincts had already brought in "a hundred or so cops who had no hope of controlling the crowd of nearly two thousand people in the streets" and it was only then that the TPF was called in.[52]

It was approximately 2:15 A.M. when the TPF units assigned to the East Village arrived in the West Village.[53] About 150 TPF officers arrived, with around one hundred of them getting out at The Corner while another fifty were dropped off at Seventh Avenue South and Christopher Street.[54]

As the TPF met with a number of high-ranking police officers at Greenwich Avenue and Christopher Street, the crowd sporadically tossed beer cans at their vans and cars. Without any warning, two police officers rushed into the crowd, plucked a youth from it at random—one who, according to Leitsch, "had done absolutely nothing"—and carried him off to a patrol wagon. As they did so, while the two arresting officers still held the young man, four other police officers began to pound the boy's face, stomach, and genitals with nightsticks. A "high shrill voice" yelled, "Save our sister!" and there was a heavy pause, during which, Leitsch recounts, "the 'butch' looking 'numbers' looked distracted." Then "momentarily, fifty or more homosexuals who would have to be described as 'nelly,' rushed the cops and took the boy back into the crowd." Like the Red Sea, which parted to let the Hebrews escape Pharaoh's army only to then close itself against that same army, the queens "formed a solid front and refused to let the cops into the crowd to regain their prisoner, letting the cops hit them with their sticks, rather than let them through."[55]

The police top brass, having finished their strategic consultations, had the TPF form themselves into flying wedges as they had done the night before. The TPF then marched up and down Greenwich Avenue, forcing parts of the crowd onto 10th Street and others onto Sixth Avenue, although from Sixth Avenue the crowds simply came back south onto Christopher Street. The TPF next marched up and down Greenwich Avenue but this time linked their arms, and as they came to a side street those on the ends of the lines broke off and "chased demonstrators down the side streets and away from the center of the action."[56]

Having cleared Greenwich Avenue, the TPF focused on opening up Christopher Street between Greenwich Avenue and Seventh Avenue South. It so happened that a number of the young men who had been hanging out in front of the Stonewall Inn had finally grown bored and decided to head to The Corner to see what was happening there when they ran right into the TPF heading toward them.[57] As the TPF advanced, they were a formidable sight. Almost three decades later, Dick Leitsch could still recall the TPF's appearance as they deployed that night on Christopher Street: "They formed a phalanx in the Greek style. They lined up, shoulder to shoulder, across Christopher Street, and they had big, plastic shields that were half-circles about four feet tall. They covered from the crotch to the top of the head, so they would protect their groin and head from bullets or bricks thrown at them. The shields were semicircular and had handles, and they were inside this half a tube. They also had riot helmets and billy sticks. So they formed this shoulder-to-shoulder phalanx across Christopher Street and then just marched, very slowly—very slowly, not rushing or anything—down the street. It was a solid wall." Charles Burch recalls the impressive sight the TPF made when deployed in line formation: "There was this huge phalanx of blue-helmeted cops with shields, and the light reflecting from their blue plastic-ness [made] an aura of silvery sheen over them."

The TPF succeeded in sweeping the crowd down Christopher Street as far as Waverly Place, where the riot police stopped, with the kids who had just before been hanging out by the Stonewall Inn at the head of the crowd. As they had the previous night, the youths again formed a chorus line and started singing and dancing right in front of the TPF.[58]

As Robert Bryan watched the face-off between the men in the kick line and the TPF, he was amazed by the gay youths' courage. "The queens—they were extremely effeminate young men—formed this kicking line all across Christopher Street, and started to do a Rockettes kick. And singing,

'We're the Stonewall Girls, we wear our hair in curls, we don't wear underwear . . . ,' as it went. And the police started moving ahead, moving towards them." The TPF advanced at a slow and steady pace, inching forward. "And the queens did not move; they just continued to kick and to sing as the police just moved closer and closer and closer; and you just wondered how long are they going to keep this up before they break and run? The police got closer and closer to them with their clubs and their helmets and their riot gear and the whole thing; and I thought it was just very inspiring, their bravery, like Bunker Hill or 'Don't fire until you see the whites of their eyes.' They were waiting until the very last minute, and it wasn't until the police were eight feet away from them that the crowd finally broke and ran."

Ironically, the TPF's psychology of using machismo to try to intimidate protesters whom society had branded as deficient in masculinity—and hence courage—ultimately raised the question of who, indeed, was braver: the TPF hiding behind their shields and helmets, equipped with guns and billy clubs, with all the force of the law and the approval of society behind them, or the gay men—with most of those in the kick line being effeminate to some degree—the objects of society's scorn and ridicule, offering their vulnerable bodies as targets and armed with nothing more than their intelligence and humor?

When the protesters finally did run, they merely repeated their tactic from the night before: as the TPF advanced up along Christopher Park toward Seventh Avenue South with the goal of clearing all of Christopher Street, the protesters turned southeast on Waverly, went up Gay Street, and again came out behind the TPF on Christopher Street forming a chorus line, all the while screaming and taunting the TPF.[59]

The guerrilla tactic of using the Village's many side streets to circumvent the police tactics for clearing the streets with sweeps of the TPF was used by the protesters over and over again, as was the kick-line routine. And just as had happened when the "nelly" men rescued a gay man from the clutches of the TPF, Leitsch noted that most of the remarkable examples of physical courage he saw during the riots were done by the more effeminate men, the real "queens":

It was an interesting sidelight on the demonstrations that those usually put down as "sissies" or "swishes" showed the most courage and sense during the action. . . . The most striking feature of the rioting was that it was led, and featured as participants, "queens," not "homosexuals." "Homosexuals" have been sitting back and taking whatever the Establishment handed out; the "queens" were having none of that. The "butch" numbers who were around the area and who participated peripherally in the action remained for the most part in the background. It was the "queens" who scored the points and proved that they were not going to tolerate any more harassment or abuse. . . . Their bravery and daring saved many people from being hurt, and their sense of humor and "camp" helped keep the crowds from getting nasty or too violent.[60]

This assertion by Leitsch is corroborated by a memory of Bob Kohler's: a "plea scrawled on the sidewalk in front of the Stonewall: BUTCHES, WHERE ARE YOU NOW THAT WE NEED YOU?"[61]

Conventionally masculine men were involved in the fighting, but in light of Leitsch's, Kohler's, and other testimony, it seems irrefutable that a highly disproportionate amount of the physical courage displayed during the riots came from the more effeminate men in the crowd.[62]

The one portion of the Village that the police could close without too much difficulty was the very focus of the protest: the block the Stonewall Inn was on. Before the night was over, the police closed off the block, allowing no one to enter Christopher Park, Christopher Street between Waverly Place and Seventh Avenue South, or Grove Street from either end of the south side of Christopher Park.[63] Shutting down what New Yorkers refer to as Sheridan Square was a victory for the police, but only a partial one, for several reasons. First, there were still plenty of gay people out on the streets challenging the police, who had seized only one small piece of the contested area, enlarged significantly since the previous night. Second, the closing came at an economic price to a number of nongay businesses. Truscott noted the loss of Saturday night business "even at the straight Lion's Head and 55 [the bar next to the Lion's Head at 55 Christopher Street]."[64] Another *Voice* columnist, Walter Troy Spencer, bemoaned that one bar owner on Christopher Street (no doubt one of these same two bars) lost $500 in one evening "of the indirect embargo."[65] Keeping the ghetto's occupants under even partial control for one evening on one block could be expensive. Indeed, things were so out of hand that on the other side of Seventh Avenue South, the United Cigar Store, Riker's restaurant, and Smilers Deli all closed down of their own volition.[66]

The TPF continued to fight to regain control of other streets beyond the Christopher Park area as the same cat-and-mouse game between police and protesters of the night before was reenacted, but this time with more police officers, more rioters, and more anger on both sides. Not surprisingly, the TPF was brutal. Leitsch simply wrote: "[T]he TPF again lived up to its reputation for violence and brutality."[67] A letter to *The Village Voice* written by Kevin Liscoe complained that he had "witnessed many senseless brutalities which there could be no justification for. One guy walking on

Sheridan Square across from the disturbance was with his chick (obviously not into it) when a TPF came from behind and just split his head open with his club."[68] Truscott reported witnessing one person getting a busted head at or near Sheridan Square and noted that "the cops amused themselves by arbitrarily breaking up small groups of people up and down the avenue."[69]

In spite of the TPF's numbers and superior equipment, the crowds of protesters were not cowed and made full use of their wit, anger, and re-sourcefulness in fighting the TPF. As the TPF moved through the streets, they swung their nightsticks with abandon, using them, Leitsch noted, like swords. But when one police officer grabbed "a wild Puerto Rican queen" and raised his arm to club him, the queen suddenly asked the cop, "How'd you like a big Spanish dick up your little Irish ass?" The officer was so star-tled he stopped his nightstick in midswing and the man escaped. On an-other occasion two police officers were chasing a crowd of a hundred or more demonstrators down Waverly Place when one of the demonstrators suddenly realized that they outnumbered the police. He immediately shouted that they should catch the police, rip their clothes off, and screw them on the spot.[70] As the crowd turned on them, the police quickly re-versed themselves and ran for blocks with the angry crowd in hot pursuit, yelling, "Catch them! Fuck them!"[71]

Amid all these sorties and skirmishes between protesters and the police, Leitsch again spotted the middle-aged woman he had seen several hours earlier telling a police officer that he should be ashamed of himself. This time she and her husband and two other heterosexual couples were in the midst of a large group of homosexuals trying to escape the TPF as they chased them with nightsticks.[72]

Still, with between two and three hundred police on the scene,[73] most of them heavily armed, the streets were reopened and most of the crowds dispersed. It had taken a major deployment of New York City's Finest to wrest control of a small section of the city back from its homosexual citi-zenry. For approximately two hours Christopher Street had indeed be-longed to the "queens."

Yet this still was not the end of the evening. While the TPF had restored order by 2:30 A.M., when the bars closed at 3:00 A.M. customers from the Village's many gay bars came by to see what was going on.[74] According to *The New York Times*, the abundance of helmeted police made the crowd even angrier than the previous night's raid on the Stonewall Inn had,[75] and the new arrivals were quickly organized into a second attempt to "liberate Christopher Street." Accounts of this attempt are extremely sketchy, apparently because with such a heavy police presence the attempt was short-lived. Still, even then, a group of the new protesters broke off and attempted to take over the IND subway line at the corner of Sixth Avenue and Waverly Place. There was a bit of a confusion during which the police tried to figure out if they could enter an area controlled by the Transit Police. After the bureaucratic and political points had been discussed, it was decided that they could, and they entered the station and chased the demonstrators out.

It was not until around 3:30 A.M. that the police finally succeeded in dispersing all of the crowds.[76] The TPF remained on the scene for some time later.[77] It is even debatable the extent to which the clearing of the streets meant a victory for the police. According to Leitsch, many men had taken advantage of the heavy police presence in the heart of the Village to go to the docks for some recreational sex. Leitsch writes: "The docks were packed tight with homosexuals having the times of their lives. After all, everything was perfectly 'safe'—all the cops were on 'The Corner'!"[78]

11

"They've Lost That
Wounded Look"

SUNDAY–WEDNESDAY

As New Yorkers walked through the Christopher Park area of Greenwich Village on Sunday, teams of gay people—each consisting of one man and one woman—passed out a flyer headlined "Get the Mafia and the Cops Out of Gay Bars." Issued in the name of the Homophile Youth Movement, the typed document proclaimed that "the nights of Friday, June 27, 1969, and Saturday, June 28, 1969, will go down in history as the first time that thousands of Homosexual men and women went out into the streets to protest the intolerable situation which has existed in New York City for many years—namely, the Mafia (or syndicate) control of this city's Gay bars in collusion with certain elements in the Police Dept. Of the City of New York." Written by Craig Rodwell, the flyer reasoned that since January 1968, when Judge Keating had ruled that even close dancing between homosexuals was legal, there was "*nothing illegal, per se, about a Gay bar.*" The flyer therefore urged gay businessmen to open legal bars that would not overcharge and that would have "a healthy social atmosphere." It also suggested that homosexual men and women "boycott places like the Stonewall," in order to "get criminal elements out of" gay bars, and write Mayor Lindsay to demand "a thorough investigation and effective action to correct this intolerable situation."

By Sunday it indeed seemed justifiable to hail the two previous nights as historic. Rodwell recalls that even after the first night, "all kinds of people [were] getting together to discuss what are we going to do, because everybody sensed that nothing's going to be the same after this. We just knew. I'm sure there were some people there that were saying, 'Oh, I don't want to get involved in this,' and ran away, but for those of us that were there—and there were many thousands of us—we sensed that it was a moment in history. There was a lot of very animated talks all over the place. 'What's going to happen now? What are we going to do?'"[1] Rodwell was not alone in sensing the importance of events: his estranged lover, Dick Leitsch, writing on behalf of Mattachine–New York titled his account of the uprising: "The Hairpin Drop Heard Around the World," *dropping a hairpin* being homosexual argot from the era for dropping a hint that one is gay.[2]

Sunday, Monday, and Tuesday nights remained relatively calm due to the police having learned several lessons from the first two nights of the riots: that in the aftermath of Friday night's raid it would take many more police officers than were initially deployed on Saturday to discourage gay men and women and their allies from attempting to seize the area around the Stonewall, which the homosexual citizens saw as their turf; that the police needed to arrive early in large numbers to preempt the gay citizenry from seizing the initiative; and that such a maneuver must be executed in a low-key manner or their mere presence might precipitate the outbreaks they were hoping to end. (At least the police used this approach on Sunday night and it worked.) The second factor working in the police's favor was that the weekend had passed. Friday and Saturday nights' events had begun late and lasted until the early morning, something most people could not do on an evening before a workday, especially if they had already done so on the previous night or two. Thirdly, some of the demonstrators felt that they had already made their point and nothing more was to be gained by again repeating what was becoming a predictable scenario. Was it worth risking more injuries and arrests, as well as damage to the neighborhood that gay people were fighting to claim as their own?

Still, Rodwell and other activists felt that the protests must continue as long as possible to try to ensure that lesbians and gay men would be heard at last, that the events of the last two days would have some kind of lasting result and not be seen as a fluke.

Mattachine–New York, however, after talking to the mayor's office and the police, joined police efforts to stop the protests. A prominent sign went up on Sunday afternoon on the front of the Stonewall Inn's east window:

> WE HOMOSEXUALS PLEAD WITH
> OUR PEOPLE TO PLEASE HELP
> MAINTAIN PEACEFUL AND QUIET
> CONDUCT ON THE STREETS OF
> THE VILLAGE—MATTACHINE[3]

Mattachine officials came to the Stonewall Inn and talked to people who showed up in an effort to discourage them from protesting.

These attempts to stop the protesters did not work. On Sunday night gay men again turned out in significant numbers on Christopher Street, including a sizable leather contingent.[4] Truscott condescendingly wrote that "Sunday night was a time for watching and rapping. Gone were the 'gay power' chants of Saturday, but not the new and open brand of exhibitionism. Steps, curbs, and the park provided props for what amounted to the Sunday fag follies as returning stars from the previous night's performances stopped by to close the show for the weekend."[5] There were fewer protesters, however, than there had been on the previous two nights, and the police presence was very high. Dick Leitsch wrote that "there were never enough people to outnumber the large squads of cops milling about" and that "all the cops in town seemed to be near The Corner again."[6] Truscott felt that "it was slow going."[7] *The Berkeley Barb* reported that on Sunday "the word passed for another gay demonstration. Help was expected from the SDS, but they never showed up."[8]

Nonetheless, there were small acts of resistance by gay people—beyond demonstrating against the police publicly for the third day in a row, which was remarkable in itself: several gay youths took daring advantage of the heavy police presence in the Christopher Street area to make a guerrilla raid on the Sixth Precinct's headquarters. They went to the police station and slapped Day-Glo blue and fuschia bumper stickers reading "Equality for Homosexuals" on the police cars, a patrol wagon, and the personal cars of cops who had left their vehicles parked while on duty.[9] Whether any police officers who drove such subverted cars home unawares were able to laugh about it is unknown, but there is evidence that at least some of the police force appreciated the use of humor by New York's gay populace during the Stonewall Riots. A member of Mattachine–New York who was detained by the police reported overhearing the following exchange between two police officers:

One [cop] said he'd enjoyed the fracas. "Them queers have a good sense of humor and really had a good time," he said. His "buddy" protested: "Aw, they're sick. I like nigger riots better because there's more action, but you can't beat up a fairy. They ain't mean like blacks, they're sick. But you can't hit a sick man."[10]

Indeed, there is good evidence that after two days the police had finally learned something about queer community relations: With the Stonewall still open as a "free store," the police were "begging" homosexuals to go inside the club, a rich irony that Dick Leitsch noted with glee.[11] And when the TPF made a sweep of the area to clear it, they did so in a noncon-frontational way, not wearing their helmets and in a "controlled and very cool" manner.[12]

Lucian Truscott was standing in front of the United Cigar Store on Sev-enth Avenue South watching things wind down when he ran into Taylor Mead, an avant-garde film and literary figure. They stood on the corner and had been talking things over for a while when up walked Allen Ginsberg.[13] Ginsberg had heard about the "Stonewall battle" the previous day and had decided to drop by to see what was going on[14] and "to show the colors."[15]

Some gay activists happened by and filled Mead and Ginsberg in on the previous two nights' events, to which Ginsberg reacted enthusiastically: "Gay power! Isn't that great! We're one of the largest minorities in the country—ten percent, you know. It's about time we did something to assert ourselves." A sudden realization seemed to come over Ginsberg, who told Truscott, "You know, I've never been in there," and decided on the spot to visit the Stonewall Inn. As Ginsberg proceeded toward the Stonewall, he practiced his lifelong belief in peace, shaped by his pilgrimage to India, where he had studied Hindu meditation and chanting techniques for calm-ing and quieting the mind. As he walked over he held up the first two fin-gers of his hand in the V shape used to signify peace in the late 1960s and greeted the members of the TPF not with the epithet "pig" but by saying "hello" to them. Truscott noted that "it was a relief and a kind of joy to see him on the street. He lent an extra umbrella of serenity to the scene with his laughter and quiet commentary on consciousness, 'gay power' as a new movement, and the various implications of what had happened."

When Truscott entered the Stonewall Inn with Ginsberg, the poet im-mediately began to bounce and dance "wherever he moved."[16] This was also the first time Truscott had been inside the club, and he noted that rock music was being played from speakers placed all around the room, suggest-ing that a sound system had been brought in, necessitated because the po-lice had destroyed the jukeboxes. Truscott thought that the club looked like "a Hollywood set of a gay bar."[17]

Truscott recounts that Ginsberg "was real excited by it all. I mean, he was just bouncing up and down with glee. He just thought it was great that all these kids had stood up to the police and that there was a revolution happening. I mean, that's the way he was behaving. And when we went into the Stonewall, he went and danced with a whole bunch of kids."

After about an hour,[18] Ginsberg and Truscott left the Stonewall Inn and Ginsberg headed toward Manhattan's Lower East Side. As Truscott walked with him, Ginsberg explained what homosexual experience used to be like, drawing the contrast with the poet's experience that evening, and concluded, "You know, the guys there were so beautiful—they've lost that wounded look that fags all had ten years ago."

The two men parted company at Cooper Square. Ginsberg waved to Truscott and yelled, "Defend the fairies!" as Truscott watched him "bounce" across the square.[19]

Ginsberg's characterization of the change the Stonewall Riots had brought about was so perceptive that when the early gay activist Allen Young interviewed Ginsberg for the literary magazine *Gay Sunshine,* the only question that Young asked him about Stonewall concerned the circumstances behind Allen's statement. Ginsberg replied:

> I wasn't there at the riot. I heard about it, and I went down the next night to the Stonewall to show the colors. A crowd was there, and the place was open. So I said, the best thing I can do is to go in; the worst that can happen is I'll calm the scene. They're not going to attack them when I'm there. I'll just start a big Om.
>
> I didn't relate to the violent part. The trashing part I thought was bitchy, unnecessary, hysterical. But, on the other hand, there was this image that everybody wanted to make that they could beat up the police, which apparently they managed to do. It was so funny as an image that it was hard to disapprove of, even though it involved a little violence.[20]

Although Ginsberg's reply to Young is the lengthiest commentary on the riots he ever provided to an interviewer, it did not speak directly to the question about the loss of the "wounded look." Truscott, the person to whom Ginsberg made the comment, thinks he understands what inspired the poet. Pointing out that Allen did not generally hang out in gay bars and using the example of the jubilant looks on the faces of the street youths in the famous Fred McDarrah photographs of the rioters, Truscott explains that "I think his idea of what a gay bar was at that time was kind of like Julius': a bunch of middle-aged men, standing around in crew-necked sweaters having a drink. What happened was he got to see this real mixed population of queens and drag queens and these young street kids, and some of them were doubtlessly hustlers. All of them were young and had long hair. I mean, this doesn't look like a bunch of middle-aged, unhappy gay men at Julius'. And that's what he was responding to: all these sort of happy-go-lucky young guys, having a good time being gay, and not unhappy about it and not unproud about it and everything. That's what he was responding to, and that's why he said they've lost that wounded look. And that was the truth. Look at the pictures. You can see it on everybody's faces."

Ginsberg later said about the Stonewall Riots: "All of a sudden at the height of the antiwar movement, at the height of the black liberation movement, after the triumph of liberation of the word [the end of print censorship], all of a sudden the cops were in there again trying to bust some guys . . . right in the center of Sheridan Square, the most bohemian traditional place in Greenwich Village!"[21]

If Sunday night was "slow," then Monday and Tuesday nights were practically dead. In fact, there is only one contemporary account of those nights, that written by Dick Leitsch for the New York Mattachine Newsletter. According to him, while both nights were calm because few gay people were on the streets, by this time both the police and the protesters had become short-tempered. One police officer tried to pick a fight with passing gay men by repeatedly challenging them, saying, "Start something, faggot; just start something. I'd like to break your ass wide open." When one man finally turned and said, "What a Freudian comment, Officer!" the cop attacked the man and arrested him, placing him in a patrol wagon to be taken to jail.

While Leitsch says that some of the police did maintain "enormous 'cool,'" it is clear that others tried to provoke violence, apparently because of their recent humiliations. Leitsch saw two officers in a patrol car repeatedly drive around the area, shouting obscenities at passersby.

However, if some police sought to cause trouble, they were not the only ones: so did some gay men. A cop, stationed at the corner of Waverly Place and Christopher Street, made a show of swinging his nightstick while tossing insults at pedestrians. He made too inviting a target for one subversive to resist. A man Leitsch describes as "[a] wildly 'fem' queen," firecracker at the ready, snuck up behind the unsuspecting pillar of society, lit the explosive, and dropped it between the officer's feet. Leitsch describes the result: "It exploded and he jumped into the air in a leap that Villella would have envied, landing on a part of his anatomy that one queen called a 'moneymaker.' He got up screaming like a peasant woman and swinging his stick." When the same man tossed another firecracker at the policeman, a general fight broke out in which members of the crowd managed to steal the badge off the policeman's shirt.[22]

Some gay men were so angry that militancy at times overlapped into aggressiveness. Journalist Tom Burke witnessed an exchange at Waverly Place between a youth and a Village resident who walked up and down the street trying to calm the gay crowd, reassuring them that the heterosexual residents sympathized with "the oppressed homosexual." The portly older man in a white shirt tried to reason with a youth with long red hair wearing an acid-green tank top. The youth was having none of it.

"The hell you say! You don't impress me," the youth shouted. "You are straight and you are my enemy! Don't give me that phoney liberal bull. *You* made the laws. Nixon's silent army!" As onlookers laughed, the young man leaned in close to the older one, the youth's face now deep red. "Now we are gonna get *you!*"

The older man's face turned ashen, and Burke could tell he wanted to flee but was too frightened of what the young man might do.

"I was in Vietnam, man, how does that grab you? Huh? Huh? And, man, I'll screw your daughter. *But I'll screw your son first!*"[23]

On Wednesday night the riots came back full force. The reason for the sudden resurgence was twofold. The more obvious cause was the appearance of *The Village Voice* on Wednesday evening, which gave very prominent play to Truscott's and Smith's accounts of the uprising.[24] Dominating the front page, the two stories were run next to each other along with two photographs by Fred McDarrah, one showing some of the rioters and the other the graffiti written on the Stonewall Inn's boarded-up windows. While the stories may have enticed some curious citizens who had not yet heard of the riots to the Christopher Park area to see what was transpiring, the main effect of these accounts was to inflame the gay populace. While Smith and Truscott had done a good job of reporting the rebellion, the tone of Truscott's article—while often sympathetic and objective—was at times one of derision and insensitivity, with phrases like "Limp wrists," "the Sunday fag follies," and "gay cheerleaders." That Smith's article was less offensive than Truscott's, with only two derogatory expressions (the phrase "dancing faggots" and the word "dyke"),[25] was lost on the readers who, understandably, lumped the two articles together as one. While there was a lot of purposefully effeminate behavior on the part of some in the crowd, the two articles not only focused on this behavior but also ignored the courage shown by conventionally masculine gay men. (The only woman mentioned in the two articles is the lesbian resisting arrest, characterized by both men with the same single word *dyke*).[26] Edmund White attributed the writers' tone to their wanting to assure "readers that the authors are straight."[27] Not only did *Voice* reportage enrage the gay population; it also came quite close to consuming *The Voice* itself in flames, when a group of gay people considered setting fire to *The Voice's* office that night.[28] The anger that led to this discussion of whether to burn down the *Voice* office was apparently caused by not only the reporting on the riots but also *The*

Voice's various past slights toward gay men and lesbians. Leitsch wrote: "That paper's editorial policy has long infuriated most homosexuals, as the paper pretends to be 'liberal' and avant-garde, but actually is conservative and uptight about homosexuality." Leitsch let it be known that he held *The Voice* responsible to a large degree for the flaring up of the rioting that he and others in the Mattachine Society were trying to quell: "They published two long 'put down' articles about the Christopher Street incidents which contributed heavily to the anger that incited the Wednesday rioting after two relatively peaceful days."

The second reason that rioting resumed in full force on Wednesday is because various radical Left groups came to protest. Leitsch, a man whose politics were eclectic, combining views that ranged from very progressive to those more typically held by the Right, saw the radical Left groups as "exploiters [who] had moved in and were using the gay power movement for their own ends."[29]

While Kohler, a leftist, felt less negative about the influx of nongay Left groups, his reading of the crowd's composition and its significance is similar to Leitsch's:

"A lot of people kept coming down, asking what happened, asking the kids, me, anybody that was around [for] information. You had a lot of curiosity seekers. Because something had happened. Everybody was aware that there was a riot, so a lot of people had questions.

"You had, for lack of a better word, *provocateurs* who were seeing an incident that could be used for the good of their movement or a different movement or a coalition of movements. This was one more. It was the last. There was nobody else left to riot, so people with some foresight, more foresight than I [had] at the time, could see that this could again strengthen the radical movement, that people they hadn't really thought about were now up there in the front.

"The big thing on everybody's mind, especially the police and movement people, was that these were the only rioters that had gotten the best of the police. So that gave them a special strangeness. I mean, people just [wondered], *How could that happen?* Because there'd been riots with Yippies and there'd been riots with the SDS and Abbie Hoffman, but nobody had ever gotten the best of the police before. The police were never put on the run, and suddenly they were put on the run by the fairies, so those people were very curious: did this really happen?

"There was no carnival atmosphere; it was just people wanting to know what happened. A lot of grumbling and the kids were laughing and talking it over, getting ready for the night, a couple of people leafleting. . . . But it was not an exceptional day of any kind. It was just a rehashing.

"The riot no longer belonged to the kids. That was very obvious. So, yes, there was a difference in the makeup. There were more people rioting that could not be easily categorized, and a lot of that had to do with people that came over from other areas. The straight movement moved in heavily that night as a support. I'm assuming it was as a support. They were, of course, using it for their own ends, too, but you were aware the riot did not belong to the kids [Wednesday] night."

The action on Wednesday night began around 10:00 P.M. According to one report, at that time "a motorcade of police drove down Christopher Street looking for trouble."[30] There was a crowd of at least "several hundred youths" gathered near the Stonewall Inn described by the then-sympathetic *New York Post* as "shoving and bottle-hurling."[31] *The New York Times* reported it as a chanting crowd and estimated its size at five hundred strong.[32] Leitsch characterized the crowd as composed of "Black Panthers, Yippies, Crazies and young toughs from street gangs all over the city and some from New Jersey."[33]

Around 10:30 P.M. "queens" lit some trash at the corner of Waverly Place and Christopher Street, apparently resulting in more fires being set on Christopher Street,[34] to which both the TPF and the fire department responded.[35] While some members of the Mattachine Society were trying to stop such acts, the Mattachine Society leadership was trying to use the riots to advance the cause by distributing handouts stating that "the disorders showed that 'gay people are reaching the end of their patience.'"[36]

Indeed, it appears that by Wednesday night patience was in exceedingly short supply on all sides. While the *East Village Other* reported that "everything became more than serious,"[37] *The New York Times* described the crowd as "hostile,"[38] and Leitsch wrote that:

the street people were no longer half-serious, half-camping. The cops . . . had taken the offensive and massive retaliation was their goal. Some seemed quite ready to depopulate Christopher Street the moment anyone would give them permission to unholster their guns. Failing that, some of them, particularly some of the TPF men, tried to achieve the same objective with their nightsticks.[39]

Ronnie Di Brienza described the scene he witnessed:

One really fat Bircher-type pig grabbed a friend of mine, who was promptly beaten in front of two hundred people by three other pigs, and then carted off to a waiting patrol car. This was it. From no where the crowd swelled to an estimated thousand, and the battle was on. One head, standing on the corner of Waverly, was unfortunate enough to yell out "pig" just when the man was behind him.

Well, in front of 1,000 witnesses, he was pummeled, dragged, kicked and lifted down the length of Christopher Street to a waiting squad car on Seventh Avenue. . . .

My buddy received seven stitches over his left eye for his participation in a freedom of assembly rally.[40]

Between the anger of the demonstrators and that of the police—with the police of course being better equipped and trained—it is not surprising that many demonstrators were injured. Leitsch describes the bodies of the wounded that littered Seventh Avenue South between Christopher and West 10th streets: "Young people, many of them queens, were lying on the sidewalk, bleeding from the head, face, mouth, and even the eyes. Others were nursing bruised and often bleeding arms, legs, backs and necks."[41]

Nor were demonstrators the only ones hurt. At least one police officer, Richard Adkins, a patrolman, was injured seriously enough by a bottle that hit him on the left side of his face that he was taken to St. Vincent's Hospital.[42]

There is consensus that on this night, as on the first night of the Uprising, it was the effeminate men who did most of the fighting. Di Brienza wrote: "I have never seen anything worse than an infuriated queen with a bottle, or long nails. Believe me, get their ire up, and you face the wrath of all the Gods that ever lived. . . . Revolution is being heard on Christopher Street, only instead of guttural MC-5 voices, we hear it coming from sopranos, and altos."[43] Indeed, Leitsch takes this view even further, saying that not only were the "queens" braver than the masculine gay men, they were also braver than the Black Panthers, Yippies, and other leftists who were there on Wednesday night: "The exploiters had moved in . . . blacks and students who want a revolution, any kind of revolution . . . swelled the crowd . . . but 'graciously' let the queens take all the bruises and suffer all the arrests. (If they have no more courage than they displayed on Christopher Street, their revolution is a long way off.)"[44]

Five persons were arrested on Wednesday night. The charges against four of them was harassment; the charges against the fifth person are unknown.[45]

On Wednesday night Village shops were broken into, apparently by the nongay protesters, for as Dick Leitsch pointed out, "all the most unlikely places were looted": shops whose owners were sympathetic to the homophile movement and to the street queens were broken into and the "fag shops" that exploited the gay community by selling overpriced wares were not hit.[46]

While the police and protesters fought their hardest on Wednesday night, the strife finished quickly. As Ronnie Di Brienza wrote at the end of his account of what he called, with some understatement, the Stonewall Incident, "This all ended within an hour, and peace was restored." He concluded his report with a pithy summation of the meaning of the events he had witnessed from beginning to end: "But the word is out. Christopher Street shall be liberated. The fags have had it with oppression."[47]

GAY

LIBERATION

12

Seizing the Moment

The Stonewall Riots had barely ended when Bill Katzenberg called Charles Pitts, the coproducer of the WBAI series *The New Symposium*. The 1968 radio program had been so successful that the program's producers had mounted a new series, *The New Symposium II*. Katzenberg asked Pitts if he would be interested in helping to start a gay leftist group. Pitts agreed to meet with Katzenberg and invited Pete Wilson, Randy Wicker's lover, who had often appeared on *The New Symposium II*, to come along to the meeting. Wilson had not only appeared as an openly gay man on the 1969 radio series; he had also marched in most of the early homophile demonstrations and joined the League for Sexual Freedom, an organization Wicker had cofounded that advocated sexual freedom for all along libertarian lines. When Pitts and Katzenberg met, Pitts was so immediately inspired that even before Wilson arrived, he crafted the memorable lines that captured the new defiant spirit of gay New Yorkers. Soon scores of gay New Yorkers would find a piece of paper thrust in their hands that asked: "Do You Think Homosexuals Are Revolting?" The same flyer rejoined: "You Bet Your Sweet Ass We Are," before promising: "We're going to make a place for ourselves in the revolutionary movement."[1] The flyer urged all who wanted to help in this new endeavor to show up at the July 24 Alternate U. meeting, the same date that O'Brien and Katzenberg had reserved at Alternate U. before the Stonewall uprising.[2]

Unbeknownst to Katzenberg, O'Brien, and Pitts, a young man named Michael Brown who had witnessed the riots sensed an opening to join newly politicized gay men with blacks, antiwar activists, and other forces on the Left. Although Brown worked in an interior decorating firm on Wall Street and had been on the staff of Hubert Humphrey's 1968 presidential campaign, he considered himself both a socialist and countercultural. He had been thrilled during the riots to see so many gay men be public about their sexuality, for he felt disgusted by the secrecy of gay life and the sordid tone that sometimes resulted from leading such a shadow life. Brown had thrown himself into the effort to support the Stonewall Riots, primarily by helping Dick Leitsch mimeograph and distribute Leitsch's account of the riots, "The Hairpin Drop Heard Around the World." The mimeographed "Hairpin" hailed the event as "the first gay riots in history" and "the opening shot" of what could be "a long, hot summer" unless reforms were made.

When Brown explained his ideas and feelings to Dick Leitsch before the riots were even over, Leitsch told him to be realistic and underlined the importance of Mattachine–New York not jeopardizing its relationship with those in authority. But Brown insisted that it was an absolute necessity for Mattachine to respond to the riots proactively.

David Scott was a twenty-one-year-old who had gotten caught up in supporting the riots when he met Michael Brown handing out mimeographed copies of "The Hairpin Drop" near Christopher Park. Scott was so eager that nearly every night after work he went up to volunteer at the Mattachine offices, helping to mimeograph flyers and then distribute them in the area around Christopher Park. While he was at the Mattachine offices he met Marty Robinson, John O'Brien, Dick Leitsch, and Madolin Cervantes, a heterosexual Mattachine member and one of its most enthusiastic supporters. He recalls a major discussion that he heard about a week after the riots among Madolin, Marty, Michael, Dick, and possibly John. "I remember Madolin saying, 'Oh, we should be nice. Gay people are known as being nice, sweet people.' And like Marty and [others] of them said, 'No! This has all got to change. It's time to get radical. The civil rights movement didn't get where they are by being nice and quiet. The antiwar movement didn't get where it is. We have to be militant, and we have to confront the authorities.'"

Leitsch yielded to Brown's entreaties and agreed to form an Action Committee and to schedule a meeting where all concerned could express their feelings and reactions to the riots. The meeting was scheduled for July 9 at Freedom House in midtown. Headed "GAY POWER," the flyer advertising the meeting was circulated during the riots over July 1 and 2. The flyer declared that the riots had shown "that gay people are reaching the end of their patience. At the bottom of the calls for GAY POWER and HOMOSEXUAL EQUALITY is a realization that we can influence our existence—if we can only come together."[3] By July 5 a new flyer appeared. This one, titled "Homosexual Liberation Meeting," recognized that the riots presented a rare opportunity for movement forward that must not be lost:

"Many of us in the community have been heartened by the appearance of a new spirit this past two weeks. Now is the time to take a stand on our own behalf. We cannot let the homosexual community fall back into a period of indifference and inaction because we have seen that this leads to persecution and explosive bitterness." It concluded with a tenet of the Left: "[N]o one is free until everyone is free!"[4]

How ready the times were for such a new direction is demonstrated not only by the riots themselves but also by how individuals were affected by the uprising in terms of political awareness. When Marty Robinson witnessed one of the kick lines squaring off with the TPF on the first night of the riots he had had a kind of epiphany, discovering in that moment that gay men's sexuality was "something precious, something worth fighting for." That night, he had lain awake in bed, unable to sleep as he thought about "the responsibility of being in the movement and the importance of doing things that are good for people." He concluded: "If I go out and politicize and repeat and demonstrate this liberation over and over again we will change the way homosexuals live." In Marty's mind, that night sealed his commitment to the gay political movement.[5]

Martha Shelley, who had only recently resigned as one of the officers of New York's small branch of the Daughters of Bilitis, had seen the riots on their second night as she was showing the Village to some DOB members visiting from Boston. She had not been aware that she was witnessing a homosexual riot, so that when her visitors had asked her what was going on she had played the New York sophisticate, calmly saying, "Oh, just a riot. We have them here all the time," and had continued her walking tour. But on reading the Sunday *New York Times* the following afternoon and learning the nature of the riot, she received a jolt. She, too, had barely slept, and not only because she had missed the last bus home to New Jersey after showing her guests around. "I was slightly feverish from lack of sleep, so I lay on my couch tossing and turning, so excited by it, thinking, 'We have to do something. We have to have a protest march.' I thought, *What am I going to do?* I thought, *I can make a speech or something.* I said, 'Yes, stand up in public and get shot at.' [But] that part of me that says, *You'd rather die than be called a coward,* came to the fore and said I have to do it." Martha went to the phone and called Jeannie and Eleanor, a lesbian couple who kept the local DOB running. After explaining what was going on, Martha said, "Look, we've got to do something. Let's have a march." Jeannie and Eleanor suggested that Martha go to the Mattachine Society. "If they agree to it, we'll jointly sponsor it."[6]

Michael Brown, Martha Shelley, and Marty Robinson were not the only ones to sense the change in the air. According to historian Toby Marotta, several homosexuals with New Left or countercultural values went to

Mattachine–New York, Daughters of Bilitis, and Craig Rodwell to urge radical new action. Those who called on Mattachine–New York and DOB found that "their budding ideas about gay political activity were very different from the homophile outlooks of the leaders in charge." Those who went to Rodwell, who was trying to get people to join HYMN, agreed with him that his "need to keep his bookstore legal and self-sustaining" limited the kind of activities that HYMN, as an extension of the bookstore, could undertake.

As Brown hustled to find recruits for his Action Committee, one of the first he got to join was Bill Weaver, a gay man he had worked with to organize the large New York City antiwar march down Fifth Avenue. Soon Earl Galvin, Marty Robinson, and Martha Shelley were members as well.

How word had spread through connections at Alternate U. showed how ripe the time was for a new kind of movement. Susan Silverman, the director of programming at Alternate U., had helped set up the July 24 meeting. Silverman had started to think about women's issues in 1967 when only seventeen and a member of the Queens College SDS chapter. There she had been encouraged by feminist Robin Morgan to join New York Radical Women, New York City's first such feminist group. Through New York Radical Women she had participated in some of the key events in the new women's liberation movement, such as the 1968 feminist protest at the Miss America Pageant. Although these demonstrations had given an outlet to Silverman's passionate interest in feminist issues, they had done nothing to help her integrate her lesbian feelings, which she kept secret. Feeling isolated within WITCH, the radical feminist guerrilla theater collective, she quit the organization and began to work at Alternate U. She also ran a feminist workshop at Alternate U. in which she met Lois Hart, a follower of the recently deceased silent Eastern master, Meher Baba. Hart was the first woman Silverman had ever met who was willing to talk about being a lesbian, and both would attend the July 24 meeting.[7]

But even before the first community meeting was held at Freedom House, another event took place that showed how ambiguously some in the gay community viewed the recent riots, as well as the extent to which the incipient movement would have its work cut out.

Ironically, Randy Wicker, the homophile movement's first East Coast militant, had been horrified by the riots. For years he had worked hard to counter stereotypical portrayals of homosexual men, and the reports he heard of the riots sounded like his worst nightmare come true: effeminate boys were in the streets camping it up while drag queens joined gay men in a chorus line to kick their heels at cops and others set trash cans on fire. And they were getting more press than Randy had received even on his best day. Wicker feared that a crazed queen might set one of the Village's old residences on fire and a grandmother or a child might be incinerated alive, obliterating overnight all the progress homophile activists had so painstakingly achieved over the past decade. Wicker had also gone up to the Mattachine–New York office to beseech Leitsch, but to calm things down rather than rev them up. Wicker proposed diverting energy into a positive and peaceful channel, such as the effort the organization already had under way to raise money to replace the trees the vigilantes had cut down in Queens. Somehow the management of the Electric Circus, one of Manhattan's biggest and hippest nightclubs, which was just beginning to see business slacken, heard of the riots and had the idea of opening its doors to gay men and women. Mattachine accepted the offer and the nightclub put out a flyer titled *Oh Boy!*, extolling itself as offering the city's best recorded sound and light show and saying: "We don't think it's necessary for gay people to be quizzed at the door, packed into over-crowded, over-heated, over-priced, Mafia-controlled sewers. If you all come, and if the experiment works—it could be beautiful . . . beautiful enough to do every week." The flyer noted that "we'll be open to the general public as usual, but we're especially encouraging gay people to come—and we really hope that everyone will dance together and dig one another." The Electric Circus invited gay people to come and dance on the night of July 6, a Sunday, promising that all the proceeds would go to the Mattachine fund to buy new "Trees for Queens."

When July 6 did come around, everything began smoothly. An acid rock band played a medley of popular songs, and some straight couples even joined gay ones on the dance floor. When the music stopped shortly after midnight, Wicker, wearing an American flag shirt (similar to the one that Abbie Hoffman had stolen from him and had been famously seen wearing on television), addressed the crowd and began talking about "gay power," the phrase made famous by the riots. But Wicker also criticized the Stonewall Riots, saying: "Rocks through windows don't open doors." Apparently the Circus had not bothered to inform all of their staff about their guests that Sunday evening, for after Randy had spoken only a few words, one of their employees suddenly realized he might be surrounded by homosexuals. He asked a blond youth standing next to him if he was "with them" and when the man replied affirmatively began to pummel him. Jack Nichols, who witnessed the scene, wrote that after the staff member was quelled, he was "led from the premises screaming and shouting like a madman." The violence ended the evening, and Wicker offered to give the bloodied youth a ride home. In the car, Randy learned that the young man had fought at the Stonewall Riots. When Randy asked him what he thought about it all, the youth answered, "All I know is that I've been in this movement three days, and I've been beaten up three times."[8]

When the July 9 meeting called by the Mattachine was held, close to a hundred people attended. One of those present was Bob Kohler, who stood up and tried to get attention for the street youths by asking for dona-tions of money or clothing for them: "We're on the brink of something here. Organizations are forming, and we're hearing 'gay liberation,' but these kids are sitting in the park. I'm doing what I can." But those at the meeting were not in a charitable mood and told him to "sit down and shut up." Most of those at the meeting wanted to hold a demonstration to protest police harassment. A vote was taken and the idea of the march won overwhelmingly. The people who wanted to have a march were told to hold a planning session in a room to the rear, to which Martha Shelley and oth-ers repaired. It was a hot day, and the newly formed march committee opened cans of beer to quench their thirst as they began to work. The ac-tivists decided that the committee should have a name. As various names were proposed, someone put forward "the Gay Liberation Front," a name modeled on the Communist Vietnamese National Liberation Front. Martha Shelley recalls her spontaneous reaction when she heard the phrase: "I started pounding on the table, saying, 'That's it! That's it! We're the Gay Liberation Front!'" In her enthusiasm, Shelley hit her hand on her beer's pop top over and over until she began to bleed, as she continued to scream, "Oh, all right!"

The group raised such a ruckus in their joy that Dick Leitsch came in demanding, "What's going on here? What is this Gay Liberation Front?" Shelley recalls: "He was really upset. He thought that we were going to have another organization. There were seven gay organizations in New York, some consisting only of two people and a newsletter. He wanted there to be one gay organization, with him at the head of it. So we hastened to re-assure him, 'Oh, no, we're not starting an organization. We're just a march committee.'"[9]

But Brown wanted something still more militant in tone and pressed for a second meeting, urging that it be held in the Village, since it was "the heart of the gay community."

The next meeting was therefore planned to take place at St. John's Epis-copal Church on Waverly Place on July 16. In the meantime, it was decided that the action should be both a protest and a commemoration of the Stonewall Riots. There would be a rally with speeches in Washington Square Park, followed by a march to the Stonewall Inn on the one-month anniversary of the riots. An ad was placed in *The Village Voice* that an-nounced the July 27 demonstration as co-sponsored by the Daughters of Bilitis and Mattachine–New York. The display ad urged the reader to "SUPPORT GAY POWER" by attending the demonstration and wearing a lavender armband.[10]

Between the meetings of July 9 and 16 Brown recruited Earl Galvin, Bill Weaver, and Martha Shelley to join the Mattachine Action Committee, or MAC. As members of MAC were leafleting for the July 16 meeting, they saw flyers advertising a special picket to be held on Bastille Day at the House of Detention for Women in support of the inmates, especially Black Panthers Afeni Shakur (mother of the future rapper Tupac Shakur) and Joan Bird. To show that gay people were now ready to join other oppressed minorities, MAC members joined the July 14 demonstration, which included John O'Brien. For the first time the two streams that had been independently moving toward starting a militant gay activist organization converged. They also got their first press coverage as militant and radical homosexuals in *Rat*: "[T]he demonstrators, chanting and singing, marched around the Women's House led by black people who had come to visit their friends inside and who had joined the solidarity demonstration. Then gay people, who now call themselves 'Pink Panthers,' . . . led the parade from the Women's House to the Stonewall Inn—scene of the Christopher Street riots."[11]

The flyer put out by Mattachine–New York on July 10 called for gay people to end their isolation and apathy by attending the second gay liberation meeting, claiming that the "positive response" to the first gay power meeting had shown that "homosexuals are no longer going to sit back and be apathetic pawns for every politician who comes along."[12]

As it turned out, apathy would be the least of Mattachine's problems at the July 16 meeting. On that night, around two hundred people gathered in a large room with a low ceiling. Things got off to a bad start when Dick Leitsch arrived late. From there it went downhill—or uphill, depending upon one's point of view. Tom Burke recorded what happened:

> Dick Leitsch, in a staid brown suit, strides to the front. With professional aplomb, he reopens the meeting. Police brutality and heterosexual indifference must be protested, he asserts; at the same time, the gay world must retain the favor of the Establishment, especially those who make and change the laws. Homosexual acceptance will come slowly, by educating the straight community, with grace and good humor and . . .
>
> A tense boy with leonine hair is suddenly on his feet . . . "We don't want acceptance, goddamn it! We want respect! Demand it! We're through hiding in dark bars behind Mafia doormen. We're going to go where straights go and do anything with each other they do and if they don't like it, well, *fuck them!* [. . .]

"Well, now, *I* think," says [Mattachine's secretary] Mrs. Cervantes, "that what we ought to have is a gay vigil, in a park. Carry candles, perhaps. A peaceful vigil. I think we should be firm, but just as amicable and sweet as . . ."

"Sweet!" The new speaker resembles Billy the Kid. He is James Fouratt, New Left celebrity [. . .]

"Sweet! Bullshit! There's the stereotype homosexual again, man! Soft, weak, sensitive! Bullshit! That's the role society has been forcing these queens to play, and they just sit and accept it. We have got to radicalize, man! Be proud of what you are, man! And if it takes riots or even guns to show them what we are, well, that's the only language that the pigs understand!"

Wild applause.[. . .]

Dick Leitsch tries to reply, but Fouratt shouts him down.

"All the oppressed have got to unite! The system keeps us all weak by keeping us separate.[. . .]"

Again and again, Dick Leitsch tugs frantically at his clean white tie, shouting for the floor, screaming for order. He is firmly ignored.[13]

The old wineskin was not able to contain the new wine. Nor was the Mattachine meeting on July 16 the first indication that the gay youth inspired by Stonewall would not follow the forms that an earlier generation had. As Craig Rodwell had ridden to Philadelphia on July 4 on the bus he had chartered for the Annual Reminder, he noticed that the people on the bus, most of whom he had personally recruited, were very animated. Much of the talk on the bus was about the Stonewall Riots, which had ended only a little more than twenty-four hours before the bus had departed New York.

When Lilli Vincenz arrived from Washington, D.C., for the Annual Reminder, she immediately noticed a change. Instead of a small and sedate group in conservative dress, she found a boisterous crowd double the usual size, wearing jeans and T-shirts and brimming over with excitement about the riots. "It was clear that things were changing. People who had felt oppressed now felt empowered," she recalls.[14]

When the demonstration started, its organizers told the demonstrators to follow the stringent rules always used at the Annual Reminder: pickets had to walk in a circle, single file and without chanting. For half an hour Craig marched in silence in the terrible heat, with no shade, clad in a suit and tie. Inwardly, he and others were seething to cut loose, to "really make a statement." Then he noticed that two young women right in front of him were simultaneously breaking two of the picket demonstration's rules: they were not marching single file and they were holding hands. Craig was just thinking, *Oh-h-h, isn't that wonderful!* when Frank Kameny, his face red as a beet, moved in between the two women and Craig and with a karate-chop blow broke their hands apart, saying, "None of that! None of that!"[15]

Furious, Craig immediately convinced about ten couples he had brought from New York to march holding hands. Bill Weaver scratched out the bland slogan on his picket sign and scrawled: "SMASH SEXUAL FAS-CISM!" on it. Rodwell noticed that the media were "going crazy" at the sight of queers actually holding hands in public as they marched in front of Independence Hall on July Fourth. He then spotted Kameny talking to a journalist. By prior agreement, the event's organizers had designated Kameny as the official spokesman, the one person authorized to talk to the media. Rodwell strode up to Kameny and barged in. "Did you hear about what's going on in New York and the riots last week?" Craig demanded. "We're tired of not being able to hold hands in public, and the leadership of our demonstration has to change."

The bus ride back to New York City was just as animated as the one going down had been, but this time instead of the talk being about the Stonewall Riots, it was about the Annual Reminder and dress codes. As he listened, Craig realized that he had just attended the last of the Annual Reminders. Never again would gay people agree to such a controlled demonstration.

The July 24 meeting at Alternate U. drew about forty people, including Katzenberg, O'Brien, Pitts, Wilson, Hart, Silverman, Brown, Weaver, Galvin, Shelley, Fouratt, and Hoose. The crowd of mostly radical homosexuals was astonished at their own numbers. They decided to have each attendee introduce him- or herself and talk a little about his or her background. After these introductions, the group agreed to meet again in one week. By this time, Brown, Weaver, and Galvin had quit MAC, whose leadership was assumed by Marty Robinson and Martha Shelley.

Robinson and Shelley were the main speakers at the Gay Power vigil and march to the Stonewall Inn six days after the first Alternate U. meeting. By 2:00 P.M. five hundred gay men and lesbians had gathered around the fountain in Washington Square Park. A new logo for the nascent revolution was displayed that day: a lavender banner with two female symbols interlinked on the left and two male symbols interlinked on the right was unfurled. Lavender armbands and sashes were distributed to the crowd. Martha Shelley stood on the fountain's rim to address the throng. She praised those present for their courage in attending such an open meeting: "The time has come for us to walk in the sunshine. We don't have to ask permission to do it. Here we are!" As she developed her theme, Shelley's tone became more militant: "Brothers and sisters, welcome to this city's first gay-power vigil. We're tired of being harassed and persecuted. If a straight couple can hold hands in Washington Square, why can't we?" The crowd applauded and went into a delirium of screams, giggles, and shouts of "Sock it to 'em!" and "Long live the queen!" Shelley continued, "We will no longer be victimized by straight people who are guilt-ridden about sex. We're tired of flashlights and peeping-tom vigilantes. Tired of marriage laws that punish you for lifting your head off the pillow." After Shelley finished by naming some famous homosexuals, Marty Robinson addressed the crowd.

The passionate young carpenter declared that "Gay power is here! Gay power is no laugh. There are one million homosexuals in New York City. If we wanted to, we could boycott Bloomingdale's, and that store would be closed in two weeks." He asked everyone present to join with groups like Mattachine–New York and Daughters of Bililis to press the fight for equality. "We will not permit another reign of terror. Let me tell you, homosexuals, we've got to get organized. We've got to stand up. This is our chance!"

The crowd then marched down 4th Street to Sheridan Square in a four-by-four column, clapping in cadence and shouting "Gay power" and other slogans. As traffic was halted for them to cross Sixth Avenue, the protesters gained confidence. This was the first openly gay march not only in New York City but on the East Coast and many could not believe what they were seeing. As *The Village Voice* reported, "Even 4th Street's resident gypsies unearthed an Instamatic from the bowels of their trailer and snapped away. . . . Maybe it wasn't just a joke. Maybe there really was a gay power."

As the crowd assembled in and around the park across from the Stonewall Inn, Marty Robinson appealed for money, as well as for the creation of a gay newspaper. At this point there was tension among some of the protesters, for according to John O'Brien, Robinson had made an agreement with him that after reaching Sheridan Square they would march on the Sixth Precinct station. When someone shouted out that they should march on to the police station, Robinson ignored it and the crowd sang "a curiously moving 'We Shall Overcome'" before Robinson and Shelley both urged the crowd to disperse, apparently afraid of potential violence if the march continued to the police station. O'Brien felt betrayed and decided that from then on he would have nothing to do with the Mattachine Society. To the *Village Voice* reporter it seemed that "[g]ay power had surfaced. . . . A mild protest to be sure, but apparently only the beginning."[16]

On July 31 at the second gay militant meeting at Alternate U., the assembly voted to call the new organization the Gay Liberation Front. They chose the name in part as a tribute to the National Liberation Front in its war with the South Vietnamese and U.S. governments. They also selected the name in hope that the new political entity would indeed be a "front," that is, not simply a new organization but a unified alliance with all other gay and lesbian groups. But the vote on the new name would be one of the few noncontroversial votes in the Gay Liberation Front's short and highly fractious history.

Ironically or fittingly, the big fight at the first official meeting of the Gay Liberation Front (or GLF, as it soon became known), as Charles Pitts, one of the founders, explained, was over whether the new group "should be [about] self-enlightenment (as a kind of consciousness-raising type thing) or integration immediately with other revolutionary or militant movements." The meeting voted and a slight majority, around 52 percent, favored concentrating on homosexual issues for the immediate future. The outcome caused a lot of shouting and disruptions as the more radical members, intent now on forming their own group, walked out. At this point many people who had attended, including Marty Robinson, were so disgusted they walked out of what now appeared to be a divided movement, leaving the floor to the more revolutionary types. In the second room a more organized meeting proceeded, so that many who had voted against joining the SDS-type radicals joined those in the second room. Jerry Hoose, who was not a leftist, stayed. He explained in retrospect that "the victory of the radicals was sealed when the responsibility for preparing a statement for *Rat* announcing GLF's birth was delegated to Michael Brown, Lois Hart, and Ron Ballard," the last two members in particular being among the most radical of all of GLF's members.

The article for *Rat* in which the Gay Liberation Front made its debut was done in the form of an interview, with the supposed interviewer unidentified. To the first question, "What is the Gay Liberation Front?," the answer given was direct, if grounded in theory:

> We are a revolutionary homosexual group of men and women formed with the realization that complete sexual liberation for all people cannot come about unless existing social institutions are abolished. We reject society's attempt to impose sexual roles and definitions of our nature. We are stepping outside these roles and simplistic myths. We are going to be who we are. At the same time, we are creating new social forms and relations, that is, relations based upon brotherhood, cooperation, human love, and uninhibited sexuality. Babylon has forced us to commit ourselves to one thing . . . revolution.

The answer to the second question indicated the strong Marxist strain that would dominate the organization. This ideology influenced both GLF's

analysis of the plight of lesbians and gay men as well as the position held
by a majority of its members, that true homosexual revolutionaries should,
indeed must, ally themselves with other groups oppressed by capitalism:

> *What makes you revolutionaries?*
>   We formed after the recent pig bust of the Stonewall, a well
> known gay bar in Greenwich Village. We've come to realize that all
> our frustrations and feelings of oppression are real. The society has
> fucked with us . . . within our families, on our jobs, in our education,
> in the streets, in our bedrooms; in short, it has shit all over us. We,
> like everyone else, are treated as commodities. We're told what to
> feel, what to think [. . . .] We identify ourselves with all the op-
> pressed: the Vietnamese struggle, the third world, the blacks, the
> workers . . . all those oppressed by this rotten, dirty, vile, fucked-up
> capitalist conspiracy.[17]

Asked how capitalism oppressed homosexuals in particular, GLF pointed
to the closet, which it saw as the result of a social "system of taboos and in-
stitutionalized repressions" to control "sexual expression." GLF's analysis of
the gay political situation appropriately brought in both Freud and femi-
nism, for marriage was named "one of the most insidious and basic sustain-
ers of the system" of sexual repression because, through it, "a male worker
is given the illusion of participating in the power of the ruling class through
economic control of his children and through the relation he has with his
wife as sexual object and household slave."

To end gay oppression, GLF said that it would "[relate] the militancy
generated by the bar bust and by increasing pig harassment to a program
that allows homosexuals and sexually liberated persons to confront themselves and society." GLF said it would achieve this through creating encounter groups, holding demonstrations, putting on dances, starting a
newspaper, "and just by being ourselves on the street," emphasizing the
value of being "out of the closet" that would, in contrast to the homophile
movement, be one of the hallmarks of the gay liberation movement. GLF
already had "specific plans" that included opening a coffeehouse and starting both "a working commune, and experimental living communes."[18]

While the analysis and the language used by GLF in its coming-out
announcement were both revolutionary and highly militant, in practice, as
historian Donn Teal recognized, "GLF did not become SDS-type revolutionary. Its public appearances ranged, as did its membership, from support of Movement-sponsored protests to confrontations over American
anti-homosexuality, personal, political, and organizational." Toby Marotta
concurred: "Although Brown, Hart, and Ballard took steps [in the *Rat* arti-

cle] to identify GLF with all the major concerns of the Movement, they made concessions to win the support of activists eager to deal first with gay issues."

It is also true that because of some of the positions GLF adopted at its inception, particularly that of trying to form alliances with other radical causes, less than four months after its birth GLF would fatally split. In the meantime, the single most important thing that needed to happen did: enough people had recognized the unique opportunity created by the Stonewall Riots to form a new, radically militant homosexual organization. The energy that the riots had released was not allowed to dissipate.

13

"We're the Gay Liberation Front!"

On a Friday night Martha Shelley spun around joyously in the dance hall to the pounding beat of the rock music that filled the room. It mattered little that this room enlivened by happy faces and animated bodies usually functioned as an Alternate U. meeting room or that the blaring music came from a makeshift stereo and tape deck system. What did matter to Martha and the hundreds of other gay men and lesbians crowded into the room was that they had come together to create this celebratory event where they felt free. Intense bursts of color generated by a light show obscured the political posters that normally provided the plain hall's only decoration. While some men and women taking a break between dances sat in the wooden folding chairs lined up along the sides of the room, others sat in the windows overlooking the street, their feet dangling three floors above the sidewalk. As everyone gathered on the floor to participate in the line dance, the primal tribal feeling grew stronger. The men and women joined together and snaked around the room hooting and shouting, then spiraled into a tight mass before quickly unwinding with such terrific force that Nikos Diaman's glasses snapped in two as he was thrown into another reveler's body.[1]

Martha loved the joy and freedom she found in these communal rituals. Such celebratory dances felt entirely different from her experiences of lesbian bars before the summer of 1969. The watering holes she had frequented were dimly lit and small. As she had danced in those small bars she had felt uptight and uncomfortable. At the GLF dances the coat check was free and a beer cost a quarter. At these dances, friendly GLF hosts wearing name tags constantly circulated looking for anyone who seemed alone, and when they found a wallflower they talked to the man or woman and encouraged him or her to dance. Here the lights were low enough to be romantic, but not so low as to suggest you were in hiding. Off this main room couples found smaller, dimly lit rooms furnished with mats and chairs, a setting that invited quiet conversation and romantic encounters. These elements created an atmosphere of sexiness and camaraderie, as shown by the way the dancers smiled, hugged, kissed, and even pinched each other.

Soon there would be dances exclusively for GLF women, which made them even more ecstatic: "I remember when we had the lesbian-only dances, we could get undressed. We danced, you know, naked to the waist. Some people even took off all their clothes. I never went that far, but any chance to take off my shirt—Ooh, all right! You know, hot night, summer in the city. And we danced in circles that were like an expression of community, not just coupling off. I'm sure we did too [many] drugs, though I never had that much of a problem with it. People slept around. Sometimes they stayed in couples for long times. But there was this feeling of ecstasy and freedom. It was great."

Jim Owles was equally enthusiastic about the GLF dances: "The first time I danced with a man was at a GLF dance, and I really loved it! It was terrific!" A born fighter and individualist, he had never had sex with another man until his twenty-second year, after he had been discharged from the air force, primarily for protesting the Vietnam War. Jim was still twenty-two when he arrived in New York City just in time to read news accounts about the Stonewall Riots. When he saw a notice about a meeting of "militant homosexuals" he decided to attend. At first he felt unsure about whether he should join the more radical group that was forming or stay with MAC. He discussed his reservations with Marty Robinson, who, like Jim, wondered if the radicals' only real intention was to provoke violence to bring about a revolution. Eventually Jim and Marty became lovers and both ended up joining GLF. Although out of the closet for less than a year, Jim wholeheartedly threw himself into the most militant gay organization ever. The young radical even became GLF's treasurer.[2]

The GLF dances were so popular that people came not just from Long Island or New Jersey but also from as far away as Amherst and Baltimore.[3] While other groups that used Alternate U. sometimes had dances, they attracted only small groups of people. For these gay dances, the line stretched down the block.[4]

The reasons for the dances' success were clear to Jerry Hoose and Bob Kohler, who organized them. Kohler recalls, "For the first time—hallelujah!— gay dances would be non-Mafia-run. It would be the first time that it would be gay dances by gay people for gay people, with the money that was handed in at the door going to gay issues and gay causes. This was a fabulous first. I get chills when I think about it. I mean, what had we had up till that point? Our entire existence revolved around oppressive, Mafia-run gay establishments where they hated faggots, where you risked your life." For Hoose, who disliked gay bars, the contrast could not have been more marked. He hated everything about the Stonewall Inn except its dance floor and had witnessed Ed Murphy brutalizing a customer at one of the other establishments at which Murphy worked: "If you got drunk or did anything wrong [in a Mafia gay bar] you not only could get thrown out, you could get murdered. I mean, no one cared." Not only did GLF offer gay men and women a free and supportive environment, but also the dances were reasonably priced and those who could not afford to pay were let in for free. Hoose recalls that "it was such a good feeling at the door because lots of people didn't have a penny and they were treated just as nicely as people who were handing us ten dollars instead of five dollars or three dollars." The dances were so appreciated that those who gave more than the suggested donation outnumbered those who asked to be excused from contributing.

Nor were gay and lesbian bars neglected as GLF began to exercise its philosophy of street-level activism there. John O'Brien recalls, "One of the things we had to win from these bars was the right to post flyers. We demanded, and won, the right to have bulletin boards. A lot of gay people today take that for granted, that the cigarette machine has newspapers on top of it or that there are bulletin boards in these places. That was a demand won. That was something that was given with reluctance by these bar owners. And the bigger the mob connection, the less likely they wanted to have bulletin boards or material distributed. They wanted their customers as ignorant and as controlled as possible, with the bouncers at the door serving watered-down liquor. And if you didn't like something, they'd push you around. It was okay for the police to come and raid, because they paid off the police anyway and occasionally there would be a raid. So what? They don't care what happens to you, and they certainly didn't care if you were beaten up on the street outside of a gay bar."

When two lesbians dancing in a Mafia lesbian bar refused to let a businessman cut in on them, the man punched one of them in the face while a Mafia hood watched and did nothing. When this was reported to GLF, a group of GLF men and women organized a takeover of the bar. As the group arrived, they started playing the jukebox and dancing while making a point of not buying any drinks. The owners did not understand what was happening, and Martha Shelley was selected to go talk to them. "We were a little afraid because, you know, Mafia, right? You don't know if they're going to bring out the submachine guns and start blowing you away. So I go up to talk to this guy, and I'm standing there with my knees shaking, and I tell him why we're there, to protest that our people aren't getting taken care of, et cetera, et cetera. He says, 'Do you know who I am?' I said, 'I don't know, and I don't care, but we're the Gay Liberation Front!'"

While such moments were scary, they were also empowering. In those early, heady days of gay liberation, the moments of exuberance certainly outnumbered those of fear. GLF reveled in puncturing the smug superiority most heterosexuals of the era felt about their own sexual orientation. Shelley recalls such an instance from GLF's first winter when she took to the streets to sell the organization's newspaper. As she stood in the snow on a Village street corner in a pair of sneakers and a torn leather jacket, yelling "Get your copy of *Come Out!*, newspaper of the Gay Liberation Front," a well-dressed middle-class couple passed by, pushing a stroller and looking at Shelley with horror. Just as they passed her, Shelley said, "Get your copy of *Come Out!* Read what your kid's going to be like when he grows up." Shelley recalls, "And they jumped, and I just loved it. It was a way of giving the world the finger for what they were doing to me."

There was also a special joy in the simple fact of being openly gay twenty-four hours a day in the public square, as practiced, for example, in demonstrations. Shelley described participation in a typical GLF demonstration as "marching down the streets, arm-in-arm, shouting, 'Power to the people. Give me a *G*; give me an *A*; give me a *Y*.' Shouting at the top of our lungs. Dressed in whatever wild and freaky costumes we felt like. Forget the nylons, unless you were a drag queen, I guess. It was let it all hang out. Unzip your fly, and it's all out there, or unzip your mind." As John Lauritsen, who had been involved with two homophile groups in Boston before joining GLF, wrote, "The Gay Liberation Front was a quantum leap forward. No more special pleading. No more apologies. Here was a radical organization, wild, woolly, and wonderful, ready to fight militantly for homosexual freedom."[5]

Flush with money from the success of its dances, GLF had moved quickly to fund a series of radical projects: a bail fund for its members, an underground-style newspaper, and a program of free lunches for the poor.

It was the launch of *Come Out!* that precipitated GLF's first major demonstration and its first victory. Immediately after its official formation on July 31, and true to its word in *Rat*, GLF set to work on its own publication. GLF composed an ad for the August 7 *Village Voice* with the provocative lead-in "Gay Power to Gay People." The ad's purpose was to solicit articles, photographs, and artwork for the new gay publication. After accepting the ad and payment for it, *The Voice* ran it without the lead-in. Furious GLFers expressed "general outrage" at their regular Sunday meeting and discussed an action against *The Voice* but decided they did not have enough evidence of bad faith to justify it. The group decided to submit another ad using the word *gay* for *The Voice's* next issue. That ad for a GLF dance carried the lead-in "Gay Community Dance." After the ad was again accepted with no comment, the person who had placed the ad got a phone call from *The Voice* the following day, explaining that it was the newspaper's policy "to refrain from printing obscene words in classified ads." Asked why anyone would consider the word *gay* obscene, the person representing *The Voice* said that "the staff had decided 'Gay' was equatable with 'fuck' and other four-letter words." Either the ad would have to be changed or it would not run. Since GLF wanted the ad to run and the word *homosexual* was not an acceptable substitute, GLF accepted *homophile* to get the ad run, with Leo Martello remarking that the then-outmoded word sounded like a nail file for homosexuals. *The Voice* promised that it would provide GLF with a written explanation of their opposition to the words *gay* and *homosexual*.

GLF had asked for the written explanation because they planned to use it as part of the basis for a lawsuit against *The Voice*. The promised explanation was never delivered, and GLF initiated its suit, which necessitated GLF's serving a copy of a letter stating their proposed action to *The Voice's* publisher, Ed Fancher. When Fancher continually refused to meet anyone from GLF at his office, GLF was forced to serve him at his apartment. As the letter was delivered, GLF asked to speak with Fancher about *The Voice's* classified policy. He refused to do so, mumbling that GLF "should not have done such an outrageous thing as to come to his place of residence" before firmly closing the door in the GLF representatives' faces.

Feeling that Fancher had literally and figuratively closed the door on dialogue, at its next general meeting GLF decided to hold an action and a demonstration aimed at *The Voice*. On the morning of September 12, at 9:00 A.M., GLF threw a picket line up around the *Voice* offices, mere feet from the Stonewall Inn. GLF protesters recalled Smith's and Truscott's casual use of terms such as *faggot* and *dyke* in their coverage of the Stonewall Riots and Walter Troy Spencer's column in which he had referred to the riots as the "Great Faggot Rebellion." In his column, instead of worrying about basic issues of justice and decent treatment of the city's lesbian and gay male population, Spencer had bemoaned that "one Christopher Street bar operator estimates that a single night of indirect embargo cost him $500 business" and that the riots may have caused friction among the Sixth Precinct, the TPF, and the Public Morals Division of the police department. Was this the newspaper that Fancher himself had envisioned, and therefore named, as the *voice* of "the displaced, disaffected, dissatisfied, and the unhappy"?

GLF set up a table to give out coffee and collect signatures on a petition condemning *The Voice*'s policy. They also brought along 5,000 copies of a flyer explaining the GLF action. When Fancher arrived at 10:00 A.M., he was presented with a proclamation of GLF's grievances before he quickly disappeared inside *The Voice*'s offices. All through the day the picketing and petitioning continued, accompanied by chanting. By late afternoon not many of the flyers remained and many signatures had been gathered on the petition. At 4:30 the GLF submitted a classified ad saying: "The Gay Liberation Front sends love to all Gay men and women in the homosexual community." Soon after, Howard Smith emerged from the building and requested three GLF representatives to meet with Fancher.

Once inside, the representatives were greeted with a cry of outrage: how could the GLF have chosen the so-liberal *Voice* as a target? But negotiations were soon undertaken. While Fancher explained that it was *Voice* policy not to censor the content of the copy its writers submitted (which GLF accepted with the proviso that they reserved the right to oppose anything *The Voice* did print), he soon relented on the advertising policy, saying that henceforth the newspaper would not alter ads after payment and would print the words *gay* and *homosexual* in its classified ads. One of the GLF emissaries leaned out the window and flashed a V-for-Victory sign to the crowd below. The *Voice* triumph came just in time for GLF's first issue of its own publication, *Come Out!* On its cover a banner line proclaimed: "*Village Voice* Goes Down." A victory dance was held in celebration.[6]

Arthur Evans and his lover, Arthur Bell, had read about the Stonewall Riots, but the event had not made a big impression on them. Evans, then a student at Columbia University, confesses that although he was a political activist, he had never made a connection between his gayness and the political struggles that were roiling the country. Regarding Stonewall, he says, "I didn't realize the implications of it. It just went over my head."

But two months after the riot, Evans and Bell were walking in the Village on a balmy, foggy night when a youth, apparently Orphan Annie, handed them a leaflet announcing the existence of GLF. They both decided to attend a meeting to see what it was like. As Evans was to say over three decades later, "It changed our lives, both of us, forever."

Evans was immediately captivated: "It was exciting because we met people there who were very proud of being lesbian and gay and had a developed sense of politics and political struggle, and who were concerned about the great issues of the day, which were imperialism, racism, and peace. So it was wonderfully exciting to see all this great consciousness bursting out in a gay and lesbian context. The two lobes in my brain came together, making me realize, *Oh, well, my political life is related to my sexual life. There's a connection here.* I saw that connection by just interacting with people there. It wasn't a preached connection; it was a lived connection. They were real people, who embodied it in who they were. That's the most powerful example of all. It was an electrifying, wonderful experience."

Around the time that GLF was confronting *The Village Voice*, an important evolutionary change occurred that would have great implications for the organization. Members of the organization were encouraged to form cells within GLF, structures that would generally function autonomously. When the cell structure began to be implemented, Evans helped start one called the Radical Study Group, most of whose members would later become published authors. One of the first books the group read was Engels's *The Origin of the Family, Private Property, and the State*, which had a great influence on Evans's thinking. For Evans, participating in the Radical Study Group was the most meaningful learning experience in his life in terms of reading, a marked contrast with his experience at Columbia, where he was still enrolled. "The graduate students were walking around, sort of in a daze, trying to get through their exams. The professors were still pretending that the 1960s hadn't happened. The idea that a gay and lesbian sensibility could be relevant to philosophy, they would scoff at that, or scoff at the idea of gay and lesbian history. It was just totally beyond the faculty's comprehension. So I would be in that academic environment, which was so backwards and rigid and foolish, and then get together with my friends, where we were discussing these texts, and it was so lively and invigorating and wonderful, because we were bringing our personal experience to it."

Even before Jim Owles and Marty Robinson had joined GLF, as members of MAC, they had discussed how to mobilize gay people into an effective political force. Numerous actions that were taken just before and after the formation of GLF had been conducted under Marty Robinson's scrutiny as experiments in militant organizing: the march on the one-month anniversary of the Stonewall Riots' outbreak, the "Hang Out" that was held on Christopher Street stoops, and the protest held where the trees in Kew Gardens had been cut down. While Marty did not complete his formal education, he had an extraordinary native intelligence, as Arthur Evans attests: "Marty Robinson is the smartest person I've ever known. He wasn't the most learned, but I've never known anybody as smart as Marty was: a brilliant thinker, theatrical, and funny. Marty was a true genius." After analyzing his experiences with the July and August actions, Marty, with Jim's assistance, was ready to take their past tactics a creative step further in September as New York's mayoral race moved into its final phase.[7]

On a warm autumn day, Mario Procaccino, the Democratic nominee for mayor, was campaigning in Queens, with his entourage not letting most citizens get too close. When his guards let a short youth with a Beatle hair-cut through to shake the candidate's hand, Procaccino pumped the young man's hand and beamed at him. The youth suddenly asked him, "Mr. Pro-caccino, what are you going to do about the oppression of the homosex-ual?" The smile disappeared and a look of concern came over his face as the candidate began to pat Jim Owles's hand as if in condolence: "Young man, I can see that you're very interested in this problem. That is one of the many problems that we must face in New York. It is sick rather than criminal, and we must show understanding and compassion for them."

At the Gotham Young Republican Club, State Sen. John Marchi, the far-right-wing Republican nominee, had just finished a speech on urban crises when a member of GLF stood up and asked, "Senator Marchi, are you aware of the emerging militancy within the homosexual community, and how does this relate to your views on law and order? Will homosexuals become targets or will you be responsive to their needs?" A stunned silence hit the room and, a reporter noted, "For the first time that evening the Sen-ator lost his cool, elegant articulate style." Marchi tried to avoid answering by saying that he did not feel it necessary to speak on the matter, for "it was being considered by some committee and was a topic for the state leg-islature." The questioner persisted, "Senator, it's not just for the legislature. As mayor you have control of the police force. How will this affect the lives of New York's eight hundred thousand homosexuals?" Marchi an-swered in a staccato voice, "I will enforce the laws and prevailing mores of society." He would be questioned two more times about the issue before he left the room.

As a candidates' forum organized by the League of Women Voters on October 1 at the Temple Torah in Queens began, thirteen GLF members were scattered in the audience of two thousand. In advance, they had all submitted questions about homosexuality. After the forum had droned on for an hour and a half, it was clear that, as they had suspected, none of their questions would be addressed by the candidates. A decision had been made prior to the meeting to target the most reactionary candidates, Marchi and Procaccino. Suddenly Marty Robinson stood up in the middle of the audience and said, "It's 1776, Mr. Procaccino! The homosexual revo-lution has begun!" As Marty and then other GLF members peppered Pro-caccino and Marchi with questions, the audience, many of its members young, began to take their side, hooting at the candidates. When the police tried to remove Marty and Jim Owles, members of the League of Women Voters surrounded them to protect them. When the GLF protesters went outside, much of the audience followed them to talk with them, finding the rest of the proceedings inside boring. Gay liberation politics made the news, with the October 1 confrontation covered by NBC-TV's one o'clock news and the *New York Post*. It would not be the last time.[8]

After returning from the Fifth Annual Reminder, Craig Rodwell developed his own idea about how to propagate the energy released by the Stonewall Riots: create a gay holiday by moving the date of the Reminder from July 4 to the riots' anniversary and by changing the place of observance to New York City, the site of the riots. At first he shared his idea only with his lover, Fred Sargeant, and two lesbian friends of theirs who were members of the New York University Lesbian and Gay Student Union, Linda Rhodes and Ellen Broidy. They all liked the idea and, in October at another meeting of the foursome in Rodwell's Bleecker Street apartment, they outlined plans for the event.[9]

Fittingly, the move to make the celebration official came in Philadelphia at the November 1969 Eastern Regional Conference of Homophile Organizations (ERCHO). Since Rodwell had offended protocol with his outburst at the Fifth Annual Reminder, he realized that if he was too publicly identified with a resolution to create the holiday it might fail. He therefore let Ellen Broidy take the lead in introducing the resolution. It read:

> That the Annual Reminder, in order to be more relevant, reach a greater number of people, and encompass the ideas and ideals of the larger struggle in which we are engaged—that of our fundamental human rights—be moved both in time and location.
>
> We propose that a demonstration be held annually on the last Saturday in June in New York City to commemorate the 1969 spontaneous demonstrations on Christopher Street and this demonstration be called CHRISTOPHER STREET LIBERATION DAY. No dress or age regulations shall be made for this demonstration.
>
> We also propose that we contact Homophile organizations throughout the country and suggest that they hold parallel demonstrations on that day. We propose a nationwide show of support.

The resolution passed with the support of all the organizations except for Mattachine–New York, which abstained.[10]

———

For all of its creative and passionate radicalism, GLF also had a dark side. Over time, events convinced Robinson and Owles that the revolutionaries in GLF were, as Marotta has pointed out, opposed to "securing reforms that would only make homosexuals complacent about the system" the revolutionaries wanted to overthrow. For example, to make the gay population more politically aware, Marty Robinson had encouraged Ralph Hall to write a column in *Gay Power,* a gay underground-style newspaper that had sprung up in the wake of the Stonewall Riots, taking its name from the riots slogan that seemed to best express the event's meaning. Some GLF members then wrote an article for *Come Out!* that dismissed *Gay Power* as "an enterprise designed to make money." When an open meeting was held to review material being considered for the GLF newspaper, a consensus was reached to not print the article critical of *Gay Power.* The *Come Out!* cell then went ahead and printed the article anyway. When a GLF assembly voted not to print a second issue of *Come Out!* but to use the money instead to start a community center, the *Come Out!* cell declared its independence. Lois Hart, who belonged to the *Come Out!* collective, described the secession as a natural "evolution," to which Marty Robinson and others responded that this was "nothing less than an attempt to steal GLF's mouthpiece, which belonged to all because it had been financed with money raised by all."

There was no shortage of self-righteousness and shrill pronouncements (not to mention extraordinary rudeness) to be heard at GLF meetings and found in the pages of *Come Out!* When Barbara Gittings and Kay Tobin came to meetings, they were sharply questioned because of their age and more conservative styles of dress about why they were attending. Kay was called a fascist for wearing a LINDSAY FOR MAYOR button. Madolin Cervantes, who had worked hard for homosexual equality for years, was rudely challenged about her right to participate in a conference of homophile organizations because she was heterosexual. Consciousness-raising sessions often amounted to little more than character assassinations. As Martha Shelley put it, "The downside is that we had so much anger that we also turned it against each other. . . . It was like if you disagreed, you were a threat." Even Bill Katzenberg, the organization's prime mover, quit the organization before it was three months old "because he thought the radicals spent a ridiculous amount of time criticizing him because he was not open about his homosexuality when working in SDS."[11] It was not long before the other main founder, Michael Brown, also quit GLF in disgust.

Most infuriating for many of GLF's members was the way in which the organization through striving for the purest form of democracy became both inefficient and undemocratic. The examples given earlier illustrate how democracy was subverted in the name of autonomy. But it was also the case that any matter that had once been decided could be reopened at any future meeting, parliamentary procedures being considered too restrictive by GLF. Given the freewheeling style of GLF meetings, it could take a very long time to reach consensus on any matter. Understandably, it tried the patience of many to see matters that had been painstakingly discussed and decided reconsidered over and over at meeting after meeting, a practice that drove Arthur Evans in particular to distraction.

But of all the contentious issues that wracked this most contentious organization (which claimed not to be an organization at all but a loose collection of individuals and small groups of individuals), the most divisive of all was the issue that had bedeviled it from its first meeting, whether it should be a one-issue organization or whether it should ally itself with all other progressive causes.

In mid-November 1969, that issue came to a head over whether GLF should make a large contribution of money to the Black Panthers. John O'Brien had introduced a motion to donate $500 to the Panthers because he wanted to achieve solidarity with them.[12] After ferocious debate, the motion was defeated. Those who opposed the motion made many arguments against it. Among the most compelling points was that the Panthers often employed language even more virulently homophobic than anything used by the reviled Marchi or Procaccino. In a move to reopen debate on an issue that had already been decided, the following week there was a call for a recount, and the motion passed.

Following the vote, Jim Owles resigned as treasurer. Marty Robinson had already quit a couple of weeks prior. That night many members walked out, something that had never happened before. These resignations marked the beginning of the end for the fledgling gay liberation organization, but the birth of another one.[13]

14

The Heroic Age

Arthur Evans had become friendly with Marty Robinson and Jim Owles not long after joining GLF because he felt a strong affinity with their approach to gay politics. It was natural, therefore, that when he began to have thoughts about the need for an alternative to GLF, he turned to one of these men. On a rainy Sunday early in November, Arthur invited Jim to join him and Arthur Bell for brunch. At the end of the meal, over coffee, Evans broached the subject of starting a new group.[1]

Jim told the two Arthurs that he and Marty had been thinking along the same lines. In fact, they had already discussed the idea with some of their closer friends. Jim expanded on his analysis of what he saw as one of GLF's main weaknesses, that in trying to align itself with all other oppressed groups, "homosexual needs were being sluffed over for the big picture." He cited how a recent weekly Sunday night meeting had been disrupted by someone arriving with a report that women were being discriminated against at the Electric Circus, whereupon half the people attending left to join in a protest at the Circus. A month prior, in early October, Jim and Marty had considered forming a group dedicated exclusively to the cause of gay liberation, with a constitution, preamble, goals, and purposes.[2] Everyone in the group who wanted to support other causes would be free to do so on their own. All this sounded good to Evans and Bell, and so Jim invited them to meet with him and Marty at Jim's apartment the following night. And so it was that the three men—Marty Robinson, Jim Owles, and Arthur Evans—who would be the most important figures in forming the new gay liberation group, as well as the three persons most prominently identified with it, began work to make it a reality in early November of 1969.

The small group invited only trusted friends to form a core group of thirteen who would meet during November and December to debate just what form the new group should take. Specifically, they worked on language for a preamble and constitution. Those thirteen were Marty Robinson, Jim Owles, Arthur Evans, Arthur Bell, Kay Tobin, Donn Teal, Tom Doerr, Fred Orlansky, Fred Cabellero, Robin Souza ("Gary Dutton"), Leo Martello, Richard Flynn, and Steve Adams.[3] The first meeting of all who wanted to participate in the "new group," as they initially called themselves, took place on November 24. (Arthur Evans missed the meeting to attend a reading by Allen Ginsberg.) After everyone agreed to screen new potential members to keep spies from GLF out, the new group's purpose was discussed. The activists agreed that the group would be radical and activist and "would take responsible actions only, carefully planned within the framework of our society . . . without violence." Various possible undertakings were discussed, as well as the issue of what they should call themselves. Brainstorming for a name produced nothing satisfactory, and it was at a later meeting that the group settled on the straightforward Gay Activists Alliance. They also agreed that the group should first draw up "a strong preamble" and then use that text as a basis to further structure the group. The task of drafting the preamble was assigned to Arthur Evans.

After taking suggestions, Evans sat down to work. He recalled: "What I was concerned about in writing the preamble for the Gay Activists Alliance and the work on the constitution was to incorporate personal lived experience. I had become very suspicious of abstract political rhetoric, even when I agreed with it. I've been heavily influenced by Marxist and anarchist thinking, but I felt that in our movement we had to start with experiential confrontations first: the light would come out of the events themselves. Let's set up the stage so that the right events happen and the light will come out of that.

"That's what I experienced when I was in Chicago at the demonstration there . . . that the experience of the activity transcends any ideology. The ideology is important; I'm not saying it's not: I'm a philosopher. I'm interested in ideas and ideology. But . . . the lived experience . . . always transcends it. . . .

"And that's what I saw GAA as doing and saying. You want to talk about revolution, the really revolutionary thing is . . . the situation of people on the street acting, in that dramatic context. . . . That releases an energy that goes on forever and keeps transforming people's lives, and that just can't be captured in any ideological formula. . . . That was one of my objections to

GLF. I kept feeling they were trying to capture revolution in an ideological formula, and my feeling was that all formulas are lies."

At the next meeting, Evans distributed his draft of the preamble, and later took critical feedback over the telephone. As the constitution evolved, it contained two critical provisions: that GAA would not endorse any candidates for public office and that meetings would follow *Robert's Rules of Order* in order to keep the organization democratic.

After one more meeting and some revisions, the final versions of the preamble and constitution were refined and adopted at a meeting attended by nineteen people in Arthur Bell's apartment on December 21, which happened to be the winter solstice. The group of activists held an election and selected Jim Owles as their president and Marty Robinson delegate at large. To celebrate the birth of their new organization, they drank champagne.

The preamble as adopted read:

We as liberated homosexual activists demand the freedom for expression of our dignity and value as human beings through confrontation with and disarmament of all mechanisms which unjustly inhibit us: economic, social, and political. Before the public conscience, we demand an immediate end to all oppression of homosexuals and the immediate unconditional recognition of these basic rights:

The right to our own feelings. This is the right to feel attracted to the beauty of members of our own sex and to embrace those feelings as truly our own, free from any question or challenge whatsoever by any other person, institution, or moral authority.

The right to love. This is the right to express our feelings in action, the right to make love . . .

The right to our own bodies. This is the right to treat and express our bodies as we will, to nurture them, to display them, to embellish them . . .

The right to be persons. This is the right freely to express our own individuality under the governance of laws justly made and executed . . .

To secure these rights, we hereby institute the Gay Activists Alliance, which shall be completely and solely dedicated to their implementation and maintenance, . . . disdaining all ideologies, whether political or social, and forbearing alliance with any other organization except for those whose concrete actions are likewise so specifically dedicated.

It is, finally, to the imagination of oppressed homosexuals them-

selves that we commend the consideration of these rights, upon
whose actions alone depends all hope for the prospect of their lasting
procurement.[4]

According to Arthur Evans, he used the word *activist* in the first paragraph to emphasize that the members of the organization were not just
thinkers but people who acted to secure gay rights. Evans modified the Declaration of Independence's phrase "let facts be submitted to a candid
world" to "before the public conscience" to place GAA's call to arms firmly
in the American revolutionary tradition.

Evans considered the right to feelings particularly important, especially
as it was mentioned nowhere in the U.S. Constitution. As Evans believed
that rights begin with feelings, he thought it necessary to acknowledge the
right to feelings and not to only thought and behavior as traditional law did.
That is, "It doesn't matter what your morality is or what your laws are or
what your thoughts are: We are entitled to our feelings, and we're especially entitled to feelings of love and beauty. The right to one's own body
was written partly in affirmation of people who today are called transgendered people."

In the penultimate paragraph Evans intended to draw the major distinction between GLF and GAA, as he felt the imperative task was to seize the
opportunity to create a vehicle that could create an uncompromised sense
of gay and lesbian identity. To Evans this identity seemed the necessary
bedrock at that historic juncture.

The final paragraph was intended as an appeal to all living in the closet.
As Evans saw it, "I'm appealing to myself as that lonely child, saying, 'This
is the avenue through which you can grow and express your power and become a person.'"

GAA had forged a revolutionary document. Remarkably, GAA often
succeeded in living up to its lofty ideals.

An advertisement was placed in *The Village Voice* for the first public meeting of GAA. The event was held at what would become the organization's
regular meeting place, the Church of the Holy Apostles on 28th Street and
Ninth Avenue. Marty Robinson reported that GAA's first action would be a
petition to present to none other than Carol Greitzer, the councilwoman
who had often called on the police to arrest gay men. The GAA petition
demanded that Greitzer introduce a bill outlawing discrimination in employment on the basis of homosexuality and that she work to end all dis-
criminatory restrictions on gay businesses and remove state laws that
criminalized homosexual conduct. Blank petitions were handed out for cir-

culation. This, the activists reasoned, would provide them with a means to meet the public while introducing many citizens to the idea of gayness as a political cause.

Further progress was soon made in organizational structure. Committees were set up for publicity and political action, as well as a street committee to distribute petitions and pamphlets and to make signs for demonstrations, and a combination pleasure and fund-raising committee. When Marty Robinson ran into *Gay Power*'s editor, he offered to run a regular GAA column if someone from the group would write it. Arthur Bell volunteered for the job.

As the eager activists busied themselves with these and other projects, they also fired off letters to newspapers that had made denigrating comments about homosexuals; met with a senior columnist at the *New York Post* to complain about the same matter; and paid surprise visits to VID and VID's Human Rights Committee to begin to soften up Greitzer as a target.

The media-savvy group realized that it could be highly beneficial to have a logo or symbol, which was provided by Marty Robinson's new lover, Tom Doerr, a graphic design artist. (Marty and Jim had broken up as a couple in the fall around the same time Marty got involved with the shy and attractive Doerr.) The symbol Doerr suggested was that of the lambda, the eleventh letter of the Greek lowercase alphabet, which resembles an inverted letter Y. Tom designed the symbol as chrome yellow on a blue background. The lambda was chosen because in chemistry and physics it symbolizes a complete exchange of energy, "that moment that's witness to absolute activity."[5]

By the end of February GAA had already grown from fifteen to forty members and thus had adequate mass to plan a large action. On the morning of March 5, GAA members traveled to city hall, planning to enter the building and demand that Mayor Lindsay—newly reelected in large part thanks to gay voters who remembered his actions to end entrapment—take a public stance to end both job discrimination and police harassment. Apparently someone had tipped off both the press and city hall, for GAA members getting off the subway carrying posters were greeted by photographers and reporters. As they approached city hall they saw that police were present in overwhelming numbers, with many on horseback. When the GAA members tried to enter city hall, the police stopped them. They asked the police why other citizens were allowed to enter city hall and they were not. The police answered that "only private citizens" could enter, not groups. The activists were warned to "keep out" and "get back," but the slight Jim Owles, whom Marty Robinson would later affectionately call "the scrappiest little faggot in New York City," tried to push past the police. After the police bodily evicted Jim, they put up barricades around the city hall promenade. A minor city functionary offered the members of GAA a meeting with a slightly less minor official. GAA stood their ground, insisting on a meeting with the mayor. They were told no dice, that Lindsay was in Buffalo. The activists were not so easily dissuaded, however. They threw up a picket line and stayed for hours, chanting and holding their signs high when not talking to the press. Men kissed men as cameras recorded the scene, and a guitar player with long hair began to improvise songs about Lindsay, sodomy, love, and "the little piggies that protect city hall." The lunch crowd generally reacted favorably, seeming to enjoy the demonstrators. Arthur Bell described the scene:

> The sight . . . they saw and the answers [the press] got quickly negated any concept of namby-pamby homosexuality. Here, for all Wall Street, City Hall, and the press of America, were honest-to-God flesh-and-blood gorgeous, gorgeous gays. Stereotypes? Gone with the wind.

Finally Michael Dontzin, the mayor's counsel and adviser, walked up to the protesters and agreed to meet with Jim Owles, a photographer from *Gay Power,* and Arthur Bell, armed with his tape recorder. A general discussion ensued about harassment of gay folk, including specifics about bars, bathhouses, and entrapment by the Transit Police. Whereas Dontzin insisted that the mayor was supportive and sensitive to the issue and cited the progress of recent years, Owles insisted that the days of backroom promises were over: what they wanted was a public stand from the mayor. Moreover, Lindsay and other political figures from now on were going to have to listen to gay gripes, talk to the gay community in public forums, and "help us when help was needed." Dontzin assured them he would present the mayor with their demands when he returned from Buffalo and, as the protesters left, promised to get back to them shortly. Owles recognized Dontzin's talk as political softshoe, however, and did not take it seriously, though Bell thought Dontzin sincere. All the same, as Bell left City Hall that Thursday, he reasoned that it was best to remain prepared to attack whoever attacked the community next.

He did not have to wait long. The following night Seymour Pine raided the gay bars the Zodiac and 17 Barrow Street. On Saturday night he raided the Snake Pit, an after-hours illegal but non-Mafia bar that, in spite of its name, had a reputation for being one of the friendlier bars in town.

Pine claimed that he had had a great many complaints against the Snake Pit for noise and that he was closing down illegal bars, gay or not. Certainly the bar was patently illegal, having neither a liquor license nor a certificate of occupancy, and like the Stonewall Inn was an overcrowded firetrap with only one exit. Around two hundred men were crowded into an area with only one exit that probably would have had an occupancy limit of sixty customers if it had been inspected and licensed by the city.

When Pine raided the Snake Pit he had trouble identifying the management, who had slipped into the crowd of customers. But more seriously, Pine was once again faced with a crowd of customers who milled about outside a raided gay bar and did not disperse. The scene seemed explosive to Pine, and the last thing he wanted was a repeat of last summer's rioting. He surveyed the situation and made up his mind: at the Stonewall raid he had let the customers go. Now he had another crowd of gay club customers on his hands as he had at the Stonewall. To prevent a recurrence of that dreaded night of last June, he decided to handle it differently this time: he would arrest all the customers still inside and sort out the bar's management from them at the station house.

It took a long time for the police to transport over 160 customers in small groups via patrol wagons from the bar to the Sixth Precinct station house. One of the customers who was held inside the Snake Pit the longest was Alfredo Diego Vinales, who had recently started frequenting the bar. Vinales was a twenty-three-year-old Argentinean with an expired visa living in East Orange, New Jersey. Before he was put into a patrol wagon, one of Vinales's friends noticed that he seemed very nervous and extremely frightened. Lawrence (not his real name), one of the club's employees, asked one of the police, "What rights do we have?" The cop simply answered, "Shut your fucking mouth."[6]

Vinales and the 162 other men taken to the Charles Street station were herded up to the station's second floor, where the scene was chaotic. The police were also verbally abusive of the arrested men, repeatedly calling them faggots and making other derogatory remarks and threats. As summons were about to be issued to all the men taken from the Snake Pit, Pine explained that their identification would not be checked and that no one would have to pay bail.

The Spanish-speaking Vinales either did not hear or did not grasp the implications of Pine's explanation. Terrified of being deported for being homosexual, Vinales suddenly bolted up a flight of stairs. As one person present in the station house would later recall, "Suddenly I heard a sound, like something falling, then screams." The screams he heard were those of Vinales, who had tried to escape by jumping from a window to the roof of the next building. He had missed and fallen onto a fence below, where he had been impaled on six of its fourteen-inch-long ice pick–sharp iron spikes. When it became obvious that the police could not simply lift Diego off of the fence, Rescue Company No. 1 of the city fire department was called in to use an electric saw to cut off a portion of the fence so that they could transport Vinales to the hospital.

After the firemen arrived, a police officer said to one of them, "You don't have to hurry, he's dead, and if he's not, he's not going to live long."

While the police may have initially intimidated those they had arrested, these were men who had witnessed the birth of a new militancy within the gay community over the last nine months. As word spread through the station of what had happened to Vinales, the men inside first talked to one another to keep their spirits up. Then, as the crowd had done at the beginning of the Stonewall Riots, they began to sing. First "America the Beautiful." Then the more political "We Shall Overcome." Then a chant first heard during the previous summer's riots began to resound inside the Sixth Precinct station: "Gay power! Gay power! Gay power!"

As the police became preoccupied with Vinales, some of the arrested men wandered into what apparently was the captain's office and took over a pair of phones. They called *The New York Times*, the *New York Post*, and the *Daily News* to apprise them of what had happened. *The Times* and the *Post* were not responsive, but the *Daily News* seemed keenly interested and dispatched a photographer to the Charles Street station. One man called a lawyer. Another man called Marty Robinson and Jim Owles.[7] To even up the score some more, they took record books from the office and dumped them down a shaft.

At ten o'clock on Sunday morning, Arthur Bell felt groggy as he wandered into his bathroom and turned on the radio. As he listened to the news, word came of a police raid on an after-hours bar in Greenwich Village in which two hundred were arrested and an unidentified man had been seriously hurt. The injured man had been taken to St. Vincent's Hospital. Bell jolted awake as he immediately realized that a gay bar had been raided once again. Bell roused Evans, signaling to him to listen to the news as Bell went to the phone and started making calls to learn what had happened.

News of the tragic incident had spread throughout the gay community, interspersed with rumors that Vinales had died or was dying, so it did not take Bell long to grasp what had happened. When he could not reach Jim or Marty, he called Bob Kohler and suggested that GLF and GAA and all the rest of the homosexual community join in a protest action that evening. Kohler did not think a protest could be pulled together on such short notice. At noon, Bell finally reached Jim and Marty, who had already gotten the news via the phone call from the police station.

It was Bell who suggested that all GAA members be called to an emergency meeting. Only two hours later, thirty GAA members were gathered at Jim and Marty's apartment. Everyone agreed that it was essential to act that day to signal the community's outrage. A protest march was decided on, to be followed by a vigil at St. Vincent's Hospital, where Vinales, who had not obliged the police by dying, lay in a coma.

A pamphlet was written by Marty Robinson about the incident, which he began with the resounding lines: "Any way you look at it—that boy was PUSHED!! We are ALL being pushed." The march would be on the Sixth Precinct station and would start from Christopher Park, the site of the riots. GAA swung into high gear as Robinson managed to find a mimeograph machine on a cold Sunday. GAA members divided into teams to deliver the flyers to different parts of the gay world. Bell worked the phone, talking to the news media and encouraging them to cover the evening's protest. Bell found that a number of the reporters with whom he spoke remembered him from the City Hall protest a few days earlier.

Later in the day, Bell noticed that Marty "was like a tiger on the prowl, pacing back and forth excited and jumpy": GLF had invited a number of nongay movement groups, so a very large turnout was expected.

By 9:00 P.M. five hundred demonstrators had assembled at Christopher Park, the site of the Stonewall Riots. The crowd included men and women from GAA, GLF, Homosexuals Intransigent (another recently formed gay organization), and HYMN, many gay people who were not members of organizations, heterosexuals, Yippies, members of a women's liberation group, as well as the Reverend Robert O. Weeks, the very supportive pastor of the Church of the Holy Apostles. From the park the angry demonstrators marched to the Sixth Precinct, chanting "Say it loud: gay is proud" and "Stop the killings," as well as the emblematic refrain from the Stonewall Riots: "Gay power!" It had been decided the tone was to be angry but orderly, and marshals from GAA and GLF supervised the march to keep it from spilling over into the streets. As the GLF banner accompanied the marchers, Villagers gay and straight spontaneously left their apartments to join the march, while others watched astonished from their windows.

When the crowd arrived at the police station they found that busloads of blue-helmeted TPF officers had been brought to greet them, as well as hundreds of uniformed police officers and "countless" plainclothesmen who encircled the area, guarding the station.

But the protesters were not cowed by this show of police force, massive as it was. Instead, the crowd called for Salvatore Salmieri, the captain, yelling, "We want Salmieri! We want Salmieri!" When Salmieri did not appear, the crowd chanted, "Who gets the pay-off? The police get the pay-off!" and "There's the Mafia in blue!"

Owles and the Reverend Weeks approached the police, and Jim suggested that a few representatives from the crowd be allowed to enter the station and talk to the commanding officer to lower the risk of rioting by the crowd. His request was turned down.

Owles turned from the police to the agitated crowd. He shouted, "Our brother lies near death at St. Vincent's Hospital! We've made our point to the police by our numbers! Now we will march in solemn procession to the hospital." The crowd calmed down somewhat and walked over to the hospital, with hundreds carrying lighted candles. There the crowd held a silent vigil march across the street from the hospital. They then returned to Christopher Park, but only after retracing the footsteps of the rioters from the previous summer by spontaneously detouring onto Gay Street as they headed up Christopher Street. To have been able to turn out a crowd half a thousand strong in cold weather in a few hours to march on a police station on behalf of gay rights was a measure of how far the new gay liberation movement had progressed in the seven months since its birth.[8]

The raid on the Snake Pit and Diego Vinales's tragic accident received fairly intense media coverage in New York City, the most attention the issue of homosexuality had received since the Stonewall Riots. The substantial media coverage that the Snake Pit raid received was a direct result of the way the Stonewall Riots had politicized the gay world: there were presently not only two organized groups of highly militant, activist gay men and lesbians but also three gay newspapers where before there had been none: in addition to *Gay Power* and *Come Out!*, there was *Gay*, which had been started by Jack Nichols and Lige Clarke. The erotic and wildly successful newspaper *Screw* had given Lige and Jack a column to write on homosexuality in 1969, called "The Homosexual Citizen." The column had proven so popular that Lige and Jack had soon realized that a gay newspaper might be financially sustainable. Also, after Stonewall the couple realized that the homosexual community was entering a historic phase, and they wanted to create a newspaper of record for the era. *Screw*'s publisher, Al Goldstein, agreed to finance the new paper, and Jack and Lige hired some of their friends from the old homophile movement, such as Kay Tobin, Dick Leitsch, and Randy Wicker, to help record the unfolding history of gay liberation.

While both *Gay* and *Gay Power* had around twenty-five thousand readers each, the new movement was also having some success with the nongay press. The protest at City Hall was covered by the *New York Post, Women's Wear Daily, Long Island Press*, WCBS, WINS, WBAI, and WABC-TV, as well as making the front page of the Spanish-language newspaper *El Diario*.[9] *The Village Voice* noted that the number of gay bars in New York City seemed to have doubled since the Stonewall Riots.[10]

For these and other reasons, the Snake Pit incident got so much attention that it galvanized the just-born gay liberation movement. Not only did the raid pump more energy into a movement that was already highly ener-gized, but it also inspired GAA to take their previous strategy of creative, direct confrontations a critical step forward to create a new form of politi-cal protest, combining militancy, guerrilla theater, and gay sensibility in the form of camp. It was this innovative tactic of bold, face-to-face encoun-ters, created by Marty Robinson, that eventually won the fledgling move-ment significant media coverage and finally put the issue of lesbian and gay rights permanently on the political map.

Arthur Evans recalled how the Snake Pit incident (and GAA's political analysis of the root cause) inspired the invention of what GAA came to call a zap: "John Lindsay was the mayor of New York who had gotten elected by a plurality of black and gay votes, a Republican liberal with a nice plastic smile, very gracious on television but really unwilling to put any teeth in his rhetoric. As a result, there was a step-up of police raids on gay bars.

"The Snake Pit incident truly outraged us, and we put out a leaflet say-ing that, in effect, regardless of how you looked at it, Diego Vinales was pushed out the window and we were determined to stop it. We decided that the politics that were going on that allowed this to happen [was some-thing that] we felt in our personal lives: it wasn't just an abstract political issue with us. People were being impaled. People were terrified, being ar-rested, careers broken. There was no division for us between the political and personal. We were never given the option to make that division. We lived it.

"So we decided that people on the other side of the power structure were going to have the same thing happen to them. The wall that they had built protecting themselves from the personal consequences of their politi-cal decisions was going to be torn down and politics was going to become personal for them. That meant, in effect, that we were going to disrupt Mayor Lindsay's personal life and the personal life of his family as a result of the political consequences of his administration. So we decided that every time he appeared in public or every time we could get to him, we would make life as personally uncomfortable for him as we could and re-mind him of the reason why."[11]

As April began, it seemed timely to call on the mayor anyhow, as Jim Owles's estimate of Dontzin's sincerity had been accurate: in the month since their meeting Dontzin had neither taken any phone calls nor an-swered any letters from GAA.

Monday, April 13, 1970, dawned a perfect spring day, which seemed appro-priate for the ceremony planned for that day, the one hundredth anniversary of New York City's most prominent cultural institution, the Metropolitan

Museum of Art. At 9:55 in the morning Mayor Lindsay ascended the front steps of the city's great temple of culture, where he was greeted by the museum's director, Thomas Hoving. A band played the national anthem, and then Mr. Hoving wittily introduced the mayor as "our landlord," bringing a grin from Lindsay.

Lindsay began to speak, thanking museum patrons for caring "deeply enough about the city and art to recognize their mutual dependency." As Lindsay spoke, no one seemed to pay any attention to a young man with dark hair, wearing a baseball jacket, who was slowly walking up the museum's steps. Lindsay was saying that for an entire century the city and the museum had "nourished each other" as the young man got closer to the podium. The mayor had just begun to praise the museum's new plaza for "extending the museum's beauty out into the street," when Marty Robinson spoke into the microphone, his voice suddenly interrupting Lindsay's bland address with the question, "When are you going to speak out on homosexual rights, Mr. Mayor?" Lindsay smiled but did not say a word as two helmeted policemen rushed Marty off the scene.

GAA members were scattered throughout the crowd, armed with leaflets, and ready to get in a line that was to form to shake the mayor's hand. As GAA members shook Lindsay's hand, they asked him questions about why he was not supporting gay rights and attempted to give him their leaflets. Some held on to the mayor's hand so long that the police had to pull them apart. While Lindsay toured the museum, one activist stuck a leaflet in his hand. Jim Owles then walked up to Lindsay and said, "You have our leaflet. Now when the hell are you going to speak to homosexuals?" Lindsay never quit smiling, nor did he ever say anything in response.

Six days later Lindsay was blindsided again. The mayor had a weekly half-hour television program on WNEW titled *With Mayor Lindsay* that was taped three hours before it aired. GAA had decided weeks in advance to target the April 19 show, so its members had been writing in for tickets for weeks. By mid-April they had around forty tickets for the April 19 date, enough to make up a third of the audience. That Lindsay still had not responded to the organization gave them a legitimate reason to "zap" him a second time.

At four o'clock thirty-seven men and at least one woman, Kay Tobin, gathered in Bell's apartment. There Arthur Evans coached them on when and how to chant, applaud, and stamp their feet in order to make the experience as unnerving as possible for Lindsay, hoping either to get him to loosen up or for some of them to be arrested. Two hours later they left Bell's apartment, which was near the television studio, departing in small groups so as not to attract attention. They had taken care to dress in a number of different styles so as to blend in with the rest of the studio audience.

At the studio Arthur Bell ran into Lindsay's counsel, Dontzin.

"I see you have some of your people here."

"Why haven't we heard from you?"

"I didn't know I was to get back to you. Let's get together next week and talk."

That must have struck Bell as more than odd, as he had left many messages with Dontzin's secretary. When Bell pointed this out to him, Dontzin apologized, saying that he "was over his head with work" and really was eager to meet with Bell and Jim Owles. In fact, he would tell his secretary to set up an appointment with them for the following week.

Dontzin then tried to home in on what GAA had planned. How many GAA members were in the audience? Bell played dumb.

When Lindsay appeared on the set, it was obvious that he and his staff knew that the deck had been stacked, for Lindsay was visibly nervous. His hands crammed into his trouser pockets, he crossed and uncrossed his legs repeatedly.

Soon the music that announced the show's opening was played, which, providentially, was Leonard Bernstein's "Something's Coming." The guest that day was Arthur Godfrey, who was appearing as an advocate for the new ecological movement.

The show started without incident as Lindsay read a Passover greeting off a TelePrompTer, but when Godfrey and the mayor began discussing ecology, the mayor's hands twiddled and he crossed his legs yet again. Marty Robinson's political innovation was already succeeding in tearing down the invisible but real wall that insulates the powerful from the negative emotional impact of their policies.

When Godfrey observed that "soot is what the housewife sees the most of," Arthur Evans rushed up to the mayor shouting, "Homosexuals want an end to job discrimination!" as another GAA member followed him, saying, "Let that man speak!" Security guards grabbed the disrupters and pulled them through an exit door. There was a huge noise created by dozens of stamping feet, accompanied by shouts of "Answer the question! Answer the question!" A member of the audience yelled out, "Are you in favor of repeal of the sodomy laws?"

The television cameras stopped rolling, and Lindsay quietly spoke: "My counsel, Michael Dontzin, will meet with those who want to see him outside." The mayor's good-cop act was followed by a member of his staff who darkly but incoherently threatened, "You cannot disrupt a public meeting under threat of arrest. You either leave in peace or are under arrest." As

Bell would later write in his *Gay Power* column, "Nobody pays him [any] mind."

Both Lindsay and Godfrey, Bell wrote, looked "terribly uncomfortable." As a cameraman said, "Let's pick it up from . . ." a GAA member heard a straight person behind him say, "Lindsay is phony as hell. He has to read off tapes. He can't answer questions unless he has prepared answers. Now he's threatening arrest."

When the taping resumed, GAA members in the audience proceeded according to plan, taking statements made by Lindsay or Godfrey, reinterpreting them in gay terms, and firing them back. When Godfrey mentioned abandoned cars, Phil Raia shouted, "And what about abandoned homosexuals?" The camera stopped and Raia was escorted out of the studio. When Lindsay made a comment about one-way bottles, Jim Owles shouted, "What about a one-way mayor—nonreturnable?" Owles gave a V-for-Victory sign as he was led outside. The funniest improvisation came when Lindsay's observation "If you're stuck in a traffic jam, it's illegal to blow your horn," elicited the response: "It's illegal in New York to blow anything." At that point, according to Bell, the looks on the faces of Godfrey, Lindsay, and the program directors said, *What next?*[12]

Ten days later, Marty Robinson, Jim Owles, and Arthur Evans were ushered into Michael Dontzin's City Hall office, accompanied by Arthur Bell and Kay Tobin to cover the meeting for their respective gay newspapers, *Gay Power* and *Gay*. Present from the city besides Dontzin were Deputy Mayor Aurelio and Harry Taylor, chief of patrol for the New York Police Department, who was there to act as Police Commissioner Leary's representative.

Aurelio started the meeting by saying that he did not like GAA's public confrontations with the mayor, which he hoped would cease. Bell retorted that if Lindsay would speak publicly on gay issues, there would be no need for the confrontations.

Marty Robinson then opened a notebook that contained a list of demands. First on the list was a "moratorium on police raids and harassment to give time to the authorities to work on solutions to the underlying problems of the State Liquor Authority and Police Department corruption." Bell noticed that Chief Taylor winced as the indictment of his police force was read, inspiring Bell to say, "Since the raids on the Stonewall and the Snake Pit and the resulting riots, homosexuals will no longer sit back and take shit from the police. One of the reasons we're here is to forewarn you that spontaneous riots might break out again this summer if police harassment continues." Bell's statement in turn inspired Taylor to chime in that

Seymour Pine had been transferred back to Brooklyn. Aurelio added, "It's not the policy of the police department to harass homosexuals per se."

Arthur Evans spoke up next, observing that there were two kinds of harassment that homosexuals experienced: harassment that has a legal basis and harassment the police did while knowing that there was no legal justification, making the arrests only for the purpose of intimidation. Evans was insistent: "This last type of harassment must stop immediately. We will not tolerate it. Often police direct verbal abuses at homosexuals that are disgusting. We demand that a directive go out that this police practice stop."

After more demands by the GAA representatives and assurances by the public officials that they understood GAA's concerns and would work with GAA to address them, the meeting ended. This time it was Bell who left the room doubting the city officials' sincerity about a summer moratorium on raids.

GAA was growing steadily by leaps and bounds, yet Craig Rodwell was having difficulty getting GLF or GAA to regularly send representatives to the meetings he was holding to organize the first Christopher Street Liberation Day (CSLD). After the resolution endorsing the creation of CSLD had passed at ERCHO the previous November, all groups that were ERCHO affiliates were invited to send representatives to the meetings to plan the first observance of the "gay holiday." But few did. This was in part because of distance, for most ERCHO organizations were outside New York City.

Craig and a small number of workers labored on to plan the observance, with Fred Sargeant, Michael Brown, and GLF treasurer Marty Nixon doing most of the work, assisted by Mattachine member Foster Gunnison.[13]

As was so often the case with lesbian and gay organizing, ideology tended to derail the work at hand. Craig had to ride herd constantly over members of the committee to keep them focused on making the CSLD march a success. As each meeting began, Rodwell tried to forestall debates by reminding the other committee members that although all of them came from different political, sexual, and racial backgrounds, their job was "to put together a mass community march" that would bring all the elements of the community together. When discussion did veer off into the theoretical, Craig would let the discussion go on for a while before raising a practical point with a remark such as, "Who's going to take these leaflets up to the Bronx? 'Cause this woman is offering to put leaflets around on telephone poles. Somebody has to take them up to her."

Once when Craig made a motion to put a notice in *The Village Voice* to advertise the march, a self-styled radical went off on a tirade, asking, "How can we spend a hundred and twenty dollars on ads when there are people starving to death in this city?" Craig then made a motion to scrap the advertising budget for the march and spend the money instead on buying hot dogs to pass out in the Bowery. Taken aback, the man opposed to buying the ad suddenly withdrew his objections.[14]

By May of 1970 GAA had collected six thousand signatures on their petition addressed to Carol Greitzer, but the councilwoman had refused to accept the petitions. On May 11, Jim Owles met with Greitzer at City Hall and got a frigid reception, with Owles reporting that she "didn't want anything to do with [GAA]." She would neither sponsor nor cosponsor an employment discrimination bill, nor would she testify at the City Human Rights Commission.

From an article in *Gay Power:*

> Two evenings later . . . thirty-five members of Gay Activists Alliance confronted Mrs. Greitzer at an open meeting of the Village Independent Democratic Club.
>
> . . . Before entering the big meeting hall, she . . . made small talk with a man she called Marty. But then she entered, and suddenly, bedlam. A roar she will never forget.
>
> Poor Carol fidgeted. . . . She told Marty she was going to leave. She was persuaded to hear it out. . . . And she and all of those V.I.D.'ers . . . heard Arthur Evans say, "Carol Greitzer refused to accept the petitions. She said she would not sponsor a job discrimination bill. . . . If she doesn't relate to the homosexual cause, the Village Independent Democratic Club doesn't relate and we are prepared to sit in."
>
> Mrs. Greitzer turned to platform chairman Robert Egan, and said, under her breath, "I don't want to make a statement. . . . Tell them I have a terrible cold. I didn't refuse those petitions. . . . I had too many things to carry. . . ."
>
> . . . Carol reneges. Her dark eyes flash. . . . "The Attorney General is the person who has done most this past year with civil rights legislation. . . . I can't get it done."
>
> Someone says, "You refuse to represent us in City Council?"
>
> Mrs. Greitzer says, "Is there a specific piece of legislation you're talking about?"

Arthur Evans says, yes, and elaborates the points in the petition.

Greitzer retorts, "My stand is there is no way of getting this through . . . not even with bombs."

Jim Owles says, "The very least we expect is a commitment, Mrs. Greitzer. . . . You've never issued a positive statement about homosexuals. You are guilty of a crime of silence."

All join in, [chanting] "Guilty of a crime of silence." . . .

"Will you back us up?" asks someone from G.A.A.

"Yes," says Mrs. Greitzer . . .

"Will you co-sponsor a bill?"

"Yes," says Mrs. Greitzer in a tone that can only be described as exasperated defeat.

"Do you accept the petitions?"

"Yes," says Mrs. Greitzer, who fortunately has one free arm for lugging that night.[15]

As a week of celebrations to commemorate the Stonewall Riots was in full swing, members of GAA planned their own special celebration by sitting in at the Republican State Committee headquarters. Arthur Evans, Marty Robinson, Tom Doerr, Jim Owles, Phil Raia, Cary Yurman, and Arthur Bell and a few other GAA members arrived at the headquarters a little after noon on June 24.

They were greeted by an emissary who said, "If you have legitimate grievances, I will see to it that they are forwarded to the right party."

Arthur Evans replied, "We want Rockefeller to come out and fight for homosexual rights. Rockefeller is guilty of a crime of silence, and we are not leaving until we get a satisfactory answer to our demands."

The employee with whom they were speaking complained, "You did not call for an appointment! You have not made a legitimate request!"

Arthur Bell described GAA's quick response to the bureaucratic runaround the employee was trying to pull on them: "We just unwound and made ourselves comfortable on the floor of the reception room until they got the picture."

Meanwhile, downstairs, in midtown Manhattan, a GAA picket line had been thrown up, with demonstrators chanting, "Two-four-six-eight, gay is just as good as straight! Three-five-seven-nine lesbians are mighty fine!" and, "Say it loud: Gay is proud!" As the day wore on, the pickets began to hold hands, kiss, and hug. Every half hour a member of the sit-in contingent would send a report downstairs that nothing was happening. TV and other news media went inside to photograph and interview the GAA members as they sat in.

At 5:00 P.M., with the protesters still there, the office could not be closed. At 6:30 a phone call came from the chair of the New York Republican Party agreeing to meet with a representative of GAA. Jim Owles said he would do it provided a member of the press could come along. The chairman would not agree to that, and Owles would not give in on his demand. The police soon showed up, and those sitting in huddled and agreed that Evans, Owles, Raia, Robinson, and Doerr would remain to be arrested—the first people ever arrested for a gay sit-in in New York.

The five arrested men, soon dubbed the Rockefeller Five, were then taken to be arraigned. Activists worked the phones and by 8:00 had forty people at the Criminal Court. As the five entered, the forty GAA members stood up and held hands, causing a commotion in the courtroom.

All five were booked on a charge of criminal trespass and let free on their own recognizance. A trial was set for August 5. Outside the courtroom, Marty Robinson made a statement to a *New York Post* reporter: "We are trying to use political power to achieve changes that will benefit homosexuals in the state. We want homosexuals to know who has been responsible for inaction regarding their civil rights, and we also wish to charge the state with corruption, such as the State Liquor Authority's nonissuance of licenses to gay bars."[16]

Recalling the quotation he had often read on the arch in Washington Square, "Let us raise a standard to which the wise and the honest may repair," Arthur Evans says, "I think that that's what GAA was doing. We were setting an example for people who were ready to come to that standard and join the struggle and make an example of their lives. That was extraordinary because it was a concept of democracy that almost doesn't exist in this society, a Walt Whitman type of democracy. Walt Whitman speaks of democracy and adhesiveness and the dear love of comrades. All that was in GAA. Democracy for us wasn't voting once every four years in an election which the Supreme Court would then throw out. It wasn't that kind of democracy.

"It was a direct, immediate democracy. We decided how we were going to govern ourselves and we governed ourselves that way. We decided who our leaders were. We elected them; we knew them all, face-to-face. We went into battle with them. We put ourselves at risk with them. We evaluated in person what we did. When we made a mistake, we evaluated it; we corrected it.

"So what was wonderful about it, I think, was that we discovered what democracy is. We learned that what we call democracy in this society is really a shadow of democracy. We learned to create a democratic life of work and struggle and sex and love and commitment, and we controlled it all, in person, face-to-face.

"So we were inspired to take that seed of lived democracy and make it spread into the body politic, to make it spread into the world. And that, I think, was one of GAA's greatest achievements. GAA was a school for democracy."

In the future lay many more zaps that would be planned and executed with brilliant panache and inspiring courage. It came to GAA's attention that an agency named Fidelifacts routinely collected information on individuals who were homosexual and sold that information to prospective employers. GAA inquired about the practice only to be told that "if it walks like a duck and quacks like a duck, we call it a duck." Members of GAA organized a picket demonstration against the company and Marty Robinson came dressed as a duck. When *Harper's* magazine printed a highly insulting article on homosexuality and then refused to print an apology or a rebuttal by GAA, members of GAA showed up at their offices unannounced bringing cookies and coffee and while some approached staff members saying, "I'm a homosexual; have a doughnut," others occupied the office of the magazine's editor. When a member of the city's marriage bureau made gratuitous insults about homosexuals wanting to marry, that office was taken over by GAA members who answered the phones and informed callers that "today we're only issuing marriage licenses to homosexuals. Are you a homosexual?" And when John Lindsay continued to withhold his full backing to passage of a gay rights law for New York City, GAA members sabotaged the announcement of his bid for the U.S. presidency by handcuffing themselves to the railings of the top balconies of Radio City Music Hall the moment Lindsay strode to the podium. As Lindsay tried to speak, the activists released hundreds of flyers stating their demands on the audience, all the while shouting for Lindsay to address their concerns.

These brilliant tactics and much more—the constant organizational work done by GAA and GLF, the dances they held, the publications they put out, the centers they started—succeeded in making the gay liberation movement flourish. As Frank Kameny stated, "By the time of Stonewall, we had fifty to sixty gay groups in the country. A year later there was at least fifteen hundred. By two years later, to the extent that a count could be made, it was twenty-five hundred."[17]

Legal gay bars also proliferated in New York City in the early seventies. While Mattachine–New York had done much of the work to make this possible through its legal efforts, Dick Leitsch feels that the main reason for their spread was Diego Vinales's impalement as a result of the raid on the

Snake Pit: "The photos of that sickened the public and outraged even the cops. The public attitude was that the cops (and liquor agents) were out of control [and] being unnecessarily brutal."[18]

As for the Stonewall Inn, the club that played such a pivotal role in bringing about this revolution, it survived the riots by about three months: passersby noticed a STORE FOR RENT sign appeared in its window sometime in the month of October 1969. There are several reasons that could explain its quick demise. First, as an expression of anger at Mafia exploitation, Craig Rodwell urged the gay populace to boycott the club. Second, the bar tried to do business as a juice bar, no longer serving alcohol. This is linked to the third reason, which is probably the true reason the club failed: Chuck Shaheen said that after the riots, the club was too notorious to remain open. Shaheen attributed this in part to timing, for the media was beginning to focus on the issue of police corruption. Shaheen explains, "We were told, This is it. Forget this. This has gotten too much notoriety, too much everything. We can never let this place open again."[19] As for Fat Tony, Chuck Shaheen merely stated that he was "eventually" killed without providing any further details. In another part of the interview Shaheen said that Fat Tony, who was a heavy user of drugs, including crystal methamphetamine, talked freely when he was on drugs and that Fat Tony had become an "embarrassment" to other mobsters. This is one reason that Shaheen knew as much as he did about the Stonewall's business operations, including things Shaheen said he should not have known. If what Shaheen was told about his former boss's demise is true, perhaps Fat Tony died because he was not careful enough about observing the Mafia code of silence.

The Mafia-owned bars were initially opposed to the annual celebrations of the Stonewall Riots. But Ed Murphy, seeing that the marches doubled in size between the first and second marches, founded the Christopher Street Festival Committee in 1972 and by 1974 had succeeded in reversing the march's direction. Whereas the first marches began in the Village at the site of the riots and went up to Central Park, Murphy manipulated matters so that the march started uptown and went down to the Village, so that he and his cronies could once again make money off the gay populace as they drank in the bars and ate food at the festival. As the Stonewall Riots became more famous, he took to riding in the annual marches in a car, calling himself "the first Stonewaller" to try to take credit for making the riots happen in the first place.

Murphy officially "came out" in 1978, claiming to have quit both his careers as a criminal freelancer and an FBI informer because he wanted to work for gay liberation. He then began to put in appearances at political events to talk about gay rights. He told one prominent gay publication that "he is the only person from Stonewall who is still interested in gay rights; the others 'are too interested in making money in bars.'" The last place Murphy worked at before his death from AIDS in 1989 was Trix—a hustler bar. In 1992, Randy Wicker led a fight to wrest back control of the festival from Murphy's associates.[20]

As for the gay street youth, the main instigators of the Stonewall Riots, Bob Kohler dragged some of them to the first meetings of GLF and tried to get them involved. But the youths lacked the political understanding, experience, and emotional maturity to participate in a meaningful way. While they sometimes took part as foot soldiers in the early gay liberation movement—handing out flyers or attending demonstrations—they did not play a role in the politicization of the gay world.

On Sunday, June 28, 1970, Craig Rodwell went to Sheridan Square to prepare for the first Christopher Street Liberation Day march, not quite sure what to expect. Crowds were to assemble on two nearby streets, Washington Place and Waverly Place between Sixth and Seventh avenues. The first signs were not encouraging. People were throwing eggs from buildings in the assembly areas at those preparing to march, and probably fewer than a thousand people had gathered. Still, Craig told himself, a thousand would be the largest gay demonstration ever. Even his friends on the committee who had planned the event with him had predicted that they would never get more than a thousand people to march all the way from the Village to Central Park, where there was to be an assembly, or Gay-in, at the Sheep Meadow.

The police did not want to let Craig delay starting the march, despite his desire to do so. He felt certain that more people would eventually show up. Before the march began, those in the crowd were warned not to wear glasses or loose jewelry around their necks in case someone attacked them. A number of local heterosexuals had shown up to watch. How would they react? The crowd seemed nervous. Sam Agostino and his friend had brought their dogs along so that if the marchers were attacked, they could just leave the march and claim that they were out walking their dogs. Half of the gay crowd that had gathered hung back on the sidewalks, trying to decide if they should join in and step out into the street.

When the march started, participants walked so quickly because of their fear of violence that later the event was jokingly referred to by some as the "first run" rather than the "first march."

But step off it did, led by a simple banner at the head of the march that read: "Christopher Street Gay Liberation Day 1970." Alongside the banner a blond youth carried an American flag, followed by the Gay Activists Alliance contingent, two hundred strong. Lesbians and gay men had come from Philadelphia, Washington, and Baltimore to participate. Representatives of the Mattachine Society of New York marched, as did members of the Daughters of Bilitis. A new radical lesbian group, the Lavender Menace, joined in, along with representatives from Yale, Rutgers, and New York University. Marching with the Gay Liberation Front contingent were some of the homeless street youth. All in all, approximately twenty different groups were represented.

Right away those marching could see that there were a lot of gay people on the sidewalks, trying to decide if it was safe to join in. Bit by bit they did. The march grew larger and larger, expanding beyond what had seemed probable or even possible. As the numbers increased, the crowd became more and more excited and spirited, inspiring still more gay people on the sidelines to join. Foster Gunnison had come up with his own scheme for calculating the crowd's size, and as the march progressed, he dashed back and forth tracking numbers and performing computations. Finally he ran up to Craig and excitedly announced that at least two thousand people were marching.

Fortunately, there was no violence, which Craig attributed in part to bewilderment on the part of heterosexual onlookers: "I think people were so shocked to see thousands of queers. At first they just can't believe it. 'Queers' was that one person they saw walking their French poodle with the rhinestone collar about ten years ago. . . . They just couldn't deal with it. They would stand with their mouths open, a blank face."[21]

The Village Voice recorded the astonished looks: "No one could quite believe it, eyes rolled back in heads, Sunday tourists traded incredulous looks, wondrous faces poked out of air-conditioned cars."[22]

As various high points along the route were reached, marchers could look back and get a sense of the march's size. Many could not believe its length. Some marchers in the middle were even more amazed when they noticed that looking in both directions they could see neither the head nor the end of the march.

The GAA contingent started to chant, "Out of the closets and into the streets!" over and over.

Another group chanted, "Give me a G!"

"G!"

"Give me an A!"

"A!"

"Give me a Y!"

"Y!"

And on until, "What do you have?" was answered with full-throated yells of "Gay power! Gay power! Gay power!"

The march was fifteen blocks long by the time it hit 22nd Street, where a

woman leaned out of an office window to throw streamers of film to celebrate the marchers, who in turn applauded her. As the sun shone brightly,
more and more men removed their shirts, lending an erotic cast to the march.
Signs included: "I am a lesbian and I am beautiful," "Hi, Mom!," "Smash Sex-
ism," "Me too" (on a dachshund), and "Homosexual is not a four-letter word."

The cathartic moment for most marchers was yet to come, however. As
the marchers reached first Central Park and then the Sheep Meadow, they
came to a high point by a granite outcropping that gave an almost
panoramic view of the march. There, at that high point, many stopped and
cried tears of joy in a moment they would never forget, as they looked out
at the vast numbers of gay men and lesbians who had turned out to support each other by marching proudly in the open.

Franklin Kameny could hardly believe the crowd of thousands he saw in
the Sheep Meadow. It had been only five years and three months since he
and Jack Nichols had organized the first picket demonstration by a gay organization. On that day the ten people who participated had been worried
that rocks would be thrown at them and so they had not alerted the press
about their plans.

It had been Kameny who had coined and propagated the phrase "Gay is
good," and in his 1968 essay with that title he had written: "I say that it is
time to open the closet door and let in the fresh air and the sunshine; it
is time to doff and discard the secrecy . . . to live your homosexuality fully,
joyously, openly, and proudly, assured that morally, socially, physically, psy-
chologically, emotionally, and in every other way: *Gay is good.* It is."[23] At
that first Stonewall Riots commemoration in 1970, it must have seemed to
him that his 1968 vision was already coming true.[24]

Conclusions

The received wisdom about the Stonewall Riots is that such an event was inevitable. This proposition is untenable, however, for there were many raids on gay bars before and after the raid at the end of June 1969 on the Stonewall Inn, and none of them resulted in any kind of sustained uprising.[1]

It is equally untenable to maintain that the riots' occurrence around the particular club, the Stonewall Inn, was simply fortuitous, that the events that took place there could have happened at any number of gay bars. On the contrary, the Stonewall Inn both as a social institution and as a geographic site had a number of unique or special features that, taken together, explain why the riots erupted there: the club was located in a large homosexual ghetto, so thousands of gay men and women could learn of the event quickly and become involved; within that ghetto, the club was strategically located, being only about two hundred feet from the ghetto's epicenter, The Corner; the club was centrally situated among several major transportation systems and nodes, which made it easy for those who wanted to become involved to get there quickly; the layout of the streets around the club was a hub design, which gave the rioters the advantage of controlling the streets around the Stonewall, for this pattern made it easy for them to enter and exit the area and correspondingly difficult for the police to seal it off; the combination of being a transportation nexus, having a hublike design, and having a lot of foot traffic meant that there were many public telephones within feet of the club that those supporting the riots could use to notify the press and friends; the club was the city's largest gay club; the club had a significant amount of open space in front of it, so that there was room for a sizable crowd to collect; most of the streets in the Stonewall's immediate vicinity were narrow, one-way streets that gave the advantage to pedestrians and the disadvantage to police vehicles; the street pattern around the club is highly irregular, which made it confusing for the riot police, many of whom lived in other boroughs, whereas many of the demonstrators lived in or frequented the Village and were familiar with the area; unlike most gay bars of the era, which were short-lived, the Stonewall had been in existence for years, which contributed to the sense of identification with the club felt by a significant number of its patrons; the club was popular with all segments of the community, so that when it was attacked, the entire community felt under attack; its broad appeal notwithstanding, the Stonewall Inn was particularly popular with the most marginal members of the gay community, gay homeless youths, so that they felt a special loyalty to the club; because of their anger, their age, and their alienation, these gay homeless youths were ideal candidates to fight in a riot; the club was across the street from one of the main places where these marginalized persons congregated; and the club offered the largest venue for dancing for gay men and lesbians and was the place where they could dance most freely, endowing the club with a special meaning as a site for full and free self-expression. These factors came together with others to create the Stonewall Riots.

Several conditions that helped precipitate the event relate to timing: the raid occurred during an election campaign (which had traditionally been the time for the worst harassment operations), making gay people assume that the raid's only purpose was to oppress them; it came late on a Friday night in an entertainment district in the week that schools were letting out, which meant that the club was very crowded and that there were many persons out on the streets; that the raid, atypically, took place late in the evening also meant that the crowd inside the bar had had adequate time to consume alcohol, lowering their inhibitions; it was the first hot weekend of the summer, and riots often coincide with high temperatures, apparently because heat increases irritability; the raid came shortly after a campaign of harassment by vigilantes in Queens, and some gay people present at the Stonewall that night were aware of those incidents; it was the last in a series of raids on gay bars, all in the same neighborhood; and it was the second raid that week on the Stonewall Inn.[2]

That the Stonewall Inn was located in New York City further contributed to the riots' success: only in a very large city were there gay activists with the specialized skills to take on leadership roles to help shape and direct the event so that it could realize its potential. Consider Craig Rodwell and John O'Brien. The first was a gay activist who knew all the other gay activists in the city, and the second a radical who knew street-fighting tactics. That two such activists happened upon the riots within minutes of each other is not something that could have occurred in many other places. New York's size is relevant to another contributing factor: the riots took place not just in the world's media capital but on a block with two significant media sites: *The Village Voice,* the country's leading alternative newspaper at the time, was only about fifty feet away, and the Lion's Den, the Village's main social center for journalists, was even closer. That, of all the reporters who covered the riots, Howard Smith, Lucian Truscott, and the unknown *Rat* reporter—the three who wrote the most detailed accounts of the riots' outbreak—simply stumbled across the event is a striking coincidence. It demonstrates how the power of certain features of the Stonewall's physical and social geography, key in creating the riots, was exponentially enhanced by being in New York City: had the Stonewall's immediate geography been the same, for example, but located in another city that was not a media center, would the event have been covered by the press at all and, if it had been, would such local coverage have mattered?[3]

There are other factors behind the riots that are significant on the macro level. First, Greenwich Village in the 1960s was both the best-known gay community in America and the place where homosexuality was most aggressively policed. This demonstrates that the basic preconditions were in place for a possible revolt by the members of that ghetto. Second, historians have observed that revolutions tend to happen after periods of liberalization. From all I have learned about the history of the homosexual community in New York City during the 1960s, I feel that this principle is an underlying cause of the Stonewall Riots. Indeed, one sees the same phenomenon occuring in another gay and transgendered community in the 1960s that almost exactly parallels the situation in New York City. Compton's Cafeteria in San Francisco was the principal refuge for that gay community's most marginalized members, transgendered persons and gay street youth. After both of these communities were given hope—by transsexual surgery becoming obtainable and by ministry provided by the Glide Memorial Church and the Council on Religion and the Homosexual—these communities rioted when their sole place of refuge was endangered. Like the Stonewall Riots, this smaller but also violent uprising occurred during a period when harassment was easing in San Francisco because of successes by a local homophile movement.[4] Given the same results in parallel situations, to ignore this principle noted by historians would be to willfully ignore the evidence. It would also make the riots' occurrence during the Lindsay administration difficult to explain: that is, why did the riots occur during the most enlightened administration on matters homosexual New Yorkers had ever seen, particularly as it followed the most repressive administration gay New Yorkers had ever endured, that of Mayor Wagner?

New York Mattachine's at-times ambivalent response to the riots aside, given this historic tendency it seems probable that without the successful campaign by the Mattachine Society of New York to end entrapment and its partial success in legalizing gay bars, the riots might not have occurred. Indeed, this view was espoused by none other than Craig Rodwell. When Michael Scherker, a historian of the riots, asked him whether "in the month or weeks before the Stonewall Riots . . . was there anything different . . . that . . . was a preparation?" Rodwell answered, "I think the four or five years before the Stonewall Riots were preparation. . . . Mattachine finally got going. . . . We finally started having a large membership and . . . we started to get some media coverage of our issues. . . . I think largely through the actions of the gay organizations, SIR in San Francisco, Mattachine here in New York in particular, and Mattachine in Washington."[5]

Finally, that the Stonewall Riots occurred during a period of great social change and unrest—the civil rights and the antiwar movements in particular—has to be added to the list of factors that caused the riots. The sixties was a time so open that even society's basic beliefs about sex, gender, and sexuality were being questioned on multiple fronts: by the reborn movement for women's rights, the sexual revolution, and androgynous styles in fashion. Challenging bedrock beliefs about sex and gender led to questioning assumptions about sexual orientation.

This intersection of many varied factors—geographical, social, political, and cultural—at the Stonewall Inn on Christopher Street shows that when Craig Rodwell, pressed by Michael Scherker to explain what had caused the riots, answered, "There are certain . . . events in history where . . . everything comes together at one particular moment," he was closer to the truth than he suspected. Certainly it was an event of a kind rare in history, one where without any planning of any kind all the necessary elements came together in just the right way to start a revolutionary change in human consciousness that is profoundly for the better. Rather than being an inevitable event that could have happened almost anywhere, the riots could have occurred only at the Stonewall Inn.

Finally, that the preconditions existed for such an event to not only occur but to bear such positive fruit is demonstrated by the beginnings of a new gay militancy first on the West Coast, as evidenced by, for example, Leo Laurence's activism and Carl Wittman's "Gay Manifesto," and later on the East Coast with Bill Katzenberg trying to start a gay Left group in the months before the riots and *Queen's Quarterly* urging gay men to learn judo and karate. These attitudes and actions show the influence of the New Left, another critical element of the event's underpinning.

Having considered what did cause the riots, it is worth considering another event that is often said to have caused them, the death of Judy Garland. The bibliography—that humble and uniquely useful research tool—gives us four essential pieces of information relevant to the theory that Garland's death caused the riots: (1) No eyewitness account of the riots written at the time by an identifiably gay person mentions Judy Garland. (2) The only account written in 1969 that suggests that Garland's death contributed to the riots is by a heterosexual who sarcastically proposes the idea to ridicule gay people and the riots.[6] (3) "D.D.'s New York," the gossip and news column of the *New York Mattachine Newsletter,* discussed the riots once; that column begins with a description of how the local gay world has been changed since the riots and about halfway through the two-page column there is a lament over Garland's death, with other news items interposed. What makes this last piece of writing so striking is that the author is enamored of celebrities, much of the regular fare of the column being social events, movies, plays, and entertainers. The other purpose the author used the column for was to boost gay politics. Having a strong interest in both gay politics and entertainers, he was precisely the kind of person who, had there been a causal connection between the two events, would have noticed and touted it. On the contrary, what is conspicuous here is that the gossip maven makes the fallout from Stonewall the leading story, places six news items between Garland's death and the Stonewall Riots, and never connects the two events. Rather than being linked in the *only* piece of indisputably gay writing at the time of the riots where Garland's death and the riots are both mentioned, the two events are not related.[7] (4) *Esquire* magazine carried an article at the end of 1969 about the emergence of the "New Homosexual" in the riots' wake that briefly discusses Garland but does not credit her death with inspiring the riots. The sexual orientation of the author, Tom Burke, is not clear from the article, but it is clear that he is conversant with and appreciative of gay society and culture. Although the author notes that Garland's passing coincided with the riots, he sees this as symbolic, because he sees Garland as emblematic of the "Old Homosexual," who, already out of touch, became hopelessly passé with the changes the riots precipitated.[8] Rather than inspiring the riots, Garland is seen as symbolically allied with the old order the riots ended and hence as a contrasting or oppositional symbol.

If the preceding is not sufficient to demonstrate that this great artist's tragic and untimely death could not have caused the riots, consider that the main fighters in the riots were street youths. These young men were not of the generation that listened to Garland, their music being rock, soul, or both. Finally, author and activist Vito Russo, a great fan of Garland's, went to pay his respects at her casket on the day the riots would begin and then witnessed the riots that night. He wrote that "it wasn't good old Judy's death or even the full moon that caused all the trouble that night."[9] Like the author of the *Esquire* article, Russo saw Garland's funeral taking place on the day the riots broke out as symbolic of a sea change, not as its cause. He told historian Eric Marcus, "[Her burial that day] historically marks the end of the old gay world and the beginning of a new one."

The question of who gets credit for starting the riots is one that deserves consideration. The question, however, contains a premise: that an individual or group of individuals can be singled out as the prime mover in a complex process that many persons collectively created. This is important for two reasons. First, as John O'Brien pointed out, there was a continuum of resistance ranging from silent persons who ignored the police orders to move to those who threw objects at the police. O'Brien maintains that it was because of those persons standing around and blocking the streets and sidewalks and keeping the police from being able to operate efficiently that he and others were able to engage in their tactics as effectively as they did: if there had been only about fifteen youths lobbing objects at the police the young men would have been quickly caught or chased away. Second, I wrote the account of the first night to reflect my understanding of what happened, namely, that until the definitive outbreak of rioting when the police retreated inside the Stonewall Inn, there was throughout the evening both a *gradual* buildup of anger and, correspondingly, a gradual escalation in the release of that anger. In the course of that buildup there were numerous turning points, some more critical than others. With these qualifications noted, I think it is clear that special credit must be given to gay homeless youths, to transgendered men, and to the lesbian who fought the police.[10] Among these, we can name three individuals known to have been in the vanguard: Jackie Hormona, Marsha Johnson, and Zazu Nova.

A common theme links those who resisted first and fought the hardest, and that is gender transgression. While we do not know how the lesbian who fought the police saw herself, we do know that her clothing was masculine, in keeping with her general demeanor. We know from Pine's testimony that the first significant resistance that he encountered inside the bar came from transvestites, and Joel S. places them among the first outside the bar to resist.[11] Marsha Johnson and Zazu Nova were both transvestites, and, as the reader has seen, the street youth were, generally speaking, effeminate men. All available evidence leads us to conclude that the Stonewall Riots were instigated and led by the most despised and marginal elements of the lesbian, gay, bisexual, and transgendered community. My research for this history demonstrates that if we wish to name the group most responsible for the success of the riots, it is the young, homeless homosexuals, and, contrary to the usual characterizations of those on the rebellion's front lines, most were Caucasian; few were Latino; almost none were transvestites or transsexuals; most were effeminate; and a fair number came from middle-class families.

What can one make of Seymour Pine's claims that he was ordered to put the Stonewall Inn out of business because it was being used as a site to blackmail gay men who worked in the Wall Street area? Having researched the matter as far as possible, I have concluded that Ed Murphy was using the Stonewall Inn for just that purpose. Most of the information on Murphy and blackmail that I found I came upon incidentally as I gathered other material. That I happened upon most of this information piecemeal and inadvertently increases my confidence in this evidence.

There is no definitive evidence to say conclusively whether Pine is telling the truth on this point. Because his role was so critical and a full report of his account has not been available, I have given his version of the events concerning the Stonewall Riots and have checked it where possible. Having compared his statements about the events with others, most of which were unpublished and thus unknown to him, I can say that the other accounts have on some matters corroborated his, including, for example, statements made by Ed Murphy. For example, Pine said that one of the undercover policewomen who were sent inside the club was from Chinatown's Fifth Precinct; that the two women were chosen based on their sizes (one petite and one large-framed) to look like a butch-femme couple; and that he suspected that one reason they had not exited on time was that they had been indulging in some partying. Murphy said that "the two cops were drunk. . . . Even the policewoman was half-crocked. She was a Polynesian broad. And she's been coming there as a dyke."[12] Finally, no account I know of disproves any statements by Pine.

Professionals who have studied the reliability of witness testimony have established two hallmarks of veracity: a willingness to acknowledge what one does not know and a consistency over time in one's recollections. The following factors weigh strongly in favor of Pine's account of the cause of the raid. When I interviewed Pine, he did not hesitate to say when he did not know, could not remember, or was not positive about information. On one occasion, he made an error, noted it, and later drew it to my attention.

He has also been consistent over the years in what he has said on the subject. For example, in Morty Manford's papers I found a January 1972 term paper that he wrote while at Columbia University in which he analyzed gay milieux. In the section on gay bars he writes: "The Gay bar scene has improved considerably in the past few years (since the *Stonewall* Rebellion). Gays are not hiding as much (opportunities to blackmail Gay clients don't work as well for the syndicates as they used to), and Gay Liberation has flexed its muscles on a number of occasions, keeping individual bar managements in line." A footnote appended to the parenthetical statement about blackmail states that "New York City Police Lieutenant Seymore [*sic*] Pine reported to me that the syndicate's main source of income from Gay bars was not on the liquor, but rather on the securities information they were able to blackmail out of the bar's Wall Street clients."[13]

Pine's consistency as demonstrated by this quotation is all the more remarkable in that it dates back to, at most, thirty months after the riots, long before there was the intense historical examination of them that began, approximately, with the approach of their twentieth anniversary. Pine gave the same explanation to David Isay in 1989 that he gave to me and also informally to tourists in Israel when he was living there in the mid-1990s.[14]

Further corroboration of Pine's version of events was found in Dick Leitsch's papers. The following statement is from testimony Leitsch gave before the New York State Assembly at its "Hearings on Homosexuality" on January 7, 1971:

Last year, following a wave of thefts from Wall Street brokerage houses, the State issued an order that all employees in the financial industry be fingerprinted. Because of this, many old and trusted employees had to be let go, because bonding companies will not insure known homosexuals and the fingerprint checks turned up evidence of old arrests. Banking and many other fields requiring bonds are off-limits to homosexuals because of this policy of bonding companies.[15]

This testimony corroborates Pine on several points: first, that there had been an unusual quantity of thefts ("a wave") from brokerage houses; second, that "many" of those who were in a position to steal such bonds were, in fact, homosexual; third, the time given in Leitsch's testimony fits the time line given by Pine, who says he got the information about the thefts around mid-1969. Leitsch's testimony, given in January 1971, refers to the fingerprint order being issued "last year," or in 1970, *following* the wave of thefts. If the connection between the stolen bonds and Mafia extortion of Wall Street workers only came to light in late 1968 or early 1969, then a new policy put into effect roughly a year later, sometime in 1970, corroborates

Pine's chronology. Further, if Pine was trying to fabricate a cover story based on these historical events to make himself look better in the eyes of history, it seems probable that he would have pointed this material out to me or to someone else or suggested that such material be searched for. Not only did he not point directly or indirectly to the policy changes Leitsch described, but I have found no indication anywhere that he was aware of this information. Moreover, on two occasions where Pine's versions of events at the riots differed substantially from accounts given by others whose presence there is indisputable, I have determined to my own satisfaction that Pine's statements were the accurate ones.

Finally, it is notable that Pine's narrative has its own internal logic when looked at in the context of other new information contained in this history. If Murphy had the goods on J. Edgar Hoover, as I believe he did, then the investigation's origin overseas in Interpol makes perfect sense. Hoover did not control Interpol, and the results of the New York Police Department investigation, as far as Pine says he was told it went, did not implicate Hoover. Therefore, no alarms would have been sounded that would have alerted Hoover to try to quash the investigation.

If Pine is telling the truth about the reason he was told to shut down the Stonewall Inn, which seems highly probable, and if Murphy was using the Stonewall Inn to blackmail homosexual men on Wall Street, which seems certain, does this change the meaning of the Stonewall Riots? First, common sense and a historical sense would lead us to conclude that the police department's fervor for closing down the Stonewall Inn would have been inspired more by a concern for protecting the wealth of powerful persons and institutions and only secondarily, if at all, by a concern for protecting gay men. Second, while such a cause would give the riots a new context, I do not feel that it changes their meaning. The portrait of the Stonewall Inn as an institution that emerges from the historical record is a very mixed one: while it was a site of refuge and safety for some so that it functioned almost as a sort of community center, for others it was a site of exploitation and degradation. Does this mean that the Stonewall Riots should not serve as a symbol for lesbian, gay, bisexual, and transgendered people today?

I feel that the riots can and should still serve as a potent and inspiring story. The reasons I feel this way are twofold. First, by way of analogy, let us look at the history of race riots in the United States. The first race riot in American history in which African-American people were not the victims of violence but its instigators took place in New York City in 1935. The specific incident that sparked that riot was a belief that the police had beaten or even killed a youth of color. After the riot was over, it turned out that the alleged event never took place. For me, this mistake does not at all diminish the rightness of those who rioted. The affected community was routinely exploited in many ways, including by white merchants who refused to hire black workers. In other words, those who rioted may have been incorrect on that occasion about that specific injustice, but they were certainly right in the aggregate that their community was being ruthlessly exploited by merchants. The 1935 riot was an attempt by the powerless to end that injustice.[16] Just so, several persons I interviewed told me that they felt that the terrible anger that erupted on the first night of rioting at Stonewall was not simply anger at the injustices of that night or of recent weeks but anger that went back to the harsh mistreatment of the community by Mayor Wagner. While I do not support the use of violence as a method of social and political change, I think there are exceptions to this principle. I agree with prominent author, essayist, and editor of gay and lesbian books, Michael Denneny that in this case, given that the community had no reason to believe anything other than that it was being oppressed, the violence was not only justified, it was also necessary: gay men had always been stigmatized in our culture for their perceived lack of masculinity, and their violent resistance against the police proved that these gay men possessed both moral and physical courage.

Second, Craig Rodwell's response is relevant, for the Stonewall Inn had no harsher critic than Rodwell. Yet when he saw the bar being raided he reacted with anger. As the reader has seen, he became the riots' primary supporter, doing his utmost to keep the riots going and to publicize them. Moreover, it was Rodwell who had the idea of celebrating the riots annually. His example shows that it is possible to recognize the ambivalence of the Stonewall Inn while celebrating the lesbian and gay resistance to the oppression that occurred there. In celebrating the event, the emphasis has always been placed on gay militancy and not on the club: thus the gay community was urged to boycott the Stonewall Inn after the riots, and the celebrations were originally called Christopher Street Liberation Day to underline the idea that gay people were claiming their own territory.

In conclusion, let me quote from the article "Where It Was," published in a gay periodical on the riots' fifth anniversary:

The gay Stonewall was actually an illegal after hours club, operated against the laws . . . the hoods tending the door and roaming the floors were only too obvious. The place was packed, overcrowded and a fire hazard to boot. But "they" just kept piling them in. . . . Two and sometimes three bars dispensed drinks until sun up. . . . There were dark hidden corners where anything went and where some of the "customers" dispensed other things. . . . Before its arrival . . . that area of Christopher Street was relatively quiet. . . . Then came the throngs hanging around on the streets in front of the Stonewall. They sat on cars . . . pushed [drugs] in Sheridan Square. . . . Finally the neighborhood was up in arms, and rightly so.[17]

Morty Manford, then president of GAA, wrote in reply:

"Where It Was" . . . bemoans the appropriateness of the Stonewall Inn as a rallying point for the Gay Liberation Movement. There is no question the bar was illegal, dirty, dingy and exploitative: in 1969 it was virtually all we had. . . . Crumby as it was, it was ours. . . . The raid was like a number of other raids I'd been in with the important exception that we fought back. A spirit of pride encapsulated in anger was articulated for the first time in modern history by Homo-sexuals as a group. That spirit said both explicitly and symbolically: "We are sick of being pushed around; we are sick of being denied our Constitutional rights; and we will persevere until injustice, exploita-tion, harassment and discrimination end." There is no getting away from the fact the Stonewall Inn is a symbol of the past. It was a de-parture point for Gays like the Bastille was for the French people.

Manford concludes his letter by reminding us of some fundamental truths: "We have undertaken a struggle of tremendous proportions that will understandably be tough, face its set-backs and take a long period of time. It is our struggle. We owe it to ourselves to discern our own best interests and support united efforts with other gays to achieve our liberation."[18]

Manford is correct: the true legacy of the Stonewall Riots is the ongoing struggle for lesbian, gay, bisexual, and transgender equality. While this fight is far from over, it is now a worldwide movement that has won many significant victories, most of them flowing from those six days in the sum-mer of 1969 when gay people found the courage to stand up for themselves on the streets of Greenwich Village.

The Stonewall Riots are the critical turning point in the movement for the rights of gay men and lesbians as well as for bisexual and transgendered people. This six-day struggle by gay people with the police for control of a gay ghetto constitutes an important event in American and world history, for it ultimately led to the inclusion of sexual orientation as a protected category in the civil and human rights movements. This was a significant broadening of these important historic movements and the beginning of the reversal of millennia of oppression.

As is true of so many gay men and lesbians, I have long been fascinated with this historic turning point. One of the reasons the event has been so captivating is that it seemed to both erupt out of nowhere and effect radical change with precipitate speed: less than six months after the Stonewall Riots *Esquire* magazine announced the birth of the "new homosexual"— and that was before the Gay Activists Alliance (GAA) was born. When I began work on this book, it was my intent to discover everything that I could about the riots in the hopes of creating a much fuller account of this event than had previously existed. I also hoped that I would be able to offer new insights into the event itself as well as to discover explanations for some questions that had long resisted resolution. Having completed this history, I feel I owe it to the reader to give some brief account of how I conducted the research for this volume.

For the most part I relied on standard methodology: a careful survey of the bibliography, thorough research in archives, and extensive interviewing of witnesses and participants. I interviewed not only persons who were at the riots, but people who participated in the movement for homosexual equality before and after Stonewall, as well as a few others who were simply participants in gay life in the Stonewall era. Those not at the riots were interviewed because they had information that would help explain the context in which the riots occurred and the immediate political changes they precipitated. To understand how radical political changes grew out of the riots and what these changes were is important because the political sea change that occurred after Stonewall is the reason the riots are important. In other words, the Stonewall Riots are important because of the political change they brought about *through* the birth of the gay liberation movement, a wave of new gay and lesbian political organizations characterized by New Left values, including activism and militancy. Journalists and other writers, however, tend not to connect the events, instead explaining the significance of Stonewall as if one day there was a riot in New York City by gay men and then, in some mysterious way, as a result gay people across the nation formed political organizations. The truth of the matter is that Stonewall intimately links two interdependent phenomena. Bob Kohler made this salient historical point with admirable pithiness when we met one day on Greenwich Avenue. He said, "The Stonewall Riots would be totally insignificant if the Gay Liberation Front hadn't been formed after the riots." After a pause, he added, "Of course, I guess it took something like Stonewall to make the Gay Liberation Front possible."

I began my research with a careful survey of the known bibliography, concentrating especially on the accounts written at the time of the riots. I then searched archives and discovered a number of articles published in 1969 that had not been previously noted. An unpublished letter, handwritten by an eyewitness in 1969, was discovered by historian James Sears as I was researching this book. The final addition to previously unknown 1969 reports came from a person I interviewed who had recorded a radio interview with an eyewitness either during the riots or a few days afterward. Access to interviews conducted by previous researchers with witnesses who were either dead or not locatable provided critical information, as did earlier interviews by other researchers with persons I was able to further interview. When it is not indicated in the body of this work whether someone is speaking to myself or to another interviewer, that information is contained in the notes or in the list of oral histories.

While many persons have claimed that the 1969 accounts of the riots either conflict with each other or are not credible, the more I studied them, the more I felt that they were both highly reliable and did not conflict with one another. I discovered that if I simply reversed the order of two events in one account, then there were no major discrepancies among the 1969 accounts.* I then collated them all into one document, arranged chronologically and organized by subject matter. I found not only almost no contradictions among these accounts, but that collectively they provided a fairly detailed history of this event, and especially of the riots' outbreak.

I was able to supplement these contemporary accounts with a wealth of information from oral histories. While interviewing witnesses and participants, I used maps of the area around the Stonewall Inn and asked interviewees to mark on the maps the places where they saw events occur and the position of persons and vehicles as well as where they themselves were situated. This technique sometimes provided corroboration of the testimony of other witnesses. The issue of corroboration leads to what I consider the most important aspect of the interview process for this history. Because the events at the Stonewall Riots have been so disputed, I was careful not to tell any interviewee prior to the interview what other persons had told me nor of the conclusions I had reached based upon my research. This is a critical point, for the reader will see that I was able to achieve anywhere from a moderate to a high degree of corroboration of many of this history's new findings based solely on the many interviews conducted. Further corroboration for new information was also generally obtained from archival and bibliographic materials. I did not give information about the accounts of other interviewees or share my conclusions not only so as not to influence the testimony each person might give me, but also—and primarily—because there has been a small number of persons whose spurious accounts, while having entered the bibliography, do not withstand careful scrutiny. It is in part because of this mere handful of persons that the contemporary accounts of the Stonewall Riots have come to be viewed with a degree of mistrust. This false testimony has naturally also made the informed public quite skeptical of most if not all accounts of the riots, and therefore I have not referred to these inaccurate accounts.

By a stroke of good fortune, my residence is only a block and a half from the former Stonewall Inn. It is also the collective good luck of those who care about gay history that the Greenwich Village Historic District, which encompasses the area where the Stonewall Riots occurred, was created the very month the insurrection occurred. While the creation of this historic district did not freeze the Village as if in amber, it did preserve the vast ma-

---

*I am referring to the Howard Smith account published in the *Village Voice*: If one reverses the order of the arrest of Dave Van Ronk and the police retreating into the Stonewall Inn bar (and key witnesses disagreed with Smith's chronology on this one matter, saying that Van Ronk was arrested before the police retreated into the bar, not afterward) then there is no real disagreement about the events portrayed in the 1969 accounts, other than some disagreements about the meaning of these events.

jority of the buildings around the locality where the riots occurred and has
kept the layout of the streets essentially the same as it was in the summer
of 1969. Thus I have been able to walk by the site of the riots countless
times during the decade it took me to research and write this book. Being
able to contemplate the setting frequently has given me a number of insights about the riots and the factors that caused them.

While I have made every effort to quote accurately from the oral histories used in this volume, I have made the normal kinds of editorial
changes, such as editing out false starts; deleting sentence fragments that,
leading nowhere, would tend to confuse the reader; and supplying words
(indicated by brackets) to clarify the speaker's meaning. On several occasions I have combined two or more quotations by the same person from
different interviews (or, very rarely, combined an interview with a written
record they left, such as a published article) into one quotation for the sake
of clarity. Whenever this has been done, the sources of the original quotations are given in the notes.

Names that are given in quotation marks when they first appear indicate
use of a pseudonym created for this book. There are three instances in this
history where accounts refer to persons without even a first name being
known. As noted in each case, I created names for those persons for narrative effect: Tano, Tom, and Lawrence. I chose these names to honor the
memory of deceased friends and a family member, all of whom died of
AIDS. Tom Casteel and Tano Delgado, lovers in the mid-1980s, were the
first new friends I made when I moved to New York. Lawrence Goudreau
Jr. was the brother of my sister-in-law, Lynn.

It is part of gay culture that some gay men refer to other men with feminine pronouns, often quickly switching the gender references about one
person back and forth. I have sometimes used this device when it was employed by the persons whose interviews I am quoting, not to confuse the
reader but to convey the feeling and flavor of the milieu and personalities.

I have generally tried to use the terminology of the 1960s in writing this
history except when doing so might cause confusion or the effect might be
jarring. I have also used more current terms when it seemed preferable for
the sake of clarity. I have used the current term *transgender* sparingly for
two reasons: first, because the word is of recent mintage, and second, because it is an umbrella term, encompassing both transvestites (cross-
dressers) and transsexuals, and it usually seemed worthwhile to preserve
the specificity of these more precise terms.

Finally, this history is one in which the major actors were male: the Mattachine Society of New York, whose leadership was practically all male,
was the only gay political organization in New York City before the riots
with any political clout; the Stonewall Inn's clientele was overwhelmingly

male; men probably predominated in the riots even more so than they did inside the Stonewall Inn; and most of the founders and leaders of the Gay Liberation Front (GLF) and the Gay Activists Alliance (GAA) were also male.* Given the need to keep the main thread of the story moving forward, it has not been possible to cover lesbian life in a full or representative way, any more than it has been to give a full picture of transgender or bisexual life at the time. I have tried to limit myself to describing events, persons, and communities only to the extent necessary to give the reader an adequate understanding of what led up to the Stonewall Riots and how the riots in turn led to the creation of the gay liberation movement. The same logic applies to the emphasis on New York in this history: since the Stonewall Riots took place in New York and GLF and GAA were born there, activities elsewhere have been brought in only when they seemed directly relevant to the story at hand.

An archivist who assisted me patiently for years as I worked on this book worried aloud that if too much information was definitely known about the Stonewall Riots, the event would lose its mythological power, the power to inspire. I can only say that for myself, the new material is as complex and ambiguous as life itself, making the story richer. On a more personal note, I would like to add that while working on this book, I met some of the most intelligent, generous, and interesting persons I have ever had the pleasure of knowing. Together they taught me much about life and about human nature, so that I will always be grateful for all that Stonewall has taught me.

DAVID CARTER
Greenwich Village
1994–2004

---

*I deeply regret that Lois Hart, a key figure in GLF, appears to have left no account of her role in that organization.

ACKNOWLEDGMENTS

The first persons I must thank are those who granted me interviews, entrusting me with their personal histories. I was often touched by the openness with which so many people spoke about their lives. I also am deeply appreciative of how patiently the persons I interviewed answered every question I had, asking them to recall details about events that took place decades ago. While I offer my sincere thanks to all those I interviewed, I would feel negligent if I did not name certain persons who showed extraordinary patience and generosity in answering my every question over numerous interviews: Thomas Lanigan-Schmidt, Danny Garvin, John O'Brien, Bob Kohler, Seymour Pine, and Jack Nichols. Tommy Lanigan-Schmidt also went to extraordinary lengths to help me understand several aspects of gay life critical to this history: without him I never would have understood either the gay street youth or what the Stonewall Inn meant to them, and thus would have missed the most critical elements of this history.

Dick Leitsch not only gave me many interviews and faithfully provided detailed answers to follow-up queries, but gave me unfettered access to his personal papers, which proved to be an extremely valuable source. Other pioneering figures who shared their personal papers include Randy Wicker, Barbara Gittings, Kay Tobin Lahusen, Jack Nichols, and Bob Kohler. A special thanks to Joe Kennedy and Robin Souza for assistance in finding GAA sources and documentation, and to historian Donn Teal for help with various leads.

My work has necessarily built upon the work of previous researchers, whether they have been historians who have made a particular study of the

Stonewall Riots or writers who included Stonewall as one of their many interests. Of special usefulness has been the work done by early researcher
Tina Crosby, the pioneering work done by writer Michael Scherker, the
first real historian of the Stonewall Riots, the interviews conducted by
David Isay for his 1989 radio documentary, the research of historian Martin Duberman for *Stonewall*, his history of the Stonewall Riots, and interviews conducted by Eric Marcus for his book, *Making History*. David Isay,
Martin Duberman, Eric Marcus, Nikos Diaman, Paul Cain, and the family
of Michael Scherker all generously made the material relevant to the
Stonewall era in their possession available to me. Historian John Loughery
was generous in sharing documents with me and providing leads. Ken
Lustbader provided me with early drafts of his master's thesis on homosexuality in Greenwich Village and also provided me with floor plans and other
documentation on the Stonewall Inn. The late Joel Honig kindly provided
me with copies of documents and generously shared his unbridled enthusiasm for gay history. It is an honor to thank historians Jonathan Ned Katz
and Joan Nestle for their encouragement and support. Frank Toscano, retired from the New York Police Department, assisted me with several questions about the NYPD.

The number, quality, and accessibility of lesbian and gay archival collections has greatly increased over the last decade and a half, and this book
would not have been possible without them. Much basic work remains to
be done in collecting and preserving gay history, and I urge the readers of
this book to donate materials and funds to your local gay and lesbian
archives. Among the many wonderful amateur and professional archivists
and librarians I met during my research, I must single out Rich Wandel,
founder and archivist of the Lesbian and Gay Community Services Center
National Archive of Lesbian and Gay History in New York City, for special
thanks. Rich is one of the many unsung heroes of the gay community who
volunteers countless hours selflessly, does high-quality work, and seeks no
recognition for himself. I must also give a special nod to Henny Brand-
horst, Vincent van der Kaap, and Jack van der Wel, the director of Homodok, at Homodok, the Gay/Lesbian Archives and Information Center in
the Netherlands, which did amazing bibliographic research for this history.
I also wish to thank the librarians and staff of the following archives and
libraries: the New York Public Library's Manuscripts and Archives Division, where I made extensive use of various collections, but particularly the
International Gay Information Center Archives; the map division of the
New York Public Library; the Irma and Paul Milstein Division of United
States History, Local History and Genealogy Division of the New York
Public Library; the Lesbian Herstory Archives of the Lesbian Herstory Ed-
ucational Foundation, Inc., in New York City; Columbia University's Oral

History Research Office, with special thanks to Mary Marshall Clark; the Rare Book and Manuscript Library of Columbia University's Butler Library; the Tamiment Institute Library of New York University; the Pat Parker/Vito Russo Center Library in New York City; the Gay, Lesbian, Bisexual & Transgender Library/Archives of Philadelphia, with special thanks to Steven Capsuto for transferring interviews taped in the early 1970s to MP3 files so that they could be studied; the Human Sexuality Collection in the Division of Rare and Manuscript Collections of Cornell University, in Ithaca, New York, with thanks to collection curator Brenda Marston; the Museum of the City of New York; Jim Lomax, head of the Heritage Committee and archival programs of the SAGE Oral History Project in New York; the Gay, Lesbian, Bisexual, Transgender Historical Society of Northern California in San Francisco, with special thanks to Executive Director Susan Stryker, Paul Gabriel, and Willie Walker; the June L. Mazer Lesbian Archives of Los Angeles, California; the Dodd Research Center of the University of Connecticut Libraries in Storrs, Connecticut, with thanks to Rutherford Witthus, Curator, Literary and Natural History Collections, for help with the Foster Gunnison papers; the One Institute and Archives in Los Angeles; the James C. Hormel Gay & Lesbian Center of the San Francisco Public Library, with thanks to Jim Van Buskirk, program manager; the Gerber/Hart Library of Chicago, with thanks to Karen C. Sendziak, Gerber/Hart historian and curator, archives; and the Special Collections Library of Duke University in Durham, North Carolina, with thanks to Elizabeth Dunn and Virginia Daley; and Mike Lanza at New York's criminal court records division.

For very generous assistance in fund-raising, I would like to thank Bob Rosenthal and the Committee on Poetry, as well as Phillip Ward, Larry Maas, and David Tsang. David Tsang is a jewel of a friend and helped support me in many different ways during the years I worked on this book.

I was honored to receive a grant from the Greenwich Village Society for Historic Preservation to write a nomination to place the site of the Stonewall Riots on the National Register of Historic Places. The nomination, which also created the Stonewall Historic District, later resulted in the district being declared a National Historic Landmark. The nomination could not have succeeded without the three preservationists who were coauthors of the nomination: Andrew Dolkart, Gale Harris, and Jay Shockley.

Deborah Lattimore did an outstanding job of producing a great number of accurate interview transcripts under tight deadlines. Amy Endler also did wonderful work as a transcriptionist. Thanks to Peter Hale for transferring MP3 files of interviews to CD-ROM format.

Thanks to all the periodicals that helped me find persons to interview, and a special thanks to Rex Wockner for helping me reach the gay media with requests for witnesses to interview.

Thanks to Tony Carini for his plumbing expertise.

Many friends and family members have been very generous in their support during the decade I have researched and written this book. Without trying to name them all, and in no particular order, I would like to thank Mark Christianson and John Kretch; Nina Mankin; Hiram Perez and the late Ray Wenner for providing wonderful hospitality in Miami; Jack Nichols for help with housing arrangements in Cocoa Beach; Henry Santiago; J.; Craig Smith; Stephen van Cline; John Jeseren; Charles Haynes and Christopher Wilson; Charles Lombardo; Steve Wolf; Jane Greenlaw; Pauline Park; Jean-Pierre Bochêne and Olivette Halton; Tad Crawford; E. E. Krieckhaus; Allan Vogt; Robert Locke; Scott Barton; Steve Silberman; Tracy Turner; and Gregg Firth.

Perhaps my greatest debt of all is to Michael Denneny, who first encouraged me to write this book and who gave me unstinting support both as an editor and as a friend. Conversation with a man of true culture like Michael was always a pleasure, and I learned much from him. Because of his seminal role in gay publishing, I consider myself honored to have worked with the man I think of as the dean of gay letters.

When Michael Denneny left St. Martin's, I was fortunate that Keith Kahla was the editor who picked up where Michael had left off. Keith's ability to identify the weak spots in a manuscript is fortunately equaled by his ability to suggest practical solutions for fixing them. Keith's assistant, Steve Eichinger, also provided valuable assistance in completing this volume. Robert Cloud expertly shepherded the book through the final stages of revision and correction. My thanks also go to Doric Wilson, not only for granting me an interview but also for his careful preparation of this book's index.

My brother, William C. Carter, and his wife, Lynn, were very supportive of me as I researched and wrote. Bill was very kind to review the manuscript with the utmost care, and his many valuable suggestions greatly improved this history. My niece, Josephine Monmaney, and her husband, Terry, provided wonderful hospitality during my stay in Los Angeles.

Arlo McKinnon not only carefully read various drafts of this book and gave me invaluable, sensitive, and intelligent feedback, he was a mainstay of support as I worked to bring the book to completion. Helping in many different ways without stint, he was the soul of generosity: friends do not come any truer.

Finally, a special thanks to my parents who, while not alive to see this work published, made it possible by inculcating in me an interest in and a respect for history.

More than a hundred people were interviewed during the course of researching this book. In addition, several other historians made available to me their independent interviews. Some of these interviews were used only as background information. Others are quoted or summarized within the text. When not otherwise cited in the notes below, a quotation will be from these interviews.

In these notes, Mattachine–New York is abbreviated as MSNY. The full titles of the *New York Mattachine Newsletter (NYMN)* and some other sources are also abbreviated, and the shortened form is noted the first time that the source is cited.

P R O L O G U E

1. In June 1969, the month the Stonewall Riots began, Connecticut became the second state to legalize homosexual sex.

I : G R E E N W I C H V I L L A G E , U S A

1. The last names of Fat Tony and his father, Ernie, are not given here. (Lauria is not the family name.) Information in this chapter on Fat Tony, his father, and other Mafia owners of the Stonewall Inn is taken from the Shaheen-Duberman interview.
2. Bill Morgan, *A Walking Tour of Jack Kerouac's City* (San Francisco: City Lights Books, 1997).
3. The history of how the Village was colonized by gay men and lesbians is recounted in George Chauncey's *Gay New York: Gender, Urban Culture, and the Making of the Gay Male World, 1890–1940* (New York: Basic Books, 1994).
4. Nancy Adair and Casey Adair, *Word Is Out* (San Francisco: New Glide Publications, 1978), p. 335, and Jonathan Katz, *Gay/Lesbian Almanac: A New Documentary* (New

York: Harper and Row, 1983), p. 304, and *Gay American History* (New York: Thomas Y. Crowell, 1976), pp. 548–556.

5. Extreme notoriety of Bonnie's Stone Wall: Rick Beard and Leslie Cohen Berlowitz, eds., *Greenwich Village: Culture and Counterculture* (New Brunswick: Rutgers University Press, 1993), hereafter *GV*, p. 49. That Bonnie's Stonewall Inn was located at 51 and 53 Christopher Street is established by a 1940s menu, displayed in January 2003 on www.villagewaterfront.org, the Web site of the Federation to Preserve the Greenwich Village Waterfront & Great Port.

6. On Village tearooms, see Terry Miller, *Greenwich Village and How It Got That Way* (New York: Crown, 1990), pp. 38–39 and 223–224; Luc Sante, *Low Life* (New York: Farrar Straus Giroux, 1991); and Caroline F. Ware, *Greenwich Village, 1920–1930* (Berkeley: University of California Press, 1994), especially pp. 52–54 and 96–97.

7. *GV*, p. 36.

8. *GV*, p. 38, and Kenneth T. Jackson, ed., *The Encyclopedia of the City of New York* (New York: New-York Historical Society, 1995), hereafter *Encyclopedia*, p. 506.

9. Miller, *Greenwich Village*, p. 2. The author is grateful to preservationist Ken Lustbader for making available his very valuable master's thesis, "Landscape of Liberation: Preserving Gay and Lesbian History in Greenwich Village" (Columbia University, 1993), as well as construction plans and diagrams relating to the original Stonewall Inn Restaurant and the later Stonewall Inn club.

10. *GV*, p. 42.

11. Nos. 51 and 53 built as stables: *The Greenwich Village Historic District Designation Report*, Vol. 1, p. 117 (New York: New York City Landmarks Preservation Commission, 1969), hereafter *Report*. Introduction of taxicab fleet: *Encyclopedia*, p. 68. Information on Saks Fifth Avenue horses supplied by Matt McGhee, who heard it from the stable employee's grandson.

12. New York Public Library, Irma and Paul Milstein Division of United States History, Local History and Genealogy, Views of New York, Microfiche 795, D4, D6, D7, and E1.

13. Lustbader.

14. *Report*, Vol. 1, p. 13.

15. Lustbader.

16. "The Hairpin Drop Heard Around the World," *New York Mattachine Newsletter,* hereafter *NYMN*, July 1969.

17. *Report*, p. 153. The space around the Stonewall Inn was much more open in the 1960s than it is today. A traffic divider was added at the east end of Christopher Park in the 1990s and a viewing garden was installed in Sheridan Square, which was only covered by asphalt in the 1960s. Unfortunately, the small amount of open space in Village streets diminishes with each passing decade.

18. *GV*, pp. 291–92.

19. Kitty Davy, "Baba's First World Tour, 1932," Part II, *Awakener* 12: 3, Summer 1968, p. 3, and Meher Baba House, October 16, 1994, letter re 88 and 90 Grove Street; *84 Questions and Answers on Avatar Meher Baba* (compiled and published by A. C. S. Chari, India: 1969), p. 49.

20. This discussion of Greenwich Village history is generally drawn, except where otherwise noted, from *GV* (especially the chapter "Straight Down Christopher Street"), *Report*, and *Encyclopedia*.

21. *Coronet*, September 1950, pp. 101–8, quoted in Neil Schlager, ed., *Gay/Lesbian Almanac* (NY: St. James Press, 1998), p. 63.

22. Information on Blick and Hoey is taken from David K. Johnson's "Homosexual Citizens," *Washington History*, Fall/Winter 1994–95, pp. 44–63, and William N. Eskridge

Jr., *Gay Law: Challenging the Apartheid of the Closet* (Cambridge: Harvard University Press, 1999), pp. 68–72.

23. Arno Karlen, *Sexuality and Homosexuality* (New York: W. W. Norton, 1971), p. 609.
24. Eskridge, *Gay Law*, p. 98.
25. New York Penal Code; "'Drag' and the Laws—and a Drag Ball," *NYMN*, January–February 1967; and "Ku Klux Klan Says It Will Seek Permission for a Masked Rally in City," *New York Times*, hereafter *NYT*, May 2, 2000.
26. Karlen, *Sexuality and Homosexuality*, p. 610, and Peter Fisher, *The Gay Mystique* (New York: Stein and Day, 1972), pp. 133–34.
27. Barry Miles, "The Beat Generation in the Village," in *GV*, p. 165.
28. Martin Weinberg and Colin J. Williams, *Male Homosexuals: Their Problems and Adaptations* (New York: Oxford University Press, 1974), pp. 31, 44–45. The authors did their fieldwork between 1966 and 1968, supplemented by two weeks in 1970.
29. Chauncey, *Gay New York*.
30. Eskridge, *Gay Law*, p. 44. Eskridge points out that although the vice societies were originally organized to combat prostitution, during and after World War I homosexuality became an important focus of their activities.
31. Chauncey, *Gay New York*, pp. 338–42, cited in Eskridge, *Gay Law*, p. 46.
32. Eskridge, *Gay Law*, p. 46.
33. Karlen, *Sexuality and Homosexuality*, p. 610.
34. Stuart Timmons, *The Trouble with Harry Hay* (Boston: Alyson, 1990).
35. Molly McGarry and Fred Wasserman, *Becoming Visible: An Illustrated History of Twentieth-Century Gay Life in America* (New York: New York Public Library, 1998), p. 43.
36. Unless stated otherwise, the information on Frank Kameny used in this book comes from Kay Tobin and Randy Wicker, *The Gay Crusaders* (New York: Paperback Library, 1972), Eric Marcus's *Making History* (New York: HarperCollins, 1992), and Paul D. Cain's interview with Kameny.
37. *The Voice* eventually relented after Wicker kept returning with the same ad copy over and over.
38. Dan Wakefield, "The Gay Crusader," *Nugget*, June 1963, pp. 51–52, 71–72.
39. "Jack O'Brian Says," *New York Journal-American*, July 9, 1962. Details about the taping come from "Minority Listening," *Newsweek*, July 30, 1962, p. 48.
40. *NYT*, July 16, 1962, p. 47; *Realist*, August, September, October 1962; *Variety* and *Herald Tribune* cited in Edward Alwood, *Straight News* (New York: Columbia University Press, 1996), p. 47; and *Escapade*, February 1963, cited in John D'Emilio, *Sexual Politics, Sexual Communities: The Making of a Homosexual Minority in the United States* (Chicago: University of Chicago Press, 1983), p. 159.
41. Toby Marotta, *The Politics of Homosexuality* (Boston: Houghton-Mifflin, 1981), p. 27.
42. John D'Emilio, *Sexual Politics*, p. 160.
43. Leitsch letter to Bob Amsel, September 7, 1967. The author is indebted to Dick Leitsch for unfettered access to his papers, hereafter Leitsch papers.
44. Mark is not the real name of Tommy's friend.

2 : OPPRESSION, RESISTANCE, AND EVERYDAY LIFE

1. Kay Tobin and Randy Wicker, *The Gay Crusaders*, pp. 67–68.
2. Edited together from Tree-Carter interview and Tree, "Beating Around the Bush," *Private Lives*, September 1991.

3. As Jerry Hoose has explained to the author, there were places other than directly on the waterfront where numerous empty trucks were parked that were used by gay men for sex in this era, but those directly on the waterfront were the best known. All of the locations that Hoose knew about were on the western end of the Village and thus proximate to the waterfront.

4. 1960 crackdown: Leitsch letter (unsent?) to Stephen M. Goldfarb, n.d., Leitsch papers; on the effect of the World's Fair crackdown, see Steven A. Rosen, "Police Harassment of Homosexual Women and Men in New York City 1960–1980," *Columbia Human Rights Law Review* 12, No. 2, Fall–Winter 1980–81, pp. 167–68, and Lustbader.

5. Lustbader.

6. Leitsch letter to Amsel, September 20, 1967, and Leitsch-Marcus interview.

7. On Leitsch's reaction to Rodwell's turning onto Christopher Street, conversation with Dick Leitsch and Jonathan Ned Katz at the Candle Bar.

8. Leitsch-Marcus interview and Leitsch letter to Amsel, September 22, 1967.

9. Leitsch interview with Paul D. Cain, August 16, 1995, quoted here. Leitsch's tone toward Craig in interviews changed markedly after the publication of Martin Duberman's *Stonewall* (New York: Dutton, 1993), which only gives Craig's version of events, Duberman having never met or interviewed Leitsch. In the interviews before the publication of *Stonewall*, Leitsch's tone is positive or neutral about Rodwell; afterward his tone is entirely negative. Leitsch told me that he always wondered why he was overlooked by historians writing about the era. After reading Rodwell's account of the era's history in *Stonewall*, Leitsch says he realized that Rodwell had been "poisoning the well of history" for decades by giving erroneous accounts of events, especially with regards to Leitsch. To sort out all such claims and counterclaims between Rodwell and Leitsch and their respective supporters and detractors would take an entire volume in itself. I have tried to limit myself concerning Leitsch and Rodwell to reporting what both seems to be immediately relevant to the story at hand and can be reasonably established. Whatever future research may reveal, there is no doubt that both men played vital roles in recent gay history and that each of them also made very significant contributions to the movement for homosexual equality.

10. D'Emilio, *Sexual Politics*, p. 166, and Marotta, *Politics of Homosexuality*, p. 30.

11. Leitsch-Marcus interview.

12. Leitsch-Carter interview. "Police Are Added in Washington Sq.," *NYT*, August 5, 1964; "'Village' Assured of Added Police," *NYT*, August 10, 1964; Randy Wicker, "The Wicker Report—It's Koch vs. DeSapio Again," *Eastern Mattachine Magazine*, July 1965, pp. 9–10; and "Politicians Make Strange Bedfellows!" *Gay*, May 25, 1970.

13. In later years a member of the Mattachine Society told Leitsch that he was himself a vice police officer and that a number of the officers who volunteered for this kind of work were homosexual, suggesting that some of the men on the vice squad who had sexually interacted with other gay men at least acknowledged their homosexuality to themselves: Leitsch-Carter interview. Indirect corroboration of the possibility that a good number of such officers could have been homosexual themselves comes from an interaction Leitsch had during a chance encounter with a judge who recognized him as "the guy from that homosexual organization." Complaining about a Transit Police officer who regularly brought men he had arrested in bathrooms before him, the judge told Leitsch that "every defendant" the officer brought in "said it was the cop who went down on them, then arrested them because they wouldn't pay him. . . . I told him the next time he showed up, I'd give him three months in prison for sucking cock in public, and I wrote a letter to his boss, telling him the same thing." Leitsch letter to Amsel, n.d., Leitsch papers.

14. "The World of the Homosexual," *Star Chronicle,* third in a series of articles that began on September 27, 1965.

15. Martin Duberman gives a different version of the events surrounding Hodges's resignation. He did not, however, attempt to interview Dick Leitsch for his recollections of these events.

16. This account of the meeting at Judson Church is taken from "Public Meeting on MacD.: Pirandello Writes Script," *Village Voice,* April 7, 1966; eight-page undated, untitled typescript in Leitsch papers; "Meeting on Village Cleanup," *NYMN* 11, no. 3; "Garelick Urges Public to Report Police Trapping of Homosexuals," *NYT,* April 2, 1966.

17. An eight-page undated typescript and an eleven-page undated, untitled typescript, apparently notes for the 1966 annual report by Leitsch to MSNY, the latter hereafter referred to as 1966 Annual Report, Leitsch papers. See also "Lindsay Placates Coffeehouse Set," *NYT,* May 3, 1966. Leitsch-Carter interview (on Koch jumping up).

18. Ten-page untitled speech on the Stonewall Riots, hereafter Stonewall Speech, and undated letter from Leitsch to Stephen M. Goldfarb, Leitsch papers; Leitsch-Carter interview; and Randy Wicker letter to *NYT,* October 23, 1963, Wicker papers.

19. Stonewall Speech. On SLA corruption, see, for example, "Ex–F.B.I Agent Links State Liquor Aide to Mafia," *NYT,* November 30, 1967, p. 50. Mentioned in this article is Matthew Ianello, the Genovese crime family member who controlled mob activity in the Village and was thus considered the "real" owner of all the Mafia's gay bars in the Village.

20. Frank Patton Jr. of Ellis, Stringfellow & Patton, representing Mattachine–New York, "Memorandum [of Law]: The Homosexual and the New York Alcoholic Beverage Control Law," Leitsch papers.

21. Leitsch's 1966 Annual Report, Leitsch papers.

22. Telegram sent to twelve members of the press, April 20, 1966, Leitsch papers.

23. Leitsch-Carter interview and "3 Deviates Invite Exclusion by Bars," *NYT,* April 22, 1966.

24. "S.L.A. Won't Act Against Bars Refusing Service to Deviates," *NYT,* April 26, 1966.

25. Booth letter to Leitsch, June 16, 1966. Leitsch papers.

26. "Gay Is Good," Craig Rodwell, *Queen's Quarterly,* Summer 1969, p. 39.

27. "Signs of the Times," *Hymnal* 1, No. 1, February 1968.

28. Charles Grutzner, "Mafia Buys Clubs for Homosexuals," *NYT,* November 30, 1967.

3 : ON THE STREET

1. Material for this chapter on the street youths is taken primarily from interviews of Thomas Lanigan-Schmidt, Bob Kohler, Martin Boyce, and Jerry Hoose by David Carter. An interview of Lanigan-Schmidt by Martin Duberman was also used, as was the article "From Night of Rage, Seeds of Liberation," by Rick Bragg, *NYT,* June 23, 1994. The primary source for material about Birdie Rivera is the interview of him by Michael Scherker.

2. When I interviewed Bob, he asserted that the street youth always hung out in Christopher Park. Tommy Lanigan-Schmidt, however, is emphatic that the park was just one of many places the youths frequented. He recalls sitting more often on stoops on Christopher Street than in Christopher Park. It makes sense that Bob would overemphasize the park, since that is both where he first met the youths and where he continued to meet them. The material about Bob Kohler is inserted here even though Bob did not meet the youths until the spring of 1969, for this is where the material fits logically.

3. Overpriced hamburgers: Barbara Judith Marie, "Stonewall Remembered Book 1," www.inch.com/~kdka/stonewall.htm.
4. Because of Hormona's fair features and youthful good looks, he probably could have easily passed as a woman had he wanted to, adding plausibility to Hoose's contention that Jackie did not have a transgender identity and did not want to undergo sexual re-assignment surgery. Female hormones were not that difficult to obtain at the time, and had this been Jackie's wish, one would think that had he gone in drag he could have made a fair amount of money as a cross-dressing prostitute because of his good looks and then been able to purchase hormones, which he did not do. We know this to be so, for in the early 1980s Jackie Hormona moved in next door to Hoose. Hoose noted then that the mildly effeminate side of Jackie had totally disappeared so that his presentation was quite conventionally masculine. Note, too, that Hoose is not sure what kind of makeup Jackie applied to smooth over facial imperfections but is sure it was something of the nature of foundation or facial powder. I have chosen fa-cial powder as Hoose stressed the subtlety of the effect.

   Hoose believes that it was around 1968 that he first saw Jackie Hormona.
5. Physical appearance: O'Brien-Carter interview.
6. Lanigan-Schmidt–Carter telephone conversation, June 31, 1998.
7. Prison, murder, muscular: Hoose-Carter interview.
8. Boyce-Carter interview.
9. Sources used for Marsha Johnson are Steven Watson, "The Drag of Politics," *Village Voice,* June 25, 1979; Andy Newman, "Death of a Drag Queen," *Hoboken Reporter,* July 19, 1992; Boyce-Carter interview; and Heide-Carter interview. I am grateful to Steven Watson for making available to me a copy of his *Voice* article as well as a copy of his original interview with Marsha. Randy Wicker kindly provided me with a copy of the *Hoboken Reporter* article.

4 : THE STONEWALL INN

1. Painted black after fire: Leitsch-Carter interview; contemporary description: Angelo d'Arcangelo, *The Homosexual Handbook* (New York: Ophelia Press, 1968).
2. Shaheen-Duberman interview. Duberman states that the three partners grew up on Mulberry Street in Little Italy and cites as his source his interview with Chuck Sha-heen, but this information is not in the interview. Joey is a made-up name: Shaheen could never remember this person's name in the interview. An Anthony Verra was ar-rested during the Stonewall Riots and charged with unlawful sale, consumption, and storage of liquor according to the *Sunday [New York Daily] News* (Dennis Eskow, "3 Cops Hurt As Bar Raid Riles Crowd," June 29, 1969, hereafter Eskow), but there is no further information in the article that would allow one to determine whether this per-son was one of the bar owners.
3. Fred W. and Timothy S. McDarrah's *Gay Pride: Photographs from Stonewall to Today* (New York: A Cappella Book, 1994), p. 2, has a photograph of the Stonewall Inn Restaurant taken in mid-1966 with Greek Revival columns and much of the second floor's brick wall exposed by the deterioration of the old stucco. I am grateful to Stephen van Cline for the detail about the columns.
4. License: Beard-Scherker interview; names on bottles: Shaheen-Duberman interview.
5. Beard-Scherker interview.
6. Oak and steel doors: Ed Murphy, "1969 at Stonewall," *Equal Times,* June 1, 1989; locks: Beard-Scherker interview. The *Equal Times* article, after describing "two big oak doors," says: "Inside that were steel doors," which seems to describe two separate

sets of doors but could be read to mean steel encased in oak. Openings in door: See photo by Diana Davies in illustration section of this volume.

7. Describe the inside: unpublished paper by David C. Scott. Blond Frankie's last name may have been Esselourne, according to an article supposedly written by the doorman that appeared in *Gay Community News* (Frank Esselourne, "Doorman Remembers," June 23, 1979, p. 10). Worked at many gay clubs before Stonewall: Hampton-Marcus interview.

8. Rotated ticket colors: Perrin-Carter and Shaheen-Duberman interviews; lamp with blue light: Shaheen-Duberman interview.

9. Garvin-Scherker interview.

10. Book used to discourage straight customers and signing false names as protection against police: Garvin-Scherker and Garvin-Carter interviews; book could be used in court: Shaheen-Duberman interview; campy names signed in book: Sheldon Ramsdell, letter to Michael Scherker, June 17, 1988.

11. Step down: Garvin-Scherker and Beard-Scherker interview; "through an inner door that was usually open": Beard-Scherker interview.

12. "Many round stools": Lanigan-Schmidt–Carter interview.

13. Conclusions on age and race based on numerous interviews.

14. Garvin-Carter interview.

15. Lanigan-Schmidt–Carter and Perrin-Carter interviews.

16. See, e.g., *Gay Activist*, June 1971.

17. Garvin-Scherker interview.

18. Vito Russo, "Still Outlaws," *Gay News*, No. 170, p. 16.

19. Garvin-Carter interview.

20. Manford in Tina Crosby, "The Stonewall Riot Remembered," January 1974, Lesbian Herstory Archives: "The atmosphere was cavern-like; it was very dark"; Arcangelo, *The Homosexual Handbook*, describes "the inky atmosphere."

21. Perry Brass in Crosby, "Stonewall Riot": "there was no ventilation"; *Gay Activist*, June 1971: "the fetid, incredibly smoky air."

22. Lanigan-Schmidt–Carter interview.

23. Lanigan-Schmidt–Carter interview.

24. Garvin-Scherker interview.

25. Joel S.-Carter interview.

26. Perrin-Carter interview.

27. Joel S.-Carter interview.

28. This room was referred to as the back room because it was the last room one entered: one could not enter it directly from the front door. It was not a back room in the sense of a place for having sex. Lights were dimmer in back room: Joel S.–Carter and Beard-Scherker interviews.

29. Tables: Beard interview; benches: Beard-Scherker and Fader interviews; ledge: Garvin interview; paneling is visible in McDarrah photograph (see McDarrah and McDarrah, *Gay Pride*, p. 4). Number of waiters: Garvin; their aggressiveness: Lanigan-Schmidt.

30. Lanigan-Schmidt–Carter interview.

31. Lanigan-Schmidt–Carter interview; Shaheen-Duberman interview.

32. Joel S.-Carter interview.

33. Beard-Scherker interview.

34. Garvin-Scherker interview.

35. Lanigan-Schmidt–Carter interview; drawings by Garvin and Michael Konnon; Shaheen-Duberman interview.

36. May 10, 1998, conversation with Larry, employee at the Waverly Theatre, who told author he attended the wedding reception for his sister at the Stonewall Inn Restaurant in 1958.

37. Lanigan-Schmidt–Carter interview.

38. Lanigan-Schmidt–Duberman interview.

39. Russo, "Still Outlaws."

40. Karla Jay and Allen Young, eds., *Out of the Closets: Voices of Gay Liberation* (New York: Douglas Book Corp., 1972), pp. 6–7.

41. Garvin-Scherker interview.

42. Crosby, "Stonewall Riot."

43. "Hardy"-Carter interview. Hardy is a family name created by the author at Jennifer's request.

44. It should be noted that the terms *drag queen, crossdresser,* and *transvestite* are being used here because these are the predominant terms from the era and we do not necessarily know how these people identified themselves in that era.

45. Garvin-Carter interview. Tommy Lanigan-Schmidt points out that today people tend to equate the scare drag of the sixties with the gender-fuck (men purposefully donning female attire without trying to pass as women by, for example, simultaneously wearing dresses and beards) movement that emerged in the seventies in San Francisco. Tommy emphasizes that much of the scare-drag look (e.g., the shirt tied at midriff that could be quickly untied) was about being able to quickly change from a male to a female persona to avoid being arrested or attacked.

46. Note that even by contemporary New York City standards, the Stonewall Inn would still be considered a moderate-sized bar.

47. I use this date because Danny Garvin is able to date the club's opening since he had been discharged from the navy that very day. He also remembers the event because it opened on the weekend of St. Patrick's Day and he had just turned eighteen.

Further corroboration for this date is found in an interview of Kevin Dunn by Michael Scherker on June 5, 1989, in San Francisco, in which Dunn states that he first went to the Stonewall Inn in March of 1967. When Scherker asked him, "How did you end up at the Stonewall?" Dunn replied, "Some guy told me about this hot *new* bar" (emphasis added).

48. "Mike"-Carter interview. (Mike is a fictitious name for the former porter of the Stonewall Inn.)

49. Rodwell-Scherker interview.

50. Craig Rodwell, "Mafia on the Spot," *Hymnal* 1, No. 1, February 1968, pp. 1–2.

51. Brew quoted in Crosby, "Stonewall Riot."

52. Rodwell, "On the Spot."

53. Leitsch letter to Amsel, September 18 [1967], Leitsch papers. While Leitsch's letter does not state that the police were in uniform or from the Sixth Precinct, that seems a reasonable assumption, as it was normally the vice squad's job to investigate and catch corrupt police officers.

54. Murphy gave the $1,200 figure to *The Village Voice,* to Emerald City Television, and to the organization Seniors in A Gay Environment (SAGE). The SAGE account was used in a SAGE theatrical presentation in 1988, and excerpts from the play were published in *Equal Times* in 1989. See Bob Dolan, "When the Law Reaches into Your Pocket," *Pageant* 23, No. 2, August 1967, pp. 40–46; Arthur Bell, "Skull Murphy: The Gay Double Agent," *Village Voice* 23, No. 19, May 8, 1978; Murphy, "1969 at Stonewall"; and Murphy interview with Gene Stavis of Emerald City Television. Note that the $1,200 a month figure agrees with Shaheen's estimate of several hundred dollars a week.

55. Tree-Carter interview.

56. *Ladder,* "Gay Power in New York City," October–November 1969, p. 40. Rodwell related in "On the Spot" how he tried to report the unsanitary conditions to various city agencies and how unresponsive the agencies were.

57. "Mike"-Carter interview.

58. I am indebted to plumbing consultant Tony Carini for explaining to me how a substantial volume of water poured into a toilet could cause a delayed overflow.

59. Carl Lee, "It's What's Happening," *Hymnal* 1, No. 5, June–July 1968.

60. Seating capacity information on floor plans of the Stonewall Inn filed with the City of New York gives the total capacity of the club at 190: "185 persons and 5 employees." However, Seymour Pine said that on the evening he raided the club it had 200–300 persons inside.

61. A number of people pointed out the club's dangers as a fire trap after the bar closed, e.g., Perry Brass in Crosby, "Stonewall Riot." Other comments on the lack of fire exits are: "The Stonewall couldn't get a license because it lacked a rear fire exit." ("Stonewall 'Historic'?" *Advocate,* August 15, 1973, p. 16), and "there were no fire exits" (Leitsch, *NYMN,* August 1969). Note, too, that the windows were carefully boarded up.

62. Rodwell in Crosby, "Stonewall Riot."

63. Russo, "Outlaws," p. 16.

64. Garvin-Scherker interview.

65. Shaheen-Duberman interview.

66. Tree telephone conversation, ca. June 1999.

67. "Beating Around the Bush," *Private Lives,* January 1993, p. 100.

68. Enid Girling is also known from the period for being one of the few attorneys available for helping gay men arrested as a result of entrapment, but is controversial for charging large fees for doing so.

69. Dick Leitsch, "The Stonewall Riots[:] The Gay View," *NYMN,* August 1969, pp. 13–14.

5 : THE SKULL

1. Lanigan-Schmidt–Duberman and Lanigan-Schmidt–Carter interviews. Note that Ed Murphy was known to be especially attracted to Latino and black youths, which could lend credibility to the rumor that the kidnapped Puerto Rican was a boyfriend of Murphy's. Tano is a made-up name for the man Tommy and his friends called Miss Polka Dot, as his real name is unknown.

2. Stephen van Cline–Carter telephone conversation, April 21, 1996.

3. This account of Murphy's life is based on interviews he gave. The sources used are Arthur Bell, "Skull Murphy: The Gay Double Agent," *Village Voice,* May 1978, pp. 1, 17–19; John Hoglund, *New York Native* obituary, March 27, 1989, "Eddie Murphy—from Hellion to Hero," *Private Lives* 2, Issue 6, December 1987; "SAGE Stories," *Equal Times,* June 1, 1989. Some of the details in the preceding sources are corroborated in a general way by Glenn Person, "CS People," *Christopher Street,* Issue 66, July 1982; in an interview by Gene Stavis on Emerald City Television; and in an interview given to Chris Davis, n.d. (apparently 1983 or 1984, since Murphy refers to the gay rights bill having been introduced before the city council of New York City for "thirteen years"). Regarding the violent incidents in his early life, Murphy consistently portrays himself as a victim standing up for himself against his oppressors, a line that interviewers Bell and Hoglund apparently bought, e.g., (Bell): "One day when shining shoes for quarters, a nasty Irish cop laced into him [Murphy] and broke his shoeshine box. The natural

thing to do was to hit the sonovabitch over the head with a milk bottle." Hoglund, after characterizing Murphy as "above all else, a fighter for [. . .] human dignity," quotes Murphy as saying that "the teacher hit me—and I hit back!!!"

4. "Detective at Hotel Is Held in Extortion," *NYT*, August 5, 1965, p. 19.

5. All of the information in this chapter about the blackmail ring quoted as coming from contemporary news accounts is from the following newspaper and magazine articles: "Gay Bar Closed," *NYMN*, March 1968, p. 5; "Nine Seized Here in Extortion Ring," *NYT*, February 18, 1966; "17 Indicted in Hush-Money Shakedown," *Herald Tribune*, 1966; "Nationwide Ring Preying on Prominent Deviates," *NYT*, February 3, 1966; "3 Indicted Here as Sex Extorters," *NYT*, June 1, 1966; "Grab City Cop as Sex-Blackmail Kingpin," *Chicago Sun-Times*, June 25, 1966; "Detective Accused as a Top Extorter," *NYT*, July 1, 1966; "Blackmailer of Deviates Gets 5 Years," *New York Post*, August 16, 1966; "Gets 5 Years in Extortion of Homosexuals," *Daily News*, 1966; "Blackmailer Gets Five-Year Sentence in Homosexual Case," *NYT*, August 17, 1966; "Gets 5 Yrs. in Extortion of Homos," *Daily News*, August 17, 1966, p. 9; "Lands at JFK, FBI Is There," *Daily News*, September 18, 1966; "More Indictments Due in Blackmail Case," *New York Post*, September 28, 1966, p. 62; "Blackmail Paid by Congressman"; *NYT*, August 17, 1967; "Member of 70-Man Ring Preying on Homosexuals Given 5 Years," *NYT*, July 12, 1967; and "2 Found Guilty in Chicago in Extortion of Homosexual," *NYT*, December 9, 1967.

Although most of the victims, including those men who were married and had children, were undoubtedly homosexual or bisexual, it seems possible from contemporary accounts that some small percentage of the victims may have been strictly heterosexual.

6. William McGowan, "Before Stonewall," *Wall Street Journal*, June 16, 2000, p. W13.

7. These nine articles are from Dick Leitsch's personal papers.

8. Richard Inman, letter to Jack Nichols (Warren Adkins, pseud.), September 19, 1965, quoted in James T. Sears's *Lonely Hunters: An Oral History of Lesbian and Gay Southern Life, 1948–1968* (Boulder, Colo.: Westview Press, 1997), p. 244.

9. Ginsberg–Benz interview.

10. *Straight News*, p. 269, and Donn Teal, *The Gay Militants*, p. 65. Description of Hoover is on p. 267 of what appears to be either the first edition of Arcangelo, *The Homosexual Handbook*, or a pirated copy of it.

11. Ginsberg–Benz interview.

12. John Paul Ranieri had a lifetime of mental health issues, and I did not always find his accounts of events to be reliable. For these reasons, I only used information from him that was corroborated by other sources.

13. Murray Weiss, "J. Edgar's Slip Was Showing," *New York Post*, February 11, 1993. I am grateful to Randy Wicker for providing me with a copy of this article. Very suggestive in this context is that Murphy would publicly say in 1978—before it became public information, as it did in the 1990s, that the Mafia had photographs of Hoover involved in sex acts—that he knew that J. Edgar Hoover "was one of my sisters" (see Bell, "Skull Murphy").

14. It is very suggestive of Murphy's powers to silence opposition that while the aforementioned article ends with the statement: "We also have other information on Mr. Murphy that will be printed here next month," the following month's newsletter did not so much as mention Ed Murphy's name.

15. *New York City Gay Scene Guide*, Vol. 2, p. 11 (1969).

16. Stonewall Speech. The relevant passage says: "A man who seemed to be the manager of the place had been arrested several times for shaking down homosexuals and had

been recently named as a member of a national blackmail ring preying on homosexuals." It is interesting to note that Leitsch originally typed "blackmailing" before changing the wording to "shaking down." Leitsch also wrote: "A man named 'Scumback' Murphy was always around the Stonewall, and was said to be one of the operators of the place." Dick Leitsch, "The Snake Pit Raid: Some Afterthoughts," *Gay* 1, No. 10, April 13, 1970.

17. Arcangelo, *Homosexual Handbook*, p. 130.

18. Shaheen-Duberman interview.

19. Garvin-Carter interview.

20. Lanigan-Schmidt–Duberman interview.

21. Kohler-Carter telephone conversation, January 11, 1999. In the *Emerald City* interview, Murphy talks about being involved in a counterfeit ring but claims that he was acting in the ring as a government agent to break the ring.

22. The only published references to this the author is aware of are Miller, p. 42, which also speaks of rumors and Robert Heide and John Gilman, *Greenwich Village: A Primo Guide to Shopping, Eating, and Making Merry in True Bohemia* (New York: St. Martin's Griffin, 1995) p. 138.

23. *Equal Times*, June 1, 1989, p. 19.

24. Carl Lee, "It's What's Happening," *Hymnal* 1, No. 6, August–September 1968, p. 2.

25. In our talks, as with all the other persons interviewed for this book, no indication had been given to Ranieri of the author's knowledge of the Stonewall Inn's operations nor any other information collected nor conclusions reached, so as not to prejudice testimony. Thus Ranieri had never been told by the author of this history of the rumors that the second floor of the Stonewall Inn was used for prostitution.

26. Ranieri-Carter conversation, June 27, 1998. My handwritten notes on the entrance say: "Gambino headquarters [were at the] back of 2nd floor—[one] entered by garage. [Ranieri] Thinks front of 2nd floor [was] junk and storage. There may've been an emergency connection from back of 2nd floor to front of 2nd floor, [Ranieri is] not sure."

27. "Beating Around the Bush," *Private Lives*, February 1992, August 1993, and December 1993.

28. Barry Perrin shared his memories of what he had been told about blackmail at the Stonewall Inn spontaneously, without any prompting from the author.

   The question naturally arises about the likelihood that a well-known person would risk giving information about himself to a membership club. A letter by Leitsch to his lover Bob Amsel documents that Cardinal Spellman himself signed the guestbook of the gay bar the Mystique: "[John Lassoe and I] mapped out a tentative campaign for revising the sodomy and solicitation laws. . . . We're gambling that we can get enough grass-roots support . . . to counter-balance the inevitable Roman Catholic opposition. John thinks it's useless, but I'm going to begin another campaign to talk to Cardinal Spellman and see if I can persuade him to remain neutral, if he won't support reform. His name is in the guest book of the Mystique, and he's been seen other places, and I'm not above a little blackmail if it keeps him in line!" Leitsch letter to Amsel, n.d., Leitsch papers.

29. McGowan, "Before Stonewall."

30. New York Public Library Manuscripts and Archives Division, International Gay Information Center tape 02851, dated February 5, 1978: Morty Manford with Bob Battenberg and Arthur Bell re Ed Murphy. Arthur Bell also reacted with skepticism to Murphy's claims of being an informant: "I don't believe it. Four or five years ago . . . the guy in charge of the Joint Strike Force Against Crime . . . showed me trees [that

diagrammed] how everyone [in the mob] was related to everybody else, and he told me Ed Murphy was a dangerous guy and someone to watch out for."

31. Information in this chapter on Seymour Pine's career and the order to close the Stonewall Inn comes from Pine-Carter interview.

32. Pine-Isay interview.

33. When Pine was interviewed by Carter he had trouble remembering when he was transferred to Manhattan but thought it was in 1969. He told Isay in 1989 that he had come into Manhattan in 1968. *The Village Voice*, which interviewed him in 1970 (Jonathan Black, "The Boys in the Snake Pit: Games 'Straights' Play," March 19, 1970), says he arrived in May 1969, so I have used that date. Note also that many press accounts of the Stonewall Riots talk about a "new" commanding officer, although some say new at the Sixth Precinct. Asked if there had there been any recent change of commanding officers at the Sixth Precinct, Pine said that there had not been.

6: DAWN IS JUST BREAKING

1. "McCarthy Wins Poll," *Hymnal* 1, No. 4, May 1968.

2. The summation given here of gay organizing in San Francisco in the 1960s is taken from D'Emilio's *Sexual Politics*, pp. 182–91.

3. Date of July 1966 is from "Young Rejects Form Own Organization," *Cruise News & World Report* 2, No. 7, July 1966, which announces the start of the new organization.

4. "Exiles of Sin, Incorporated," *Berkeley Barb*, November 11, 1966.

5. *We Protest*, flyer, Donald Lucas papers, Gay and Lesbian Historical Society of Northern California. I am indebted to Susan Stryker for calling this flyer and all the other materials quoted here on Vanguard to my attention.

6. Jean-Paul Marat, "On Prejudice," *V* 1, No. 2, October 1966, p. 1.

7. Stryker-Carter interview.

8. "Young Homos Picket Compton's Restaurant," *Cruise News & World Report* 2, No. 8, August 1966, and "History of Christopher Street West," (San Francisco) *Gay Pride* program, June 25, 1972.

9. Evans–Carter interviews. Although the perception is still widespread that Whitman was the major influence on Ginsberg's poetic development, Ginsberg was clear that Blake was his main inspiration. It is notable that Evans was moved by both Blake and Whitman, both important to Ginsberg, and then was heavily influenced by Ginsberg as well. See, e.g., Allen Ginsberg *Spontaneous Mind: Selected Interviews 1958–1996*, ed. David Carter (New York: HarperCollins, 2001).

10. Garvin-Carter interview and Garvin-Scherker interview.

11. Garvin-Scherker, Garvin-Carter, Shaheen-Duberman, and Beard-Scherker interviews; "The Night They Raided Stonewall," *Gay Activist*, June 1971; Russo, "Still Outlaws"; *1969 New York City Gay Scene Guide*, Vol. 2; and Arcangelo, *The Homosexual Handbook*.

12. White-Carter interview and Crosby, "Stonewall Riot."

13. "Gay Power Gains," *Hymnal* 1, No. 6, August–September 1968. The date of the *Wall Street Journal* article was July 17, 1968; the letters to the editor column containing responses to the article was published in August.

14. "It's What's Happening" and "On Stage," *Hymnal* 1, No. 5, June–July 1968.

15. Lori Reid, *The Complete Book of Chinese Horoscopes* (Shaftesbury, Dorset; Rockport, Mass.: Barnes & Noble Books, 1997), p. 123.

16. "Transit Cops Shake Down Wrong Man" and "More Police Harassment," *NYMN*, February 1969.

17. "Cop Kills Two—May Go Free" and "Docks, Darkness and Danger," *NYMN*, March 1969.

18. Bathhouse wrecked and no bribes paid: *Los Angeles Advocate*, April 1969, p. 22. "Bathhouse Raided," "Dock Killings," and "Your Friendly SLA," *NYMN*, April 1969.

19. D'Emilio, *Sexual Politics*, p. 230, and *Vector*, April 1969.

20. "Gay Rebel Gets Shafted by Uptight Boss," *Berkeley Barb*, April 11, 1969.

21. "Pink Panthers Gay Revolution Toughening Up," *Berkeley Barb*, April 18–24, 1969.

22. "Killer Cops at Large" and "Gay Strike Turns Grim," *Berkeley Barb*, April 25–May 1, 1969, and "Group Will Act" and "Gay Strike Hits Southern Front," *Berkeley Barb*, May 2–8, 1969.

23. "Gays Get Tougher," *Berkeley Barb*, May 23–29, 1969.

24. Carl Wittman, "A Gay Manifesto," in Karla Jay and Allen Young, eds., *Out of the Closets: Voices of Gay Liberation* (New York: Douglas Book Corp., 1972), p. 330.

25. "Coming Mayoralty Contest," *NYMN*, May 1969.

26. Alternate U. history from telephone conversation with Mike Bradley, October 26, 2003.

27. Tobin and Wicker, *Gay Crusaders*, p. 173. I conclude that this approach was made by Katzenberg because he was the main person pushing the idea for such an organization and Hoose and O'Brien have no recollection of making the pitch to Marty Robinson. Further evidence that the approach to Robinson came from Katzenberg or someone in his group is that the first press mention of the group that would very soon become known as the Gay Liberation Front is of a demonstration that John O'Brien was present at and it says that the group called itself the Pink Panthers. "From Outside the Pen," *Rat* 2, No. 15, late July 1969, p. 4.

    Hoose says he has no memory of meeting O'Brien before the riots and thus does not count himself as a founder of the group that would become the Gay Liberation Front, but when I first interviewed O'Brien, he told me that he had spoken to Jerry Hoose about this and that Hoose did not recall these conversations and meetings. If O'Brien were fabricating this, it seems highly unlikely that he would include Jerry Hoose in the roster of those trying to start a militant gay group before Stonewall when he knew that Hoose would deny any memory of these events. Moreover, in an article in the program of San Francisco's first gay pride march (*Gay Pride*, June 25, 1972), an article about how gay pride observations began ("History of Christopher Street: How It All Began!") lists Hoose as one of four founders of the Gay Liberation Front. (The other three it credits are Michael Brown, Martha Shelley, and Jim Owles.) Incidentally, Jerry Hoose told the author in an October 26, 2003, telephone conversation that it was he who had coined the phrase *gay pride* at one of the meetings planning the first celebration of the Stonewall Riots.

28. *Rat*, July 24, 1969.

29. *NYMN*, June 1969.

30. David Bird, "Trees in a Queens Park Cut Down As Vigilantes Harass Homosexuals," *NYT*, July 1, 1969; Don Jackson, "Reflections on the N.Y. Riots," *Los Angeles Advocate*, October 1969, p. 11.

31. Letter to the editor signed by Kevin Liscoe, July 10, 1969, *Village Voice*, p. 4; "Gay Power in New York City," p. 40; and "Reflections."

32. "Dawn Is Just Breaking . . . ," *Queen's Quarterly* 1, No. 3, Summer 1969, p. 5. Most ellipses are in the original editorial.

33. Ronnie Di Brienza, "Stonewall Incident," *East Village Other* 4, No. 32, July 9, 1969, p. 2.

34. Di Brienza, "Stonewall Incident," and Pine-Carter interview.

7 :   A   F R I D A Y   N I G H T   O U T

1. The experiences of persons recounted in this chapter are based upon interviews and the following: "Steve" Ritter's talk at "The Forgotten Stonewall," a Stonewall commemoration, June 16, 1994, and Garvin-Carter telephone conversation, December 12, 1999. In this chapter, for dramatic reasons, most of the thoughts and feelings of the persons reported in interviews have not been given as direct quotations.

2. That the search warrant, number 578, dated June 26, 1969, was over twenty-four hours old when the police initiated the raid is significant, for there have been several variations of a rumor that the raid on the Stonewall Inn the night of June 27 began because of a dispute between the police and the bar earlier that day. Information on the search warrant is from the police log for June 28, 1969, obtained by Michael Scherker under the Freedom of Information Act.

3. "Satisfaction" played prior to police raid: Barry Cunningham, *Gay Power: The Homosexual Revolt*, (New York: Tower Publications, 1971.)

8 :   " W E ' R E   T A K I N G   T H E   P L A C E ! "

While the account in this book of the Stonewall Riots is based on many sources, it makes extensive use of the invaluable accounts published at the time, especially Lucian Truscott's "Gay Power Comes to Sheridan Square" and Howard Smith's "Full Moon over the Stonewall" (both in *Village Voice*, July 3, 1969), Dick Leitsch's "The Hairpin Drop Heard Around the World" (*NYMN*, August 1969), Ronnie Di Brienza's "Stonewall Incident" (*East Village Other* 4, No. 32, July 9, 1969), and the anonymous "Queen Power: Fags Against Pigs in Stonewall Bust" (*Rat* 2, no. 14, July 9–23, 1969).

1. According to the Sixth Precinct's log for June 28, 1969, obtained by Michael Scherker under the Freedom of Information Act, the raid began at 1:20 A.M. This agrees with the account given in the underground newspaper *Rat*, which gives the time of the raid as "[a]bout 1:15." By all evidence, the *Rat* account of the riots is possibly the most precise reporting of the events of Friday night. That the official police account coincides with an unofficial account within five minutes is very strong corroboration.

2. Established from photograph by Joseph Ambrosini in Eskow.

3. Morty Manford, May 1978, student paper, "The New York Gay Political Movement, 1978: An Organizational and Strategy Critique," hereafter Manford 1978, and a 3-page incomplete typescript, "Stonewall Remembrances," hereafter Manford "Remembrances." All Manford manuscripts cited are from the Morty Manford Papers, Manuscripts and Archives Division, the New York Public Library, Astor, Lenox and Tilden Foundations. These accounts of the riots were eventually published as part of an article, "Why We Should Postpone New York's Gay Rights Bill: A New Look at Gay Political Strategy," in *Gaysweek*, October 16, 1978, pp. 10–16.

4. Pine-Carter interview.

5. According to Pine's 1989 interview with David Isay, they called for backup just before entering the Stonewall Inn, but since that is Pine's recollection twenty years after the event, I have chosen to go with what Howard Smith was told by the police, presumably Pine, in 1969: they phoned after all the officers were inside the Inn: Smith, "Full Moon." Also, I have chosen to go with Pine's later statement to Isay that they "requested a couple of police officers and patrol wagons," since a patrol wagon did indeed come, rather than accept the *Voice* version that he requested "a patrol car and some officers."

6. Note, however, that according to one patron who claimed to be inside the bar when the raid began, the police initially "kept the music and dancing going so's not to get everyone up.": *Rat,* July 9, 1969. Perhaps this seeming inconsistency could be explained by the presence of the two undercover female police in the bar before the raid.

7. Manford later described the raiding officers as a combination of federal Treasury officials and Sixth Precinct policemen. Morty Manford interview with Eric Marcus, hereafter Manford 1989, and Manford "Remembrances." Manford identified some of the raiding officers as federal Treasury officials in not only the 1978 and 1989 accounts but also a January 1972 paper, "A Comparative Study of Gay Liberationists and Columbia Homosexuals," hereafter Manford 1972. (See also Manford, "Why We Should Postpone.") This assertion suggests Pine told Manford this, as the Bureau of Alcohol, Tobacco and Firearms is part of the U.S. Department of Treasury and Manford 1972 has a footnote citing Pine.

    Photograph accompanying Eskow article shows that the suits plainclothes officers were wearing that night were dark.

8. Manford 1978 and Manford 1989.

9. Manford 1989.

10. Eagles-Carter interview.

11. Pine-Carter interview. Pine added that "I guess they had a few drinks, too. You know, that was their job, to be part of that crowd."

12. Pine-Carter interview.

13. Pine-Carter interview.

14. Pine-Carter interview. Pine demanded to see identification and noted the man's name.

15. Eagles-Carter interview. Possible corroboration of this account of lesbian resistance inside the club soon after the raid began comes from Bruce Shenton, who told the author that he heard about a week after the riots that the genesis of it all was a lesbian confrontation inside the bar. Shenton-Carter interview.

16. "Confusion and uncertainty": Manford 1978, and "ten or fifteen minutes": Manford 1989.

17. Pine-Carter interview.

18. Alcohol found in storage room: Pine-Carter interview.

19. Paper attached to each container and evidence book: Pine-Carter interview.

20. Quantities of alcohol seized: Eskow. That it was Smythe who cataloged the alcohol: Pine-Isay and Pine-Carter interviews. Cataloging their names and addresses: Pine-Carter interview.

21. Pine estimates the length of time it took between the beginning of the raid and getting all the customers he chose not to arrest outside as from fifteen to twenty minutes. Pine-Carter interview.

22. *Rat,* July 9, 1969.

23. Manford 1989. Manford saw symbolism in their being held in this area, as if inside a closet. "Little did the police know the ironic symbolism of that. But they found out fast."

24. While this account never explicitly states that the complaining about the raids on the Stonewall took place inside the Stonewall Inn itself, it all but says so, leaving one with that tacit understanding, Di Brienza, "Stonewall Incident."

25. Jackson, "Reflections."

26. Jackson, "Reflections."

27. Walter Troy Spencer, "Too Much, My Dear," "Last Call" column, *Village Voice,* July 10, 1969, p. 36.

28. "Gay Power in New York City," p. 40.

29. Manford 1978.

30. Lanigan-Schmidt–Duberman interview.

31. Truscott, "Gay Power."

32. Manford 1989.

33. Smith, "Full Moon."

34. Truscott, "Gay Power," and Smith, "Full Moon," p. 1. Tom is a made-up name for the anonymous *Rat* reporter.

35. Joel S.–Carter. The direction of the patrol wagon is corroborated by other witnesses, including Maria Ritter.

36. This is Joel S.'s description of the scene at the time the first paddy wagon arrived.

37. Rodwell-Ardery interview. "The raid was just starting at that time. And we noticed the crowds. We went over there," and Rodwell-Duberman: "When we first arrived there . . . it was a small crowd . . . it had just started to gather." Game of bridge: Randy Shilts, *The Mayor of Castro Street* (New York: St. Martin's Press, 1982), p. 42.

38. Rodwell-Scherker interview. While in 1986 Craig Rodwell told Scherker that when he arrived there were two police cars in front of the Stonewall Inn, when he gave an account of the riots to Breck Ardery in 1970 he said that when he arrived "there was a paddy wagon pulled up." I have decided to use the Ardery account concerning the police vehicles present, not only because it is so close in time to the event itself but also because according to Ed White's letter to Alfred Corn, it was while Mafia owners were being loaded into the van that "[s]omeone shouted 'Gay Power,'" for White's letter has the ring of someone noting the cry for the first time. He even says "others took up the cry," which sounds similar to Rodwell telling Scherker, "I can remember yelling 'Gay power' at one point, and people cheering, like this was the first time they'd ever heard something like that, you know. And then people throwing pennies or something." Note, too, that most accounts do not have money being thrown until a patrol wagon is on the scene and being loaded with prisoners.

39. Rodwell-Scherker interview.

40. Rodwell-Ardery interview.

41. Pine-Isay and Pine-Carter interviews. Although Pine describes activities in the back room as happening mainly while the patrons were leaving, it is reasonable to assume that they began these activities while the patrons were lined up and waiting. Otherwise, what would the eight police officers have been doing during that time? Note, too, that in the Eskow account the police "began clearing the bar [. . .] [a]fter 28 cases of beer and 19 bottles of liquor were confiscated" (emphasis added). In the Isay interview, Pine stated that the real motivation for removing the bars was to put pressure on the club's owners.

　　Pine never did learn who was giving the orders to disregard his calls for more patrol wagons and reinforcements. As the Sixth Precinct was well paid by the Stonewall Inn and as Pine had violated protocol by not informing them of the raid in advance and the Sixth Precinct was able to countermand the orders, it seems probable that these cancellations did originate from the Sixth Precinct in retaliation.

42. Pine was quite clear in his interviews with the author that he made sure everyone he did not want to arrest was outside the club before he attempted to load any prisoners into vehicles.

43. White-Corn letter. Both White and Truscott ("Gay Power") report negative and positive reactions from the crowd as the bar owners and employees are arrested. The accounts are ambiguous and could suggest that they were being either booed because of their own exploitation of gay people or cheered because of their connection

with a bar that was a gay institution. Similarly, one could read the accounts as suggesting that the police were being booed (or cheered) for arresting them. White: "As the Mafia owners were dragged out one by one and shoved into the wagon, the crowd would let up Bronx cheers and jeers and clapping. Someone shouted 'Gay Power,' others took up the cry—and then it dissolved in giggles. A few more prisoners— bartenders, hatcheck boys—a few more cheers." Truscott: "Suddenly the paddy-wagon arrived and the mood of the crowd changed. Three of the more blatant queens—in full drag—were loaded inside, along with the bartender and doorman, to a chorus of catcalls and boos from the crowd." While it is quite possible that different persons in the crowd reacted differently (some seeing the police as the enemy for arresting the mobsters, others applauding these arrests, and still others feeling that both were the enemy), I have interpreted the boos and catcalls at this point at being aimed primarily at the Mafia members and associates, per the account given by Vito Russo to Eric Marcus: "People were . . . screaming at who they perceived to be the enemy, . . . the owners of the bar—people who worked there." Even though Russo told Marcus he arrived later, after the patrol wagons had left, if some members of the crowd were screaming at the Mafiosi then, it seems probable that they would have done so earlier as well.

44. Joel S.–Carter interview: "Sound carried very well that night."
45. White-Corn letter.
46. Fader-Carter interview. Harry Beard also saw John in the paddy wagon. Scherker-Beard interview.
47. White-Corn letter.
48. It is worth noting, however, that humor can be a way of sublimating anger, and various writers have noted over the years that as an oppressed minority, homosexuals found—and continue to find—a number of creative ways to express that anger, with camp humor being one of them.
49. White-Corn letter.
50. Truscott, "Gay Power," p. 1.
51. White-Corn letter.
52. Based on numerous reports.
53. *The New Symposium II,* a WBAI Sunday gay radio program, broadcast transcript. The precise date of the program is unknown. The broadcast begins with an introductory statement by Charles Pitts saying, "On *The New Symposium* tonight we will hear an interview with a gay bar owner. But first we want to play a tape we recorded yesterday when we talked to a young man who was in the vicinity of the Stonewall bar during the riots there Friday and Saturday nights of last week." If Pitts considered Sunday to mark the beginning of a new week, then it is possible the program was taped on June 29, but it seems more likely from the description of the riots as taking place "last week" (instead of "over the last two days," for example) that the interview with Sargeant was taped on Saturday, July 6, 1969.
54. There can be practically no doubt that this was Tammy Novak that the *Rat* reporter saw exiting. Not only does the description of Tommy fit Tammy Novak, but also Tree explained in a telephone conversation during the summer of 1999 that Tammy Novak's name as a boy was Tommy.
55. When Ritter says "older" we need to note that she had just turned eighteen, so she just means older than herself.
56. See Duberman, *Stonewall,* p. 197, Rodwell-Duberman interview, and Maida Tilchen, "Mythologizing Stonewall," *Gay Community News,* June 23, 1979, p. 16.
57. Note that the descriptions of her clothing given by several witnesses agree to a con-

siderable degree, especially when one considers that the *Voice* articles give no description of her clothing or any other details about her. Indeed, a careful reading of the two *Voice* articles shows that only *one* word, *dyke*, is employed in the entirety of the *Voice's* reporting to describe this woman. It is therefore remarkable that witnesses Yates's, Hardy's, and Beard's accounts describing her appearance and dress agree in such detail, since the *earliest* of these was given twenty years after the event. Also, Scherker's interview with Beard has never been published (although it is quoted in *Stonewall*) and when I interviewed Yates he had no particular interest in the lesbian, his interest centering more on his friend Gino's reaction to her mistreatment, for Yates thought it was perhaps Gino's cobblestone toss that had triggered the riots. In Mike Long's *San Francisco Sentinel* article ("Stonewall: The Night the Girls Said No!" June 22, 1989, pp. 3–4) she is described as wearing "a man's black leather suit." Beard described her to Scherker as being "fully dressed in male clothing." It should be noted that while Duberman cites inconsistencies between Beard's accounts as given to Scherker and to the *San Francisco Sentinel,* this is not necessarily the case, for while Beard's is the only name quotations are attributed to in the article, some quotes in the article are *not* attributed, and the article begins by stating that "three men [are] determined to set the record straight." (The other two men, shown in a photo with Beard, are Gene Huss and Don Knapp.) Also, whereas Duberman says (p. 299, n. 39) that Beard "describes the cop as 'hitting her over the head with his billy club,'" in the article this is not a direct quotation but a statement by the reporter. Duberman assumes that this information came from Beard, but it could just as well have come from Huss or Knapp. Still, I consider Beard a source to be used with some care, seeming at times given to exaggeration, as when in his interview with Scherker he said that twenty-five drag queens lined up in a chorus line and, under Beard's leadership, kicked the front door of the Stonewall Inn open.

Descriptions of the lesbian's clothing are as follows: "fully dressed in men's clothing" (Beard-Scherker interview); "a man's black leather suit" (Beard and/or Knapp and/or Huss in Duberman, *Stonewall*); "Dark suit. Sport coat, white shirt, tie," which Yates summed up as "fancy, go-to-bar drag for a butch dyke"; and "I think she was in pants" (Hardy, when asked about her clothes).

The similarities in the independent descriptions of the woman's body are also striking, again, especially after so many years. Yates describes her as "beefy, good-sized, . . . probably in her late thirties, dark, very short . . . mannish haircut, typical New York butch, not Anglo, probably Italian or Jewish: dark hair, dark features." Hardy described her as "bigger, huskier, not a femme, not a real feminine person. Not even a feminine person. Bigger size, nasty temper. She was at least as tall as I am; I'm five-seven. If I remember right, she had darker hair." Asked her impression of the lesbian's age, Hardy emphasized that she was only seventeen in June 1969 and has never been a good judge of age and therefore could only guess "late twenties, early thirties."

The descriptions of this woman as a butch or bull-dyke type further increase the likelihood of these accounts being accurate because of another important piece of unpublished evidence. In the Lesbian Herstory Archives among the records of the film *Before Stonewall* is the paper written by Tina Crosby on the Stonewall Riots as a piece of folk historical research, "The Stonewall Riot Remembered." Crosby interviewed eight people, seven of whom either went to the Stonewall Inn or had participated in the riots. Crosby wrote that "each person I talked with remembered the Stonewall as an exclusively male bar, with the only exception being an occasional *tough* lesbian [emphasis added] or female friend of one of the male patrons." This paper is dated January 1974. The early date of Crosby's interviews, combined with the paper's unpublished status, make it valuable corroboration on this point.

58. Hardy, who at five feet, seven inches, is tall for a woman, says that the arrested lesbian was at least as tall as she.

59. Yates-Carter interview.

60. This letter (referred to as the "Rhoda letter") was discovered by James T. Sears, who published an excerpt from it in his book *Lonely Hunters*. The letter is found in the Atlanta Lesbian Feminist Alliance Papers, Special Collections Library, Duke University. Unfortunately, not all pages of this letter have been preserved. Also, the manuscript at Duke is a photocopy of the original letter and not the original itself. Whether the original manuscript survives is unknown.

61. Beard-Scherker interview.

62. Long, "Stonewall," June 22, 1989. Note that the two possibilities are not mutually exclusive: the lesbian could have both requested that the cuffs be loosened and protested the rough treatment.

63. Beard's versions of the events surrounding the lesbian seem all the more plausible given the role in them of the handcuffs bothering the lesbian, for the role of handcuffs was also very much on the mind of Dave Van Ronk. Van Ronk explained that the handcuffs the police used on him were Spanish cuffs, metal handcuffs specifically made so that if one struggles to escape, they automatically tighten. However, the cuffs can also tighten simply from general movement. Van Ronk remembers this well because he made his living playing guitar: his cuffs had tightened and by the time he was released from the handcuffs he had lost some feeling in one of his hands. Note also that Steve Yates remembers the lesbian having her hands cuffed *behind* her back, which is the way Van Ronk remembers his hands being cuffed, another indirect corroboration: it makes sense that the police would cuff all or most of the prisoners arrested in the same place at the same time in the same manner and (presumably) with the same kinds of handcuffs.

64. Truscott, "Gay Power," p. 1, and Smith, "Full Moon," p. 25.

65. Leo E. Laurence, "Gays Hit N.Y. Cops," *Berkeley Barb*, July 4–10, 1969, p. 5. Laurence wrote: "Ironically it was a chick who gave the rallying cry to fight." The *Magpie*, a Los Angeles gay publication, in an August 1969 article by Bobbie Huff, "N.Y. Police Scream at Queens" (p. 14), appears to quote the *Barb* account but instead of calling the woman a "chick" identifies her as a "female customer."

66. Laurence, "Gays Hit N.Y. Cops."

67. However, chronologically the event in *Rat* seems too early in the evening and may very possibly have involved a male prisoner. Harry Beard, "I Was There . . . the Stonewall Riot," *New York Gay Press* 1, No. 1, July 1980, p. 5. "The squad car tried to escape with its prisoner. Too late . . . the cops weren't going anywhere on four slashed tires." That police vehicles' tires were slashed is corroborated by four separate mentions in three independent accounts: the *Rat* account, Beard's account, and two quotations by Morty Manford: a single short phrase in Manford 1978, "Slashed tires of the paddywagon," and Manford 1989: "I can't claim credit for the small acts of violence that took place. I didn't break any windows. I wasn't the one who had a knife and cut the tires on the paddy wagon. I didn't hit a cop and I didn't get hit by a cop."

68. Yates-Carter interview. Note that according to Yates, Gino told everyone he was Italian, although Yates said he and his friends "knew" Gino was Puerto Rican.

69. Hardy-Carter interview.

70. According to "I Was There," by Harry Beard, the patrol car he saw the lesbian put in had all of its tires slashed, which suggests the lesbian originally in the police car

might have been subsequently placed inside the patrol wagon to make driving the police car easier.

71. Dunn-Scherker interview.

72. That Eagles thinks that the injured lesbian he saw had blood on her head suggests that this may be the same lesbian Beard says he saw get hit on the head. If this is the case, it could bolster the scenario laid out in note 70 whereby the lesbian in the police car could have been moved to the patrol wagon, which would also mean that the same lesbian could have been seen entering two vehicles, and thereby magnifying the impression some people had of the number of lesbians present. However, I accept the testimony of Beard, Eagles, and Dunn that more than one lesbian was present, although I think there were probably only two or three lesbians at most inside the Stonewall Inn on this occasion. Another difficulty with Eagles's account about the lesbians is that the arrested Raymond Castro was placed inside a patrol wagon with a lesbian and it is very clear that she was not injured.

73. There can be little doubt that Castro was the person Tom saw fighting the cops, for note both that Tom puts the man "at the door" of the Stonewall where Castro was by his own account and Tom writes that "5 or 6 cops . . . tried to subdue him." Castro told the author that when he got to the police station an officer of higher rank suggested that he was an animal because it had taken five policemen to subdue him. It was very probably Ray whom Fader also had in mind when he said, "I think there was a fellow—he was a strong guy, and I think he got in kind of a fight with them. They put him in the wagon." Fader-Carter interview. Castro's arrest Friday night is also corroborated via Carter's interviews with both Joel S. and Perrin.

74. Manford-Marcus interview. Manford attributed this act by the local police to their being conscripted into the raid by "treasury police," but a more reasonable interpretation is that the Sixth Precinct was angry about not being notified by the Public Morals Division of the raid until the last moment, especially if this would endanger their payoffs from the Stonewall Inn. One also has to wonder whether from where Manford was standing he could see the police struggling to subdue Ray Castro. If not, Manford may not have known why the police were leaving the rear of the van.

75. Murphy-Davis interview.

76. The original account has a typographical error here: "tried the resting the guy"; *assisting* is the only word that would seem to both fit the context and be capable of being misread as "the resting."

77. Smith, "Full Moon," p. 25.

78. Truscott, "Gay Power."

79. The slashed tires may also help explain why it took the patrol wagon so long to return: perhaps the tires were changed at the Sixth Precinct or another patrol wagon had to be found.

80. Smith, "Full Moon." That the officer Pine spoke to was one of the drivers of the vehicle: Pine-Isay interview. In that interview Pine does not say which driver of which vehicle he spoke to.

81. Smith, "Full Moon."

82. Eskow identifies the officer as Gil Weissman.

83. Pine-Isay interview; Smith, "Full Moon": "the only uniformed cop among them." He is identified as Gil Weissman in Eskow; see note 82.

84. Van Ronk's birthday was not until the thirtieth of the month, so he was celebrating early, presumably because, as was the case with Steve Yates, it was the weekend closest to his actual birthday.

85. *NYT*, June 29, 1969, and Leitsch, *NYMN*, July 1969.

86. "Pennies were flung at the door of the bar and the mass of evicted homosexuals tittered in defiance." Manford 1978.
87. "Dirty Copper!": Leitsch, *NYMN*, August 1969.
88. Smith, "Full Moon."
89. Under the eye: Smith, "Full Moon." Right eye: Police log, June 28, 1969. Pine in his interview with the author gave a very different account of the incident: Pine is very clear that he saw Van Ronk purposefully approach Weissman and flip a coin directly into his face, causing the injury. Pine further asserts that far from picking someone at random, he knew who had injured Weissman and followed him into the crowd.
90. Smith, "Full Moon."
91. Smith, "Full Moon."
92. Pine-Isay interview.
93. Smith, "Full Moon."
94. Pine-Isay interview.
95. Van Ronk explicitly rejects Howard Smith's account of the police beating him, even going so far as to say that the scene inside the Stonewall Inn was so confused that he is not sure whether the kicks he received were purposeful or inadvertent. Van Ronk–Carter interview.
96. Smith, "Full Moon." Note that according to Pine, it was Smith who approached him: "At that point, a reporter from the *Village Voice* came up and asked if he could stay on our side to see what we were doing, and he would cover it from that angle, rather than from out front. He showed me his press card; that was okay with me." Pine-Carter interview.
97. Smith, "Full Moon."
98. Smith-Carter interview.

9 : LANCING THE FESTERING
WOUND OF ANGER

1. Pine-Isay interview.
2. Truscott, "Gay Power."
3. Truscott-Carter interview.
4. Truscott-Carter interview. Note how closely this agrees with the account in *Rat* of the meaning of what happened at that time: "A few pigs outside had to flee for their lives . . . and barricade themselves in. It was too good to be true. The crowd took the offensive."
5. Fader-Carter interview. Note the similarity to a quote published a year later on Stonewall's first anniversary: "It was our Verdun: Thou shalt not pass and all that." Hans Knight, "'Other Society' Moves into the Open," *Sunday Bulletin*, July 19, 1970.
6. David Isay, *Remembering Stonewall*, 1989 Pacifica Radio Archive.
7. *Newsweek*, October 27, 1969.
8. Manford 1989. Photographic corroboration of Manford's account can be seen in a photograph by Diana Davies taken of the front of the Stonewall Inn shortly after the riot, that shows the lower left pane of the double window immediately above the Stonewall Inn's entrance broken.
9. Manford 1989.
10. Bruce Voeller, "Stonewall Anniversary: Assessing the Activist Years," *Advocate*, July 12, 1979, p. 30. Voeller continues: "Stories about the following events differ. In some, a transvestite picked up a rock and threw it at the police; in others, the young Puerto Rican, who may have been nongay, threw a beer can. Whoever acted first started an

avalanche." That it is Voeller who wrote this is all the more interesting, given Voeller's strong interest in the Stonewall Riots. Unfortunately, Voeller does not say if he was at the riots, whether he witnessed any of this, and, if not, what his sources are.

11. The photograph by Ambrosini is reprinted on the cover of this book.

Hoose-Carter interview. The quote is what Hoose remembers his friend the deceased John Goodman telling him immediately after Hoose arrived. Robert Bryan corroborates John Goodman's presence at the riots on Friday. Besides the testimony of Goodman about the leading role of Zazu Nova, we have John O'Brien's testimony that he saw Nova there the first night and in the company of Marsha Johnson, although O'Brien did not see Nova fighting but getting her photo taken on a corner with Marsha. Still, O'Brien arrived after the initial outburst that forced the police to retreat inside the Stonewall Inn, so he could not have seen the first instigators of violence.

Testimony about the primacy of Marsha Johnson's role is widespread but generally second- or even thirdhand. For instance, both Robert Heide and John O'Brien saw Marsha in the crowd outside the club on the first night and both independently described her as being in semidrag, not full drag. Heide says he saw her "just in the middle of the whole thing, screaming and yelling and throwing rocks and almost like Molly Pitcher in the Revolution or something. I mean, a loud yelling and screaming, 'You can't do that. Who the hell, who the fuck!'" He is also clear, however, that he cannot say that she was the first to throw an object: "I didn't see this, but I did speak with someone who claims that Marsha was the first one to throw a stone at a policeman." Heide-Carter interview.

As is true here with Heide, several others interviewed for this history said that soon after the first night of the riots they heard that she was the person who really started it. There is also an intriguing account that Robin Souza told the author that he heard first from Marty Robinson in the fall of 1969 and from Morty Manford in the mid-1970s: that after the police entered the bar Marsha threw a shot glass into a mirror, saying, "I got my civil rights!" and that Morty said that was what started the riots. Souza said that in the Gay Activists Alliance that was called "the shot glass that was heard around the world." While I believe Souza is telling the truth when he says that Morty told him this story, there are several problems with it. First is that Morty left several accounts of the riots before his death, including several written by him, and did not once include any mention of Marsha. (This raises the possibility that Morty may have censored his own recorded accounts, fearing that to publicly credit a severely mentally ill transvestite prostitute with starting the Stonewall Riots, and thus indirectly the gay liberation movement, could have been used effectively by the movement's opponents.) Second, Seymour Pine said that there were no black transgendered persons inside the bar.

It seems clear that whether it was Jackie Hormona who was the first person to be violent (or to perform the first act of violence that precipitated an outpouring of violence), it seems reasonable to conclude that Marsha Johnson was almost indubitably among the first to be violent that night and may possibly even have been the first. Marsha's inability to speak with any coherence and focus is no doubt the reason we do not have a clear account of her own recollections.

To this date there are no known interviews or accounts by Zazu Nova. This may have something to do with her apolitical nature. According to John O'Brien, who knew Nova from the trucks, "Basically Nova was very much into her looks. I mean, she was very narcissistic . . . very much so . . . was worried about her looks and her

face and everything. . . . She was an attitude queen, but not a political queen."
O'Brien-Carter interview.

12. Truscott, "Gay Power."
13. Manford 1989.
14. "No place for Gaiety," *New York Post,* June 28, 1969.
15. O'Brien noted that the main concentrations of people doing most of the action were at the west end of the Stonewall Inn, close to the stoop that Craig Rodwell and Fred Sargeant had climbed to witness the action and directly across the street from the stoop. Truscott, who the reader will remember had perched himself on top of a garbage can on the east side of the stoop to better witness the action, also remembers the way the crowd focused its anger on the Stonewall's west window.
16. O'Brien, like Kohler, was aware of the meter being loose.
17. O'Brien's description of one of the men who uprooted the meter is corroborated by Fader: "I remember one guy, kind of a muscular, heavy guy, blond guy—some people had started to pull a parking meter." (Fader-Carter interview.) O'Brien's description of the men uprooting the parking meter being masculine in appearance but also with a street feel to them also matches Edmund White's description of the same scene: "Some adorable butch hustler boys pull up a *parking meter* [emphasis in original], mind you, out of the pavement and use it as a battering ram." White-Corn letter.
18. Eskow agrees that "windows were smashed."
19. White-Corn letter.
20. White-Corn letter.
21. Smith, "Full Moon."
22. *Rat,* July 9, 1969, and Di Brienza, "Stonewall Incident."
23. Kohler-Carter interview.
24. Smith, "Full Moon."
25. Beard, "I Was There," p. 5. That a piece of glass was thrown in this manner at the police through the open door is corroborated fully by Sargeant's account given to WBAI and partially by *Rat*'s statement: "the cops inside were scared shitless, dodging projectiles and flying glass."
26. Kohler-Carter interview.
27. Rodwell-Scherker interview October 9, 1986, and Rodwell-Duberman interview.
28. While Smith wrote that it was a "large wrench," Pine is adamant that it was the Stonewall Inn's fire ax that Smith took to protect himself with and not a wrench: Pine-Carter interview.
29. Leitsch-Carter interview.
30. Used hose to put fire out: Eskow and Leitsch, "Hairpin."
31. *Rat,* July 9, 1969.
32. Smith, "Full Moon."
33. Pine cannot recall whether it was he or Smythe who discovered a way to get the policewoman outside the bar. Since Pine states that his main focus was very much on keeping his men from firing, I have written this account as if it was Smythe who got the policewoman out, which Pine told an interviewer he finds a logical assumption.
34. Smith-Carter interview.
35. "Wooden wall . . . was forced down": *Rat,* July 9, 1969.
36. "[T]he mob will pour in": Smith, "Full Moon."
37. Smith, "Full Moon."
38. Truscott, "Gay Power."
39. "[C]ome up with another assault": Truscott, "Gay Power."

40. "[T]he door is broken down": White-Corn letter. The account of lighting a fire inside the Stonewall is corroborated by Dave Van Ronk, who told the author that he recalled walking past the Stonewall Inn shortly after the riots and seeing that the bottom part of the entrance door had been burned.

41. "[L]it a trash can full of paper afire and stuffed it": *Rat*, July 9, 1969.

42. Manford 1989.

43. The symbolism of the coatroom being burned was noted by Eric Marcus in his interview with Morty Manford.

44. Di Brienza, "Stonewall Incident." Craig Rodwell similarly recounted, "I remember [a] person coming up and squirting lighter fluid into the broken windows and then throwing matches in," though, Rodwell added, "it never caught." Rodwell-Scherker interview.

45. Smith, "Full Moon."

46. In the last paragraph of page 1 of Manford "Remembrances," Manford makes a kind of impressionistic and dramatic collage of the evening's high points and mentions "fire trucks circling; the hosing-down of the crowd."

47. White-Corn letter. Note that Manford's use of the plural in note 46 is a corroboration of White on there being more than one fire truck at the scene: "fire trucks" and "two fire engines."

48. Manford 1989. Original has "started" rather than "start."

49. TPF: Pine-Isay and Pine-Carter interviews.

50. Smith, "Full Moon."

51. Police clearing the crowds away from the Stonewall Inn's entrance: Pine-Carter interview.

52. Garvin-Carter interview.

53. Sixth Precinct police log for June 28, 1969.

54. Police predesignated: Pine-Carter interview.

55. Calling ambulance: Pine-Carter interview.

56. St. Vincent's Hospital: Sixth Precinct police log for June 28, 1969.

57. Van Ronk–Carter interview. Location of patrol wagon corroborated by Marle Becker.

58. Becker-Carter interview. Asked how he could be sure they were transvestites from such a distance, Becker responded that they were all wearing dresses and that the only people he regularly saw at the Stonewall Inn in dresses were men.

59. Pine-Carter interview.

60. Pine-Carter interview.

61. Apparently Rodwell means Christopher Park. In the manner of most New Yorkers, he seems to be referring to the park as Sheridan Square.

62. Rhoda letter. Note that the evidence that it was the fire truck hoses that were used on the rioters is inferential, for the Rhoda letter uses the plural, *fire hoses,* and by all accounts there was only one fire hose in the Stonewall Inn. That the fire trucks' hoses were used on the crowd is confirmed by a brief mention in the collage-style paragraph written by Morty Manford ca. 1978: "the hosing-down of the crowd," which immediately follows the phrase "fire trucks circling." (See note 46 above.) One suspects that for propaganda purposes most witnesses have not wanted to recall the hosing down of the crowd, for it would be the one definite instance during the riot when the protesters were humiliated.

63. Rodwell-Scherker interview.

64. Telephone conversation with John Fisk, October 21, 1997.

1. Babick-Scherker interview.
2. Truscott, "Gay Power."
3. I am grateful to Danny Garvin for providing the fuller text of this slogan, the beginning of which is not visible in the McDarrah photographs, making it clear that the slogan is referring to the Vietnam War.
4. Fred McDarrah, the *Village Voice* photographer, took photographs of some of the rioters on Saturday night. The first slogan quoted here is visible in one of those photographs. The photograph of the second slogan was made the same weekend, if not on Saturday. For a copy of the photographs with these slogans, see McDarrah and McDarrah, *Gay Pride,* pp. xxxvi and 3.
5. Dick Leitsch, "The Stonewall Riots[:] The Police Story," *NYMN,* August 1969, pp. 5–6.
6. *NYT,* June 30, 1969.
7. Rodwell, from leaflet titled *Get the Mafia and the Cops Out of Gay Bars.* Rodwell issued the flyer in the name of HYMN.
8. Truscott, "Gay Power."
9. Rodwell-Ardery interview.
10. Rodwell-Duberman interview.
11. Within two to three hours: Rodwell-Ardery interview.
12. While Rodwell told Duberman that "people started to come down here in the early evening, eight o'clock probably or something like that," most contemporary accounts have the crowds assembling late in the evening and early morning. Fred Sargeant, Craig's lover, told WBAI Radio within days of the riots that the crowd assembled around 12:00 A.M. (This latter is from my notes made after hearing the WBAI interview, so it is based on my memory and not a transcript.) While it is possible that people began to filter into the neighborhood around 8:00 P.M., it does not sound as if the crowds were truly sizable and identifiable as crowds until around midnight.
13. Rhoda letter.
14. *NYT,* June 29 and 30, 1969; Leitsch, *NYMN;* and Truscott, "Gay Power."
15. *NYT,* June 30, 1969; Leitsch, *NYMN,* July 1969; and Laurence, "Gays Hit N.Y. Cops." Craig Rodwell told Martin Duberman that people started "to come down here in the early evening, eight o'clock probably ... and gradually it got to be 8:30, 9:00 o'clock. . . . Just thousands of people. Spilling over into the street. And that's when we decided to block off the street." However, Rodwell told this to Duberman over twenty years after the events. I have noticed in my many interviews with Stonewall Riots witnesses that the element they consistently are the least reliable on is that of time, and they also tend to consistently place times of events earlier than they in fact happened. I base my attribution of error to them because both news and police reports recorded at the time of these events tend to generally agree on the timing of events. Since contemporary news and police reports agree that the crowd started to act up probably around 12:45 A.M. at the earliest, I give these contemporaneous records more weight than Rodwell's much later interview with Duberman.
16. Truscott, "Gay Power."
17. Leitsch, *NYMN,* July 1969.
18. Leitsch, *NYMN,* August 1969.
19. *NYT,* June 30, 1969.
20. Unfortunately, the accounts that mention the handing out of literature do not make it clear what pieces were handed out except that Edmund White's letter to Alfred

Corn states that the Mattachine Society was handing out the pamphlet *What to Do If You Are Arrested*. It would appear very likely that what was handed out by Rodwell was an earlier draft of the leaflet he gave out on Sunday, *Get the Mafia and Cops Out of Gay Bars*, and that similarly the Mattachine Society of New York was also handing out an early version of Leitsch's "The Hairpin Drop Heard Around the World."

21. White-Corn letter. Note that White's account corroborates O'Brien's assertion that he invited members of the Crazies to the demonstration and that they came.
22. Truscott, "Gay Power."
23. Leitsch, "Hairpin."
24. Leitsch, "Hairpin."
25. Truscott, "Gay Power."
26. Di Brienza, "Stonewall Incident."
27. Babick-Scherker interview.
28. Leitsch, *NYMN,* July 1969.
29. Sign on door: *NYT,* June 29, 1969.
30. Owners trying to coax customers into the Stonewall Inn as chants grew louder and more frequent: Truscott, "Gay Power."
31. Crowd growing restless: Truscott, "Gay Power."
32. Laurence, "Gays Hit N.Y. Cops"; Rodwell-Duberman interview.
33. Old lady trying to get through crowd: Leitsch, *NYMN,* July 1969.
34. As of 2003, June 28, 1969, was still the hottest June 28 in New York City history: http://www.weather.com/weather/climatology/USNY0996?climoMonth=6.
35. Rodwell-Duberman interview. Leitsch's account corroborates Rodwell on the crowd's overflowing from the sidewalks into the street: "As the mob grew, it spilled off the sidewalk, overflowed Sheridan Square Park, and began to fill the roadway." Leitsch, *NYMN,* July 1969.
36. When they decided to block off Christopher Street: Rodwell-Duberman interview. According to Leitsch ("Hairpin"), as the crowd began to spill over into the streets "[o]ne of the six cops who were there to keep order began to get smart and cause hostility." Leitsch's very next sentence begins: "A bus driver blew his horn at the meeting, and someone shouted, 'Stop the Bus!'" which seems to suggest that the decision to occupy Christopher Street may have been instigated by hostility from unsympathetic heterosexuals, but both Rodwell's and Sargeant's accounts carry no such suggestion. The reader needs to remember that Leitsch was writing as the head of Mattachine–New York and, while his account is both an admirable job of reporting and an important historical record, one should expect it to carry somewhat of a bias in favor of the protesters by emphasizing negative behavior on the side of the police and downplaying any such behavior by the demonstrators.
37. Sargeant on WBAI interview late June or early July 1969 and Rodwell-Ardery interview. It is significant that this assertion is made by both individuals independently in two interviews very close to the time of the riots, yet this aspect of the riots has never been commented upon in any of the literature on the Stonewall Riots.
38. In 1990s terminology, this would be the right to gay (or queer) space. This interpretation of the meaning of excluding nongay traffic is the author's own and is not based on interviews with any Stonewall Riots participants.
39. A witness indicates that vehicles of people who showed support for gay people were allowed through.
40. Leitsch, "Hairpin."
41. Rodwell-Duberman interview.

42. Dick Leitsch wrote to the author in an October 30, 2003, e-mail that he had never heard of this purported death and believed it to be urban legend, but Kohler wrote about it in 1970 and in an e-mail to the author, also on October 30, 2003, confirmed that Rodwell had criticized him "for being insensitive to the cab driver's death by using it in an article," confirming that Rodwell also believed the man to have died. The article "Where Have All the Flowers Gone" (*Come Out!* 1, No. 2, January 10, 1970), about the street youths, reminisced about the riots. In it Kohler wrote: "I remembered when . . . Christopher Street was a battleground . . . and the Cab Driver who had a heart attack when his cab was overturned (in time of peace and war—the man said— many sparrows fall!)." Like Rodwell, Kohler also recalls the incident as taking place on the night of Saturday, June 28, 1969. Kohler told the author in a phone conversation on the same day that he sent the e-mail that he remembered that the man was very old.

43. In 1969 author Jamake Highwater went by the name J. Marks. He is quoted extensively on Saturday night's events by Leo Laurence in "Gays Hit N.Y. Cops."

44. Unfortunately, Rodwell did not describe the situation in enough detail to make the meaning of this incident clear. Again, since most New Yorkers refer to Christopher Park as Sheridan Square and as a group of policemen had been stationed in front of the Stonewall Inn and in the account just before this Craig is positioned on Christopher Street close to Greenwich Avenue, there can be no doubt that he is talking about Christopher Park, as Sheridan Square is not visible from Christopher Street close to Greenwich Avenue. According to Rodwell, the barrage injured people (at least some of them police, presumably) and made the police very angry.

45. Youth bouncing garbage can lids and shopkeeper scolding the police: Leitsch, *NYMN*, July 1969.

46. Howard Brown, M.D., *Familiar Faces, Hidden Lives: The Story of Homosexual Men in America Today* (New York: Harcourt Brace Jovanovich, 1976), pp. 12, 19–20.

47. Wilson to Carter in conversation, September 4, 2003; Babick-Scherker interview.

48. Leitsch, "Hairpin."

49. Leitsch, "Hairpin."

50. Highwater (J. Marks) quoted in Laurence, "Gays Hit N.Y. Cops."

51. *NYT*, June 30, 1969.

52. Leitsch, "Hairpin."

53. *NYT*, June 30, 1969.

54. Leitsch, "Hairpin."

55. Leitsch, "Hairpin."

56. Leitsch, "Hairpin."

57. Truscott, "Gay Power."

58. Truscott, "Gay Power," and Highwater (J. Marks) in Laurence, "Gays Hit N.Y. Cops."

59. White-Corn letter.

60. Edited together from two *NYMN* articles. The first and last sentences of this extract are from the August 1969 issue of *NYMN*; the rest is from the July 1969 issue.

61. Kohler, "Where Have All the Flowers Gone."

62. Note also in this regard that in Leitsch's statement he qualifies his own words by saying "for the most part" and "participated peripherally." He is not saying, of course, that all the physical courage and bravery was on the part of the more effeminate members of the crowd but that as a group, they were the most courageous.

63. Although none of the accounts state explicitly that Grove Street, running on the south side of Christopher Park, was shut down between Waverly Place and West 4th Street, it is only logical to assume that it was, given the apparent police objective of

controlling the area around the Stonewall Inn, which was the focal point of protests on both Friday and Saturday nights.

64. Truscott, "Gay Power."
65. References to Spencer are from Walter Troy Spencer's "Last Call" column in the July 10, 1969, *Village Voice*, titled "Too Much My Dear," a highly insulting piece of reportage, p. 36.
66. White-Corn letter.
67. Brutality of TPF: *NYMN*, August 1969.
68. Kevin Liscoe letter to the editor, *Village Voice*, July 10, 1969, p. 4.
69. Truscott, "Gay Power."
70. Demonstrators on Waverly Place realizing they outnumbered their pursuers: Leitsch, *NYMN*, July 1969.
71. Jack Nichols and Lige Clarke, "Homosexual Citizen" column, *Screw*, July 25, 1969, p. 16.
72. Three heterosexual couples fleeing TPF with homosexuals: Leitsch, *NYMN*, July 1969.
73. Number of police officers between two and three hundred: Leitsch, *NYMN*, July 1969.
74. Bars closing at 3:00 A.M. and patrons coming to Sheridan Square area: Leitsch, *NYMN*, July 1969.
75. *NYT*, June 30, 1969.
76. Truscott, "Gay Power."
77. According to the June 30 *NYT*, the TPF was withdrawn at 4:00 A.M.; Leitsch puts the time of withdrawal at 5:30 A.M. *NYMN*, July 1969.
78. Leitsch, *NYMN*, July 1969.

11: "THEY'VE LOST THAT WOUNDED LOOK"

1. Rodwell-Scherker interview.
2. See chapter 8, introductory unnumbered note.
3. The sign is visible in a photograph taken by Fred McDarrah on Sunday, June 29, 1969. Leitsch told the author that the message was written by the Stonewall's owners, who asked him to okay it, and that he barely glanced at it, telling them that he didn't care if they put it up or not. Such a claim does not seem likely when one compares the literacy and neat lettering of this sign with the crudeness and semiliteracy of the signs put up by the Mafia. Even if the sign were the Mafia's idea, okaying the sign (as Leitsch says he did, however offhandedly), especially with the use of the name of the organization he headed attached to it, Leitsch became obligated to take a large amount of the responsibility for the sign.
4. Crowd turnout Sunday, leather contingent: Leitsch, "Hairpin."
5. Truscott, "Gay Power."
6. All the cops at The Corner: Leitsch, "Hairpin."
7. Truscott, "Gay Power."
8. Laurence, "Gays Hit N.Y. Cops."
9. Leitsch, "Hairpin." Colors of bumper stickers: Tom Burke, "The New Homosexuality," *Esquire*, December 1969, pp. 178, 304–18.
10. Police conversation reportedly overheard by Mattachine–New York member: Leitsch, "Hairpin."
11. Police begging homosexuals to go to the Stonewall Inn: Leitsch, "Hairpin."
12. Nonhelmeted TPF sweep: Truscott, "Gay Power."
13. Mead and Ginsberg in front of United Cigar Store: Truscott-Carter interview.

14. Alison Colbert, "A Talk with Allen Ginsberg," *Partisan Review* 38, No. 3, 1971, pp. 289–309, reprinted in Allen Ginsberg, *Spontaneous Mind: Selected Interviews 1958–1996*, David Carter, ed. (New York: HarperCollins, 2001).

15. "To show the colors": Ginsberg interview by Allen Young, first published in *Gay Sunshine*, No. 16, January–February 1973, pp. 1, 4–10, reprinted several times, including in Ginsberg, *Spontaneous Mind* (see note 14).

16. Ginsberg walking to Stonewall and dancing: Truscott, "Gay Power."

17. Appearance inside Stonewall: Truscott, "Gay Power."

18. "After about an hour": Truscott-Carter.

19. Truscott walking Ginsberg home: Truscott, "Gay Power."

20. Young, *Gay Sunshine*.

21. Ginsberg interview for film *Before Stonewall* transcript, Lesbian Herstory Archives.

22. Cop at Waverly Place as victim of firecrackers and having his badge stolen: Leitsch, "Hairpin." (The badge was found the following day by the police stuck in a string of pickled pig's feet hanging from a tree in Washington Square Park.) Edward Villella was principal dancer with the New York City Ballet in the 1960s.

23. Burke, "New Homosexuality." The article does not give the date Burke witnessed this encounter, but it is clearly several days into the riots.

24. The date of the *Voice* pieces can easily lead to confusion about chronology. The edition with Truscott's and Smith's articles is dated July 3, Thursday, but although *The Voice* was dated Thursday it came out late on Wednesday night (another useful corroboration that events on Wednesday night happened late in the evening, incidentally).

25. I do not think it fair to characterize Smith's phrase "the gay customers freshly ejected from their hangout, prancing high and jubilant in the street," as derogatory. As the reader has seen from the accounts in this volume, there was a great deal of very flamboyant behavior at the time of the riots. This was especially true on the first night at the very time Smith is reporting on with the preceding phrase, i.e., the time when the customers were leaving the Stonewall Inn before the protest began to turn serious. A more objective assessment would be that in this instance Smith probably was quite accurate in his recording of the prevalent tone of the camp protest at that particular moment.

26. Smith, "Full Moon," and Truscott, "Gay Pride."

27. White-Corn letter.

28. Leitsch, *NYMN*, August 1969.

29. Leitsch, *NYMN*, August 1969.

30. John Thomas, letter to the editor, *Village Voice*, July 10, 1969, p. 4.

31. *New York Post*, July 3, 1969.

32. *NYT*, July 3, 1969.

33. Leitsch, *NYMN*, August 1969.

34. Protesters' setting trash on fire at Waverly and Christopher: Di Brienza, "Stonewall Incident"; fires set along Christopher Street: *NYT*, July 3, 1969.

35. The TPF and fire department responding: Di Brienza, "Stonewall Incident." Besides the TPF, the only other police presence reported in the media for Wednesday night is that of the Sixth Precinct. *NYT*, July 3, 1969.

36. *New York Post*, July 3, 1969.

37. Di Brienza, "Stonewall Incident."

38. *NYT*, July 3, 1969.

39. Leitsch, *NYMN*, August 1969.

40. Di Brienza, "Stonewall Incident."

41. Leitsch, *NYMN*, August 1969.
42. "Cop Injured 5 Seized in Village," *New York Post*, July 3, 1969. *NYT* (July 3, 1969) similarly noted that "members of the Tactical Patrol Force and police of the Charles Street station [. . .] were the targets occasionally of bottles and beer cans."
43. Di Brienza, "Stonewall Incident."
44. Leitsch, *NYMN*, August 1969.
45. While the July 3 *NYT* reported that "at least four" were arrested, according to both the letter from Thomas published in the *Voice* and the July 3 *New York Post*, five persons were arrested.
46. Leitsch, *NYMN*, August 1969.
47. Di Brienza, "Stonewall Incident." The July 3, 1969, *New York Post* account, the only other published account that addresses the duration of Wednesday's rioting, corroborates Di Brienza's statement that Wednesday night's events lasted approximately one hour.

1 2 :   S E I Z I N G   T H E   M O M E N T

1. The account in this chapter of the series of meetings and actions that took place during the month between the Stonewall Riots and the founding of the Gay Liberation Front, unless otherwise noted, is based primarily on Toby Marotta's *The Politics of Homosexuality* and secondarily on Donn Teal's *The Gay Militants*.
2. While Katzenberg had started to organize a gay Left organization before the riots, the radicalizing effect the street actions had is demonstrated by the difference in tone between the two ads for the same meeting that appeared in *Rat*. The ad placed by Katzenberg and O'Brien before the riots stated: A group of young radical homosexuals will meet this week to develop a critique of heterosexual supremacy, both in society and within the movement. The second ad used Pitts's language: DO YOU THINK HOMOSEXUALS ARE REVOLTING? YOU BET YOUR SWEET ASS WE ARE. We're going to make a place for ourselves in the revolutionary movement. We challenge the myths that are screwing up this society.
3. *Gay Power* flyer with date notated, "7/1/69–7/2/69," Leitsch papers.
4. *Homosexual Liberation Meeting* flyer with date notated "7/5/69–7/6/69," Leitsch papers.
5. *Gay Crusaders*, pp. 173–74; Raul Ramirez, "I Remember Stonewall," *San Francisco Examiner*, June 4, 1989.
6. Shelley-Scherker interview.
7. Marotta, *Politics of Homosexuality*, p. 71.
8. *Oh Boy!* flyer, Leitsch papers; Leitsch-Carter interview; Wicker-Marcus interview; [Lige] Clark and [Jack] Nichols, "Remember the Stonewall," *Gay*, June 29, 1970; McDarrah and McDarrah, *Gay Pride*, p. xxxv. While the claim of three days doesn't quite seem to fit with the chronology of the riots and the event at the Electric Circus, these are the youth's words as Wicker remembers them.
9. Shelley-Scherker interview. Bob Kohler heard Shelley proclaiming the name Gay Liberation Front and so has always incorrectly credited her with inventing the name.
10. *Village Voice*, July 24, 1969, Leitsch papers.
11. "From Outside the Pen," *Rat* 2, No. 15, [late July] 1969, p. 4; O'Brien-Carter interview.
12. Mattachine–New York flyer, Leitsch papers.
13. Burke, "New Homosexuality."
14. Kimberly Scott, "Stonewall's Aftermath Spurred D.C. Successes," *Washington Blade*, May 25, 1994.
15. Kameny disputes Rodwell's contention that he used a blow to separate the two

women's hands, saying that he simply walked up to the women and passed his hand between them, thereby separating them.

16. Jonathan Black, "Gay Power Hits Back," *Village Voice,* August 1, 1969, pp. 1, 3; "Gay Power in New York City," quoted in Gay Community News 20, Nos. 1–2, June 1994, p.3; O'Brien-Carter interview.

17. Ellipses are in the original article.

18. "Gay Revolution Comes Out," *Rat,* August 12–16, 1969.

13: "WE'RE THE GAY LIBERATION FRONT!"

1. Jonathan Black, "The Boys in the Snake Pit," *Village Voice,* March 19, 1970, and N. A. Diaman's *Making Gay History,* an unpublished manuscript. I am indebted to Diaman for letting me quote from *Making Gay History* for the description of a GLF dance and the GLF meetings where votes were taken over donating money to the Black Panthers.

2. Tobin and Wicker, *Gay Crusaders,* pp. 29–45.

3. Diaman, *Making Gay History.*

4. O'Brien-Carter interview.

5. John Lauritsen, "The First Gay Liberation Front Demonstration," *New York Native,* June 26, 1989, p. 20.

6. Mike Brown, Michael Tallman, and Leo Louis Martello, "The Summer of Gay Power and the *Village Voice* Exposed," *Come Out!* 1, No. 1 November 11, 1969, pp. 10–11.

7. On Robinson using the early actions as experiments, see Marotta, *Politics of Homosexuality,* pp. 135–39, and Evans-Carter interview.

8. Teal, *Gay Militants,* pp. 48–50; Tobin and Wicker, *Gay Crusaders,* p. 168; and *Come Out!,* November 11, 1969.

9. Rodwell told Duberman in the 1990s that he had the idea for the event on the bus ride back from the Fifth Annual Reminder, but he had told Michael Scherker in 1986 that he had the idea some weeks after his return to New York City. However, on the record "June 28, 1970: Gay and Proud," made for the occasion of the first Christopher Street Liberation Day, Rodwell told interviewer Breck Ardery in 1970 that he and his three friends had brainstormed the entire concept in October of 1969, without saying if or when he himself first had the idea.

10. [Craig Rodwell], "Gay Holiday," *Hymnal* 2, No. 1, January 1970, p. 8; Rodwell-Scherker interview; Rodwell-Duberman interview; Marotta, *Politics of Homosexuality,* pp. 164–65; and Teal, *Gay Militants,* p. 300.

11. Marotta, *Politics of Homosexuality,* p. 90.

12. O'Brien-Carter interview.

13. Teal, *Gay Militants,* pp. 89–90, and Arthur Bell, *Dancing the Gay Lib Blues,* p. 16.

14: THE HEROIC AGE

1. Unless otherwise indicated by a note, this account of the history of the formation of the Gay Activists Alliance and the first six months of its existence is drawn from Bell, *Dancing,* and Teal, *Gay Militants.*

2. Date of early October is from *GAA Reunion* 1, No. 6, December 3, 1994, hereafter *Reunion.* Jim and Marty conceived of the organization at 29 Jones Street.

3. GAA 1971 flyer, quoted in *Reunion.*

4. Bell, *Dancing,* pp. 21–23. The text of the preamble is given here exactly as printed in Bell.

5. Bell, *Dancing,* p. 31, and Souza-Carter interview.

6. "Lawrence" is a made-up name for the Snake Pit employee who anonymously gave Arthur Bell an account of the raid and subsequent events at the Sixth Precinct police station in *Gay Power,* No. 13.

7. This is an inference drawn from a report of the men inside the station calling GAA and another report that Owles and Robinson received a phone call at around that same time notifying them of what was happening, though there are other ways that the news could have reached Robinson and Owles.

8. This account of the Snake Pit raid and the accident Vinales suffered is based on Bell, *Dancing;* Teal, *Gay Militants;* Disk Leitsch, "The Snake Pit Raid: Some After-thoughts," "The Snake Pit Raid:" "500 Angry Homosexuals Protest Raid," "Patrons Tell of Raid from Inside," and "Responsible Cop Cops Out," all in *Gay* 1, No. 10, April 13, 1970; Leo Louis Martello, "Raid Victim Impaled on Fence," *Los Angeles Advocate,* April 29–May 12, 1970; Arthur Irving (pseud. for Arthur Bell), "Gay Activists Alliance News and Other Events" and "The Morning of the Snake Pit: An Interview," *Gay Power,* No. 13; "Jumper's Condition Still Grave," *New York Post,* March 10, 1970; and Philip Mc-Carthy, "Impaled, Saved by Fire 'Docs,'" *Daily News,* March 9, 1970. Salmieri's name is misspelled in the article "500 Angry Homosexuals." Thanks to Frank Toscano, formerly of the Sixth Precinct, for verifying the spelling of the captain's name.

   Fortunately, Vinales lived, despite the seriousness of his injuries.

9. Martello, "Raid Victim."

10. Black, "Boys in the Snake Pit."

11. Scherker-Evans interview.

12. Teal, *Gay Militants;* Bell, *Dancing;* "Gay Activists Alliance News," *Gay Power,* No. 16; and "GAA Confronts Lindsay at Channel 5," *Gay* 1 No. 14, May 11, 1970.

13. Marotta, *Politics of Homosexuality,* pp. 166–67.

14. Rodwell-Scherker interview.

15. "Zapping with Carol: Hello Bella," *Gay Power* 1, No. 18. International Gay Information Center Archives, Manuscripts and Archives Division, The New York Public Library, Astor, Lenox and Tilden Foundations.

16. *Gay,* "5 Gay Activists Arrested in Sit-in," 1, No. 23, July 13, 1970.

17. Franklin Kameny interview for *Stonewall: Myth, Magic and Mobilization,* Public Radio International, 1994. While Kameny may exaggerate slightly here, consider that John Paul Hudson's *The Gay Insider, USA* (New York: Stonehill Pub, 1972), published in 1972 (and very likely therefore reflecting the gay world of 1971), takes 627 pages to discuss gay places and groups in America. It lists, for example, merely under the category of gay "Religious Organizations," eighty of them. It also lists 108 gay publications and 386 "gay liberation" groups. See also Marotta, *Politics of Homosexuality,* pp. 322, 324–25; Teal, *Gay Militants,* pp. 196, 205, 310; and D'Emilio, *Sexual Politics,* p. 238.

18. E-mail from Dick Leitsch to author, October 29, 2003.

19. On the date of the Stonewall's closing, see Carl Lee, "It's What's Happening," p. 2 (this closing date is corroborated by the "Bar Beat" column in *Gay Power* 1, No. 3); Shaheen-Duberman interview.

20. On the march's doubling in size each year, see Craig Rodwell's "Gay and Free," *QQ Magazine,* December 1971; on gay bars opposing the commemorations of the Stonewall Riots, see Craig Rodwell quoted in Arthur Bell, "Hostility Comes Out of the Closet," *Village Voice,* June 28, 1973, pp. 1, 16, 18; on Murphy's founding of the Christopher Street Festival Committee, see February 12, 1993, open letter from Randy Wicker to members of Community Board 2; on Murphy's funeral and last place of employment, see "A Call About Ed Murphy," *New York Native,* February 20, 1989; for Murphy quoted in a prominent gay publication see Glenn Person, "CS Peo-

ple," *Christopher Street*, Issue 66, pp. 10–11; on Wicker's attempt to displace Murphy's associates from the festival, see J. Pederzane, "Charges of Skimming Roil '92 Christopher Street Festival," *NYT*, June 26, 1992.

21. Rodwell-Scherker interview.
22. Jonathan Black, "A Happy Birthday for Gay Liberation," *Village Voice*, July 2, 1970, pp. 1, 58.
23. Tobin, *Gay Crusaders*, p. 134.
24. Bell, *Dancing*; Teal, *Gay Militants*; Duberman, *Stonewall*; Lacey Fosburgh, "Thousands of Homosexuals Hold a Protest Rally in Central Park," *NYT*, June 29, 1970; Black, "Happy Birthday"; Rodwell-Scherker interview; Agostino-Carter interview; and Leo Skir, "Notes from the Underground—The Road That Is Known," *Evergreen Review*, September 1970, pp. 16, 20, 74–77.

CONCLUSIONS

1. I am indebted to John O'Brien for making this point to me.
2. For the effect of high temperatures on behavior, see Emma Brockes and Oliver Burkeman, "Blame It on the Sunshine," *The Guardian*, May 30, 2001, as well as the report of the National Advisory Commission on Civil Disorders. Note that the fighting at Compton's Cafeteria also occurred during hot weather. Rodwell also cited the weather as a factor: "I immediately knew that this was the spark we had been waiting for for years. It's hard to explain. It has to do with the weather and the time of the day and the week and who's around and circumstances, whatever." Rodwell-Duberman interview.
3. It seems possible that at least one of the other journalists who initially covered the event may have also come from the Lion's Head, for the *Daily News* account features a photograph by Joseph Ambrosini, a freelance photographer. The picture was taken at the very beginning of the outbreak from *behind* police lines at a time when the police were trying to keep people away from the Stonewall Inn. Was Ambrosini also in the Lion's Den and did he call the newspaper to alert them to the story?
4. See, e.g., D'Emilio, *Sexual Politics*, and Marcus, *Making History*. Given the several parallels, it is worth asking whether the interest Bob Kohler took in the homeless gay youths a couple of months before the riots played any part in their willingness to fight.
5. Scherker-Rodwell interview.
6. Spencer, "Too much my dear."
7. "D.D.'s New York," *NYMN*, August 1969.
8. Burke, "New Homosexuality."
9. Russo, "I Remember Stonewall."
10. Charles Kaiser suggested to the author that Stormé DeLarverie (see *The Gay Metropolis: 1940–1996* [Boston: Houghton Mifflin, 1997], p. 198) was this woman, but she could not have been. To cite only a few of the problems with this thesis, DeLarverie's story is one of escaping the police, not of being taken into custody by them, and she has claimed that on that night she was outside the bar, "quiet, I didn't say a word to anybody, I was just trying to see what was happening," when a policeman, without provocation, hit her in the eye ("Stonewall 1969: A Symposium," June 20, 1997, New York City). DeLarverie is also an African-American woman, and all the witnesses interviewed by the author describe the woman as Caucasian. Finally, there has been much speculation about who this woman could have been if a lesbian did play a key role. Stormé was well known in the local lesbian community at the time of the riots and has remained so ever since, and it is highly improbable that this woman who was

seen by hundreds of people could have been a person of note in the community, else she would have been identified at the time or shortly thereafter.

11. It is remarkable—and no doubt inevitable given human psychology—that in the popular imagination the number of transvestites at the riots is always exaggerated. Readers will note that in the McDarrah photos of the riots there is one transgendered person and none of the persons I interviewed, some of whom knew her, ever saw her actively involved in the riots. (Note that the McDarrah photographs, which do feature the street youths, were taken late on Saturday night during one of the lulls in rioting, when nothing in particular was happening. Truscott-Carter interview.) The Ambrosini photo does not show a single transvestite. Craig Rodwell told researcher Michael Scherker that "one of the myths about Stonewall is it was all drag queens. I mean, drag queens are part of what went on. Certainly one of the most courageous, but there were maybe twelve drag queens . . . in thousands of people." Scherker-Roadwell interview.

12. Stavis-Murphy interview.

13. Manford 1972.

14. David Isay, *Holding On* (New York: W. W. Norton, 1996); letter from Nancy LaMarr, *Transgender Tapestry,* issue 80; Fall 1997, pp. 9–10.

15. "Testimony of Dick Leitsch/Executive Director Mattachine Society Inc. of New York/ Hearings on Homosexuality/New York State Assembly/January 7, 1971," p. 8, Leitsch papers. The same news was noted in two gay publications in March 1970: "Wall Street Purge Causes Job Losses," *Gay* 1, No. 8, March 15, 1970, p. 3, and "Wall Street Purge," *NYMN,* March 1970, pp. 7–8. The latter article states that a "rash of thefts of negotiated stocks and bonds from banks and securities brokers" led Attorney General Louis Lefkowitz to decree that "all employees in the financial district must be fingerprinted. This was because of a reputed Mafia connection with the thefts." The mention of a "Mafia connection" is further corroboration of Pine. See also "361 Arrest Records Uncovered by Wall Street Fingerprinting," *NYT,* February 5, 1970.

16. This history is given in the PBS series *New York City: A Documentary History*.

17. Gene Heil, "Where It Was," *Where It's At,* July 15, 1974, pp. 30–31. International Gay Information Center Archives, Manuscripts and Archives Division, The New York Public Library, Astor, Lenox and Tilden Foundations.

18. Morty Manford, letter to the editor, *Where It's At,* July 21, 1974, Morty Manford Papers, Manuscripts and Archives Division, The New York Public Library, Astor, Lenox and Tilden Foundations.

BIBLIOGRAPHY

Adair, Nancy, and Casey Adair, *Word Is Out: Stories of Some of Our Lives*. San Francisco: New Glide Publications, 1978.

Advocate. "Stonewall 'Historic'?" (August 15, 1973): 16.

Alwood, Edward. *Straight News: Gays, Lesbians, and the News Media*. New York: Columbia University Press, 1996.

Beard, Harry. "I Was There . . . the Stonewall Riot." *New York Gay Press* (1:1; July 1980): 5.

Beard, Rick, and Leslie Cohen Berlowitz, editors, *Greenwich Village: Culture and Counterculture*. New Brunswick: Rutgers University Press, 1993.

Bell, Arthur. *Dancing the Gay Lib Blues: A Year in the Homosexual Liberation Movement*. New York: Simon and Schuster, 1971.

———— [pseudonym Arthur Irving]. "Gay Activists Alliance News and Other Events." *Gay Power* (No. 13): 4.

———— [pseudonym Arthur Irving]. "The Morning of the Snake Pit: An Interview." *Gay Power* (No. 13): 5.

———— [pseudonym Arthur Irving]. "Gay Activists Alliance News." *Gay Power* (No. 16).

———— [pseudonym Arthur Irving]. "Zapping with Carol: Hello, Bella." *Gay Power* (No. 18): 4.

————. "Skull Murphy: The Gay Double Agent." *Village Voice* (May 8, 1978): 1, 17–19.

Berkeley Barb. "Gay Rebel Gets Shafted by Uptight Boss" (April 11, 1969): 11.

————. "Pink Panthers Gay Revolution Toughening Up" (April 18–24, 1969): 11.

————. "Gay Strike Hits Southern Front" (May 2–8, 1969): 11.

————. "Gay Strike Turns Grim" (April 25–May 1, 1969): 7.

————. "Group Will Act" (May 2–8, 1969): 11.

Bird, David. "Trees in a Queens Park Cut Down As Vigilantes Harass Homosexuals." *New York Times* (July 1, 1969).

Black, Jonathan. "Gay Power Hits Back." *Village Voice* (July 31, 1969): 1, 3.

————. "The Boys in the Snake Pit: Games 'Straights' Play." *Village Voice* (March 19, 1970): 1, 61–64.

————. "A Happy Birthday for Gay Liberation." *Village Voice* (July 2, 1970): 1, 58.

Bragg, Rick. "From Night of Rage, Seeds of Liberation." *New York Times* (June 23, 1994).

Brockes, Emma, and Oliver Burkeman. "Blame It on the Sunshine." *Guardian* (May 30, 2001).

Brown, Howard, M.D. *Familiar Faces, Hidden Lives: The Story of Homosexual Men in America Today.* New York: Harcourt Brace Jovanovich, 1976.

Brown, Mike, Michael Tallman, and Leo Louis Martello. "The Summer of Gay Power and the *Village Voice* Exposed!" *Come Out!* (1:1; November 14, 1969): 10–11.

Burke, Tom. "The New Homosexuality." *Esquire* (December 1969): 178, 304–18.

Chari, A. C. S., compiler and publisher. *84 Questions and Answers on Avatar Meher Baba.* India: 1969.

Chauncey, George. *Gay New York: Gender, Urban Culture, and the Making of the Gay Male World, 1890–1940.* New York: Basic Books, 1994.

Chicago Sun-Times. "Grab City Cop as Sex-Blackmail Kingpin" (June 25, 1966).

[Clark,] Lige, and Jack [Nichols]. "New York Notes." *Los Angeles Advocate* (April 1969): 22.

————. "Pampered Perverts." *Screw* (July 25, 1969): 16. (The title of the article, "Pampered Perverts," was chosen by Al Goldstein, the publisher of *Screw*. This article was printed in the Homosexual Citizen column of *Screw*, a forum created by Goldstein. While Nichols and Clark were the sole authors of the articles for this column, they had no control over the title Goldstein assigned to each issue's column.)

————. "Remember the Stonewall!" *Gay* (No. 21; June 29, 1970): 5.

Colbert, Alison. "A Talk with Allen Ginsberg." *Partisan Review* (38:3; 1971): 289–309; reprinted in Allen Ginsberg, *Spontaneous Mind: Selected Interviews 1958–1996,* edited by David Carter.

Crosby, Tina. "The Stonewall Riot Remembered." Lesbian Herstory Archives of the Lesbian Herstory Educational Foundation, Inc.

Cruise News and World Report. "Young Rejects Form Own Organization" (2:7; July 1966): 1.

————. "Young Homos Picket Compton's Restaurant" (2:8; August 1966): 1 and continued.

Cunningham, Barry. *Gay Power: The Homosexual Revolt.* New York: Tower Publications, 1971.

Daily News. "Gets 5 Years in Extortion of Homos" (August 17, 1966).

————. "Lands at JFK, FBI Is There" (September 18, 1966).

———— (Sunday Edition). "3 Cops Hurt As Bar Raid Riles Crowd" (June 29, 1969).

D'Arcangelo, Angelo (Josef Busch). *The Homosexual Handbook.* New York: Ophelia Press, 1968.

Davy, Kitty. "Baba's First World Tour, 1932, Part II." *Awakener* (12:3; Summer 1968): 1–21.

D'Emilio, John. *Sexual Politics, Sexual Communities: The Making of a Homosexual Minority in the United States.* Chicago: University of Chicago Press, 1983.

Di Brienza, Ronnie. "Stonewall Incident." *East Village Other* (4:32; July 9, 1969): 2.

Dolan, Bob. "When the Law Reaches into Your Pocket." *Pageant* 23:2; (August 1967): 40–46.

Duberman, Martin. *Stonewall.* New York: Dutton, 1993.

Eskow, Dennis. "3 Cops Hurt As Bar Raid Riles Crowd." *New York Daily News* (June 29, 1969).

Eskridge, William N., Jr. *Gay Law: Challenging the Apartheid of the Closet.* Cambridge: Harvard University Press, 1999.

Esselourne, Frank. "Doorman Remembers." *Gay Community News* (June 23, 1979): 10.

Federation to Preserve the Greenwich Village Waterfront and Great Port. www.villagewaterfront.org.

Fisher, Peter. *The Gay Mystique: The Myth and Reality of Male Homosexuality.* New York: Stein and Day, 1972.

Fosburgh, Lacey. "Thousands of Homosexuals Hold a Protest Rally in Central Park." *New York Times* (June 29, 1970).

GAA Reunion (1:6; December 3, 1994): 4.

Gay. "Wall Street Purge Causes Job Losses" (No. 8; March 15, 1970): 3.

———. "The Snake Pit Raid" (1:10; April 13, 1970): 2.

———. "500 Angry Homosexuals Protest Raid" (1:10; April 13, 1970): 3.

———. "Patrons Tell of Raid from Inside" (1:10; April 13, 1970): 3.

———. "Responsible Cop Cops Out" (1:10; April 13, 1970): 10.

———. "GAA Confronts Lindsay at Channel 5" (No. 14; May 11, 1970): 3.

———. "5 Gay Activists Arrested in Sit-In" (No. 23; July 13, 1970): 3.

Gay Activist. "The Night They Raided Stonewall" (1:3; June 1971): 4.

Gay Power. "Bar Beat" (1:3): 7, 18.

Ginsberg, Allen. Interview by Allen Young. *Gay Sunshine* (No. 16; January–February 1973): 1, 4–10.

———. *Spontaneous Mind: Selected Interviews 1958–1996,* edited by David Carter. New York: HarperCollins, 2001.

The Greenwich Village Historic District Designation Report, 2 volumes. New York: New York City Landmarks Preservation Commission, 1969.

Grutzner, Charles. "Mafia Buys Clubs for Homosexuals." *New York Times* (November 30, 1967).

Haines, Steve. "Killer Cops at Large." *Berkeley Barb* (April 25–May 1, 1969): 7.

Harrington, Stephanie. "Public Meeting on MacD.: Pirandello Writes Script," *Village Voice* (April 7, 1966): 1, 24–25, 28.

Heide, Robert, and John Gilman. *Greenwich Village: A Primo Guide to Shopping, Eating, and Making Merry in True Bohemia.* New York: St. Martin's Griffin, 1995.

Heil, Gene. "Where It Was." *Where It's At* (July 15, 1974): 30–31.

Herald Tribune. "17 Indicted in Hush-Money Shakedown" (1966: undated clipping): n.p.

"History of Christopher Street: How It All Began!" [San Francisco] *Gay Pride* [program] (June 25, 1972).

Hoglund, John. "Eddie Murphy—From Hellion to Hero." Part 1. *Private Lives* (2:6; December 1987): 30, 32.

———. "Obituaries: Edward F. Murphy." *New York Native* (March 27, 1989): 9.

Hudson, John Paul. *The Gay Insider, USA.* New York: Stonehill Pub., 1972.

Huff, Bobbie. "N.Y. Po-Lice Scream at Queens." *Magpie* (August 1969): 14.

Isay, David. *Holding On.* New York: W. W. Norton, 1996.

Jackson, Don. "Reflections on the N.Y. Riots." *Los Angeles Advocate* (October 1969): 11.

Jackson, Kenneth T., editor. *The Encyclopedia of New York City.* New Haven: Yale University Press; New York: New-York Historical Society, 1995.

Jay, Karla, and Allen Young, editors. *Out of the Closets: Voices of Gay Liberation.* New York: Douglas Book Corp., 1972.

Johnson, David K. "Homosexual Citizens: Washington's Gay Community Confronts the Civil Service." *Washington History* (Fall/Winter 1994–95): 44–63.

Kaiser, Charles. *The Gay Metropolis: 1940–1996.* Boston: Houghton Mifflin, 1997.

Karlen, Arno. *Sexuality and Homosexuality: A New View.* New York: W. W. Norton, 1971.

Katz, Jonathan. *Gay American History: Lesbians and Gay Men in the U.S.A.: A Documentary.* New York: Thomas Y. Crowell, 1976.

———. *Gay/Lesbian Almanac: A New Documentary.* New York: Harper and Row, 1983.

Katz, Leonard, and Norman Poirier. "Blackmailer of Deviates Gets 5 Years." *New York Post* (August 16, 1966).

Kepner, Jim. "Our Movement Before Stonewall" (booklet printed by Kepner). October 1989; revised 1994.

Knight, Hans. "'Other Society' Moves into the Open." [Philadelphia] *Sunday Bulletin* (July 19, 1970).

Kohler, Bob. "Where Have All the Flowers Gone." *Come Out!* (1:2; January 10, 1970): 14.

The Ladder. "Gay Power in New York City." (October–November 1969): 40.

LaMarr, Nancy. "Transcriptions." *Transgender Tapestry* (Issue 80; Fall 1997): 9–10.

Laurence, Leo E. "Gay Revolution." *Vector* (April 1969): 11, 25.

———. "Gays Get Tougher." *Berkeley Barb* (May 23–29, 1969): 31.

———. "Gays Hit N.Y. Cops." *Berkeley Barb* (July 4–10, 1969): 5.

Lauritsen, John. "The First Gay Liberation Front Demonstration." *New York Native* (June 26, 1989): 20.

Lee, Carl. "It's What's Happening." *New York Hymnal* (1:5; June–July 1968): 2.

———. "It's What's Happening." *New York Hymnal* (1:6; August–September 1968): 2.

———. "It's What's Happening." *New York Hymnal* (2:1; January 1970): 2.

Leitsch, Dick. "Cop Kills Two—May Go Free." *New York Mattachine Newsletter* (March 1969): 1–2.

———. "Coming Mayoralty Contest." *New York Mattachine Newsletter* (May 1969): 1–2. (Not signed.)

———. "The Hairpin Drop Heard Around the World." *New York Mattachine Newsletter* (July 1969): 21–23.

———. "Gay Riots in the Village." *New York Mattachine Newsletter* (August 1969): 1–3.

———. "The Stonewall Riots[:] The Gay View." *New York Mattachine Newsletter* (August 1969): 13–14.

———. "The Stonewall Riots[:] The Police Story." *New York Mattachine Newsletter* (August 1969): 5–6.

———. "Police Raid on N.Y. Club Sets Off First Gay Riot." *Los Angeles Advocate* (September 1969): 3, 11.

———. "The Snake Pit Raid: Some Afterthoughts." *Gay* (1:10; April 13, 1970): 13.

———. "Politicians Make Strange Bedfellows!" *Gay* (May 25, 1970).

Liscoe, Kevin. "Letters to the Editor." *Village Voice* (July 10, 1969): 4.

Long, Mike. "Stonewall: The Night the Girls Said No!" *San Francisco Sentinel* (June 22, 1989): 3–4.

Lustbader, Ken. "Landscape of Liberation: Preserving Gay and Lesbian History in Greenwich Village." Master's thesis, Columbia University, 1993.

Manford, Morty. "A Comparative Study of Gay Liberationists and Columbia Homosexuals." Student paper, Columbia University, 1972.

———. "The New York Gay Political Movement, 1978: An Organizational and Strategy Critique." Student paper, Columbia University, 1978.

———. "Why We Should Postpone New York's Gay Rights Bill: A New Look at Gay Political Strategy." *Gaysweek* (October 16, 1978): 10–16.

"Marat, Jean-Paul." "On Prejudice." *V* (1:2; October 1966): 1.

Marcus, Eric. *Making History: The Struggle for Gay and Lesbian Equal Rights, 1945–1990: An Oral History.* New York: HarperCollins, 1992.

Marie, Barbara Judith. "Stonewall Remembered Book 1," www.inch.com/~kdka/stonewall.htm.

Marotta, Toby. *The Politics of Homosexuality.* Boston: Houghton-Mifflin, 1981.

Martello, Leo Louis. "Raid Victim Impaled on Fence." *Los Angeles Advocate* (4:5, April 29–May 12, 1970): 1, 6.

McCarthy, Philip. "Impaled, Saved by Fire 'Docs'." *Daily News* (March 9, 1970).

McDarrah, Fred W., and Timothy S. McDarrah. *Gay Pride: Photographs from Stonewall to Today*. New York: A Cappella Books, 1994.

McGarry, Molly, and Fred Wasserman. *Becoming Visible: An Illustrated History of Twentieth-Century Gay Life in America*. New York: New York Public Library, 1998.

McGowan, William. "Before Stonewall." *Wall Street Journal* (June 16, 2000).

Miles, Barry. "The Beat Generation in the Village." In Beard and Berlowitz, *Greenwich Village: Culture and Counterculture*. New Brunswick: Rutgers University Press, 1993.

Miller, Terry. *Greenwich Village and How It Got That Way*. New York: Crown, 1990.

Morgan, Bill. *The Beat Generation in New York: A Walking Tour of Jack Kerouac's City*. San Francisco: City Lights, 1997.

Morty Manford Papers, Manuscripts and Archives Division, The New York Public Library, Astor, Lenox, and Tilden Foundation.

Murphy, Ed. "1969 at Stonewall." *Equal Times*, 1989 Gay Pride Commemorative Special Edition (1:10; June 1, 1989): 19.

National Star Chronicle. "The World of the Homosexual." (undated clipping: third in a series of articles that began with 5:1; September 27, 1965).

Newman, Andy. "Death of a Drag Queen." *The Hoboken Reporter* (July 19, 1992).

Newsweek. "Minority Listening" (July 30, 1962): 48.

———. "Policing the Third Sex" (October 27, 1969): 81.

New York City Gay Scene Guide, vol. 1, no. 2. New York: Apollo Book Company, 1969.

New York Hymnal. "Signs of the Times" (1:1; February 1968): 5.

———. "McCarthy Wins Poll" (1:4; May 1968): 1,3.

———. "On Stage" (1:5; June–July 1968): 5–6.

———. "Gay Power Gains" (1:6; August–September 1968): 1, 9.

New York Journal-American. "Jack O'Brian Says" (July 9, 1962).

New York Mattachine Newsletter. "Meeting on Village Cleanup" (11:3; April 1966): 1–3.

———. " 'Drag' and the Laws—and a Drag Ball" (January–February 1967): 5–7.

———. "Gay Bar Closed" (March 1968): 5.

———. "More Police Harassment" (February 1969): 14.

———. "Transit Cops Shake Down Wrong Man" (February 1969): 14.

———. "Docks, Darkness, and Danger" (March 1969): 3–4.

———. "Bathhouse Raided" (April 1969): 1–2.

———. "Dock Killings" (April 1969): 5.

———. "Your Friendly SLA" (April 1969): 16.

———. "D.D.'s New York" (August 1969): 18–19.

New York Native. "A Call About Ed Murphy" (February 20, 1989): 10.

New York Post. "Cop Injured 5 Seized in Village" (July 3, 1969).

———. "The Gay Anger Behind the Riots" (July 8, 1969).

———. "Jumper's Condition Still Grave" (March 10, 1970).

———. "No Place for Gaiety" (June 28, 1969).

New York Times. "Police Are Added in Washington Sq." (October 5, 1964).

———. "'Village' Assured of Added Police" (October 7, 1964).

———. "Detective at Hotel Is Held in Extortion" (August 5, 1965).

———. "Garelick Urges Public to Report Police Trapping of Homosexuals" (April 2, 1966).

———. "3 Deviates Invite Exclusion by Bars" (April 22, 1966).

———. "S.L.A. Won't Act Against Bars Refusing Service to Deviates" (April 26, 1966).

————. "Lindsay Placates Coffeehouse Set" (May 3, 1966).

————. "3 Indicted Here as Sex Extorters" (June 1, 1966).

————. "Detective Accused as a Top Extorter" (July 1, 1966).

————. "Blackmailer Gets Five-Year Sentence in Homosexual Case" (August 17, 1966).

————. "Blackmail Paid by Congressman" (May 17, 1967).

————. "Ex-F.B.I. Agent Links State Liquor Aide to Mafia" (November 30, 1967).

————. "2 Found Guilty in Chicago in Extortion of Homosexual" (December 9, 1967).

————. "4 Policemen Hurt in 'Village' Raid" (June 29, 1969).

————. "Police Again Rout 'Village' Youths" (June 30, 1969).

————. "361 Arrest Records Uncovered by Wall Street Fingerprinting" (February 5, 1970).

————. "Ku Klux Klan Says It Will Seek Permission for a Masked Rally in City" (May 2, 2000).

Pederzane, J. "Charges of Skimming Roil '92 Christopher Street Festival." *New York Times* (June 26, 1992).

Person, Glenn. "CS People: Ed Murphy." *Christopher Street* (Issue 66; July 1982): 10.

Queen's Quarterly. "Dawn Is Just Breaking . . ." (1:3; Summer 1969): 5.

Ramirez, Raul. "I Remember Stonewall." *San Francisco Examiner* (June 4, 1989).

Ranzal, Edward. "Member of 70-Man Ring Preying on Homosexuals Given 5 Years." *New York Times* (July 12, 1967).

Rat. "Queen Power: Fags Against Pigs in Stonewall Bust" (2:14; July 9–23, 1969): 6.

————. "From Outside the Pen" (2:15; "late July 1969"): 4.

————. "Gay Revolution Comes Out" (August 12–16, 1969).

The Realist. August 1962, September 1962, October 1962.

Reid, Lori. *The Complete Book of Chinese Horoscopes.* Shaftesbury, Dorset; Rockport, Mass.: Barnes and Noble Books, 1997.

Rodwell, Craig. "Mafia on the Spot." *New York Hymnal* (1:1; February 1968): 1–2. (Not signed.)

————. "Gay Power Gains." *New York Hymnal* (1:6; August–September 1968): 1, 9.

————. "Gay Is Good." *Queen's Quarterly* (Summer 1969): 39.

————. "Gay Holiday." *New York Hymnal* (2:1, January 1970): 8. (Not signed.)

————. "Gay and Free." *QQ Magazine* (3:6; December 1971): 22–27.

Rosen, Steven A. "Police Harassment of Homosexual Women and Men in New York City 1960–1980." *Columbia Human Rights Law Review* (12; 1980–1981): 159–190.

Roth, Jack. "Nine Seized Here in Extortion Ring." *New York Times* (February 18, 1966).

————. "Nationwide Ring Preying on Prominent Deviates." *New York Times* (March 3, 1966).

Russo, Vito. "I Remember Stonewall." *Soho Weekly News* (6:38; June 21–27, 1979): 12–13, 22. (The same article was published, slightly edited, as "Still Outlaws." *Gay News* [No. 170]: 16–17.)

Sante, Luc. *Low Life: Lures and Snares of Old New York.* New York: Farrar Straus Giroux, 1991.

Schlager, Neil, editor. *Gay and Lesbian Almanac.* New York: St. James Press, 1998.

Scott, David C. "My Autobiography." Student paper, New College of California, 1983.

Scott, Kimberly. "Stonewall's Aftermath Spurred D.C. Successes." *Washington Blade* (May 25, 1994).

Sears, James T. *Lonely Hunters: An Oral History of Lesbian and Gay Southern Life, 1948–1968.* Boulder, Colo.: Westview Press, 1997.

Shilts, Randy. *The Mayor of Castro Street: The Life and Times of Harvey Milk.* New York: St. Martin's Press, 1982.

Skir, Leo. "Notes from the Underground—The Road That Is Known." *Evergreen Review* (September 1970): 16, 20, 74–77.

Smilon, Marvin. "More Indictments Due in Blackmail Case." *New York Post* (September 28, 1966).

Smith, Howard. "Full Moon over the Stonewall." *Village Voice* (July 3, 1969): 1, 25.

Spencer, Walter Troy. "Too Much, My Dear." *Village Voice* (July 10, 1969): 36.

Tate, Laurence. "Exiles of Sin, Incorporated." *Berkeley Barb* (November 18, 1966): 5.

Teal, Donn. *The Gay Militants*. New York: Stein and Day, 1971.

Thomas, John. "Letters to the Editor." *Village Voice* (July 10, 1969): 4.

Thompson, Mark, editor. *Long Road to Freedom: The* Advocate *History of the Gay and Lesbian Movement*. New York: St. Martin's Press, 1994.

Tilchen, Maida. "Mythologizing Stonewall." *Gay Community News* (June 23, 1979): 16.

Timmons, Stuart. *The Trouble with Harry Hay*. Boston: Alyson, 1990.

Tobin, Kay, and Randy Wicker. *The Gay Crusaders*. New York: Paperback Library, 1972.

Tree. "Beating Around the Bush." *Private Lives* (September 1991): 86–88.

———. "Beating Around the Bush." *Private Lives* (February 1992): 74–78.

———. "Beating Around the Bush." *Private Lives* (January 1993): 100.

———. "Beating Around the Bush." *Private Lives* (August 1993): 86–88.

———. "Beating Around the Bush." *Private Lives* (December 1993): 84–85.

Truscott, Lucian. "Gay Power Comes to Sheridan Square." *Village Voice* (July 3, 1969): 1, 18.

Voeller, Bruce. "Stonewall Anniversary: Assessing the Activist Years." *Advocate* (July 12, 1979): 30.

Wakefield, Dan. "The Gay Crusader." *Nugget* (June 1963): 51–52, 71–72.

Ware, Caroline F. *Greenwich Village, 1920–1930: A Comment on American Civilization in the Post-War Years*. Boston: Houghton-Mifflin, 1935; reprint Berkeley: University of California Press, 1994.

Watson, Steven. "The Drag of Politics." *Village Voice* (June 25, 1979): 72–73.

Weinberg, Martin S., and Colin J. Williams. *Male Homosexuals: Their Problems and Adaptations*. New York: Oxford University Press, 1974.

Weiss, Murray. "J. Edgar's Slip Was Showing." *New York Post* (February 11, 1993).

White, Edmund. "Letter to Ann and Alfred Corn." In David Bergman, editor, *The Violet Quill Reader: The Emergence of Gay Writing After Stonewall*, 1–4. New York: St. Martin's Press, 1994.

Wicker, Randy. "The Wicker Report—It's Koch vs. DeSapio Again." *Eastern Mattachine Magazine* (July 1965): 9–10.

Wilde, Oscar. *The Complete Letters of Oscar Wilde*, edited by Merlin Holland and Rupert Hart-Davis. New York: Henry Holt, 2000.

Wittman, Carl. "A Gay Manifesto." In Jay and Young, *Out of the Closets: Voices of Gay Liberation*, 330–342.

ORAL HISTORIES

The following interviews were conducted by the author, unless a second name appears, indicating a different interviewer. The use of quotation marks around a name indicates a pseudonym.

Agostino, Sam: Feb. 26, 1998.
Babick, Christopher—by Michael Scherker: Dec. 10, 1988.
Beard, Harry—by Michael Scherker: Aug. 3, 1988.
Becker, Marle: Jul. 30, 1999.
Bockman, Philip: Aug. 14, 1999; July 13, 2001.
Boyce, Martin: Sept. 17, 1998.
"Bruce": Sept. 16, 1997.
Bryan, Robert: Sept. 3, 1999.
Burch, Charles: Apr. 10, 1998.
Callahan, Tim: Apr. 5, 2001.
Castro, Raymond: Oct. 10, 1999.
Dunn, Kevin—by Michael Scherker: June 5, 1989.
Eagles, Philip: Oct. 1, 1998; Aug. 21, 1999.
Evans, Arthur: Dec. 16, 17, 2000; Oct. 13, 2002. Also interviewed by Michael Scherker: June 8, 1989.
Fader, Michael: Apr. 8, 1998.
Gabriel, Paul: Dec. 17, 2000.
Galvin, Earl—by Nikos Diaman: Dec. 7, 1992.
Garvin, Danny: Feb. 12, Mar. 14, May 27, 1998; Sept. 29, Nov. 30, 1999. Also interviewed by Michael Scherker: Dec. 15, 1988.
Ginsberg, Allen—by Obie Benz: Oct. 17, 1987.
Gittings, Barbara: Dec. 15, 2000. Also interviewed by Paul D. Cain: n.d.
Hampton, Dawn—by Eric Marcus: Jan. 1994.
"Hardy," Jennifer: Sept. 1, 1997.

Heide, Robert: Aug. 19, Sept. 21, 1999.

Hoose, Jerry: Mar. 5, 17, 1998; Aug. 23, 2001; Oct. 16, 17, 25, 2003.

Joel S.: Jan. 5, 1998.

Kohler, Bob: Oct. 7, 17, 1997; Mar. 12, 24, 28, 1998; Apr. 5, 2003.

Konnon, Michael: May 5, 1998.

Lanigan-Schmidt, Thomas: Mar. 13, 21, Dec. 12, 1998; Sept. 30, 2000; May 6, 2001; Jul. 21, 22, 2002; Aug. 4, 9, Oct. 18, 2003. Also interviewed by Martin Duberman: May 2, 1992.

Leitsch, Dick: Dec. 9, 1997; Mar. 2, 1999; Jul. 21, 2001. Also interviewed by Eric Marcus: Jan. 23, 1989; —by Eric Marcus: Jan. 1994; and by Paul Cain: Aug. 16, 1995.

Manford, Morty: Dec. 9, 1989—by Eric Marcus.

"Mike," Stonewall Inn's porter: Mar. 2, 21, 1998.

Murphy, Ed—by Chris Davis: circa 1983; and by Gene Stavis: May 22, 1978.

Nichols, Jack: Oct. 4, 7, 8, 1996.

O'Brien, John: Mar. 21, 1997; June 23, 30, Jul. 4, 1998.

Olenick, Michael: Oct. 30, 1999.

Perrin, Barry: Jul. 14, 1999.

Pine, Seymour: Sept. 18, Oct. 26, 28, Nov. 14, 1999; Aug. 12, 2000. Also interviewed by David Isay: ca. spring 1989.

Ranieri, John Paul: Mar. 17, 24, 30, 1998.

Ritter, "Steve"/"Maria": Nov. 9, 1997; Apr. 19, 2000.

Rivera, Robert—by Michael Scherker: June 10, 1989.

Rodwell, Craig—by Breck Ardery: ca. spring 1970; by Michael Scherker: Oct. 9, Nov. 20, 1986; and by Martin Duberman: 1990, 1990, Nov. 14, 1990; and Jan. 25, 1991.

Russo, Vito—by Eric Marcus: Dec. 21, 1988.

Scott, David C.: Apr. 24, 1998; Jan. 26, 1999. Also interviewed by Michael Scherker: June 10, 1989.

Shaheen, Chuck—by Martin Duberman: Nov. 20, 1991.

Shelley, Martha: Dec. 14, 2000. Also interviewed by Michael Scherker: June 5, 1989.

Shenton, Bruce: Aug. 31, 1999.

Smith, Howard: Feb. 2, 1998.

Stryker, Susan: Dec. 15, 2000.

Tish: Jan. 15, Mar. 10, 1998.

Tree: Sept. 16, 1997.

Truscott, Lucian K.: Mar. 17, 1997.

van Cline, Stephen: Apr. 21, 1996; Apr. 18, 1997.

Van Ronk, Dave: Sept. 8, 1997.

White, Edmund: Sept. 10, 1997.

Wicker, Randy: Nov. 13, 1997; Jul. 6, 2001. Also interviewed by Michael Scherker: Aug. 8, 1988.

Wilson, Doric: Aug. 22, Sept. 4, 1999.

Wynkoop, William: Nov. 29, 1997.

Yates, Steve: Oct. 8, 1996.

CREDITS FOR THE PHOTOGRAPHS

The author gratefully acknowledges the following sources for the material reprinted in the photo section:

Photo Section pages:

2 (top) reprinted courtesy of Milstein Division of United States History, Local History & Genealogy, The New York Public Library, Astor, Lenox and Tilden Foundations.

2 (bottom) reprinted courtesy of Tree.

3 (top), 5 (middle) reprinted courtesy of Fred W. McDarrah.

3 (bottom), 7 (bottom) reprinted courtesy of Kay Tobin Lahusen.

4, 5 (bottom) reprinted courtesy of Diana Davies Collection, Manuscripts and Archives Division, The New York Public Library, Astor, Lenox and Tilden Foundations.

5 (top) reprinted courtesy of Thomas Lanigan-Schmidt.

6 (top), 7 (top), 8 (middle) reprinted courtesy of Fred N. Orlansky.

6 (bottom) reprinted courtesy of New York Daily News, L.P. Reprinted with permission.

8 (top) taken from "Gay Freedom 1970," reproduced by permission of Queen's Quarterly Publishing Co., Inc.

INDEX